"How can we improve jurors' comprehension of legal instructions? In a tour de force, Greg Byrne's remarkable book recommends a 'jury-centric approach' to addressing this perennial problem with using ordinary citizens to decide legal disputes. Greg Byrne argues persuasively that those engaged in lawmaking, developing legal procedures, and providing support to judges should also take a jury-centric approach, ensuring that their actions serve the goal of a well-informed jury. Highly recommended."

—**Professor Valerie P Hans**, *Charles F Rechlin Professor of Law, Cornell Law School, US.*

"This is a must-read book for anyone interested in juror comprehension — academics, practitioners and policy makers. It draws on a vast array of literature and combines this with a real understanding of the law and how judges and courts work to make original and practical suggestions for improved procedures."

—**Professor Fiona Leverick**, *Professor of Criminal Law and Criminal Justice, University of Glasgow, UK.*

"This book brings together the disparate strands of jury research into a coherent framework that can actually achieve reform. The 'jury-centric approach' is presented forcefully, clearly, and with great originality. Using case studies and presenting concrete proposals, this book is essential reading for anyone interested in jury reform."

—**Professor Jonathan Clough**, *Associate Dean (International), Faculty of Law, Monash University, Australia.*

Making Jury Trials Fair

This book proposes using a 'jury-centric approach' for improving laws, practices, and procedures in jury trials. Courts assume that jurors in a criminal trial understand and apply the judge's directions about the law. This assumption is based on jury verdicts and the courts' observations of jurors and inferences about juror comprehension. Research reveals that the courts' assumption about juror comprehension is fundamentally flawed. Addressing this problem is essential for fair trials. A jury-centric approach is evidence-informed and works within a fair trial framework. It asks what jurors need to understand the issues that they must determine. It also examines juror comprehension research and why judges and lawyers have often been sceptical about this research. The book illustrates and evaluates a jury-centric approach through three case studies involving structured decision-making aids, homicide laws, and misconceptions in sexual offence cases. The book proposes establishing an interdisciplinary Juries Advisory Council, drawing on judicial and legal expertise as well as expertise in jury research. The jury's task is increasingly complicated. Reform is essential to help jurors understand their task and determine the issues on their legal and factual merits. The book will be a valuable resource for academics, researchers, policymakers, and students in the areas of Criminal Law, Courts, Human Rights Law, Psycholinguistics, and Organisational Psychology, and to judges and lawyers.

Dr Greg Byrne PSM is an experienced criminal law policy adviser. He has led many significant criminal law reforms in Victoria, Australia, over the past 25 years. His research and publication interests focus primarily on juries, sexual offences, victims of crime, and criminal law reform.

Making Jury Trials Fair

A Jury-centric Approach to Criminal Laws, Guiding Juries and Juror Comprehension

Greg Byrne

Routledge
Taylor & Francis Group
LONDON AND NEW YORK

First published 2025
by Routledge
4 Park Square, Milton Park, Abingdon, Oxon OX14 4RN

and by Routledge
605 Third Avenue, New York, NY 10158

Routledge is an imprint of the Taylor & Francis Group, an informa business

British Library Cataloguing-in-Publication Data
A catalogue record for this book is available from the British Library

Library of Congress Cataloging-in-Publication Data
Names: Byrne, Greg, author.
Title: Making jury trials fair : a jury-centric approach to criminal laws, guiding juries, and juror comprehension / Greg Byrne.
Description: Abingdon, Oxon [UK] ; New York, NY : Routledge, 2025. | Includes bibliographical references and index.
Identifiers: LCCN 2025001752 | ISBN 9781032755113 (hardback) | ISBN 9781032761008 (paperback) | ISBN 9781003477129 (ebook)
Subjects: LCSH: Jury. | Fair trial. | Trial practice. | Criminal law. | Criminal procedure.
Classification: LCC K5492 .B97 2025 | DDC 345/.075—dc23/eng/20250116
LC record available at https://lccn.loc.gov/2025001752

ISBN: 978-1-032-75511-3 (hbk)
ISBN: 978-1-032-76100-8 (pbk)
ISBN: 978-1-003-47712-9 (ebk)

DOI: 10.4324/9781003477129

Typeset in Galliard
by Apex CoVantage, LLC

Contents

Foreword

As an impressionable law student 50 years ago, I remember listening with awe as the genius of the common law was reverently explained to a lecture theatre full of first year students with similarly unformed minds. Trial by jury, the right to a fair trial, the importance of precedent, and the flexibility to adapt to new and previously unforeseen circumstances were, I was led to believe, to the common law, what night following day, photosynthesis, or the laws of gravity were to students of the natural order of things. How the natural laws applied might depend on the time of year, the climate or physical characteristics, how the common law applied depended on the circumstances, but that there was a natural order was unquestioned, immutable.

That reverent awe was replaced by a growing awareness that the common law not only reflected the values of those older, privileged white men who shaped it, but that changing the common law was, if not entirely random, unpredictable, inconsistent, and slow to adapt to the social cultural and technological changes that were occurring. In my kinder moments I mused, that might have been because the time and intellectual energy invested by academics, practitioners, and judges to become more learned in the law necessarily reduced the opportunities for exposure to the noisier, messier, more diverse wider world that was developing around them.

Whatever the cause, the comfortable assumptions underpinning that early reverence for the capacity of the common law to reflect changed circumstances, namely that society was homogeneous, that judges, and the barristers who argued the cases before them, were the best placed to assess changed community behaviours and values, and that their views were representative of the community's were increasingly contestable.

A few examples, now comprehensively overturned, will suffice to illustrate the point. Provocation defences based on jealous rage or a homosexual pass, marital right as a defence to rape, and the requirement to warn it was dangerous to convict of rape on the uncorroborated account of the complainant were all common law constructs.

I was not alone in losing my starry-eyed view of the capacity of the common law to reflect changes in behaviours and values. Law reformers, and legal and social science scholars had increasingly turned their attention to whether the values and assumptions embedded in the common law definitions of offences, allowable defences, and evidentiary rules reflected contemporary values, and were evidence based. This research, too, pointed out the absence of evidentiary support for evidentiary directions that were based on an assertion of judicial experience.

Parliaments, too, had become increasingly active in codifying, or replacing the common law, and creating new offences, defences, causes of action, and evidentiary rules.

Whether attributable to these changes alone, or in combination with other factors such as the expansion of fields of forensic expertise, the increasing use of technology to capture and test evidence, or as a result of increased appellate scrutiny, trials generally increased in length and complexity. This was not necessarily a good thing.

Scholars, particularly those from the social sciences, also turned their attention to whether modern jurors, in modern jury trials, were doing what was required of them, namely apply the law, as explained to them, to the evidence they had presented to them, in order to determine whether the prosecution had discharged its onus of satisfying them, unanimously, or by a permissible majority, of the guilt of an accused of a charge.

The results are, or should be, confronting, for judges, practitioners, legislators, policy advisers, and law reformers alike. Even given the limitations resulting from the inability to interrogate jurors directly about a trial in which they participated, the overwhelming, and consistent results of the studies Dr Byrne brings together reveal many jurors did not understand and correctly apply jury directions.

Yet, trial judges are generally unaware of the research, and observations in judgments, and from empirical research conducted with judges, indicates judges remain supremely confident they know what jurors think and need. Similarly, appellate courts continue to express confidence in the ability of trial judges to understand and provide for jurors' needs.

Research reveals jurors today are representative of, or above the general levels of, education of the communities from which they are drawn. Yet they are more often than not denied the tools judges and lawyers have, and they are used to using in their daily lives, to assist in decision making: transcripts or recordings of evidence to refresh memory, written versions of the legal directions delivered orally, and aids to guide decision making. They are told both to confine their decision making to the evidence and directions presented to them in the trial, but also to use their common sense and experience of life to evaluate evidence and decide what weight to give evidence, and arguments.

In framing jury directions, and in responses to empirical research on juror comprehension, judges often refer to judicial experience. As Dr Byrne notes, there is no empirical research to support the judicial confidence their experience is representative of anything more than their own experience.

Other assumptions, untested by evidence, abound: that jurors understand and apply directions; that if an appellate judge has a reasonable doubt, a juror must, or should have also had such a doubt; that jurors are either blank slates or capable of putting aside bias or prejudice.

Some jurisdictions have introduced reforms to aid juror comprehension. As Dr Byrne reveals, the uptake is neither uniform nor high. And the restrictions on juror research means there has been no opportunity to assess the efficacy of the various aids which have been used.

These are dispiriting, if not bleak, findings for anyone who works in the criminal justice system, and believes in the right to a fair trial and retention of trial by jury.

If we are to retain trial by jury as the principal, and in some jurisdictions only, means of determining serious contested criminal charges, then the case for determining and providing juries with what they need to do so is unarguable.

After all, as Dr Byrne argues, a trial is not a fair trial if those responsible for deciding whether an accused is guilty of the charges they face are not able to understand what they need to do to make that decision. The arguments in favour of including the ability of the jury (tested by evidence, not speculation) to understand their role, to have guidance in how to go about their task, and to evaluate the evidence and understand the framework against which they must make their decision as essential components of the right to a fair trial are compelling.

The question of whether legal training should include more exposure to the social sciences, and whether judges and legislators sufficiently value what that discipline brings to clarity of expression of legislative intent, and its application to making individual trials fair, may need to be explored in other works.

There is much to stimulate thinking and provoke meaningful responses by adopting the jury-centric approach Dr Byrne proposes. From the start of the journey, when legislators are thinking of the way an offence is to be defined by statute, to the end of the trial, where a judge is directing a jury, the question of what would a juror understand is a critical, even if not determinative consideration. So, too, is developing a meaningful way of testing those assumptions by an evaluative process after verdict which does not undermine the integrity of a trial and the necessary confidentiality of a jury's deliberations. The beauty of this proposal is that it is more about reframing the thinking and approach to juror communication, to consider juror understanding, than it is about procedural or structural overlays on an already complex system.

Dr Byrne proposes an interdisciplinary Juries Advisory Council to drive the research agenda. Again, he mounts a compelling argument for the establishment of such a body. His five questions that must be considered are clear, simple, and balanced. Just imagine how much better jurors would be equipped to play their role in a fair trial if these five questions were used to evaluate every proposal for legislative or procedural reform.

Imagine if we knew the answers to some of these questions. What are the language and cultural assumptions appropriate to jurors drawn from a diverse, multicultural society? The 2021 census records that over half the Australian population was born overseas or had at least one parent born overseas, and a language other than English is spoken in one quarter of households. Other common law countries are also increasingly diverse. How best to engage with the educational and occupational profile of a modern jury? What is known about different communication styles appropriate to a diverse group of adult strangers in a modern multicultural society? What assumptions can safely be made about jurors' knowledge of their role as jurors, or of the criminal justice system generally? How to deal with the potential conflict between reliance on common sense and experience of life, and a requirement to put aside bias and prejudice, beliefs or assumptions? How to address unconscious bias?

In my dream criminal trial process, juries would be retained, trials would be shorter than they currently are, and jurors would be provided with the information and assistance evidence shows will ensure they understand their task and are best equipped to perform it.

This carefully researched and thoughtful work should be essential reading for everyone who plays a role in the administration of criminal justice.

Felicity Hampel AM SC
Melbourne
November 2024

Preface

As a criminal lawyer working at the Office of Public Prosecutions (Vic) during the 1990s, I witnessed many trials and observed different styles that judges used to manage trials and guide juries with their task. While I was interested in issues concerning the composition and representativeness of the jury, my interest in jury directions and juror comprehension was not piqued until some years later.

When working in policy and legislation in the Department of Justice (Vic), I led several major criminal law reforms, including a five-year overhaul and modernisation of criminal procedure. When informing County Court judges about the reforms in the late 2000s, one judge said: 'That's all well and good, but what are you doing about jury directions?' Jury directions had become a significant problem, making judge's communication with juries more difficult and resulting in more appeals. When guiding juries with their task, the trial judge's primary audience was becoming appellate courts rather than the jury. Victoria was not alone.

Following a report from the Victorian Law Reform Commission, the Department of Justice established the Jury Directions Advisory Group (JDAG) to develop solutions. JDAG included appellate judges, trial judges, barristers, prosecution and defence lawyers, academics with jury expertise, and a representative from the Judicial College of Victoria. Justice Chris Maxwell, then President of the Court of Appeal, and I were the co-convenors of JDAG. I was the chair of JDAG, and my team and I supported JDAG through the development of discussion papers that proposed reforms to jury directions and the judge's guidance. JDAG's work led to groundbreaking legislative reforms in the *Jury Directions Act 2015* (Vic). Critical to the success of the reform process was President Maxwell's willingness to question long-established laws and practices and County Court trial judges Judge Meryl Sexton (now Deputy Chief Judge) and Judge Felicity Hampel who identified many outdated and unfair jury directions and demonstrated their readiness to try new ways of guiding juries.

Jury direction reform whetted my appetite for new challenges, and I commenced my PhD in 2015. The PhD journey was long and challenging on many levels. While there are too many people to thank, there are several people that

I would like to mention. My supervisors (who were also members of JDAG), Professor Jonathan Clough and Associate Professor Jacqueline Horan, provided invaluable advice and feedback in developing my methodology and the ideas in my PhD. Special thanks also to Dr Steven Tudor for *voluntarily* offering to read a late draft of my thesis and for providing insightful comments. Thanks also to my family and friends for their support and encouragement along the way, and especially to Michèle, Greta, and Jasper.

Being awarded the Mollie Holman medal for best PhD in Law at Monash University in 2022 capped off my PhD journey. However, the opportunity to transform my thesis into a book which could be helpful to judges, policymakers, academics, students, and others beckoned.

This book reflects my interests in legal policy reform, jury trials, and my desire to improve the fairness of the criminal justice system. The five-step jury-centric approach that I developed is much more broad-ranging than the legislative reform of jury directions that I was involved in. However, that reform process gave me hope that judges, policymakers, academics, and students might be interested in knowing more about reforming laws, practices, and procedures to help jurors understand their task and the issues in a trial. I hope the ideas and proposals in this book might be a catalyst for further evidence-informed reform.

Dr Greg Byrne PSM

Acknowledgement of country

I acknowledge and respect the traditional owners of Australia and their continuing connection to this land. In particular, I acknowledge and respect the Wurundjeri people of the Kulin nation, the traditional custodians of the land on which I researched and wrote this book. I pay my respects to Elders past and present.

Acronyms and abbreviations

AIJA	Australasian Institute of Judicial Administration
CLR	Criminal Law Review, Department of Justice (Vic)
CSA	Child sexual assault
ICCPR	International Covenant on Civil and Political Rights 1966
JAC	Juries Advisory Council
JDA	*Jury Directions Act 2015* (Vic)
JDAG	Jury Directions Advisory Group
LRCWA	Law Reform Commission of Western Australia
MCCOC	Model Criminal Code Officers' Committee of the Standing Committee of Attorneys-General
NSWLRC	New South Wales Law Reform Commission
NZLC	New Zealand Law Commission
QLRC	Queensland Law Reform Commission
SDM aid	Structured decision-making aid
USA	United States of America
VLRC	Victorian Law Reform Commission

Glossary

Bench books Bench books provide information to assist trial judges in conducting a trial. Bench books may vary from providing examples of directions to illustrate the style of directions to being more prescriptive about what a judge should do or say. Most jurisdictions have their own bench books tailored to the laws of their jurisdiction.

Checklist A checklist is a type of SDM aid that a judge usually gives to the jury during the summing up. In a checklist, the judge turns the elements of the offence and any defence into questions for the jury to answer. The questions are not adapted, or are only adapted in a minor way, to the facts of the case (eg, name of the accused). The questions are likely to be abstract in nature, referring to the legal issue that must be determined (eg, did the accused assault the victim?).

Comment A judge may make a comment about the evidence. A judge's comment usually involves the judge's opinion or observation about what significance to attach, or not to attach, to evidence adduced in the trial. A jury is not required to follow a judge's comment.

Direction A jury direction may also be called a jury instruction. A judge gives the jury directions about the law. The jury must follow the judge's directions.

Evidentiary direction 'Evidentiary directions' relate specifically to evidence called in a case. Evidentiary directions include:

- warning a jury that they must consider certain factors before accepting evidence
- warning a jury not to use or rely on inadmissible evidence that the jury has heard
- directing the jury that they may only use evidence in a limited way or for a limited purpose or must not reason in a particular way
- informing/educating the jury about certain matters where there is a risk that a juror may have a misconception, or make a mistaken assumption, that affects their impartiality in determining the issues.

Factual question Factual questions normally form part of an SDM aid. In a factual question, the judge embeds the law into the facts of the case. As a result, the judge does not have to explain the law separately to the jury. Factual questions may start as questions in a checklist that a judge (and/or counsel) then tailors to the particular facts and the issues in the trial. Judges usually give factual questions to the jury as part of the summing up. A factual question may also be called a 'fact-based' direction or a 'question trail'.

General direction A general direction explains matters such as the jury's role, the presumption of innocence, and the standard of proof. Courts give many of the same general directions in every trial. However, while the content of a direction is unlikely to change between trials, some general directions are only relevant in some trials (eg, where there are multiple accused, or multiple charges).

Instruction A jury instruction may also be called a jury direction. A judge gives the jury instructions about the law. The jury must follow the judge's instructions.

Integrated directions Integrated directions are a form of SDM aid. The term 'integrated directions' describes the combination of factual questions with additional information and directions. In relation to each factual question, the judge may:

- identify evidence relevant to determining that factual question
- give evidentiary directions relevant to that evidence, and
- refer to the way in which the prosecution and defence have put their cases in relation to that factual question.

Question trail A 'question trail' is a type of SDM aid — the term 'question trail' is commonly used in New Zealand. A question trail contains factual questions. It may also contain information about how the parties put their case and evidentiary directions. In scope, it may vary from simple factual questions to fully integrated directions.

Route to verdict A 'route to verdict' is a type of SDM aid — the term 'route to verdict' is commonly used in England and Wales. A route to verdict contains factual questions and a decision-making path for the jury. It may be combined with information (usually in other documents) about how the parties put their case and evidentiary directions. In scope, it may vary from simple, factual questions to fully integrated directions.

Step-direction 'Step-directions' are a type of SDM aid — the term 'step-directions' is more commonly used in Canada. Step-directions contain factual questions. They may also contain information about how the parties put their case and evidentiary directions. In scope, step-directions may vary from simple factual questions to fully integrated directions.

Structured decision-making aid (SDM aid) A structured decision-making aid highlights important decision points that a jury must consider to reach a verdict. SDM aids highlight the decision-path through questions with Yes/No answers and the answer from one question leads to the next question or to an outcome. Jurisdictions use different names for SDM aids including integrated directions, question trails, route to verdict, step-directions, and checklists.

Substantive direction Substantive directions explain the elements of an offence charged, alternative offences, and any relevant defence. Unlike general directions, judges must tailor substantive directions to the offence(s) in each case.

Summing up Following the close of evidence and addresses to the jury, the judge sums up the case to the jury. A summing up may also be called a 'charge'. A summing up must identify the issues in dispute and assist the jury to determine those issues in accordance with the law. The summing up includes jury directions and may include an SDM aid, a summary of the evidence, comments about the evidence, a summary of how the parties put their case, and a summary of counsel's closing addresses.

1 Introduction

In a criminal trial, the jury's task is to decide whether the accused is guilty or not guilty of an offence in accordance with the law. When the trial commences, jurors rarely know the laws that they must apply to reach a verdict and rarely have any experience or particular skills in their task. It is the judge's responsibility to guide jurors — primarily by giving 'jury directions'[1] (also called 'jury instructions') — so that they understand the law and their task. Courts *assume* jurors understand and apply the judge's directions[2] because this assumption has 'been tested by the experience of generations of judges, lawyers, parties and jurors'.[3] What if this assumption is flawed?

If this assumption is flawed, then jurors 'cannot perform their function properly, and a just verdict will be reached only by chance'.[4] Juror comprehension research demonstrates that this assumption is fundamentally flawed: 'no matter how it is measured, jurors appear largely incapable of understanding judicial instructions as they are traditionally delivered by the judge'.[5] This book examines this flawed assumption, the problems with the ways in which courts have tested this assumption, and proposes a method for improving juror comprehension of their task — to decide whether the accused is guilty or not guilty of an offence in accordance with the law.

1 In this book I primarily use the term 'jury directions', a term that is used in Australia, New Zealand, and England and Wales. However, in some jurisdictions (eg, the United States of America and Canada) 'jury directions' are called 'jury instructions'.

2 See, eg, *Gilbert v The Queen* (2001) 201 CLR 414, 420 [13] (Gleeson CJ and Gummow J), 425 [31] (McHugh J); *R v Mirza* [2004] 1 AC 1118, 1178 [163] (Lord Rodger) ('*Mirza*'); *Taylor v The Queen* (2013) 1 WLR 1144, [25]; *R v Corbett* [1988] 1 SCR 670, 692 (Dickson CJ); *Richardson v Marsh* 481 US 200 (1987), 208.

3 *Mirza* (n 2) 1179 [164] (Lord Rodger).

4 Law Reform Commission of Canada, *The Jury in Criminal Trials* (Working Paper No 27, 1980) 76.

5 James R P Ogloff and V Gordon Rose, 'The Comprehension of Judicial Instructions' in Neil Brewer and Kipling D Williams (eds), *Psychology and Law: An Empirical Perspective* (Guilford Press, 2005) 407, 425.

DOI: 10.4324/9781003477129-1

Why is juror comprehension of the judge's guidance often limited? Jurors are conscientious.[6] Judges and law reform commissions have been trying to improve the judge's guidance to juries.[7] However, good intentions from jurors, judges, and law reform commissions are not enough. The jury's task is increasingly difficult. This difficulty arises because of new offences, new evidence gathering techniques, and increased requirements to guide the jury when considering evidence. Further, the law's requirement that a judge's directions be legally accurate usually prevails over the equally important requirement that directions be comprehensible to jurors.[8] However, there is a more fundamental problem affecting juror comprehension. This problem concerns the way in which courts (and the law more generally) determine what jurors do and do not understand.

The confidentiality of jury deliberations largely prevents courts from directly observing what jurors comprehend. As a result, courts have developed their own methods: observing jurors in the courtroom, listening to jury questions, and making their own assessment of what is or is not comprehensible to jurors. Added to this is a general sense of whether juries appear to understand the judge's guidance based on jury verdicts. The courts' methods for assessing juror comprehension developed before social science research about juror comprehension (eg, from psychology and linguistics) emerged in the 1970s and 1980s. Since then, courts have generally struggled to incorporate social science research into assessments of juror comprehension. However, some jurisdictions have made improvements that are at least consistent with social science research including rewriting directions in plain language, changing the timing of instructions, and in developing resources (eg, bench books) to assist judges when they are guiding jurors. These changes may improve juror comprehension, but significant problems remain.

Most juror comprehension literature focuses on improving the comprehensibility of jury directions because directions contain the law that provides the jury's decision-making criteria. Legal discourse concerning juror comprehension focuses primarily on the law governing jury directions. Social science juror comprehension literature also often focuses on jury directions because

6 See, eg, New Zealand Law Commission, *Juries in Criminal Trials: Part Two* (Preliminary Paper No 37, November 1999) 1 (NZLC).

7 See Jonathan Clough et al, *The Jury Project 10 Years On — Practices of Australian and New Zealand Judges* (Australian Institute of Judicial Administration, April 2019) ('*The Jury Project 10 Years On*'). Law reform commissions have also sought to address juror comprehension problems. See, eg, New Zealand Law Commission, *Juries in Criminal Trials* (Report No 69, February 2001); Queensland Law Reform Commission, *A Review of Jury Directions* (Report No 66, September 2009) (QLRC); Victorian Law Reform Commission, *Jury Directions* (Report No 17, May 2009); New South Wales Law Reform Commission, *Jury Directions* (Report No 136, November 2012).

8 See, eg, *R v Adomako* [1995] 1 AC 171, 189 (Lord Mackay LC) ('*Adomako*'); *Zecevic v DPP (Vic)* (1987) 162 CLR 645, 670 (Deane J); *R v Ménard* [1998] 2 SCR 109, 124–7.

they provide a readily identifiable — and interesting — subject for examination.[9] However, jury directions are not the only source of juror comprehension problems. If the law the judge must explain is inherently complex or unclear, strategies that focus on the language used to improve the comprehensibility of jury directions will be of limited benefit.[10]

Thinking about juror comprehension problems in terms of jury directions not only risks limiting solutions, but it also risks limiting understanding of the problem: 'if all you have is a hammer, everything looks like a nail'.[11] I expand the focus from jury directions to include the laws (eg, offences and defences), practices, and procedures that shape trials and the issues that juries must consider. Further, analysing the trial process and criminal laws from the jury's perspective is essential to fully understand what jurors need to understand their task. If the process used by our justice system is failing to assist jurors to perform their task, the system must change. Reframing the problem in this broader and more fundamental way helps in identifying and shaping a wider range of potential solutions.

The solutions must be evidence-informed, incorporating social science research about juror comprehension. It is essential for a fair trial that jurors understand their task. However, changes must work within the legal system and any changes must be consistent with other requirements of a fair trial. Given the consequences of jurors not understanding their task, juror comprehension requires considered and urgent attention.

Before discussing how I examine these issues, it is important to clarify two matters.

First, this book, and much literature, frequently refers to 'juror comprehension problems'. This description may suggest the problem concerns the capacity of jurors to understand their task. However, this term is not used to be critical of jurors and their comprehension skills and does not focus on their competence as jurors. Jurors are 'overwhelmingly conscientious in their task, and very conscious of their responsibility'.[12] It is incumbent on judges to explain the issues that the jury must determine in a manner that is readily

9 Penny Darbyshire, Andy Maughan and Angus Stewart, 'What Can the English Legal System Learn from Jury Research Published up to 2001?' (Kingston Law School, 2001) <www.sixthformlaw.info/06_misc/pdf_files/penny_darbyshire.pdf> 1.

10 Ogloff and Rose (n 5) 428.

11 Abraham H Maslow, *The Psychology of Science: A Reconnaissance* (Harper & Row, 1st ed, 1966) 16. 'Maslow's hammer' refers to a cognitive bias arising from reliance on a familiar tool.

12 NZLC, *Juries in Criminal Trials: Part Two* (n 6) 1. See also John Baldwin and Michael McConville, *Jury Trials* (Clarendon Press, 1979) 14. Some books written by individual jurors also support this conclusion: see, eg, D Graham Burnett, *A Trial by Jury* (Alfred A Knopf, 2001); Malcolm Knox, *Secrets of the Jury Room* (Random House Australia, 2005); Mary Timothy, *Jury Woman: The Story of the Trial of Angela Y Davis — Written by a Member of the Jury* (Emty Press, 1974).

comprehensible to the jury.[13] Research indicates that comprehension problems are more likely to be caused by the trial process itself — and 'the form or manner in which the information is presented to jurors'[14] — than by juror capacity.[15] Further, social science research more generally has identified that understanding the 'characteristics of the situation', rather than the 'characteristics of the person', is far more important in predicting how a person will behave.[16]

Second, the judge's role, and responsibility, is to educate jurors so that they know how to perform their task — an educational function that bears some similarities to that of a lecturer at university.[17] If the class consistently fails, that is not normally the fault of the students. However, it also may not be the fault of the lecturer. A judge may not know how best to guide (educate) jurors about the subject matter, and/or the law may constrain the judge in how they guide (educate) the jury.

A 'jury-centric' approach

To reach a verdict, jurors must understand the issues that they must determine: '[i]nformed decisions begin with informed decision-makers'.[18] To ensure a fair trial, jurors must understand their task, to determine the issues on their legal and factual merits. To address juror comprehension problems, I propose that a 'jury-centric approach' be employed to address juror comprehension problems in criminal trials. So, what is a jury-centric approach?

My definition of a 'jury-centric approach' builds on Nancy Marder's definition of a 'jury-centric' perspective.[19] Both definitions take the jury as their starting point. Marder's 'perspective' then asks what 'tools' (eg, written copies of jury directions, taking notes and asking questions) jurors need 'to perform more effectively' their task.[20] My 'approach' is broader. I ask, what do jurors need to ***understand*** their task. Broadening the lens to see and understand the problem opens new ways of addressing this problem.

13 Jonathan Clough, 'The Role of Judges in Assisting Jury Comprehension' (2004) 14 *Journal of Judicial Administration* 16, 16. See also Justice David Watt, *Helping Jurors Understand* (Thomson Carswell, 2007) 171. See also *Adomako* (n 8) 189 (Lord Mackay LC).

14 Sara Gordon, 'What Jurors Want to Know: Motivating Juror Cognition to Increase Legal Knowledge & Improve Decisionmaking' (2014) 81 *Tennessee Law Review* 751, 760.

15 Warren Young, Yvette Tinsley and Neil Cameron, 'The Effectiveness and Efficiency of Jury Decision-Making' (2000) 24 *Criminal Law Journal* 89, 93.

16 Phoebe C Ellsworth and Alan Reifman, 'Juror Comprehension and Public Policy: Perceived Problems and Proposed Solutions' (2000) 6 *Psychology, Public Policy and Law* 788, 794–5.

17 Watt (n 13) 22–5; Jacqueline Horan, *Juries in the 21st Century* (Federation Press, 2012) 52–5; Max Rogers, 'Laypeople as Learners: Applying Educational Principles to Improve Juror Comprehension Instructions' (2021) 115 *Northwestern University Law Review* 1185, 1211–12.

18 Watt (n 13) 2.

19 Nancy S Marder, 'Introduction to the Jury at a Crossroad: The American Experience' (2003) 78 *Chicago-Kent Law Review* 909, 918.

20 Marder (n 19) 918.

Judges can already improve their guidance to jurors in different ways. For example, by using plain language in jury directions, reducing the conceptual complexity of their guidance, and providing the jury with structured decision-making aids[21] (SDM aids). A jury-centric approach extends the range of matters that are potentially relevant to improving juror comprehension. Juror comprehension problems are not simply a consequence of language or conceptual complexity. Whether judges can explain laws comprehensibly depends upon the content of the laws themselves. Therefore, juror comprehension is relevant to reforming and drafting laws that judges must explain to jurors.

A jury-centric approach also brings rigour and transparency to determining how to make the issues jurors must determine comprehensible to them. This rigour begins by recognising that juror comprehension of the issues in a trial is a necessary condition of a fair trial. This extends fair trial considerations beyond that of the historically more limited conception of balancing fair trial principles between the accused and the community.[22] However, the fact that jurors understand their task does not make the trial fair. That is, juror comprehension is a necessary but not a sufficient condition of a fair trial. There are many other fair trial requirements.

A jury-centric approach provides a transparent organising framework for considering all relevant matters. It is relevant to analysing existing laws, practices, and procedures. And it applies to proposals for change that may affect juror comprehension irrespective of whether the purpose of the change concerns juror comprehension. The five steps in my jury-centric approach to jurors understanding their task involve the following questions:

(1) Is there an evidence-informed basis for concluding that a proposal (eg, to change criminal laws, practices, or procedures) will improve juror comprehension?
(2) Does the proposal conflict with another fair trial principle or human right, and if so, is it unjustifiable or inappropriate to proceed with the proposal?
(3) Are there any other relevant policy considerations (other than fair trial principles or human rights), and if so, do they outweigh the benefits of introducing the proposal?
(4) If the proposal involves an area of judicial expertise, is a judge best placed to tailor a solution to an individual case?
(5) Do judges need resources or training to implement the new practice or process?

21 Structured decision-making aids (SDM aids) 'highlight important decision points along a path to an outcome', namely a verdict: Tamsin Ede and Jane Goodman-Delahunty, 'Question Trails in Trials: Structured versus Unstructured Juror Decision-Making' (2013) 37 *Criminal Law Journal* 114, 119.

22 See, eg, *Jago v District Court of New South Wales* (1989) 168 CLR 23, 33 (Mason CJ) and 49–50 (Brennan J); *Attorney-General's Reference (No 3 of 1999)* [2001] 2 AC 91, 118 (Lord Steyn); Laura Hoyano, 'What Is Balanced on the Scales of Justice? In Search of the Essence of the Right to a Fair Trial' [2014] (1) *Criminal Law Review* 4.

The first step in a jury-centric approach is to consider evidence from juror comprehension research. Evidence is relevant to whether jurors comprehend the laws they must apply, whether they understand their task, and whether proposals for change improve comprehensibility or have unintended consequences. Evidence from juror comprehension research is essential when applying a jury-centric approach because juror comprehension is a necessary condition of a fair trial.

The next two steps in a jury-centric approach examine whether a proposal for change that improves juror comprehension, and therefore helps to ensure a fair trial, may be unacceptable for other reasons. Reform proposals that improve juror comprehension may be limited by other human rights, including other fair trial considerations. Further, other policy considerations may be relevant in defining laws, such as when determining the scope of criminal liability. Therefore, it is necessary to assess whether a reform proposal conflicts with another human right, including a fair trial principle (second step), or is outweighed by another policy consideration (third step). A jury-centric approach uses existing policy processes for analysing these kinds of human rights conflicts and competing policy considerations. However, under a jury-centric approach, the issues may be framed differently because juror comprehension of their task is a necessary condition of a fair trial.

The fourth step in a jury-centric approach concerns judicial expertise. A trial judge is traditionally responsible for determining how best to guide a jury in each case. Social science research may suggest that changes in guiding a jury would improve juror understanding. However, it is not reasonable or practicable to expect all judges to become experts in juror comprehension research. Understanding what does and does not fall within areas of judicial expertise is relevant to determining how changes to improve juror comprehension should operate. A jury-centric approach may therefore change the expectations and responsibility of each trial judge to determine how best to guide a jury in each case.

The fifth step in a jury-centric approach asks what support judges need to implement a new practice or process. Like jurors, judges may need assistance in performing their task. The nature of jury-centric changes means that judges may require more and distinct kinds of support than is usually provided. For example, judges are more likely to change their practices if they understand the benefits of doing so. If a change to the law depends upon juror comprehension research from another discipline, such as psychology, it is important to explain why a change is made in a manner that is comprehensible to judges. Further, some changes might require judges to develop new skills.

The five steps in a jury-centric approach provide a comprehensive organising framework for achieving the fair trial goal that jurors understand their task. The next section outlines why I argue that using a jury-centric approach is essential to ensure fair trials.

Outline of chapters

I argue that using a jury-centric approach is necessary to ensure a fair trial by:

(1) examining juror comprehension problems
(2) explaining why the law has struggled to address juror comprehension problems
(3) proposing a new way of addressing the problem (a 'jury-centric approach'), and
(4) using case studies to illustrate and assess a jury-centric approach.

Juror comprehension problems

To understand juror comprehension problems, I begin by explaining how courts guide jurors with their task (Chapter 2). Judges traditionally guide jurors by summing up a case and directing jurors about the law they must apply. To determine what guidance to provide to juries, courts must decide what jurors do and do not understand. The confidentiality of jury deliberations substantially limits the courts' knowledge about juror comprehension. Much of the information courts obtain about juror comprehension is indirect (eg, from jurors' questions and jury verdicts). It may also include observations about jurors (eg, whether they appear to understand based on their demeanour) or judges' assessments of what they think should be comprehensible to jurors.

Social science research provides the principal robust and transparent method for identifying juror comprehension problems. Analysis of juror comprehension problems usually focuses on jury directions as the source of problems. Juror comprehension research, primarily from the fields of psychology and psycholinguistics, consistently shows that jurors do not understand many directions as judges traditionally give them (Chapter 3). Further, while the law makes assumptions about what jurors understand and how they go about their task (eg, recording the evidence and then only considering their verdict following the judge's guidance about their task in the summing up), research shows that these assumptions are misplaced. Research also indicates that the courts have regularly overestimated what is comprehensible to jurors. In dealing with this research, it is important to understand both the limitations of the research and the extent to which research from one jurisdiction is relevant to another jurisdiction.

Why the law has struggled to address juror comprehension problems

It is the responsibility of the trial judge to tailor jury directions to the issues in each case. Consistent with this responsibility, improvements to jury guidance in Australia have often occurred 'at the level of individual judges and courts, rather than on a whole-of-jurisdiction basis'.[23] Despite increasing recognition

23 Clough et al, *The Jury Project 10 Years On* (n 7) 1.

of juror comprehension problems, in many jurisdictions, evidence-informed change has been relatively limited. Understanding why change has been limited helps to identify solutions to this problem (Chapter 4).

Within the law (including courts), the law's knowledge and processes provide the starting point for assessing whether jurors understand their task. This starting point reflects that the trial provides the law's own system for determining the truth. Despite the limitations in the law's knowledge of juror comprehension, it is difficult to dislodge this starting point. The law, and courts, are often sceptical about juror comprehension research. The research comes from an unfamiliar discipline, it may not be written for lawyers, and it may fundamentally question the fairness of long-established practices for securing fair trials. Understanding social science and the law as different disciplines, with different systems of knowledge, goals, values, and methodologies, helps to define the problem and explain why juror comprehension has not been adequately addressed.

A new way of addressing juror comprehension problems

While judges are traditionally responsible for tailoring their guidance to the jury's needs in each case, judges are not, and it is unreasonable to expect them to be, experts in juror comprehension research. A Juries Advisory Council should lead the reform process to improve juror comprehension (Chapter 5). The Council should be interdisciplinary in nature. Reforms must work seamlessly within a myriad of trial permutations. Combining expertise from the law and the courts on the conduct of trials with juror comprehension expertise is essential to ensure reforms are effective. The Council should apply a jury-centric approach.

A 'jury-centric approach' provides a five-step organising framework for determining the suitability of laws, practices, and procedures in terms of juror comprehension (Chapter 6). Some jury-centric reforms can be added at the end of the law reform processes and practice improvements, for example, plain language improvements and SDM aids. However, the laws, practices, and procedures may limit the improvements that can be made by applying a jury-centric approach. Therefore, a jury-centric approach is potentially relevant to the review and development of any laws, practices, or procedures relevant to juror understanding of their task and the issues in a trial.

Applying a jury-centric approach requires evidence in relation to laws, practices, and procedures. The breadth of evidence required poses challenges for applying a jury-centric approach to all aspects of criminal trials and to all reforms. However, it is not always necessary to assess every proposal in every jurisdiction for juror comprehension. This is because reasonable inferences can be drawn from research. Whether direct evidence is necessary or reasonable inferences are sufficient, will be matters of judgment. In making that judgment, familiarity with juror comprehension research will be essential. A Juries Advisory Council has the interdisciplinary expertise to perform this role.

While a jury-centric approach draws on features that are familiar to review and reform processes (eg, dealing with competing fair trial principles and assessing different policy considerations), the effect of the five-step process is unique. Its goal is to ensure a fair trial where jurors understand their task and determine the issues on their legal and factual merits. It is evidence-informed. It considers matters within a fair trial framework. Defining juror comprehension problems as a necessary condition of a fair trial turns the problem of juror comprehension from one that exists in social science research into a problem that is more familiar to lawyers. Appellate courts do not usually discuss juror comprehension as a fair trial consideration. Defining the problem of juror comprehension within traditional legal terms makes it more accessible in the law. However, while juror comprehension is a necessary condition of a fair trial, it is not a sufficient condition of a fair trial — other policy factors must be considered (eg, to distinguish the offences of murder and manslaughter).

A jury-centric approach expands the focus of the enquiry into the causes and potential solutions to juror comprehension problems. It operates as a complete method for improving the comprehensibility of criminal laws and trials for jurors. Because a jury-centric approach is potentially relevant to every aspect of the conduct of a criminal trial and any criminal offence triable before a jury, the scope of such an examination would be enormous. It is not possible to discuss every way in which a jury-centric approach may improve criminal trials. Therefore, I use case studies to illustrate the application of a jury-centric approach and to determine whether it should be employed to address juror comprehension problems.

Using case studies to illustrate how a jury-centric approach works

The case studies concern critical issues from trials that research shows juries have difficulties understanding. The case studies illustrate how all five steps of a jury-centric approach work, although not every step is relevant to every proposal.

The first case study (Chapter 7) discusses several ways in which using SDM aids could reshape the judge's guidance to the jury. For example, by transforming directions about the elements of offences and defences into factual issues for the jury to determine, providing the jury with written material at the commencement of the trial that explains the issues in the case, and requiring the accused to disclose their defence when the trial commences. Parts of the case study go beyond the way in which any jurisdiction currently uses SDM aids. The proposals in this case study highlight how each step in a jury-centric approach is relevant and provides a robust and transparent method for conducting evidence-informed law reform to improve how the judge guides jurors in their task.

The second case study (Chapter 8) examines how a jury-centric approach is relevant to the formulation of criminal offences by focusing on the offences of murder and manslaughter and excessive self-defence laws. Many of the complexities with jury directions stem from the complexity of the law in criminal offences.[24] The extent to which a judge can transform directions about the law into factual questions for the jury to determine depends upon the terms of the law (eg, does the law contain fine legal distinctions). This case study illustrates how traditional policy approaches have given insufficient weight to the comprehensibility of laws to jurors when defining homicide laws. This case study also shows how a jury-centric approach can affect policy choices, even with an offence that is the result of many policy choices.

The third case study (Chapter 9) examines using a jury-centric approach to address the risk of bias in sexual offence cases. The representativeness of a jury is one of the safeguards for addressing different biases (including misconceptions) that jurors, like all people, may have. However, some misconceptions, for example, about the relevance of the time taken to make a complaint about a sexual offence, are more prevalent in the community and therefore potentially in juries. Where misconceptions exist, there is a risk that a jury will not be impartial and will not decide the legal and factual issues on their merits. Therefore, to ensure a fair trial, a judge may need to address misconceptions. But how will a judge know what misconceptions jurors are likely to have and in what circumstances they may arise?

A jury-centric approach challenges the traditional view that the trial judge is in the best position to tailor jury directions to the specific circumstances in each case. Determining the best way of guiding jurors requires legal expertise and expertise in juror comprehension research. Therefore, a jury-centric approach deepens analysis of what is and is not an area of judicial expertise and judicial responsibility. It also provides a transparent approach for dealing with controversial issues of this nature, providing an evidence-informed pathway for addressing problems while being cognisant of the need for the judge to remain impartial.

The need to use a jury-centric approach

I argue that a jury-centric approach *should* be employed to address juror comprehension problems (Chapter 10). Doing so will improve juror comprehension, and this is essential for a fair trial. A jury-centric approach provides a robust and transparent decision-making framework. It incorporates expertise from the law and from social sciences. Further, a jury-centric approach provides a mechanism for resolving conflicts between proposals that address juror comprehension and other fair trial principles, human rights, and other policy considerations. A jury-centric approach employs a systemic approach to a systemic problem. It recognises that there are limits to judicial expertise in how best to guide jurors. Further, while a jury-centric approach focuses on

24 Justice Mark Weinberg, 'Jury Directions on Trial — A Pathway through the Labyrinth?' (Speech, Supreme and Federal Court Judges' Conference, 5–9 July 2014) 60.

supporting jurors in understanding their decision-making task, it recognises that judges need more support to guide jurors more effectively. However, the change process will be lengthy, and we know that juror comprehension problems exist that affect the fairness of trials. Therefore, it is necessary to consider whether, and if so how, to proceed with jury trials before all criminal laws, practices, and procedures are reviewed through a jury-centric approach.

Focus of this book

Criminal trial by jury is an essential and valuable feature of common law criminal justice systems. Therefore, the most critical issue is how, and how well, trial by jury 'works'.[25] My discussion focuses on how trial by jury works in terms of juror comprehension of their task, including the issues they must determine. To assess this, I have relied on the significant amount of existing juror comprehension research. I have not added to this research by conducting original research concerning the proposals in my case studies. It is not necessary to add to this research for this book. My focus is demonstrating why, and how, a jury-centric approach should be used to change criminal laws, practices, and procedures to improve juror comprehension.

Juries are part of the justice system in many common law and civil law jurisdictions.[26] Unless otherwise stated, my book focuses on juries in criminal trials in Australia, England and Wales, New Zealand, and Canada. However, I also draw on research from the United States of America (USA) and Scotland. The number of different jurisdictions in the USA and different practices in jury trials in the USA and Scotland require specialised analysis to determine the applicability of the kinds of changes that I discuss. Similarly, a jury-centric approach may be relevant to civil trials by jury, trial by judge alone (eg, strategies to make the issues in a trial clearer), and to criminal trials in other jurisdictions that use some form of lay participation in the decision-making process,[27] but this would require further analysis.

25 Lord Justice Moses, 'Summing Down the Summing-Up' (Speech, Annual Law Reform Lecture, Inner Temple, 23 November 2010) 2.

26 See, eg, Valerie P Hans, 'Jury Systems around the World' (2008) 4 *Annual Review of Law & Social Sciences* 275; Sanja Kutnjak Ivković et al, 'Introduction' in Sanja Kutnjak Ivković et al (eds), *Juries, Lay Judges, and Mixed Courts: A Global Perspective* (Cambridge University Press, 2021) 1, 19.

27 '[N]early two-thirds of *all* nations currently involve lay citizens as decision-makers in their justice systems': Ivković et al (n 26) 19. And 56 countries use juries in criminal trials: Valerie P Hans, 'The Surprising Endurance of Trial by Jury: A Perspective from the United States' in Nicola Monaghan (ed), *Contemporary Challenges in the Jury System: A Comparative Perspective* (Routledge, 2025) 117, 123.

2 How courts determine what guidance jurors need

Introduction

This chapter discusses how courts determine what guidance jurors need to perform their task of deciding whether the accused is guilty or not guilty of an offence in accordance with the law. Good decision-making requires that a decision-maker understands their task. Therefore, to make a good decision, jurors must understand the issues that they must determine and the law that they must apply. Almost invariably, jurors do not know all the laws that they must apply. Therefore, judges must guide the jury with their decision-making task. I will explain key components of the way in which judges traditionally guide jurors.

Guiding jurors has become increasingly difficult because more cases are difficult (eg, sexual offence cases), the evidence can be more difficult (eg, arising from developments in science and technology), and there are many offences and appellate decisions that judges must apply. In recent decades, some courts have recognised that there are problems with the guidance they provide to jurors based on matters such as the number of appeals and their own assessment of the complexity of the guidance they must provide. This chapter briefly discusses some of the more significant changes that some jurisdictions have introduced to improve jury guidance.

It is also implicit in the development of jury directions that judges know what guidance jurors need. Therefore, I will examine how courts determine what jurors know and how jurors are likely to reason. Identifying the limits of the courts' knowledge about jurors is critical to understanding how juror comprehension problems exist and why they remain.

Chapter 3 then examines research assessing whether courts have correctly identified what jurors need to know and the effectiveness of judges' guidance to juries. Chapter 4 then discusses why in most jurisdictions social science research has only played a limited role in changing the law and criminal trials to address juror comprehension problems.

DOI: 10.4324/9781003477129-2

How the judge traditionally assists jurors with their task

The core components of the judge's assistance to jurors

The presentation of evidence in a trial through witnesses limits the ability of the parties to present the evidence as one coherent story. Jurors must work out what evidence they accept and apply the relevant laws to that evidence. Jurors are unlikely to know the relevant laws that they must apply. Therefore, the task of the judge is to bring the law and the evidence together to assist the jury to decide whether the accused is guilty or not guilty.

The way in which the judge assists the jury continues to evolve. However, traditionally, following the close of evidence and counsels' addresses to the jury, the judge sums up the case to the jury and explains their task. This is commonly known as the 'summing up', though different descriptions are sometimes used (eg, the 'charge' or final instructions'). The purpose of a summing up is 'to ensure a fair trial of the accused'.[1] The summing up therefore must identify the issues in dispute and assist the jury to determine those issues in accordance with the law.[2] A traditional summing up involves blocks of information including directions about the law, a summary of the evidence, a summary of how the parties put their case, and a summary of counsel's closing addresses.[3]

Jury directions (or instructions) inform the jury about their task, the law they must apply, and aim to prevent errors in jury reasoning processes. The jury *must* follow the judge's directions when determining whether the accused is guilty or not guilty. The term 'jury directions' is sometimes used to describe the summing up. However, a judge may give jury directions at the start of a trial or during a trial. There are three types of jury directions: general directions, substantive directions, and evidentiary directions. Jurisdictions use different descriptions for these directions.

First, judges give 'general directions' (sometimes called 'procedural directions', 'preliminary directions', 'preliminary instructions', and 'preliminary remarks') in almost every trial and the directions are virtually the same in each

1 *RPS v The Queen* (2000) 199 CLR 620, 637 (Gaudron A-CJ, Gummow, Kirby and Hayne JJ). See also *R v Barker* [2010] EWCA Crim 4, [43] (Lord Chief Justice of England and Wales) ('*Barker*'); Justice David Watt, *Helping Jurors Understand* (Thomson Carswell, 2007) 30.

2 See, eg, *Alford v Magee* (1952) 85 CLR 437 ('*Alford*'); *Stevens v The Queen* (2005) 227 CLR 319 ('*Stevens*'); *R v Adomako* [1995] 1 AC 171, 189 (Lord Mackay LC) ('*Adomako*'); *R v MacKinnon* (1999) 132 CCC (3d) 545, 555 (CA) (Doherty JA).

3 Queensland Law Reform Commission, *A Review of Jury Directions* (Report No 66, September 2009) 273 [9.88] (QLRC). See also Nancy Marder, *The Power of the Jury: Transforming Citizens into Jurors* (Cambridge University Press, 2022) Ch 4 ('*The Power of the Jury*').

trial. For example, directions concerning the presumption of innocence, and that the prosecution must prove the accused's guilt beyond reasonable doubt. By contrast, a judge must tailor substantive directions and evidentiary directions to the circumstances of each case.

Second, 'substantive directions' explain the elements of an offence charged and any relevant defence that is open on the evidence. This may include explaining alternative offences and different bases of liability such as complicity or incitement or a definition used in an offence (eg, what constitutes 'sexual penetration' in a sexual offence).

Third, an 'evidentiary direction' (sometimes called a 'warning') usually involves directing the jury to consider certain factors before accepting evidence (eg, identification evidence), or providing that the jury may only use evidence in a limited way or must not reason in a certain way (eg, for post-offence conduct evidence). An evidentiary direction may also address misconceptions that jurors might have (eg, about sexual offences or family violence). The purpose of evidentiary directions is to ensure a fair trial (or to avoid a miscarriage of justice).[4] This has, for example, produced many similar kinds of directions in England and Wales and in Australia.[5]

General directions and substantive directions are long-standing features of the modern adversarial system. If a judge does not admit certain evidence in a trial, the judge does not need to give evidentiary directions about that evidence. As laws have increasingly changed to admit more evidence, the risk that jurors may make an error with how they use evidence has also increased. This has led to the growth in evidentiary directions in recent decades.

Tailoring the judge's assistance to the jury

A judge must tailor their summing up, including jury directions, to the specific circumstances of each case.[6] The judge must transform appellate court judgments and legislation to explain how the law applies to the 'real' issues in the case, in a form that is intelligible to the jury.[7] Lord Mackay said that

4 See, eg, *Bromley v The Queen* (1986) 161 CLR 315, 325 ('*Bromley*'); Judicial Studies Board, *Crown Court Bench Book: Directing the Jury* (2010) <https://issuu.com/forensicmed/docs/crown_court_benchbook_-_judicial_studies_board> 4; Watt (n 1) 199–204.

5 See eg, *R v PS* [2013] EWCA Crim 992, [35]–[37] on the obligation to direct the jury about the accused's disadvantage in defending an allegation of historical sexual abuse and *R v Beck* [1982] 1 WLR 461 and *R v Makanjuola* [1995] 1 WLR 1348, 1351D, where a witness's evidence may be unreliable. See also Jeremy Gans et al, *Criminal Process and Human Rights* (Federation Press, 2011) 478–9; Judicial College, *The Crown Court Compendium — Part I: Jury and Trial Management and Summing Up* (July 2024) <www.judiciary.uk/wp-content/uploads/2024/07/Crown-Court-Compendium-Part-I-July-2024-1.pdf> ch 10 ('*Crown Court Compendium*').

6 See, eg, *Alford* (n 2) 466; *R v Lawrence* [1982] AC 510, 519 ('*Lawrence*'); *R v Ménard* [1998] 2 SCR 109, 124–7 [26]–[31].

7 *Alford* (n 2) 466; *Stevens* (n 2); *Attorney-General's Reference (No 3 of 1994)* [1998] AC 245, 272F-G (Lord Hope); Watt (n 1) 70–1.

the 'supreme test' for a jury direction is that it should be 'comprehensible to an ordinary member of the public who is called to sit on a jury and who has no particular acquaintance with the law'.[8] Therefore, directions should not be 'ritualistic formulations',[9] should not simply quote legislation or appellate decisions,[10] and 'should avoid . . . over-subtle distinctions . . . that may actually be counter-productive to the end sought'.[11] However, because of the financial and emotional cost of a retrial, trial judges are particularly concerned to 'appeal-proof' their directions by not departing significantly from the words of an Act, case, or jury directions manual.[12] As a result, trial judges often focus much more on whether jury directions are legally accurate than whether jurors understand the directions.[13]

The goal is for jury directions to be both accurate and comprehensible. Indeed, 'there has been a constant struggle to balance legal correctness with comprehensibility and comprehension is very often the loser'.[14] It can be difficult to explain complex legal concepts in comprehensible language. It can be difficult for experts in the law to see how statements may be ambiguous or misinterpreted by jurors. It can be difficult to explain laws when the level and nature of jurors' existing understanding of the law is not known. It can also be difficult to state some laws accurately: if a law 'is incoherent no amount of redrafting of . . . instructions is going to result in jurors understanding it'.[15] Further, in some cases, appellate courts have descended into considerable detail concerning the directions a judge must give,[16] thereby limiting a judge's capacity to adapt directions to make them comprehensible. As a result,

8 *Adomako* (n 2) 189 (Lord Mackay LC). To a similar effect in Canada, 'instructions should . . . [tell jurors] in language *they* understand, what *they* need to know to decide the case *they* are trying': Watt (n 1) 160 (emphasis in original).

9 *Doggett v The Queen* (2001) 208 CLR 343, 346 (Gleeson CJ).

10 See, eg, *R v Rodgerson* [2015] 2 SCR 760, 785 [51] ('*Rodgerson*').

11 *Zoneff v The Queen* (2000) 200 CLR 234, 260 [65] (Kirby J) (footnotes omitted) ('*Zoneff*').

12 Nancy S Marder, 'Two Weeks at the Old Bailey: Jury Lessons from England' (2011) 86 *Chicago-Kent Law Review* 537, 545; Lord Justice Moses, 'Summing Down the Summing-Up' (Speech, Annual Law Reform Lecture, Inner Temple, 23 November 2010) 11; James R P Ogloff, Jonathan Clough and Jane Goodman-Delahunty, 'Enhancing Communication with Australian and New Zealand Juries: A Survey of Judges' (2007) 16 *Journal of Judicial Administration* 235, 236; *Rodgerson* (n 10) 785 [51].

13 Justice Marcia Neave, 'Jury Directions in Criminal Trials — Legal Fiction or the Power of Magical Thinking' (Speech, Supreme and Federal Court Judges' Conference, 23 January 2012) ('Jury Directions in Criminal Trials').

14 Roger M Young, 'Using Social Science to Assess the Need for Jury Reform in South Carolina' (2000) 52 *South Carolina Law Review* 135, 154.

15 J Alexander Tanford, 'The Law and Psychology of Jury Instructions' (1990) 69(1) *Nebraska Law Review* 71, 102. See also Rabeea Assy, 'Can the Law Speak Directly to Its Subjects? The Limitation of Plain Language' (2011) 38(3) *Journal of Law and Society* 376.

16 See, eg, *Edwards v The Queen* (1993) 178 CLR 193; *R v Bauer* (2018) 266 CLR 56, 97–8 [86].

some jury directions are extremely complex and may be unintelligible to most jurors.[17]

Courts operate on the assumption that jurors do understand the judge's guidance.[18] However, courts accept that directions are not necessarily always clear to jurors. Indeed:

> [j]udges probably accept that there is an element of sophistry in the presumption that juries always follow their instructions. But the presumption 'is a pragmatic one, rooted less in the absolute certitude that the presumption is true than in the belief that it represents a reasonable practical accommodation of the interests of the state and the defendant'.[19]

This 'practical accommodation of the interests of the state' recognises that it is difficult to assess whether every juror properly understands every issue they must determine. The practical accommodation of the interests of the defendant recognises that there may sometimes be an unacceptable risk that jurors will not understand (or apply) the judge's directions,[20] creating an unacceptable risk that a trial will not be fair. As a result, for example, a judge may rule that certain evidence is inadmissible because of the risk that jurors will use the evidence impermissibly.

These assumptions are also pragmatic because, as discussed next, courts do not have a transparent and reliable method for determining whether jurors do comprehend the judge's directions. Compounding this, it is much easier for appellate courts to assess legal accuracy than comprehensibility. Ensuring legal accuracy is part of the raison d'être of appellate courts — it avoids 'judicial idiosyncrasy, variance and individual inclination'.[21] It is much more difficult to appeal on the ground that a jury direction was not comprehensible or was confusing.[22]

The growth in the number and nature of jury directions that judges must give also makes it more challenging for judges to provide comprehensible guidance to juries.

17 See, eg, Justice Mark Weinberg, *Simplification of Jury Directions Project*, Supreme Court of Victoria (2012) <www.supremecourt.vic.gov.au> vi. See also Marie Comiskey, 'Initiating Dialogue about Jury Comprehension of Legal Concepts: Can the "Stagnant Pool" be Revitalized?' (2010) 35 *Queen's Law Journal* 625, 665–6.

18 See, eg, *Gilbert v The Queen* (2001) 201 CLR 414, 425 (McHugh J); *Taylor v The Queen* [2013] 1 WLR 1144, 1153 [25]; *R v Corbett* [1988] 1 SCR 670, 692 (Dickson CJ) ('*Corbett*'); *McIntosh v Her Majesty's Advocate (No 2)* [1997] SLT 1320, 1324 (Ross CJ); *Richardson v Marsh* 481 US 200 (1987), 208 ('*Richardson*').

19 *Zoneff* (n 11) 260 [65] (Kirby J) quoting *Richardson* (n 18) 211.

20 *Richardson* (n 18) 207–11.

21 *Melbourne v The Queen* (1999) 198 CLR 1, 45 (Kirby J).

22 Neave, 'Jury Directions in Criminal Trials' (n 13) 3.

Providing comprehensible guidance to the jury has become more difficult

The role and importance of jury directions has grown. In recent decades, changes to evidence laws have allowed the admission of more evidence by limiting the scope of common law exclusionary rules. When courts admit a wider range of evidence that they consider jurors might misuse, courts may give additional directions to prevent jury error. For example, the abrogation of corroboration requirements in Australia resulted in courts admitting more evidence and led to the High Court of Australia determining that judges need to give additional jury directions.[23]

Further, different kinds of evidence, resulting from changes to science and technology, have 'fundamentally changed the nature of evidence in the 21st century courtroom'.[24] There have been changes: in the way police gather evidence (eg, surveillance device recordings, CCTV recordings, DNA evidence); to fields of expertise (eg, emerging areas of expertise in medical fields such as psychiatric or psychological understanding of the accused's or the complainant's state of mind[25]); and to the ways in which evidence is presented to the jury (eg, much or all of the evidence may be recorded and then played to the jury at the trial[26]).

Parliaments have introduced new criminal offences including terrorism, money laundering, sexual trafficking, and many child sexual offences. England and Wales enacted more than 4,000 offences between 1989 and 2009.[27] The drafting and interpretation of some laws may also result in complex substantive directions.[28]

The purpose of jury directions has also expanded. Courts and legislatures have increasingly recognised the interests of the complainant and the community in determining what is necessary for a fair trial.[29] For example, jury directions may address the risk that jurors might rely on misconceptions about a sexual offence complainant when assessing a complainant's credibility and reliability (eg, the misconceptions that a genuine complainant would be overtly distressed and would complain immediately).[30]

23 See eg, Australian Law Reform Commission, *Evidence* (Report No 26, 1985) [489]–[490]; *Bromley* (n 4); Jeremy Gans, Andrew Palmer and Andrew Roberts, *Uniform Evidence* (Oxford University Press, 2019) 539–40.

24 Jacqueline Horan, *Juries in the 21st Century* (Federation Press, 2012) 109.

25 See, eg, Horan (n 24) 109–12.

26 This occurred in the trial of Cardinal George Pell: *Pell v The Queen* [2019] VSCA 186, [30]–[35].

27 Sir Brian Leveson, *Review of Efficiency of Criminal Proceedings*, Judiciary of England and Wales (Report, January 2015) 5 [13].

28 See, eg, Criminal Law Review, Department of Justice (Vic), *Review of Sexual Offences* (Consultation Paper, September 2013) 1–3 concerning Victoria's rape laws.

29 See, eg, *R v A (No 2)* [2002] 1 AC 45, 65 [38] (Lord Steyn), where Lord Steyn referred to a 'triangulation of interests between the accused, the victim and society'.

30 See, eg, *Crown Court Compendium* (n 5) 20–1; *Jury Directions Act 2015* (Vic) s 52; *Criminal Procedure (Scotland) Act 1995* (c.46) ss 288DA and 288DB.

Increased technicality in the circumstances in which a judge must give directions and the content of those directions often requires judges to give more and/or lengthier directions. The more complex the judge's task is, the more difficult it is for the judge to transform relevant laws into comprehensible directions that provide effective assistance to the jury. These challenges have led to a new focus on improving the guidance provided to juries.

A new focus on improving the judge's guidance

Growing concerns with the effectiveness of the judge's guidance

During the latter parts of the 20th century, courts and law reform bodies began to express concerns about whether jury directions were effectively guiding juries. For example, in 1980 only 23% of judges surveyed in Canada were 'quite certain that juries generally understand the judge's instructions'.[31] As discussed in Chapter 3, extensive research, primarily from the USA, suggested that there was a significant problem with juror comprehension of jury directions. Research, and these concerns, have continued to grow.

In 2001, Lord Justice Auld concluded that the criminal justice system in England and Wales was full of 'complexities in every corner of it'.[32] This included lengthy summaries of the evidence and detailed directions on the law. Lord Justice Auld described directions as embarrassing in their complexity and failing to provide effective guidance to jurors.[33]

Also in 2001, the New Zealand Law Commission (NZLC) found that there were 'serious problems' with how judges communicated with juries.[34] The NZLC's jury research identified that 'fairly fundamental misunderstandings of the law' arose in 35 of the 48 trials examined and that 'many jurors' were, for example, uncertain about the meaning of 'proof beyond reasonable doubt'.[35]

Because of similar concerns about jury directions, in 2002, the Australasian Institute of Judicial Administration resolved to review jury directions and the summing up. This led to a survey of Australian and New Zealand judges in 2006. Most judges surveyed considered that jurors had 'either some (48.5%) or a great deal (8.8%) of difficulty' understanding directions about the law.[36] Most judges surveyed in Victoria considered that directions had 'become increasingly more complex, creating an "over intellectualisation" of criminal

31 Law Reform Commission of Canada, *The Jury in Criminal Trials* (Working Paper No 27, 1980) 77.

32 Lord Justice Auld, *A Review of the Criminal Courts of England and Wales* (Report, September 2001) 17 [30].

33 See, eg, Auld (n 32) 534.

34 New Zealand Law Commission, *Juries in Criminal Trials* (Report No 69, February 2001) 1 [3] (NZLC).

35 NZLC, *Juries in Criminal Trials* (n 34) 54 [7.16].

36 Ogloff, Clough and Goodman-Delahunty (n 12) 252.

law . . . [and this was] . . . a major impediment to effective communication' with the jury.[37]

Appeals data also suggested that complex laws were a problem in Australia. A study of successful appeals in the High Court of Australia and intermediate courts of appeal between 1 July 2005 and 31 December 2012 identified that errors in jury directions comprised at least 25% of successful appeals.[38] A separate study in Victoria found that where there was a new trial following an appeal, the jury 'reconvicted' the accused in approximately 90% of cases.[39] The original legal error did not appear to have been relevant to the jury's reasoning.

The length of jury directions also suggested problems. In 2006, judges' estimates of the length of their jury directions revealed significant differences within Australia and between Australian jurisdictions and New Zealand. The Victorian estimates for jury directions in ten-day trials (4 hours 15 minutes) were the longest in Australia and almost the longest for five-day and 20-day trials. At each of these trial lengths, the estimated length of directions in Victoria was 2.3 to 3.4 times longer than in New Zealand.[40] Lengthy jury directions raise questions about whether directions are too complex or confusing to assist jurors in understanding their task.

In 2007 and 2008, the Law Reform Commissions of Queensland,[41] Victoria,[42] and New South Wales[43] commenced their reviews of jury directions. Each Law Reform Commission concluded that there were problems with the summing up and jury directions. Victoria proposed significant legislative reform, but Queensland and New South Wales did not.[44]

In 2010, Lord Justice Moses concluded that jury directions and the summing up in England and Wales remained long and complex. He described directions in the new Bench Book as being 'in a foreign tongue' to jurors,

37 Elizabeth Najdovski-Terziovski, Jonathan Clough and James R P Ogloff, 'In Your Own Words: A Survey of Judicial Attitudes to Jury Communication' (2008) 18 *Journal of Judicial Administration* 65, 80.

38 Judge Sydney Tilmouth, 'The Wrong Direction: A Case Study and Anatomy of Successful Australian Criminal Appeals' (2015) 40 *Australian Bar Review* 18. By combining Judge Tilmouth's categories of errors (eg, 'failure to direct', 'misdirections', and 'inadequate directions'), more than 25% of errors resulting in a successful appeal against conviction concerned directions.

39 Victorian Law Reform Commission, *Jury Directions* (Report No 17, May 2009) 152 (VLRC). The data does not indicate whether the accused was convicted of the same offence. This figure concerns cases where there was a retrial — the prosecution discontinued (formerly called a *nolle prosequi*) 30% of cases.

40 James R P Ogloff et al, *The Jury Project: Stage 1 — A Survey of Australian and New Zealand Judges* (Australian Institute of Judicial Administration, 2006) 26–8.

41 QLRC, *A Review of Jury Directions* (n 3).

42 VLRC, *Jury Directions* (Consultation Paper 6, September 2008).

43 New South Wales Law Reform Commission, *Jury Directions* (Report No 136, November 2012).

44 Chapter 4 further discusses the reasons for these differences.

containing concepts that were 'alien' to jurors, and criticised the lack of guidance provided to jurors.[45]

In 2015, Sir Brian Leveson called for further improvements to the summing up and jury directions in England and Wales.[46] Also in 2015, the Supreme Court of Canada observed that despite their efforts, after 15 years, judges had only shifted from 'quoting large extracts from appellate decisions . . . to quoting large extracts from model charge manuals to safeguard their verdicts from appeal'.[47] In 2019, Lord Simon concluded that crafting a 'succinct and concise summing-up' for the jury remains challenging.[48]

This brief sketch highlights some of the more significant steps that have drawn attention to problems with jury directions and the summing up. There have been many other reviews and calls for action.[49] These reviews and calls for action have:

- focused on improving the summing up and jury directions, and
- employed different reform pathways for improving judicial guidance to juries.

Improving the summing up and jury directions

As discussed earlier in this chapter, the judge traditionally assists the jury with its task by providing blocks of information in the summing up. Lord Justice Moses rightly criticised this process, describing the path that judges lead juries along as 'obscure, tortuous and as arduous as could possibly be devised'.[50] Instead, as Lord Justice Moses said, the judge should *guide* the jury in its task. This guidance has increasingly involved providing the jury with a decision-making framework.

A judge can structure all the information in their summing up around a decision-making framework. Jonathan Clough et al describe the judge's functions as not only a guide but as a cartographer for the jury:[51] providing the jury with a written map to follow in the form of an SDM aid that 'highlight[s]

45 Moses (n 12) 4.
46 Leveson (n 27).
47 *Rodgerson* (n 10) 785 [51].
48 *R v Reynolds* [2019] EWCA Crim 2145, [50]–[69] (Lord Simon).
49 See, eg, Justice Geoffrey Eames, 'Tackling the Complexity of Criminal Trial Directions: What Role for Appellate Courts?' (2007) 29 *Australian Bar Review* 161; Cheryl Thomas, *Are Juries Fair?* (Ministry of Justice, 2010); Criminal Law Review, Department of Justice & Regulation (Vic), *Jury Directions: A Jury-Centric Approach* (Report, March 2015); Sir John Gillen, *Gillen Review: Report into the Law and Procedures in Serious Sexual Offences in Northern Ireland* (Report, May 2019).
50 Moses (n 12) 2.
51 Jonathan Clough et al, 'The Judge as Cartographer and Guide: The Role of Fact-Based Directions in Improving Juror Comprehension' (2018) 42(5) *Criminal Law Journal* 278, 296 ('The Judge as Cartographer and Guide').

important decision points along a path to an outcome', namely a verdict.[52] This written map changes judges' traditional reliance on oral communication of the jury's task. Further, the judge can reduce the amount of law that they need to explain to the jury by embedding the law, that they would otherwise provide in substantive directions, into the facts of the case. This framework can help jurors to manage the order of their discussions, to focus on the issues in dispute and to resolve disagreements.[53] Chapter 7 discusses in detail this reconceptualisation of the judge's role in guiding jurors with their decision-making task.

Judges have also changed their traditional approach of only giving jury directions during the summing up. Judges increasingly direct the jury about some matters when the trial commences and/or during the trial.[54] A 2019 survey of Australian judges found that it is now common (93%) for judges to give some general directions (eg, the burden and standard of proof) at the start of a trial. This was a significant increase from the 2006 survey where approximately 65% of judges in Australia (and 74% of judges in New Zealand) gave such directions.[55] Further, more than 90% of Australian judges said they provide general or evidentiary directions during the trial and about 50% provide substantive directions during the trial. While more than 90% of New Zealand judges also said they provided evidentiary directions during the trial, about 70% of judges provided general directions and 24% of judges provided substantive directions during the trial.[56]

Technology and changing ways in which jurors consume information has also led to changes in the summing up. In 2001, the NZLC recognised the value of providing the jury with a transcript of the evidence in the trial in addition to the judge's references to the evidence in their summing up.[57] Courts in some jurisdictions have increasingly provided juries with this transcript as technological advancements have made it easier to do so. By 2019, 93.6% of New Zealand judges, and 89% of Victorian judges, said they always provide the jury with a transcript.[58]

Victoria has introduced the most significant changes to narrow the issues in dispute and to reduce the number of jury directions. Following the close of all evidence in the case, the prosecution and defence counsel must indicate to the judge what is and is not in issue. Having done so, counsel must then request

52 Tamsin Ede and Jane Goodman-Delahunty, 'Question Trails in Trials: Structured versus Unstructured Juror Decision-Making' (2013) 37 *Criminal Law Journal* 114, 119.

53 Ede and Goodman-Delahunty (n 52) 119.

54 See, eg, *Crown Court Compendium* (n 5) 1–3; *Criminal Procedure Rules 2020* (UK) r 25.14.

55 Jonathan Clough et al, *The Jury Project 10 Years On — Practices of Australian and New Zealand Judges* (Australian Institute of Judicial Administration, April 2019) 7–8 ('*The Jury Project 10 Years On*').

56 Clough et al, *The Jury Project 10 Years On* (n 55) 16–20.

57 NZLC, *Juries in Criminal Trials* (n 11) 130–4 [341]–[354].

58 Clough et al, *The Jury Project 10 Years On* (n 55) 40–1.

that the judge give, or not give, directions that are open on the evidence.[59] This 'statutory conversation' places greater weight on the forensic decisions of counsel.[60] Defence counsel might, for example, consider that some directions would diminish the strength of their case and therefore not want directions given. This new process has 'altered the balance of responsibility between trial judge and trial counsel', appears to reduce the number of directions the judge must give, and judges appear to support it.[61] Victoria also introduced significant statutory reforms to simplify evidentiary directions, including directions on post-offence conduct, tendency evidence, coincidence evidence, and identification evidence.[62]

In developing these improvements to the judge's guidance to the jury, jurisdictions have adopted different reform pathways.

Different reform pathways employed for improving judicial guidance to juries

Because it is the judge's duty to tailor jury directions to the specific circumstances of each case,[63] much of the responsibility for improving the judge's guidance has traditionally fallen to individual judges. Jurisdictions have adopted different approaches to reforming the laws and practices governing the judge's guidance to juries. The reform processes adopted in England and Wales and in Victoria illustrate contrasting ways of trying to improve jury guidance.

In addition to reviews conducted by Lord Justice Auld and Sir Brian Leveson discussed earlier in this chapter, the Criminal Procedure Rules Committee in England and Wales set out the judge's overarching obligations to give directions in Rules.[64] The Rules require the judge to give directions about the law at any time that will assist the jury, and to summarise, to the extent necessary, the evidence that is relevant to the issues the jury must determine.[65] These rules essentially codify the principal requirements of directions at common law and include general, substantive, and evidentiary directions.

The Judicial College of England and Wales combined previous publications involving specimen directions, the Bench Book and checklists into a

59 *Jury Directions Act 2015* (Vic) ss 11–16. See also Greg Byrne and Justice Chris Maxwell, 'Putting Jurors First: Legislative Simplification of Jury Directions' (2019) 43(3) *Criminal Law Journal* 180, 188–9.

60 See, eg, Justice Chris Maxwell and Greg Byrne, 'Making Trials Work for Juries: Pathways to Simplification' [2020] (11) *Criminal Law Review* 1034, 1049–50.

61 Byrne and Maxwell (n 59) 188, 195–6.

62 *Jury Directions Act 2015* (Vic) ss 18–37. See also Byrne and Maxwell (n 59) 192–3.

63 See, eg, *Alford* (n 2) 466; *Lawrence* (n 6) 519; *McGartland v Her Majesty's Advocate* [2015] HCJAC 23 [31]; *Ménard* (n 6) 124 [27]; *Rodgerson* (n 10) 785 [52].

64 Criminal Procedure Rules 2020 (UK).

65 Criminal Procedure Rules 2020 (UK) (n 64) r 25.14(2) and (3)(a).

Compendium, which was published in 2016.[66] The Compendium revised jury directions with the goal of supporting judges in giving more comprehensible jury directions.[67] To improve the comprehensibility of jury directions, examples of directions were reviewed by Plain English Campaign.[68]

The willingness of appellate courts in England and Wales to improve the content of their directions is evident in the development of directions to address misconceptions in sexual offence cases. The Court of Appeal in England and Wales accepted that it was appropriate for judges to give directions to counter certain misconceptions in sexual offence cases.[69] Thus, directions to address misconceptions replaced older directions founded on the misconception that a complaint of a sexual offence is 'easy to fabricate, but extremely difficult to refute'.[70]

By contrast, there is only one clear instance of the High Court of Australia overturning a previous decision for the purpose of simplifying jury directions. The High Court had developed a complex six-step formulation for excessive self-defence in *Viro v The Queen* ('*Viro*').[71] A majority of judges in the High Court in *Zecevic v DPP (Vic)*[72] ('*Zecevic*') concluded that the *Viro* formulation was complex and 'imposed an onerous burden on trial judges and juries',[73] containing 'refinements which cannot be expressed in a way which makes them readily understandable'.[74] The *Viro* test was described as 'confusing at best, and incomprehensible at worst'.[75] The High Court replaced this test with a two-step formulation in order to simplify jury directions on self-defence.[76]

Intermediate appellate courts in Australia are more constrained in their capacity to change jury directions than the High Court of Australia.[77] When

66 *Crown Court Compendium* (n 5) 1–2; Peter Hungerford-Welch, 'Helping the Jury to Do Their Job' in Nicola Monaghan (ed), *Contemporary Challenges in the Jury System: A Comparative Perspective* (Routledge, 2024) 7, 7–8.

67 Criminal Procedure Rules 2020 (UK) r 25.14.

68 Criminal Procedure Rules 2020 (UK) 22–13. Plain English Campaign helps government departments and other official organisations to provide 'clear and concise information': <www.plainenglish.co.uk/about-us.html>.

69 See, eg, *R v D* [2008] EWCA Crim 2557; *R v Miller* [2010] EWCA Crim 1578.

70 *R v Henry* (1969) 53 Cr App R 150, 153 (Lord Salmon). This misconception also formed the basis of directions in Australia and New Zealand: *Kelleher v The Queen* (1974) 131 CLR 534, 543 (Barwick CJ); *Payne v The Queen* [2011] NZCA 127 [10]. See generally, Dorne Boniface, 'The Common Sense of Jurors vs the Wisdom of the Law: Judicial Directions in Sexual Assault Trials' (2005) 28(1) *University of New South Wales Law Journal* 261, 264–6 ('The Common Sense of Jurors').

71 *Viro v The Queen* (1978) 141 CLR 88, 146–7 (Mason J).

72 *Zecevic v DPP (Vic)* (1987) 162 CLR 645, 660 (Wilson, Dawson and Toohey JJ) ('*Zecevic*').

73 *Zecevic* (n 72) 653 (Mason CJ).

74 *Zecevic* (n 72) 660 (Wilson, Dawson and Toohey JJ).

75 Justice Mark Weinberg, 'The Criminal Law — A Mildly Vituperative Critique' (2011) 35 *Melbourne University Law Review* 1177, 1181.

76 *Zecevic* (n 72) 661 (Wilson, Dawson and Toohey JJ).

77 Maxwell and Byrne (n 60) 1043.

two senior Victorian judges 'declared that jury directions had become too complicated' they said that 'the only solution was to legislate'.[78] Therefore, to improve jury directions, Victoria needed to adopt a different approach from that used in England and Wales. Following a report from the Victorian Law Reform Commission (VLRC),[79] Victoria established the Jury Directions Advisory Group (JDAG) to provide advice on proposed reforms.[80] JDAG was comprised of appellate and trial judges, representatives from the Office of Public Prosecutions, Victoria Legal Aid, Criminal Bar Association, and the Judicial College of Victoria. The reform process involved a partnership between the executive and the judiciary. The Department of Justice developed most of the proposals considered by JDAG.[81] The calls for reform in Victoria eventually led to Victoria introducing substantial (also described as 'radical'[82]) statutory reforms to jury directions,[83] especially evidentiary directions.

With the reforms that jurisdictions have made and the different pathways for improving the judge's guidance, is any more change required to improve juror comprehension?

Assessing the changes to the judge's guidance

It is possible to draw some conclusions about the scope and effectiveness of reforms made this century to improve the judge's guidance to the jury. This helps to assess the limitations with existing approaches to address juror comprehension problems.

Reconceptualising the judge's role in guiding the jury has been significant. As I will discuss in detail in Chapter 7, New Zealand introduced SDM aids (called 'question trails') to guide jurors with their task. This led to considerable research into question trails, including comparing the use of question trails in New Zealand with more traditional directions used in Victoria at the time of the research (the 'Trans-Tasman' study).[84] This study found that question trails provide significant assistance to jurors, because they can reduce the complexity of substantive directions and present information more logically to

78 Byrne and Maxwell (n 59) 184.

79 VLRC, *Jury Directions* (n 39).

80 Criminal Law Review, Department of Justice (Vic), *Jury Directions: A New Approach* (Report, January 2013) 16 (CLR).

81 Byrne and Maxwell (n 59) 185–6.

82 Justice Virginia Bell, 'Jury Directions: The Struggle for Simplicity and Clarity' (Speech, Banco Court Lecture, Supreme Court of Queensland, 20 September 2018) 20.

83 *Jury Directions Act 2015* (Vic). See generally Byrne and Maxwell (n 59) 180.

84 Clough et al, 'The Judge as Cartographer and Guide' (n 51). See also Benjamin Spivak, James R P Ogloff and Jonathan Clough, 'Asking the Right Questions: Examining the Efficacy of Question Trails as a Method of Improving Lay Comprehension and Application of Legal Concepts' (2019) 26(3) *Psychiatry, Psychology and Law* 441; Benjamin Spivak et al, 'The Impact of Fact-Based Instructions on Juror Application of the Law: Results from a Trans-Tasman Field Study' (2020) 101(1) *Social Science Quarterly* 346.

jurors. Judges increasingly provide similar guidance to juries in England and Wales,[85] Canada,[86] and Victoria.[87]

However, the extent to which courts use SDM aids like question trails varies between and within jurisdictions. Examination of the content of New Zealand's question trails for the same issues in sexual offence cases revealed significant differences in judges' directions (eg, concerning consent, belief in consent, and intoxication).[88] Further, one New Zealand judge observed that in using question trails, 'some [judges] are more experienced, better than others . . . [but] some make a complete hash of it'.[89] This is despite the fact that New Zealand has published more than 140 examples of question trails to support judges in their use.[90] In England and Wales, there are variations in practice concerning the form, structure, and style of presenting a 'route to verdict' (another SDM aid).[91] For example, judges may provide juries with multiple documents (eg, a series of questions and/or a flowchart or diagram and the judge may also provide written summaries of the law) rather than integrating different pieces of information in the judge's summing up.[92] This may split the jurors' attention and remove the benefit of this decision-making aid.[93]

In 2019, almost half of all judges surveyed in Australia (47.9% or 45/94) said they were not aware of the fact-based approach used in SDM aids like question trails.[94] Four years after Victoria introduced integrated directions,[95] where awareness of the use of fact-based directions was highest in Australia, only 20% of the judges surveyed had ever used them.[96]

Narrowing the issues at the start of a trial should also assist jurors with their task. However, at the commencement of the trial, jurisdictions use different strategies for narrowing the issues. For example, in Victoria, defence counsel must respond to the prosecution's opening, by indicating to the jury the matters in the prosecution case with which the defence takes issue.[97] In England and Wales, New Zealand, and New South Wales, the accused may, but

85 *Criminal Practice Direction 2023* (UK) 8.5. See also *R v Atta-Dankwa* [2018] 2 Cr App R 16.
86 Watt (n 1) 93.
87 *Jury Directions Act 2015* (Vic) s 67.
88 Elisabeth McDonald, *Rape Myths as Barriers to Fair Trial Process: Comparing Adult Rape Trials with Those of the Aotearoa Sexual Violence Court Pilot* (Canterbury University Press, 2020) 547–8.
89 Clough et al, *The Jury Project 10 Years On* (n 55) 51.
90 Courts of New Zealand, *A Guide to the Question Trails* <www.courtsofnz.govt.nz/for-lawyers/question-trails/>.
91 David Ormerod and Cheryl Thomas, 'Routes to Verdict — What We Know and What We Need to Know' [2021] (8) *Criminal Law Review* 615, 616.
92 *Crown Court Compendium* (n 5) 1–4.
93 See, eg, Clough et al, 'The Judge as Cartographer and Guide' (n 51) 289.
94 Clough et al, *The Jury Project 10 Years On* (n 55) 50.
95 See the *Jury Directions Act 2015* (Vic) s 67.
96 Clough et al, *The Jury Project 10 Years On* (n 55) 50. See also Judicial College of Victoria, *Jury Directions Act 2015 Evaluation: Judicial Survey Results*, discussed in Byrne and Maxwell (n 59) 199.
97 *Criminal Procedure Act 2009* (Vic) s 225.

need not, give an opening address identifying what matters are in issue.[98] In Canada, the accused may only give an opening address before the prosecution calls evidence in 'special or unusual circumstances'.[99] In Queensland, defence counsel is not permitted to open the case to the jury before the close of the prosecution case.[100]

While courts in England and Wales took steps to address misconceptions in sexual offence cases, studies suggest that judges are not giving these directions when they should, and when they do, they do not do this early in the trial when they are likely to be more effective.[101] Similarly, a study of 25 trials in Victoria found that in most of the 21 cases in which the issue of delay in making a complaint arose, directions addressing misconceptions about delay were not given mid-trial even though they could have been.[102]

The steps taken to address misconceptions in other jurisdictions have been inconsistent. In Australia, Victoria has directions that address some misconceptions, for example, that a 'real' victim will always give the same account about a sexual offence each time they are asked.[103] However, there are many misconceptions that Victoria has not addressed.[104] In 2020, the New South Wales Law Reform Commission (NSWLRC) recommended that five additional misconceptions in sexual offence cases be addressed by statutory jury directions.[105] Further, while the NSWLRC gave detailed consideration to the kinds of matters that should be evaluated, it did not cite any research that suggested its recommended directions will be effective.[106]

Further, while approximately 90% of judges surveyed in New Zealand and Victoria provide the jury with a transcript of the evidence during their

98 *Criminal Procedure Rules 2020* (UK) r 25.9(2)(c); *Criminal Procedure Act 2011* (NZ) s 107(2); *Criminal Procedure Act 1986* (NSW) s 159(2).
99 *R v Pickton* [2007] BCSC 61 [6].
100 *Criminal Code Act 1899* (Qld) s 619(3).
101 See, eg, Olivia Smith, *Rape Trials in England and Wales: Observing Justice and Rethinking Rape Myths* (Palgrave Macmillan, 2018) 60, 79–80. See also Jennifer Temkin, Jacqueline M Gray and Jastine Barrett, 'Different Functions of Rape Myth Use in Court: Findings from a Trial Observation Study' (2018) 13(2) *Feminist Criminology* 205.
102 Julia Quilter and Luke McNamara, *Qualitative Analysis of County Court of Victoria Rape Trial Transcripts: Report to the Victorian Law Reform Commission* (Final Report, August 2021) 140.
103 *Jury Directions Act 2015* (Vic) s 54D.
104 See, eg, Patrick Tidmarsh and Gemma Hamilton, 'Misconceptions of Sexual Crimes Against Adult Victims: Barriers to Justice' [2020] 611 *Trends & Issues in Crime and Criminal Justice*.
105 New South Wales Law Reform Commission, *Consent in Relation to Sexual Offences* (Report No 148, September 2020) 167 [8.85] (NSWLRC).
106 NSWLRC, *Consent in Relation to Sexual Offences* (n 105) 196 [10.17]. See, generally, Greg Byrne, 'A Pathway to Fair(er) Trials: Why We Need a Juries Advisory Council' (2021) 31(2) *Journal of Judicial Administration* 49, 58–9, 70 ('A Pathway to Fair(er) Trials'); Faye T Nitschke and Blake M McKimmie, 'The Effectiveness of Educational Jury Directions in Adult Sexual Assault Trials' in Greg Byrne and Jacqueline Horan (eds), *Sexual Assault Trials: Challenges and Innovations* (LexisNexis, 2025) ch 11.

deliberations to supplement the judge's summing up, only 19% of judges surveyed in Australia (excluding Victoria) always provide the jury with a transcript.[107] In England and Wales, a judge only provides a jury with a transcript of a witness's evidence during its deliberations in exceptional circumstances.[108]

As discussed earlier in this chapter, important indicators of problems with jury directions and the summing up in Victoria were the number of successful appeals against conviction, and the length of the summing up provided. Since the introduction of the *Jury Directions Act 2015* (Vic) (JDA) Victoria has improved by both measures.

First, successful appeals against conviction have reduced from an average of 24.8 each year (2005–12)[109] to 11.7 (1 January 2017–30 June 2020).[110] The proportion of successful appeals concerning jury directions reduced from 25–50% in 2005–12[111] to 19.5% between 1 January 2017 and 30 June 2020.[112] While changes to appeals contributed to this reduction, it seems certain that the jury directions reforms were a key factor in reducing the number of conviction appeals.[113] Second, judges' estimates of the length of their summing up have reduced by approximately 50%.[114] However, during the same period of time, judges' estimates of the length of the summing up in New South Wales also showed a substantial reduction despite there being no legislative changes[115] — it is not clear why this has occurred.

Data concerning appeals against conviction and the length of the summing up provide blunt and indirect measures for assessing the effectiveness of the judge's guidance. For example, reducing the number of successful appeals against conviction in Victoria suggests that there has been a reduction in the difficulties judges face in accurately stating the law in jury directions. However, reducing difficulties for judges does not necessarily mean that the courts' assistance to jurors has improved. Shortening the length of jury directions may reduce the cognitive load on jurors but this is not necessarily the case because legal language may be 'so dense and packed with so much information that it's impossible to express the concepts understandably without using more words'.[116] The Trans-Tasman field study found that the (traditional style) summing up in Victoria was approximately 85% longer than in New Zealand. However, the summing up in each jurisdiction measured similarly in terms of

107 Clough et al, *The Jury Project 10 Years On* (n 55) 40–1.
108 See, eg, *R v Popescu* [2010] EWCA Crim 1230; *Crown Court Compendium* (n 5) 3–29.
109 Tilmouth (n 38) 20.
110 Maxwell and Byrne (n 60) 1054.
111 Tilmouth (n 38). Data, derived from different methodologies, suggests this proportion may have been up to 50%: CLR, *Jury Directions: A New Approach* (n 80) 12–13.
112 Maxwell and Byrne (n 60) 1054.
113 Byrne and Maxwell (n 59) 196–7.
114 Clough et al, *The Jury Project 10 Years On* (n 55) 33.
115 Clough et al, *The Jury Project 10 Years On* (n 55) 32.
116 Peter M Tiersma, 'Communicating with Juries: How to Draft More Understandable Instructions' (2005–06) 10 *The Scribes of Journal Legal Writing* 1, 33.

the Flesch-Kincaid readability formula and juror perceptions of helpfulness and understanding of the summing up.[117]

Thus, improvements to the summing up and jury directions in recent years to assist jurors with their decision-making have been mixed — some jurisdictions have introduced significant changes and others very little. Change in Australia has often been 'ad hoc, occurring at the level of individual judges and courts, rather than on a whole-of-jurisdiction basis'.[118] This may also explain the inconsistent uptake of reforms in other jurisdictions. For example, scholars have described reform in the USA as 'piecemeal'.[119]

Other than strategies to improve bench books containing guidance for judges in directing juries, most jurisdictions do not have any ongoing process for improving juror comprehension. The reform process operating in Victoria between 2010–19 no longer exists.[120] Further, where jurisdictions have made changes, testing to determine whether this has improved juror comprehension has been extremely limited. For example, in Victoria, testing has involved surveys of judges' perspectives[121] or practices[122] rather than testing of jurors. There has been no testing of specific reforms to simplify evidentiary directions in Victoria.[123] No jurisdiction has a formalised ongoing process for testing juror comprehension of the judge's guidance. Academics, rather than courts or government bodies, often conduct research on juries.

One explanation for the lack of systemic change and systematic data collection is that courts have their own processes for deciding what jurors know or do not know and what jurors need to understand their task. Further, courts have traditionally viewed the judge's function in assisting the jury as something that is bespoke. Because every case is different, appellate courts have said that trial judges are best placed to determine what directions to give in a case and must tailor their directions to the specific circumstances of each case.[124] To perform this function, trial judges need to determine what jurors do or do not understand and how best to assist them. Appellate courts (in developing the law) and trial judges have been determining what jurors do and do not know long before social science research about juror comprehension developed. The courts' knowledge continues to be important. The next section discusses what this knowledge is and how it has developed.

117 Clough et al, 'The Judge as Cartographer and Guide' (n 51) 294.
118 Clough et al, *The Jury Project 10 Years On* (n 55) 1.
119 Miko M Wilford and Brian H Bornstein, 'The Disappearing Trial: How Social Scientists Can Help Save the Jury from Extinction' (2023) 29(1) *Psychology, Crime & Law* 1, 9.
120 See Byrne, 'A Pathway to Fair(er) Trials' (n 106) 58.
121 See, eg, Byrne and Maxwell (n 59) 195.
122 See, eg, Quilter and McNamara (n 102).
123 Byrne and Maxwell (n 59) 199.
124 See, eg, *Alford* (n 2) 466; *Lawrence* (n 6) 519; *Ménard* (n 6).

The courts' knowledge about juror comprehension

As discussed before, the High Court of Australia changed self-defence laws because they were too complicated and could not be explained in 'readily understandable' terms.[125] The High Court concluded that its new self-defence laws were 'readily understandable' to a jury.[126] Similarly, New Zealand's Court of Appeal concluded that its new explanation of proof beyond reasonable doubt would improve on existing practices, based on evidence about problems with its existing approach but without any evidence that its new approach would improve juror understanding.[127] How do courts determine whether jury directions are not, or will be, understandable to jurors? The direct information that courts can obtain from jurors about what jurors understand is limited. These limitations are critical in explaining why courts have relied on more indirect methods for determining what jurors know, how they reason, and what will be understandable to them.

The confidentiality of jury deliberations limits courts' knowledge about juror comprehension

Going back at least as far as the 14th century, juries generally conducted their deliberations separately from other people and often did so in secret.[128] The jury's verdict was inscrutable — reflecting its authority in having replaced other methods of trial premised upon divine intervention such as trial by ordeal.[129] The ways in which the law protects the confidentiality of jury deliberations significantly reduces the disclosure of information about what jurors know and how they reason. The confidentiality of jury deliberations is protected by:

- limits on the disclosure of jury deliberations during a trial
- limits on the use of evidence about the content of jury deliberations in an appeal against a jury's verdict, and
- laws that prohibit soliciting, obtaining, and publishing information about jury deliberations.

125 *Zecevic* (n 72) 660 (Wilson, Dawson and Toohey JJ).
126 *Zecevic* (n 72) 665 (Wilson, Dawson and Toohey JJ).
127 *R v Wanhalla* [2007] 2 NZLR 573, 586–7 [41]–[47] (William Young P, Chambers and Robertson JJ).
128 Diane E Courselle, 'Struggling with Deliberative Secrecy, Jury Independence, and Jury Reform' (2005) 57 *South Carolina Law Review* 203, 215. See also Sir Matthew Hale, *The History of the Common Law of England* (3rd ed, E. and R. Nutt, and R. Gosling, 1739) 257. However, not all deliberations were conducted in secret, where jurors reached verdicts quickly and in the courtroom during the 18th and 19th centuries: John H Langbein, *The Origins of the Adversary Criminal Trial* (Oxford University Press, 2003) 21–2.
129 Courselle (n 128) 214.

Limits on disclosure of jury deliberations during a trial

During a trial, a judge may hear evidence concerning factors that may affect jury deliberations. For example, evidence may lead the parties or the public to have a reasonable apprehension that a juror or jury may be biased or failing to act in accordance with their oath (eg, accessing information from the internet).[130] This kind of evidence may result in a jury or juror being discharged where there is a 'high degree of need' to do so.[131] In practice, discharging a jury or jurors for this reason occurs infrequently.[132] Therefore, the discharge of a jury or juror does not usually provide valuable information about what jurors generally do and do not know.

Many juror comprehension problems will only emerge during deliberations following the judge's summing up. Within the jury room, only other jurors would be able to detect comprehension problems (assuming they accurately understand their task). At least in some jurisdictions, the jury has 'a collective responsibility for ensuring that the conduct of each member is consistent with the jury oath and that the directions of the trial judge about the discharge of their responsibilities are followed'.[133] In one study, 48% of jurors said 'they either would not know what to do or were uncertain' what to do if 'something improper occurred during jury deliberations'.[134] To address this, judges may inform jurors that it is their duty to bring any concerns about fellow jurors to the attention of the judge.[135]

The effectiveness of this direction about each juror's duty is unclear.[136] Judges often give this direction in the context of directions about jurors not conducting their own enquiries, such as using the internet or social media.

130 See, eg, *Webb v The Queen* (1994) 181 CLR 41; *R v Connors* [2013] EWCA Crim 368.

131 *Crofts v The Queen* (1996) 186 CLR 427, 432 (Dawson J), 440–1 (Toohey, Gaudron, Gummow and Kirby JJ) ('*Crofts*'); *Winsor v The Queen* (1866) LR 1 QB 289, 390.

132 Between 2016–17 and 2020–21, judges in Victoria rarely discharged juries because of juror misconduct or jury interference: Paul Dore, 'Australia Gets More Serious about Juror Misconduct' *Jur-E Bulletin*, online, 20 May 2022 <www.ncsc.org/newsroom/jure>.

133 *R v Thompson* [2011] 1 WLR 200, 203 ('*Thompson*'). See also, *Papazoglou v The Queen* [2014] VR 457, 508–13 (Maxwell P), 525 (Weinberg JA); Marder, *The Power of the Jury* (n 3) 125–6.

134 Thomas, *Are Juries Fair?* (n 49) 39. However, some strategies may improve juror knowledge of their obligations: Cheryl Thomas, 'The 21st Century Jury: Contempt, Bias and the Impact of Jury Service' [2020] (11) *Criminal Law Review* 987, 995–7.

135 See, eg, *Thompson* (n 133). See also Judicial Commission of New South Wales, *Criminal Trial Courts Bench Book* <www.judcom.nsw.gov.au/criminal/> [1–480]. See *HCF v The King* (2023) 97 ALJR 978; [2023] HCA 35 [59] where the trial judge informed jurors of their duty to report, but jurors did not report to the judge internet research conducted by another juror.

136 For an example of where the foreperson did inform the judge that a juror had made inquiries on the Internet, see *Hoang v The Queen* (2022) 96 ALJR 453, 456 [6] (Kiefel CJ, Gageler, Keane, Gordon and Edelman JJ).

Jurors may feel reluctant to report their fellow jurors.[137] If, for example, one juror is intimidating another juror, it may be difficult for the affected juror to report their concerns.[138] Reporting another juror for misconduct is likely to be even more difficult for a juror than asking a question during the trial, as discussed next. Given these limits on the reporting of problems within the jury room, trial procedures have revealed little information about juror comprehension.

Limits on the use of evidence about jury deliberations in an appeal against a jury's verdict

Following the conclusion of a trial, evidence of jury deliberations is usually inadmissible except in extremely limited circumstances. These limited circumstances are governed by the so-called 'exclusionary rule'.[139] The exclusionary rule renders evidence about jury deliberations inadmissible unless the evidence concerns factors extrinsic to a jury's deliberations,[140] such as where the jurors have in effect repudiated their oath,[141] or there has been 'criminal conduct calculated to prevent free and frank deliberation'.[142] There is no 'bright line' test for determining what is 'extrinsic' to the jury's deliberations. Whether a matter is extrinsic depends primarily upon applying the policy objective of the rule.[143]

The public policy rationale for the exclusionary rule is to 'preserve the secrecy of jury deliberations, and to maintain the integrity and finality of a formally expressed verdict'.[144] The objective of the rule is to promote full and frank deliberations,[145] to protect jurors (and former jurors) from pressure and harassment,[146] and to promote public confidence in the integrity of the justice system.[147] The exclusionary rule may also suppress criticisms of trial by jury by preventing the disclosure of problems in jury deliberations. As a result, the extent of the rule has been criticised because it means that 'one must accept

137 Tasmania Law Reform Institute, *Jurors, Social Media and the Right of an Accused to a Fair Trial* (Final Report No 30, January 2020) 110–15 [3.7.34]–[3.7.60].

138 See, generally, Judith Fordham, 'Juror Intimidation: An Investigation into the Prevalence and Nature of Juror Intimidation in Western Australia' (2010) 37(5) *Brief* 8.

139 See, eg, *Vaise v Delaval* (1785) 1 TR 11; 99 ER 944; Dorne Boniface, 'Juror Misconduct, Secret Jury Business and the Exclusionary Rule' (2008) 32 *Criminal Law Journal* 18, 24–6 ('Juror Misconduct'); Courselle (n 128) 210.

140 *Smith v Western Australia* (2014) 250 CLR 473 ('*Smith*').

141 *R v Young* [1995] QB 324 ('*Young*').

142 *Smith* (n 140) 484.

143 *Smith* (n 140) 481.

144 *Smith* (n 140) 481. Similar rules apply in the United Kingdom and Canada: *R v Mirza* [2004] 1 AC 1118, 1144 ('*Mirza*'); *R v Pan* [2001] 2 SCR 344, 373–5 ('*Pan*').

145 *Smith* (n 140) 481–2; *Mirza* (n 144) 1144; *Gregory v United Kingdom* (1997) 25 EHHR 577, 594 [44].

146 *Smith* (n 140) 484.

147 Boniface, 'Juror Misconduct' (n 139) 24–8; *Pan* (n 144) 373–5.

some dubious verdicts, even in cases of the utmost gravity, as the cost to be paid for protecting the jury system'.[148]

Cases that discuss the admissibility of evidence from jurors about their deliberations in criminal cases have disclosed serious problems with juror comprehension of their task in those cases.[149] These cases include where:

- some jurors did not understand that their verdict of guilty of murder had to be unanimous — only eight of the 12 jurors supported a verdict of guilty[150]
- some jurors may not have understood that they needed to agree on a verdict of not guilty of murder before returning a verdict on the uncharged offence of manslaughter[151]
- some jurors used a Ouija board to help them reach a verdict[152]
- a jury did not understand that they could ask the judge to clarify the meaning of 'hung jury' and thought the court would hold them for another two weeks or more if they were unable to agree,[153] and
- a jury convicted the accused of manslaughter believing that was the appropriate verdict when they accepted that the accused had acted in self-defence.[154]

The stringency of the exclusionary rule means that such cases are uncommon. While this is not a complete list of every case, the paucity of examples across the last 50 years from several jurisdictions indicates how rarely appellate proceedings disclose information about fundamental juror comprehension problems. Accordingly, while the cases are disturbing, they may be aberrant rather than representative of juror comprehension problems and provide little information to the courts about juror comprehension problems generally.

There are strong public policy grounds for the exclusionary rule. Whether or not there should be any modification to the rule is beyond the scope of

148 *Mirza* (n 144) 1130 (Lord Steyn in dissent). See also *Tanner v United States* 483 US 107 (1987), 115–20 (Marshall J in dissent) ('*Tanner*').

149 For examples of cases in the USA where jurors have misunderstood jury instructions and/or the meaning of words, see Walter W Steele Jr and Elizabeth G Thornburg, 'Jury Instructions: A Persistent Failure to Communicate' (1988) 67 *North Carolina Law Review* 77, 80–3.

150 *Nanan v Trinidad and Tobago* [1986] 1 AC 860. See also *NH v Director of Public Prosecutions (SA)* (2016) 260 CLR 546; [2016] HCA 33 ('*NH v DPP*') where after verdicts had been accepted by the court, the foreperson indicated that the jury did not agree by majority that the accused were not guilty of murder.

151 *NH v* DPP (n 150).

152 *Young* (n 141). Gans argues that this case was much more complex than the case report suggests: Jeremy Gans, *The Ouija Board Jurors: Mystery, Mischief and Misery in the Jury System* (Waterside Press, 2017).

153 *R v Zacharias* (1987) 39 CCC (3d) 280. See also Boniface, 'Juror Misconduct' (n 139) 32.

154 *Sellars v United States* 401 A 2d 974 (1979), 980–2.

this book.[155] What is clear is that for both practical and public policy reasons, the exclusionary rule significantly restricts the information that courts obtain about jurors' comprehension of their task.[156]

Laws that prohibit soliciting, obtaining, and publishing information about jury deliberations

Many jurisdictions have laws that prohibit soliciting or obtaining information about jury deliberations and prohibit the disclosure or publication of information about jury deliberations. In most jurisdictions, it is an offence for jurors to discuss their deliberations with anyone who was not a member of their jury.[157] The general prohibition on discussing deliberations prevents judges, lawyers, academics, journalists, and others from asking jurors any questions about their deliberations, including questions about what jurors did or did not understand. Such questions may risk undermining the jury's verdict and may involve jurors giving evidence of their own misconduct.[158]

The strong confidentiality protections afforded to jury deliberations in most jurisdictions means that little information becomes public, and more particularly to the courts, about what jurors know, how they reason, and whether they fully understand their task. Where a case reveals some juror comprehension problems, its rarity and specificity to a case, means that juror misunderstandings appear to be evidence of individual rather than systemic problems.

Jurors' questions as a guide to comprehension

Most jurisdictions permit jurors to ask the judge questions.[159] The reliability and accuracy of jurors' questions as a source of information about juror comprehension depends on three assumptions.

155 See, eg, *Mirza* (n 144); *Tanner* (n 148); NZLC, *Juries in Criminal Trials: Part Two* (n 61) 65–6 [270]–[277]; Enid Campbell, 'Jury Secrecy and Impeachment of Jury Verdicts (Pt 2)' (1985) 9 *Criminal Law Journal* 187.

156 See, eg, Mark Findlay, 'Policies of Secrecy and Denial: Barriers to Judicial Reform' (1996) 7(3) *Current Issues in Criminal Justice* 368, 369; Comiskey (n 17) 660–1.

157 See, eg, *Juries Act 2000* (Vic) s 78; *Jury Act 1977* (NSW) ss 68A and 68B; *Jury Act 1995* (Qld) s 70; *Contempt of Court Act 1981* (UK) s 8 and *Juries Act 1974* (UK) s 20A; *Criminal Code*, RSC 1985, c C-46, s 649.

158 Justice Michael McHugh, 'Jurors' Deliberations, Jury Secrecy, Public Policy and the Law of Contempt' in Mark Findlay and Peter Duff (eds), *The Jury Under Attack* (Butterworths, 1988) 58–61.

159 Jacqueline Horan, 'Empowering Jurors to Ask Questions about the Expert Evidence in Criminal Trials' (2024) 28(4) *The International Journal of Evidence & Proof* 312 ('Empowering Jurors'). The ability to ask questions is more restricted in some states in the USA: Nancy S Marder, 'Answering Jurors' Questions: Next Steps in Illinois' (2010) 41 *Loyola University of Chicago Law Journal* 727 ('Answering Jurors' Questions').

The first assumption is that jurors will correctly identify when they do not understand a direction. As I discuss in Chapter 3, there is a significant difference between jurors' subjective assessment of their comprehension and objective tests of juror comprehension. Many jurors cannot reliably identify every direction which they do not understand.[160]

The second assumption is that jurors will always ask the judge a question to resolve their uncertainty. Justice Watt says that jurors and juries are 'not the least hesitant to report any difficulties encountered in their deliberations, including their inability to reach a unanimous verdict'.[161] Justice Watt does not cite any evidence for this proposition, and he may be relying on his experience as a trial judge of jurors reporting or asking questions about such matters. Jurors may be more likely to report an inability to reach a unanimous verdict than to ask a question, because they have no choice but to report a problem if (enough) jurors cannot agree on their verdict. However, research suggests that jurors often feel 'an overwhelming inhibition against asking questions'.[162] In New South Wales, 30% of jurors surveyed wanted further directions or explanations during deliberations but only half of those jurors sought such information.[163] Studies in other jurisdictions have also shown that a significant proportion of jurors felt intimidated, discouraged, or (mistakenly) thought that they could not ask questions.[164] In a study of 55 criminal jury trials in Australia, most jurors (93% of trials surveyed) were told at the start of the trial that they could ask questions, but 95% of jurors who had a question for an expert witness did not ask their question.[165] However, some jurors reported that they did not know they could ask questions, other jurors did not feel comfortable asking questions, were worried they were not allowed to ask their questions, or felt that they would be interrupting proceedings by asking questions.[166]

The third assumption is that the judge will understand the jury's questions. In the highly publicised trial of Vicky Pryce in London, the jury asked the judge ten questions. Having discharged the jury for failing to reach a verdict, the judge said that the jury's questions revealed 'absolutely fundamental

160 See, eg, James R P Ogloff and V Gordon Rose, 'The Comprehension of Judicial Instructions' in Neil Brewer and Kipling D Williams (eds), *Psychology and Law: An Empirical Perspective* (Guilford Press, 2005) 407; Penny Darbyshire, Andy Maughan and Angus Stewart, 'What Can the English Legal System Learn from Jury Research Published up to 2001?' (Kingston Law School, 2001) <www.sixthformlaw.info/06_misc/pdf_files/penny_darbyshire.pdf>.

161 Watt (n 1) 261.

162 Darbyshire, Maughan and Stewart (n 160) 48.

163 Mark Findlay, 'Juror Comprehension and Complexity' (2001) 41 *British Journal of Criminology* 56, 71.

164 See generally, Kate Warner, Julia Davis and Peter Underwood, 'The Jury Experience: Insights from the Tasmanian Jury Study' (2011) 10(3) *Judicial Review* 333, 340–1; NZLC, *Juries in Criminal Trials: Part Two* (n 61) 31.

165 Horan, 'Empowering Jurors' (n 159) 317.

166 Horan, 'Empowering Jurors' (n 159).

deficits in understanding'.[167] The judge's exasperation reflected a significant difference between what he expected jurors to know and what the jurors did know. The jury questions included:

- some common problems (eg, what does 'proof beyond reasonable doubt' mean)
- challenges in understanding elements of an offence (eg, what does it mean for a 'will to be overborne'), and
- cognitive challenges (eg, the difference between inferences and speculation, when jurors may use common sense, and when doing so becomes speculation).

The jurors' questions were potentially a useful source of information about what jurors did not know in that case: the judge's responsibility was to 'understand the jury's uncertainty, not to make light of it'.[168]

Accordingly, jurors do not always correctly identify what they do not understand, they may be reluctant to ask questions, and judges may not fully understand jurors' questions. As a result, information from jurors' questions provides a limited and potentially inaccurate source of information for determining what jurors know and how they reason. This is not to suggest that jurors should not ask questions. The benefit to jurors in being able to ask questions[169] is quite different from whether questions provide valuable and reliable information from which judges can determine what jurors know and how they reason.

Given the significant limitations in obtaining direct information about what jurors understand, the next section examines the courts' indirect methods for determining what jurors understand.

Judicial knowledge and experience

Courts use their 'judicial knowledge and experience'[170] to determine what jurors know, and the reasoning errors they might make, to determine what guidance is necessary to ensure a fair trial. Sometimes courts refer to judicial

167 Caroline Davies, 'Vicky Pryce Faces Retrial after Jury "Fails to Grasp Basics"' *The Guardian* (UK News), online, 21 February 2013 <www.theguardian.com/uk/2013/feb/20/vicky-pryce-retrial-jury>.

168 Steven Lubet and Kevin Chang, 'Stupid Juror Questions?' (2013) 37(2) *American Journal of Trial Advocacy* 315, 331.

169 See, eg, Marder, 'Answering Jurors' Questions' (n 159); Larry Heuer and Steven Penrod, 'Increasing Jurors' Participation in Trials: A Field Experiment with Jury Notetaking and Question Asking' (1988) 12(3) *Law and Human Behavior* 231.

170 See, eg, *Barker* (n 2) [40]; *R v Miller* [2010] EWCA Crim 1153 [21] ('*R v Miller*'); *IMM v The Queen* (2016) 257 CLR 300, 346 (Nettle and Gordon JJ) ('*IMM*').

knowledge and experience as their 'collective' 'judicial knowledge and experience', or 'collective experience', 'experience', or 'corporate' experience.[171]

Courts have not defined 'judicial knowledge and experience' and have not described how judges form it. It often involves empirical conclusions that are not based on robust data. Judicial perceptions about what is comprehensible to jurors are most likely formed by a combination of factors including what judges find comprehensible, what judges believe jurors find comprehensible, judges' observations of juror demeanour when judges direct the jury, and conclusions that judges draw from jury questions and jury verdicts about whether jurors have understood their task.

Judicial knowledge and experience is often formed based on inferences drawn from repeated conduct or events. For example, the High Court of Australia has said that 'the experience and wisdom of the law is that, almost universally, jurors approach their task conscientiously'.[172] Further, courts assume that jurors understand the judge's directions — an assumption that courts claim has 'been tested by the experience of generations of judges, lawyers, parties and jurors'.[173]

Courts can use 'judicial knowledge and experience' to decide specific matters, such as whether a direction is or is not comprehensible to a juror — without any evidence. For example, as discussed, a majority of High Court judges in *Zecevic* concluded that trial judges could not explain the *Viro* formulation of self-defence in 'readily understandable' terms. However, the majority concluded that their new test was 'readily understandable' to a jury. The judges reached both conclusions without any evidence.[174] Similarly, without relying on any empirical evidence, Lord Hughes JSC described part of the test of dishonesty as a 'test which jurors and others often find puzzling and difficult to apply'.[175] Again, without relying on empirical evidence or referring to evidence showing the difficulties jurors have with the concept of 'proof beyond reasonable doubt', the High Court of Australia said that comparing the civil standard

171 See, eg, *Barker* (n 2) [40]; *R v Miller* (n 170) [21]; *Crown Court Compendium* (n 5) ch 20–1; *IMM* (n 170) 346 (Nettle and Gordon JJ); Peter McClellan, 'Legislative Facts and Section 144 — A Contemporary Problem?' (Speech, Supreme Court of New South Wales Annual Conference 2015, 4 September 2015).

172 *Dupas v The Queen* (2010) 241 CLR 237, 247 [26]. See also *R v Abu Hamza* [2011] ECHR 211.

173 *Mirza* (n 144) 1179 [164] (Lord Rodger). Similarly, 'the experience of trial judges is that juries do perform their duty according to the law': *Corbett* (n 18) 692 (Dickson CJ).

174 *Zecevic* (n 72) 660 (Wilson, Dawson and Toohey JJ). The courts' 'experience' included the experience recounted by trial judges, see, eg, *Lawson and Forsythe v The Queen* [1986] VR 515, 547 (McGarvie J).

175 *Ivey v Genting Casinos (UK) Ltd* [2017] AC 391, 408 [57]. For empirical evidence concerning whether jurors find it difficult to apply, see Emily Finch, 'The Elephant in the Jury Room: Exploring Mock Jurors' Understanding of Different Approaches to Dishonesty' [2021] (7) *Criminal Law Review* 513.

of proof with the criminal standard of proof provided 'an effective means of conveying to a jury' the higher standard of criminal proof.[176]

When judicial knowledge and experience appears in a judgment, it often appears as an incontrovertible statement of fact. Further, courts often do not describe their conclusions as part of the court's judicial knowledge and experience. Courts can simply state a fact or conclusion, and they need not explain the basis for their conclusion. For example, a Victorian appellate judge said that 'longstanding experience has demonstrated that the . . . [direction on recklessness] is straightforward and relatively simple for juries to apply. . . . In the Court's experience, it is a test easily grasped by juries'.[177] Further, because these descriptions are so pervasive, the fact that judges use this knowledge and experience can seem unremarkable.[178] This can make it difficult to recognise this form of knowledge.

For many years, 'judicial knowledge and experience' provided the only available way for courts to form a view about juror comprehension. The courts' judicial knowledge and experience has been accurate and important in some areas. For example, in identifying that there were risks associated with identification evidence.[179] However, it was not accurate or helpful in other areas, such as sexual offences where some jury directions developed based on the incorrect assumption that a complaint of a sexual offence is 'easy to fabricate, but extremely difficult to refute'.[180] The courts' judicial knowledge and experience may have simply reflected a common misconception. For example, the High Court of Australia said that sexual offence directions on delay in making a complaint were 'based on supposed "human experience" and the "experience of the courts"'.[181] This occurred because what constitutes, or is believed to constitute, 'ordinary human behaviour' largely developed without a scientific basis. Instead, it reflected the prevailing subjective opinion or perceptions of the world of predominantly similar people (judges) in terms of gender, education, and class[182] who determine what constitutes 'judicial knowledge and experience'.

176 *R v Dookheea* (2017) 262 CLR 402, 426 [41].

177 *DPP (Vic) Reference No 1 of 2019* (2020) 284 A Crim R 19, 51 [124] (Priest JA).

178 See generally, Greg Byrne, 'The High Court in *Pell v The Queen:* An "Unreasonable" Review of the Jury's Decision' (2020) 45(4) *Alternative Law Journal* 284, 289–90.

179 See, eg, Australian Law Reform Commission, *Evidence* (n 23) [420]–[436]; Fiona Leverick, 'Jury Instructions on Eyewitness Identification Evidence: A Re-Evaluation' (2016) 49(3) *Creighton Law Review* 555, 557–9.

180 See, eg, Australian Law Reform Commission, *Family Violence — A National Legal Response* (Report No 114, October 2010) 1311–34; Boniface, 'The Common Sense of Jurors' (n 70) 264–6.

181 *Crofts* (n 131) 451 (Toohey, Gaudron, Gummow and Kirby JJ).

182 See generally, Chief Justice James Spigelman, 'The Truth Can Cost Too Much: The Principle of a Fair Trial' (2004) 78 *Australian Law Journal* 29, 39; Kylie Burns, 'Judges, "Common Sense" and Judicial Cognition' (2019) 23(3) *Griffith Law Review* 319, 329–30.

Chapter 4 further discusses the relationship between judicial knowledge and experience and judicial notice, and the reliability of judicial knowledge and experience. However, before discussing those matters, it is implicit within the idea of 'judicial knowledge and experience' that courts understand jurors.

Courts' assumptions about jurors

Judicial knowledge and experience inform the courts' assumptions about jurors. There are few clear general statements about what jurors know, how they reason, or a set of decision-making skills that courts assume an ordinary juror possesses.[183] Justice Watt says that it can be inferred that the law (including courts) operates on the assumption that the

> ideal juror is passive, an observer of trial proceedings who is the object of one-way linear communication. She or he is a complete and accurate encoder of information who suspends judgment on the evidence and issues until the end of the case. And at the end of the case, our ideal juror considers all the evidence, remembers each and every legal instruction, and applies those instructions unerringly to reach a verdict that she or he does *not* explain.[184]

Courts also assume that jurors are 'blank slates',[185] enabling jurors to 'suspend judgment' until the end of the case. However, this assumption is qualified in that many evidentiary directions have developed to address concerns that jurors may reason incorrectly or that jurors may give inappropriate weight to certain evidence. Justice Watt's description of the court's assumptions about the ideal juror focuses on jurors' capacity and reasoning processes. These assumptions accord with the court's traditional form of assistance to jurors being provided mostly during the summing up. These assumptions may be changing as judges increasingly provide some guidance during the trial. However, they remain the law's starting point when considering jurors and the starting point from which changes are made.

The traditional view of jurors as 'ready-made problem solvers' also assumes that jurors know what their role is as jurors and how they should go about their group decision-making task.[186] Rather than finding 'ready-made problem

183 Nancy Pennington and Reid Hastie, 'A Cognitive Theory of Juror Decision Making: The Story Model' (1991) 13 *Cardozo Law Review* 519. The authors say that 'psychological literature also lacks any general unified discussion, although an unflattering image of the juror can be discerned in the multitude of references to a bias-prone creature who constructs a decision from a toolbox of prejudices and heuristics': at 519.

184 Watt (n 1) 63–4 (emphasis in original).

185 See eg, Sara Gordon, 'Through the Eyes of Jurors: The Use of Schemas in the Application of "Plain Language" Jury Instructions' (2013) 64 *Hastings Law Journal* 643, 669.

186 Marder, *The Power of the Jury* (n 3) 3.

solvers', Marder explains how the jury system *makes*, rather than finds, jurors.[187] The jury system including various aspects of their courtroom experience transforms citizens into jurors who begin to understand their role and how they should perform it. For example, jurors observe courts proceedings, the roles performed by the judge and counsel, how the judge communicates with the jury throughout the trial, and jurors have their own jury box in court and a room in which to conduct their deliberations confidentially.

The courts' assumptions about jurors are also apparent when courts review jury verdicts. In most common law jurisdictions, appeal provisions specifically provide that the court must allow an appeal if the jury's verdict is unreasonable or cannot be supported having regard to the evidence.[188] Appellate courts have interpreted this ground differently. On the one hand, appellate courts in Scotland will almost never overturn a jury's verdict.[189] By contrast, the High Court in Australia has developed a test that has resulted in a significant number of jury verdicts (83 of 614) being overturned.[190] This is because the High Court has said that in determining whether 'it was open to the jury to be satisfied beyond reasonable doubt that the accused was guilty . . . a doubt experienced by an appellate court will be a doubt which a jury ought to have experienced'.[191] The High Court did not cite any evidence for the proposition that a doubt experienced by an appellate judge is a doubt that a jury (or juror) ought to have experienced.

Research in New Zealand found that while judges in 48 trials 'essentially' agreed with jury verdicts in half the cases and considered almost another quarter of verdicts to be open to the jury and therefore did not agree with a significant number of verdicts.[192] The High Court also did not explain how it reconciles its view about jury-judge doubt with its view that the 'purpose and genius of the jury system' is how it incorporates the 'ordinary experiences of ordinary people . . . in the determination of factual matters'.[193] Psychologists have said that people may construct different stories from identical evidence 'primarily because they filter the evidence through their own experiences, expectations, values, and beliefs'.[194]

187 Marder, *The Power of the Jury* (n 3) 10.

188 See, eg, *Criminal Procedure Act 2009* **(Vic)** s 276(1)(a); *Criminal Appeal Act 1912* (NSW) s 6(1); *Criminal Code*, RSC 1985, c C-46 s 686(1)(a)(i); *Criminal Procedure Act 2011* (NZ) s 232(2)(a). See also *Criminal Appeal Act 1968* (UK) s 2(a).

189 See, eg, *King v Her Majesty's Advocate* (1999) SCCR 330, 333; *Donegan v Her Majesty's Advocate* [2019] HCJAC 10 [35].

190 Tilmouth (n 38) 19–21.

191 *M v The Queen* (1994) 181 CLR 487, 494–4 ('*M*').

192 NZLC, *Juries in Criminal Trials: Part Two* (n 61) 68 [9.3]–[9.4].

193 *Doney v The Queen* (1990) 171 CLR 207, 214. See also Nancy S Marder, 'Introduction to the Jury at a Crossroad: The American Experience' (2003) 78 *Chicago-Kent Law Review* 909, 922.

194 Brian H Bornstein and Edie Greene, 'Jury Decision Making: Implications for and from Psychology' (2011) 20 *Current Directions in Psychological Science* 63, 64–5.

In practice, appellate courts have acknowledged that there may be different reasonable views of the facts.[195] Indeed, significant disagreements about factual conclusions in a case, and whether they have a doubt about the accused's guilt, are not uncommon even among appellate judges.[196] It may be that the High Court's position on jury-judge doubt reflects a policy position about when it will review a jury's verdict rather than a view that an ideal juror is indistinguishable from a judge, at least in terms of when they should have a doubt. That might explain why New Zealand and Canada have interpreted the same ground of appeal differently and expressly recognise that jurors may reach different conclusions about the facts and the question is whether that finding was open to the jury.[197]

Courts' assumptions about who jurors are

To determine what jurors know, and how they reason, it is also important to understand who jurors are and how they have changed.

In 1956, Lord Devlin described English juries as 'predominantly male, middle-aged, middle-minded and middle-class'.[198] English juries changed from being predominantly male to include females more generally in 1972.[199] Property qualifications and gender restricted jury service until they were removed in New South Wales in 1947 and in Victoria in 1956.[200] Canada[201] and New Zealand[202] have similar histories in the composition of their juries.

A common myth appears to be that juries are comprised of disproportionate numbers of unemployed people and pensioners[203] and that this contributes to juror comprehension problems. This assumes that those with higher levels of education and training 'will be able to think abstractly, follow complex evidence and feel comfortable sitting down for long periods'.[204] However, across

195 See, eg, *Kalbasi v The Queen* (2018) 264 CLR 62, 121 [159] (Edelman J); David Hamer, 'Appeals against Conviction on Indictment: Process, Outcome and NSW Reform after Kalbasi v Western Australia' (2019) 43 *Criminal Law Journal* 201, 211.

196 See, eg, *M* (n 191); *S v The Queen* (1989) 168 CLR 266.

197 See, eg, *R v Munro* [2007] 2 NZLR 87, 106–7 [87]; *Corbett v The Queen* [1975] 2 SCR 275, 282.

198 Lord Patrick Devlin, *Trial by Jury* (Stevens, 1956) 20.

199 *Criminal Justice Act 1972* (UK) s 26.

200 Jacqueline Horan and David Tait, 'Do Juries Adequately Represent the Community? A Case Study of Civil Juries in Victoria' (2007) 16 *Journal of Judicial Administration* 179, 182.

201 Regina Schuller and Neil Vidmar, 'The Canadian Criminal Jury' (2011) 86 *Chicago-Kent Law Review* 497, 501.

202 *Juries Amendment Act 1976* (NZ).

203 Cheryl Thomas and Nigel Balmer, *Diversity and Fairness in the Jury System* (Ministry of Justice Research Series 2/07, June 2007) 190; Queensland Law Reform Commission, *A Review of Jury Selection* (Report No 68, February 2011) 48–9 (QLRC).

204 Horan and Tait (n 200) 197.

Australia, jurors are likely to be better educated than the general population.[205] While not assessing education levels, research in England and Wales concluded that it was a myth that 'middle classes', and those who were referred to in the 'Auld review as "the important & clever" manage to avoid jury service'.[206] High status professions were fully represented on juries and the highest rates of jury service were from middle- to high-income earners.[207]

The jury itself faces new kinds of challenges. Changing juror demographics means that there are more jurors (including digital natives) who are used to being 'continuously online and engaged'.[208] In the information age, '[s]earch engines such as *Google* are new tools in our problem-solving toolkits'.[209] Therefore, jurors' expectations about how courts should present information to them have been changing.[210] Yet jurors are deprived 'of the very tool by which they are accustomed to learning and organizing material'.[211] Jurors are required to confine themselves to the evidence in the trial. However, research suggests that many jurors want to use the internet during a trial, and some do.[212]

Courts rarely discuss whether these kinds of changes to the composition of the jury (or even myths about its composition) have made any difference in determining what jurors know or how they reason. Limitations in understanding jurors constrains the courts' judicial knowledge and experience of what jurors know, how they reason, and what courts need to do to guide jurors with their task.

Therefore, there are limitations in both the courts' direct and indirect information about what jurors know and how they reason. At the same time, the functions performed by both judges and jurors are increasingly complicated.

205 Jane Goodman-Delahunty et al, *Practices, Policies and Procedures That Influence Juror Satisfaction in Australia* (Research and Public Policy Series No 87, July 2007) 130, Table 12; QLRC, *A Review of Jury Selection* (n 202) 48 [4.22]; Horan and Tait (n 200) 196–7.

206 Thomas and Balmer (n 203) 197–8.

207 Thomas and Balmer (n 203) 197–8.

208 *Jurors, Social Media and the Right of an Accused to a Fair Trial* (n 137) xv. 'Recent Australian survey results indicate that approximately 87% of Australians use the internet at least once per day; 60% of Australians use the internet more than five times per day; and Australians own, on average, 3.5 internet-enabled devices': at 16. See also Krislin C Nuzum, 'Letting Google into the Jury Room: A Proposed Study on the Effect of Abolishing the Juror Research Admonition' (2019) 60(1) *Jurimetrics* 105, 108.

209 Nuzum (n 208) 108.

210 Nuzum (n 208) 108; Jacqueline Horan, 'Jurors as Detectives of Truth and "Don't Search" Instructions in Sexual Assault Trials' in Greg Byrne and Jacqueline Horan (eds), *Sexual Assault Trials: Challenges and Innovations* (LexisNexis, 2025) 145, 149–55 ('Jurors as Detectives of Truth').

211 Nancy S Marder, 'Juries and Technology: Equipping Jurors for the Twenty-First Century' (2001) 66 *Brooklyn Law Review* 1257, 1285.

212 See, eg, Horan, 'Jurors as Detectives of Truth' (n 210). See also Thaddeus Hoffmeister and Ann Charles Watts, 'Social Media, the Internet, and Trial by Jury' (2018) 14(1) *Annual Review of Law and Social Science* 259, 266–7.

Judges must determine what is or is not understandable to jurors, predict potential errors in reasoning that jurors may make, craft their directions to prevent jury errors, and ensure that jurors do understand their task.

Conclusion

Assessing juror comprehension presents systemic challenges for the courts. The confidentiality of jury deliberations and the limited reliable information provided by jurors' questions means that the courts have relied on indirect methods for assessing juror comprehension. Judges generally make their own assessments of juror comprehension based on limited data and their own views of what jurors should comprehend. The number of successful appeals and the length of the summing up provide blunt indicators of juror comprehension problems. However, together, these blunt indicators and judicial assessments of juror comprehension have increased recognition of juror comprehension problems and driven some reform.

Most significantly, the courts' own assessments have led to changes in the way some judges assist jurors with their task. Reconceptualising the judge's role as a guide and a cartographer highlight ways in which trial by jury can adapt to meet juror comprehension challenges. However, change tends to come from individual judges, and this has contributed to the extent of change between and within jurisdictions varying significantly. Further, no jurisdiction has an ongoing process for conducting research on juror comprehension and apart from England and Wales (to an extent), no jurisdiction has an ongoing process for improving juror comprehension.

Chapter 3 examines what social science research reveals about whether the courts have correctly identified what jurors need to know and the effectiveness of the courts' guidance to juries.

3 Social science juror comprehension research

Introduction

Juror comprehension problems mean that jurors may not fully understand their task and therefore, not decide cases on their legal and factual merits. Chapter 2 discussed how courts assess whether there are juror comprehension problems and their pragmatic assumption that jurors understand jury directions. While courts primarily rely on indirect information about jurors that is quite limited and may be unreliable, the courts' conclusions could still be accurate. Social science research from disciplines such as psychology, linguistics, and psycholinguistics provides another method for examining juror comprehension.

Juror comprehension research is extensive. In 2001, Penny Darbyshire referred to 'the mass of sophisticated work on juror comprehension and jury instructions that has been produced in the United States and elsewhere'.[1] Dennis Devine et al described the empirical literature as so large that is 'nearly impossible to review comprehensively'.[2] In this chapter I discuss key research about juror comprehension problems, including research that examines how jurors approach their task in a trial and the differences between subjective and objective assessments of juror comprehension. I also examine the strengths and limitations of juror comprehension research, and common criticisms of this kind of research. Because this research comes from different jurisdictions, I also discuss whether, and if so to what extent, research from one common law jurisdiction can be relied on in another jurisdiction. Existing research is more than sufficient to determine whether there are juror comprehension problems and, in general terms, the nature and extent of these problems. In Chapter 4, I discuss why juror comprehension research has been of limited effect in changing the law and trials to address juror comprehension problems.

1 Penny Darbyshire, Andy Maughan and Angus Stewart, 'What Can the English Legal System Learn From Jury Research Published up to 2001?' (Kingston Law School, 2001) <www.sixthformlaw.info/06_misc/pdf_files/penny_darbyshire.pdf> 1.

2 See, eg, Dennis J Devine et al, 'Jury Decision Making: 45 Years of Empirical Research on Deliberating Groups' (2001) 7 *Psychology, Public Policy and Law* 622, 625.

DOI: 10.4324/9781003477129-3

Understanding the juror's task

The juror's task

As discussed in Chapter 2, it can be inferred that the law has traditionally assumed that jurors will passively observe trial proceedings, suspend any judgment while recording all the evidence, understand and remember all jury directions, and then apply those directions correctly to the evidence they have recorded. While the judge's guidance has continued to evolve, the fundamental components of that guidance remain the same. In broad terms, the assumptions underpinning the judge's guidance are that the jury will:

- listen to and evaluate fairly the evidence in the case
- comprehend the relevant laws from the judge's directions, and
- apply the law to the facts.

Nancy Pennington and Reid Hastie have further broken down these three functions, identifying eight steps that the law assumes the ideal juror must perform:

(1) 'encode' information from the trial — this involves listening to and remembering the evidence
(2) understand legal categories and the differences between legal categories (eg, in relation to alternative offences)
(3) select the admissible evidence and ignore the inadmissible evidence or information (eg, counsel's body language or facial expressions)
(4) construct a plausible sequence of events
(5) evaluate the credibility and reliability of witnesses — this includes assessing what witnesses say against jurors' own experience and knowledge
(6) evaluate any inconsistencies in the evidence including any directly contradictory evidence
(7) assess their findings of fact against the presumption of innocence and the standard of proof beyond reasonable doubt, and
(8) decide on their verdict.[3]

These steps can be challenging. For example, the second step involves understanding legal categories. This step usually refers to the way a judge traditionally gives jury directions about the law. Legal concepts can be amorphous and difficult to understand. In trying to understand directions, jurors 'bring their lay expectations and understandings to the task of interpreting legal instructions'.[4]

3 Nancy Pennington and Reid Hastie, 'Juror Decision-Making Models: The Generalization Gap' (1981) 89 *Psychological Bulletin* 246, 249–55.
4 Shari Seidman Diamond and Judith N Levi, 'Improving Decisions on Death by Revising and Testing Jury Instructions' (1996) 79 *Judicature* 224, 232.

Jurors may assign meaning to words and phrases that are different from their legal meaning (eg, for offences like burglary, terms like assault, and words like 'charge' which may be used in different ways).[5] It can also be difficult for jurors to follow and apply directions that contradict their intuitions or preconceptions about judicial processes (eg, jurors may think that circumstantial evidence does not carry the same weight as direct evidence).[6]

Jurors may also have pre-existing beliefs about witnesses that affect their ability to evaluate the credibility and reliability of witnesses (Pennington and Hastie's step five). For example, jurors may believe that police are specially trained observers and therefore their identification evidence is more reliable, or that the evidence of a confident witness is more accurate than a hesitant witness.[7] Further, the judge may give the jury evidentiary directions to counteract pre-existing beliefs, which courts expect jurors to understand and apply when evaluating a witness's evidence.

In addition to the discrete challenges with all eight steps, cognitive load theory is relevant to all steps that jurors engage in. Cognitive load 'can be thought of as the mental activity imposed upon an individual's finite working memory'.[8] Limits to a person's working memory may inhibit their capacity to understand their task, including jury directions.[9] The extent of cognitive load will depend upon many factors, including the quantity of evidence, familiarity with the evidence (eg, technical or scientific evidence),[10] the complexity of the law the jury must apply, and the issues that are in dispute in the trial. A trial may take many days. Jurors must decide whether the accused is guilty or not guilty of a serious criminal offence, cognisant of the significant ramifications of their decision for the accused, the victim of the crime (if there is one), and the community.[11] '[S]tress, emotions and uncertainty' may reduce

5 See, eg, Diamond and Levi (n 4) 232; Peter M Tiersma, 'Communicating with Juries: How to Draft More Understandable Instructions' (2005–06) 10 *The Scribes of Journal Legal Writing* 1, 8–11.

6 See, eg, Norman J Finkel, 'Commonsense Justice and Jury Instructions: Instructive and Reciprocating Connections' (2000) 6(3) *Psychology, Public Policy, and Law* 591; Vicki L Smith, 'Prototypes in the Courtroom: Lay Representations of Legal Concepts' (1991) 61(6) *Journal of Personality and Social Psychology* 857; Bradley Saxton, 'How Well Do Jurors Understand Jury Instructions? A Field Test Using Real Juries and Real Trials in Wyoming' (1998) 33 *Land and Water Law Review* 59, 95.

7 Elizabeth F Loftus and Edith Greene, 'Twelve Angry People: The Collective Mind of the Jury' (1984) 84 *Columbia Law Review* 1425, 1432.

8 Ryan Essex and Jane Goodman-Delahunty, 'Judicial Directions and the Criminal Standard of Proof: Improving Juror Comprehension' (2014) 24 *Journal of Judicial Administration* 75, 77. See generally, John Sweller, Jeroen J G van Merriënboer and Fred Paas, 'Cognitive Architecture and Instructional Design: 20 Years Later' (2019) 31(2) *Educational Psychology Review* 261.

9 Sweller, Merriënboer and Paas (n 8) 261–3.

10 Sweller, Merriënboer and Paas (n 8) 263.

11 Brian H Bornstein et al, 'Juror Reactions to Jury Duty: Perceptions of the System and Potential Stressors' (2005) 23(3) *Behavioral Sciences & Law* 321, 322–3.

working memory.[12] And cognitive load is likely to be higher for jurors who return a verdict of guilty.[13]

Being a juror is particularly challenging. At the start of the trial, judges may not give jurors any organising framework for the decision they will have to make. Evidence at a trial follows a question-and-answer format. Witnesses give evidence about various parts of a chain of events, fragmenting a story. Evidence laws may prevent a witness from giving 'the full story', such as evidence about reasons for their conduct, or emotional reactions that a person had. Jurors must then organise and make sense of this patchwork of information. The jury and trial processes may play important roles in transforming people into jurors who broadly understand their role.[14]

Further, jurors are often inexperienced with a decision-making task of this nature. People learn in different ways, and they must perform a complex and difficult learning task.[15] Jurors are often passively rather than actively engaged in a learning process, which may make recalling evidence more difficult, particularly for those jurors who are predominantly active learners.[16] The trial process necessarily constrains the application of best-practice educational principles, making it more difficult for both the judge in teaching and the juror in learning.[17] Jurors do not have the benefit of a dialogue with their teacher and the teacher focuses primarily on the lesson being taught rather than the needs of the learner.[18] Further, entering a novel and demanding situation, jurors are likely to have some degree of anxiety about their task which may impede their ability to absorb and organise new information.

Social science research reveals that there is a substantial difference between the courts' concept of an ideal juror and the real juror's task. The courts' ideal juror is a legal fiction — no 'research-based support can be found for this model in social science, legal, or political science literature'.[19] Therefore the next question is whether there is a better way of understanding and explaining the real juror's task.

12 Sweller, Merriënboer and Paas (n 8) 285.

13 Tamsin Ede and Jane Goodman-Delahunty, 'Question Trails in Trials: Structured versus Unstructured Juror Decision-Making' (2013) 37 *Criminal Law Journal* 114, 129.

14 Nancy Marder, *The Power of the Jury: Transforming Citizens into Jurors* (Cambridge University Press, 2022) 1–2.

15 See generally, Lora M Levett et al, 'The Psychology of Jury and Juror Decision Making' in Neil Brewer and Kipling D Williams (eds), *Psychology and Law: An Empirical Perspective* (Guilford Press, 2005) 365, 379.

16 Max Rogers, 'Laypeople as Learners: Applying Educational Principles to Improve Juror Comprehension of Instructions' (2021) 115 *Northwestern University Law Review* 1185, 1213–14.

17 Jacqueline Horan, 'Jurors as Detectives of Truth and "Don't Search" Instructions in Sexual Assault Trials' in Greg Byrne and Jacqueline Horan (eds), *Sexual Assault Trials: Challenges and Innovations* (LexisNexis, 2025) 145, 151–3.

18 Horan (n 17) 151–3.

19 B Michael Dann, '"Learning Lessons" and "Speaking Rights": Creating Educated and Democratic Juries' (1993) 68 *Indiana Law Journal* 1229, 1241.

The story model

The 'story model' is generally accepted as providing the best explanation for how jurors approach their task.[20] According to the story model, the real juror is not a passive listener, recording and then evaluating evidence at the end of the trial. This juror is 'an active participant, struggling to make sense of the trial' from the moment that they enter the jury box.[21]

The first step in the story model involves jurors using their knowledge and experience to develop a meaningful understanding of the case, by imposing 'a narrative story organization on trial information'.[22] Jurors use their knowledge and experience to understand and assess the evidence presented at trial. Each person's knowledge and experience are a type of 'schema', that is, 'a cognitive framework that helps individuals organize and interpret information'.[23] All people — including judges and jurors — have their own knowledge and experience that is relevant to how they organise and interpret information. Which of the many schemas jurors possess will be activated in a trial will depend upon how recently the juror has used or considered that schema and how the juror frames the information in the trial. 'Framing' refers to what the juror sees as relevant to understanding the issues in the trial and their task. 'Framing' helps jurors to understand, shape, and define an issue.[24] When explaining the issues to the jury, the judge's framing of the issues reflects what the judge considers to be relevant. The judge's framing of the issues may help to shape and define the issues for jurors. Understanding jurors' schemas and ways of framing issues is important not just to jury directions but to all the information presented in the trial.

Jurors may consider more than one story at a time when evaluating evidence. The story that is likely to emerge as the 'best' story is one that has the best coverage, coherence, and uniqueness.[25] A story has the best coverage if it accounts for all the evidence presented at the trial. The most coherent story is

20 See generally, Nancy Pennington and Reid Hastie, 'A Cognitive Theory of Juror Decision Making: The Story Model' (1991) 13 *Cardozo Law Review* 519; Dennis J Devine, *Jury Decision Making: The State of Science* (New York University Press, 2012) 26–9; Darbyshire, Maughan and Stewart (n 1) 22; Levett et al (n 15) 373–5.

21 Levett et al (n 15) 373.

22 Nancy Pennington and Reid Hastie, 'Evidence Evaluation in Complex Decision Making' (1986) 51 *Journal of Personality and Social Psychology* 242, 243 ('Evidence Evaluation'); Shelley C Spiecker and Debra L Worthington, 'The Influence of Opening Statement/Closing Argument Organizational Strategy on Juror Verdict and Damage Awards' (2003) 27(4) *Law and Human Behavior* 437, 438–9.

23 Sara Gordon, 'Through the Eyes of Jurors: The Use of Schemas in the Application of "Plain Language" Jury Instructions' (2013) 64 *Hastings Law Journal* 643, 649–51.

24 Gordon (n 23) 653–6; Brian H Bornstein and Edie Greene, 'Jury Decision Making: Implications for and from Psychology' (2011) 20 *Current Directions in Psychological Science* 63, 64–5.

25 See generally Nancy Pennington and Reid Hastie, 'The Story Model for Juror Decision Making' in Reid Hastie (ed), *Inside the Juror: The Psychology of Juror Decision Making* (Cambridge University Press, 1993) 192, 198–9; Levett et al (n 15) 374.

one that is consistent, plausible, and complete. If two or more stories have similar coverage and coherence, jurors will not have confidence in the story unless one of the stories is unique. Each juror organises and forms the most coherent story by assessing the evidence — or the plausibility of story events —against their own knowledge of the world and what usually happens.[26] Because each juror performs this task, jurors from the same jury who hear identical pieces of evidence may construct different stories, 'primarily because they filter the evidence through their own experiences, expectations, value and beliefs'.[27]

The second step in the story model involves jurors understanding the judge's directions, or decision-making criteria. This stage can be complex. There may be alternative offences where there are important decision-making criteria that distinguish one verdict outcome from another (eg, murder, manslaughter, and self-defence as a full acquittal to such charges).[28] Further, jurors may need to reassess their evaluation of a witness, or the relevance of evidence, in accordance with the judge's directions about the evidence.

The third step in the story model involves jurors combining the story information with the classifications and definitions in the judge's directions and determining the best match between the story and the potential verdicts.[29] This involves an assessment of the likelihood that the defendant committed the crime, and jurors must be satisfied about this likelihood beyond reasonable doubt.

Thus, research highlights how much information jurors must learn, and the complexity of the reasoning process jurors undertake. This research stands in marked contrast to what we can infer is the courts' concept of an ideal juror, and what the ideal juror knows and how they reason. However, despite the limitations in the courts' understanding of jurors, the courts' guidance might still be effective.

The effectiveness of the judge's guidance to jurors

Social science juror comprehension research has focused extensively on the judge's directions because directions provide the jury's decision-making criteria (the second step in the story model). This section examines research concerning the effectiveness of jury directions. The research involves jurors and juries from actual cases and from jury simulation studies. The research assesses both subjective and objective juror comprehension levels.

In broad terms, there have been several trends in juror comprehension research. Jury-related research grew significantly in the 1970s and 1980s,[30] and

26 See generally Pennington and Hastie, 'Evidence Evaluation' (n 22) 247; Levett et al (n 15) 374.
27 Bornstein and Greene (n 24) 64–5.
28 Pennington and Hastie, 'Evidence Evaluation' (n 22) 253.
29 Pennington and Hastie, 'Evidence Evaluation' (n 22) 253.
30 Edith Greene et al, 'Jurors and Juries: A Review of the Field' in James R P Ogloff (ed), *Taking Psychology and Law into the Twenty-First Century* (Springer, 2002) 225, 255.

one of the key questions researchers asked was whether jury directions help jurors to understand their task. Research in the USA often focused on the comprehensibility of pattern directions against the backdrop of 'plain language' movements.[31] Research then increasingly focused on assessing the comprehensibility of specific directions. As discussed in Chapter 7, another trend in juror comprehension research has occurred in Australia in the 21st century, focusing on SDM aids. Shifts in research focus reflect not only different areas of interest, but they also respond to methodological criticisms of research. For example, when jurors say they understand jury directions, are their responses reliable?

Jurors' subjective assessments of their comprehension

Numerous studies of actual jurors in criminal trials indicate that jurors report high levels of comprehension of jury directions. For example, 85% of jurors studied in New Zealand reported that the judge's directions were clear and 80% said they were helpful.[32] Jurors in New South Wales reported that they 'understood completely' or 'mostly' (94.6%) the judge's directions.[33] A study from England and Wales found that 94% of jurors surveyed said that it was 'not at all difficult or not very difficult to follow the judge's directions on the law'.[34] A study in Wyoming found that 94% of jurors found instructions were 'fairly' or 'very' helpful and 97% said that they felt they understood the instructions 'pretty well' or 'completely'.[35]

Research involving 628 jurors across three states in Australia in 2007 similarly found that 88–90% of jurors perceived the information provided by the judge to be clear about verdict options, the issues for the jury, the burden of proof, the case facts, legal principles, and the explanation of proof beyond reasonable doubt.[36] In a more recent study in Victoria and New Zealand, 463 jurors rated their judge's directions very highly 'for both perceived helpfulness (Vic: 4.81, NZ: 4.78) and perceived understanding (Vic: 4.59, NZ: 4.81)' on a scale of one to five.[37]

31 See, eg, Robert P Charrow and Veda R Charrow, 'Making Legal Language Understandable: A Psycholinguistic Study of Jury Instructions' (1979) 79 *Columbia Law Review* 1306; Amiram Elwork, Bruce D Sales and James J Alfini, *Making Jury Instructions Understandable* (Michie Company, 1982).

32 New Zealand Law Commission, *Juries in Criminal Trials: Part Two* (Preliminary Paper No 37, November 1999) 51 [7.3] (NZLC).

33 Lily Trimboli, 'Juror Understanding of Judicial Instructions in Criminal Trials' (2008) 119 *Contemporary Issues in Criminal Justice* 1, 9.

34 Michael Zander and Paul Henderson, *The Royal Commission on Criminal Justice: Crown Court Study* (Research Study No 19, 1993) [8.6.2].

35 Saxton (n 6) 85.

36 Jane Goodman-Delahunty et al, *Practices, Policies and Procedures That Influence Juror Satisfaction in Australia* (Research and Public Policy Series No 87, July 2007) 143.

37 Jonathan Clough et al, 'The Judge as Cartographer and Guide: The Role of Fact-Based Directions in Improving Juror Comprehension' (2018) 42(5) *Criminal Law Journal* 278, 294.

As discussed next, objective juror comprehension surveys produce very different results from subjective juror comprehension surveys. The differences are so significant that they 'suggest that subjective measures are relatively inconsequential in understanding comprehension and the relationship between instruction complexity and case outcomes'.[38] Subjective measures may have limited value because, for example, jurors may be reluctant to admit that their knowledge is limited, or they may think they understand something because they have given meaning to words and phrases based on their own commonsense understanding of the law.[39]

Despite their limitations, subjective measures of juror comprehension are relevant in two ways. First, they help to explain why juror comprehension problems may not be obvious in trials. If jurors did not believe they understood the judge's directions, they might ask more questions and might have more difficulty in reaching a verdict. Second, if jurors do identify that some jury directions are difficult to understand, that provides good evidence of the need to change a direction.

Objective assessments of juror comprehension

This section discusses objective assessments of juror comprehension research concerning traditional-style jury directions and SDM aids and juror comprehension research concerning 'proof beyond reasonable doubt', which is an important direction in many jurisdictions.

Objective assessments of juror comprehension of jury directions given in a traditional style

In addition to reporting high levels of comprehension subjectively, the study from New Zealand discussed earlier found 'fairly fundamental misunderstandings of the law' emerged during deliberations in 35 of the 48 trials studied (73%).[40] In 19 of the 35 trials, these misunderstandings concerned elements of the offence charged, such as the distinction between murder and manslaughter and the meaning of 'intent' (eg, what is the difference between 'purpose' and 'intent', and does 'intent' imply premeditation).[41] These errors affected how jurors approached their task and sometimes led individual jurors to agree erroneously on a verdict.[42]

38 Blake M McKimmie, Emma Antrobus and Chantelle Baguley, 'Objective and Subjective Comprehension of Jury Instructions in Criminal Trials' (2014) 17 *New Criminal Law Review* 163, 167.
39 See, eg, Louise Ellison and Vanessa E Munro, '"Telling Tales": Exploring Narratives of Life and Law within the (Mock) Jury Room' (2015) 35(2) *Legal Studies* 201, 223.
40 NZLC, *Juries in Criminal Trials: Part Two* (n 32) 53 [7.12].
41 NZLC, *Juries in Criminal Trials: Part Two* (n 32) 53 [7.13]–[7.14].
42 NZLC, *Juries in Criminal Trials: Part Two* (n 32) 55 [7.25].

The New Zealand study is unusual because it involved actual jurors. Objective assessment of the comprehension levels of actual jurors is indirectly prohibited in most jurisdictions because any assessment process will be intimately connected with the confidentiality of juror deliberations.[43] Most studies do not involve actual juries; they involve jury simulation studies. These studies have sought to identify the causes of juror comprehension problems and to evaluate what strategies are effective in improving comprehension.

In the 1970s in the USA, Amiram Elwork, Bruce Sales, and James Alfini rewrote instructions from actual cases, where they assessed one case as having complex issues and another case as having comparatively simple issues.[44] They rewrote instructions twice in the complex case — the second revision occurred following initial testing — and once in the simple case. They rewrote the standard jury instructions having regard to the need to avoid legal jargon, uncommon words, abstract words, ambiguous words, and negatively modified words. They also rewrote the instructions using the active voice and by presenting information more logically (eg, where understanding one idea flows from understanding the previous idea).[45]

The average (mean) percentage of right answers in the complex case was 51% when using the original instructions. This rose to 80% after the second rewriting.[46] Further, 49% of the improvements in answers to questions involved improvements of more than 20%.[47] In the actual case on which the case with complex issues was based, the jury found the accused guilty of battery with intent to kill, being a lesser alternative offence to attempted murder. In the simulated jury survey, using the original trial instructions, only one of 34 mock jurors (3%) could say what the difference was between these two offences.[48] With the rewritten instructions, comprehension rose so that 80% of the 86 mock jurors tested could correctly answer this question.[49]

With a similar focus on the language used in jury directions, Robert Charrow and Veda Charrow assessed juror comprehension of certain standard civil jury instructions used in California.[50] They asked mock jurors to paraphrase an instruction that was read to them on two occasions.[51] They then concluded that the mock jurors correctly paraphrased the instruction just over half the time (0.540).[52] Charrow and Charrow identified linguistic constructions

43 See, eg, Jacqueline Horan, *Juries in the 21st Century* (Federation Press, 2012) 71.

44 Elwork, Sales and Alfini, *Making Jury Instructions Understandable* (n 31) 44–5.

45 Amiram Elwork, Bruce D Sales and James J Alfini, 'Juridic Decisions: In Ignorance of the Law or in Light of It?' (1977) 1 *Law and Human Behavior* 163, 165–9 ('Juridic Decisions').

46 Elwork, Sales and Alfini, *Making Jury Instructions Understandable* (n 31) 45–6.

47 Elwork, Sales and Alfini, *Making Jury Instructions Understandable* (n 31) 48–9.

48 Elwork, Sales and Alfini, *Making Jury Instructions Understandable* (n 31) 51–3.

49 Elwork, Sales and Alfini, *Making Jury Instructions Understandable* (n 31) 51–3.

50 Charrow and Charrow (n 31) 1311.

51 Charrow and Charrow (n 31) 1312–3. The instructions were between 27 and 154 words long.

52 Charrow and Charrow (n 31) 1316.

that were impeding comprehension. These substantially overlapped with those identified by Elwork, Sales, and Alfini but their research identified additional matters. For example:

- removing or clarifying vague or ambiguous phrases
- reducing lists of items (eg, knowledge, skill, experience, training, or education) to no more than two where possible, and
- using directives such as 'must', 'should', and 'may' where appropriate (eg, in relation to juror's duties).[53]

When Charrow and Charrow removed these challenging psycholinguistic constructions, mock jurors' overall performance was 'substantially better on the modified instructions than on the original instructions'.[54] There was a statistically significant improvement for nine of the 14 instructions assessed with the mean of the mean scores improving from 0.447 to 0.592.[55] Charrow and Charrow concluded that the results of their study 'underscore[d] the fact that jury instructions are not written for their major intended audience'.[56]

Jane Goodman and Edith Greene similarly focused on the linguistic construction of jury directions and found that the terse nature of some instructions may reduce comprehension. Instructions should instead include information to distinguish potentially confusing ideas. They concluded that judges could further clarify instructions having regard to the need to avoid:

- the use of common words with uncommon meanings (eg, element, charge, burden)
- archaisms (eg, the modifier 'such')
- over precision (eg, 'evidence or the lack of evidence')
- terms with excessively flexible meanings (eg, 'reasonable person'), and
- poetic language (eg, 'fully, fairly and carefully considered').[57]

Laurence Severance and Elizabeth Loftus also revised jury directions using psycholinguistic principles of the kind used by Elwork, Sales, and Alfini and Charrow and Charrow. They found that the use of revised directions reduced the overall error rate from 29.3% for those who received no instructions to 24.3%. The overall correct application measure increased from 56% for those who received no instructions to 68% for those who received the revised instructions.[58]

53 Charrow and Charrow (n 31) 1321–6.
54 Charrow and Charrow (n 31) 1331.
55 Charrow and Charrow (n 31) 1333.
56 Charrow and Charrow (n 31) 1359.
57 Jane Goodman and Edith Greene, 'The Use of Paraphrase Analysis in the Simplification of Jury Instructions' (1989) 4 *Journal of Social Behavior and Personality* 237, 249–50.
58 Laurence Severance and Elizabeth Loftus, 'Improving the Ability of Jurors to Comprehend and Apply Jury Instructions' (1982) 17 *Law & Society Review* 153, 184–91.

However, errors in juror comprehension remain even when psycholinguistic principles are employed to rewrite directions. A meta-analysis of 121 instructions from 63 articles (involving 12,184 participants) found that as the conceptual complexity of instructions increases, efforts to simplify and clarify instructions by applying psycholinguistic principles are less effective.[59]

Another significant cause of juror comprehension errors occurs where people have their own (inaccurate) preconceived ideas of the law, sometimes referred to as 'commonsense justice' or 'prototypes'.[60] These ideas of the law may conflict with the directions and (mock) jurors may be resistant to change their views or accommodate new information.[61] Further, 'jurors seem to have particular difficulty following and applying instructions that contradicted their intuitions or preconceptions of the judicial process' (eg, in thinking circumstantial evidence does not carry the same weight as direct evidence).[62] However, jurors may not be aware that they are applying, and may not intend to apply, their own sense of the law in preference to the law contained in the judge's directions. This indicates that improving comprehension requires rewriting jury directions to be clear and accurate, and to address differences between the law and jurors' beliefs about what the law is or should be.[63]

Research has also considered the effectiveness of changes to the process of giving directions. For example, Elwork, Sales, and Alfini assessed giving directions before the trial, only after the trial, and before and after the trial.[64] Giving directions before the trial assessed whether intentional learning is more effective than incidental learning, as has been shown in other contexts. Giving jurors a framework enables them to be selective about what they remember based on what is relevant rather than based on their own assessment of what they think will be important.[65] This framework may assist jurors with Pennington and Hastie's step two (understanding legal categories) and step three (selecting admissible evidence), as discussed earlier in this chapter. Giving directions before the subjects heard the evidence reduced factual errors for two out of three key factual issues in the trial.[66] Accordingly, Elwork, Sales, and Alfini recommended that judges give instructions before the evidence is heard in addition to at the end of the trial.[67]

59 Chantelle M Baguley, Blake M McKimmie and Barbara M Masser, 'Deconstructing the Simplification of Jury Instructions: How Simplifying the Features of Complexity Affects Jurors' Application of Instructions' (2017) 41(3) *Law and Human Behavior* 284 ('Deconstructing the Simplification of Jury Instructions') 296.
60 Finkel (n 6) 608–9. See also Smith (n 6) 869.
61 Severance and Loftus (n 58) 194.
62 Saxton (n 6) 95. See also Finkel (n 6) 605–12.
63 Diamond and Levi (n 4) 232.
64 Elwork, Sales and Alfini, 'Juridic Decisions' (n 45) 171–5.
65 Elwork, Sales and Alfini, 'Juridic Decisions' (n 45) 172.
66 Elwork, Sales and Alfini, 'Juridic Decisions' (n 45) 177.
67 Elwork, Sales and Alfini, 'Juridic Decisions' (n 45) 178. See also Alan Reifman, Spencer M Gusick and Phoebe C Ellsworth, 'Real Jurors' Understanding of the Law in Real Cases' (1992) 16 *Law and Human Behavior* 539, 549–50; Smith (n 6) 224.

Objective assessments of juror comprehension when judges provide structured decision-making aids

A significant amount of juror comprehension research concerns directions given in the traditional manner. With traditional directions, juror comprehension depends upon a juror:

- recalling the direction
- understanding the law referred to in the direction, and
- applying the law to the facts.

However, as discussed in Chapter 7, several jurisdictions have been moving away from the traditional style of jury directions. When using SDM aids, the judge can embed substantive directions about the law into factual questions (decision points) that the jury must determine. The aim is to further simplify the information provided to jurors. On this approach, juror comprehension depends upon a juror:

- recalling the factual question (the judge normally provides the question in writing)
- understanding the factual question, and
- answering the factual question based on the evidence.

As a result, if the judge uses factual questions, jurors do not have to recall and understand a law to apply it. This changes what needs to be evaluated when determining whether a juror comprehends directions. For example, Charrow and Charrow used a paraphrase test, which requires a person to restate a jury direction in their own words.[68] The assumption is that a person cannot paraphrase a direction if they do not understand it. However, because jurors do not need to learn about the law to answer factual questions, their comprehension of the law embedded into a factual question is unlikely to improve.[69] With fact-based directions, the ability of jurors to understand the factual question — and thereby apply the law — is critical.[70] Further, a juror may be able to apply a direction better than they can recall and restate the components of a direction.[71]

The most comprehensive review of SDM aids occurred in the mid-2010s in a study that compared Victoria, where judges gave directions in a traditional

68 Charrow and Charrow (n 31) 1309–10.

69 See, eg, Essex and Goodman-Delahunty (n 8); Clough et al (n 37) 284–8.

70 See, eg, Clough et al (n 37) 284; Chantelle M Baguley, Blake M McKimmie and Barbara M Masser, 'Re-Evaluating How to Measure Jurors' Comprehension and Application of Jury Instructions' (2020) 26(1) *Psychology, Crime & Law* 53, 57–8 ('Re-Evaluating How to Measure Jurors' Comprehension').

71 Baguley, McKimmie and Masser, 'Deconstructing the Simplification of Jury Instructions' (n 59) 286.

style, and New Zealand, where judges used an SDM aid called a 'question trail' (the 'Trans-Tasman' study).[72] The factual questions (in which the judge embeds the law) create a 'question trail' (decision points) that lead to a verdict. Factual questions are also called fact-based directions. I discuss specific aspects of this research further, and other research concerning SDM aids, in my case study in Chapter 7.

The Trans-Tasman study assessed juror comprehension and application of directions in various ways and both before and after deliberation. The study assessed comprehension of standard directions, directions rewritten using plain language principles, directions with a checklist, and fact-based directions. When using a paraphrase test to evaluate juror comprehension, like many other studies, comprehension was below 70%. On application tests, jurors performed much better on true-false questions, getting approximately 70–80% correct, than on multiple-choice questions, getting approximately 50% correct.[73] Multiple-choice or true/false questions often indicate higher comprehension levels than do paraphrase tests.[74]

Significantly, the Trans-Tasman study found that:

- jurors in New Zealand performed 18.5% better than jurors in Victoria on application tests, and
- in contrast to other SDM aids, mock jurors who received question trails in simulated studies performed nearly equally regardless of their comprehension knowledge prior to the trial.[75]

Whether a judge gives directions traditionally or uses SDM aids, a direction that is common to each jurisdiction is that the prosecution must prove the accused's guilt beyond reasonable doubt. This common requirement reflects its shared legal, historical, and cultural provenance.[76] It therefore provides a good case study to compare jurisdictional differences in juror comprehension research.

Juror comprehension of 'proof beyond reasonable doubt'

In Australia, other than in Victoria, judges normally must not provide any explanation of 'proof beyond reasonable doubt'.[77] In Canada, New Zealand, and Victoria, judges may provide some explanation of the concept of proof

72 Clough et al (n 37).
73 Clough et al (n 37) 288.
74 Catriona McKay, Mark Nolan and Michael Smithson, 'Effectiveness of Question Trails as Jury Decision Aids: The Jury's Still Out' (2014) 21(4) *Psychiatry, Psychology and Law* 492, 493.
75 Clough et al (n 37) 292–3.
76 Barbara Shapiro, *Beyond Reasonable Doubt and Probable Cause: Historical Perspectives on the Anglo-American Law of Evidence* (Berkeley, 1991) 1–41.
77 *R v Dookheea* (2017) 262 CLR 402. See *Jury Directions Act 2015* (Vic) s 63.

beyond reasonable doubt and that explanation is quite similar.[78] In England and Wales, a judge may explain proof beyond reasonable doubt in terms of whether the jury is 'sure' that the person is guilty. This explanation overlaps with some of the terminology used in Canada and New Zealand. Federal jurisdictions in the USA refer to being 'firmly convinced' that the accused is guilty.[79]

Despite differences in the explanation of 'proof beyond reasonable doubt', and differences in the research questions used to survey jurors, research from different jurisdictions shows that jurors commonly struggle to understand this important concept. For example, in New South Wales, 55% of jurors surveyed (1,178) understood 'proof beyond reasonable doubt' to mean being sure that that a person is guilty, but they were not asked to further explain this in terms of whether it meant 100% certain or something else.[80] In Queensland, when jurors surveyed were asked to explain proof beyond reasonable doubt in their own terms, 36% (11/33) described it too onerously (eg, no doubt at all).[81] In the USA, 31% of 505 mock jurors thought the instructions meant they had to be 100% certain.[82] Research in England found that a third of jurors surveyed understood the test of 'sure' to mean 100% certain, which is erroneously high.[83]

In contrast to erroneously stringent interpretations, some jurors' understanding of 'proof beyond reasonable doubt' is erroneously low. Of the jurors surveyed in New South Wales (1,178), 22% said the phrase meant 'very likely the person is guilty' or 'pretty likely that the person is guilty'.[84] In Queensland, 31% of jurors surveyed (9/33) described 'proof beyond reasonable doubt' too lowly or not at all.[85] Similarly, research in Wyoming found that almost 30% of jurors surveyed (seriously) misunderstood a true/false statement about the

78 *R v Lifchus* [1997] 3 SCR 320; *R v Wanhalla* [2007] 2 NZLR 573 ('*Wanhalla*'); *Jury Directions Act 2015* (Vic) s 64.

79 Essex and Goodman-Delahunty (n 8) 80. See also Joel D Lieberman and Bruce D Sales, 'What Social Science Teaches Us about the Jury Instruction Process' (1997) 3 *Psychology, Public Policy, and Law* 589, 597–8.

80 Trimboli (n 33) 4.

81 Blake McKimmie, Emma Antrobus and Ian Davis, 'Jurors' Trial Experiences: The Influence of Directions and Other Aspects of Trials' in Queensland Law Reform Commission, *A Review of Jury Directions* (Report No 66, 2009) 13.

82 Geoffrey Kramer and Durean M Koenig, 'Do Jurors Understand Criminal Jury Instructions? Analyzing the Results of the Michigan Juror Comprehension Project' (1990) 23(3) *University of Michigan Journal of Law Reform* 401, 414.

83 John Warwick Montgomery, 'The Criminal Standard of Proof' (1998) 148 *The New Law Journal* 582. See also Katrin Mueller-Johnson, Mandeep K Dhami and Samantha Lundrigan, 'Effects of Judicial Instructions and Juror Characteristics on Interpretations of Beyond Reasonable Doubt' (2018) 24 *Psychology, Crime and Law* 117, 119; Michelle I Bertrand and Richard Jochelson, 'Mock-Jurors' Self-Reported Understanding of Canadian Judicial Instructions (Is Not Very Good)' (2018) 66 *Criminal Law Quarterly* 137.

84 Trimboli (n 33) 6.

85 McKimmie, Antrobus and Davis (n 81).

meaning of proof beyond reasonable doubt that asked whether a 'more likely than not' standard was correct.[86]

Research in New Zealand reported that 'many jurors' and juries surveyed were uncertain about the meaning of 'proof beyond reasonable doubt', often describing it in percentage terms and describing it as 100%, 95%, 75%, and 50%.[87]

The differences in these survey results may reflect differences in the survey methods and/or differences between jurisdictions. However, the results produce a 'convergent validity'.[88] That is, a substantial proportion of jurors/mock jurors in each jurisdiction had difficulty understanding and applying the test of 'proof beyond reasonable doubt' — applying the test at either an erroneously high level or an erroneously low level.[89]

Problems with juror comprehension of 'proof beyond reasonable doubt' are consistent with juror comprehension research more generally. While differences in testing methods may explain some of the differences in the results between studies, comprehension rates are often below, or not much better than 50%.[90] Even at the high-water mark, which is closer to 70%,[91] comprehension levels are still disconcertingly low.

So far, this discussion has assumed that juror comprehension research is reliable and that research emanating from different jurisdictions can be relied upon. It is outside the scope of this book to discuss all criticisms of juror comprehension research.[92] However, the next section discusses common criticisms of juror comprehension research.

The strengths, limitations, and criticisms of juror comprehension research

When considering the relevance and reliability of juror comprehension research, it is essential 'to be attentive to the assumptions, methods and

86 Saxton (n 6) 96–9. See also, Kramer and Koenig (n 82) 414–16.

87 NZLC, *Juries in Criminal Trials: Part Two* (n 32) 54 [7.16]. The NZLC's Preliminary Paper does not specify what constitutes 'many jurors'.

88 Phoebe C Ellsworth, 'Legal Reasoning and Scientific Reasoning' (2012) 63 *Alabama Law Review* 895, 914.

89 Significant errors in understanding beyond reasonable doubt were also evident with research involving 785 mock jurors in sexual assault cases in Australia: Thea Gumbert, 'Proof Beyond Reasonable Doubt in Sexual Assault Trials' in Greg Byrne and Jacqueline Horan (eds), *Sexual Assault Trials: Challenges and Innovations* (LexisNexis, 2025) 193, 202–03.

90 See, eg, Lieberman and Sales (n 79) 596–7; Baguley, McKimmie and Masser, 'Deconstructing the Simplification of Jury Instructions' (n 59) 285.

91 See, eg, Baguley, McKimmie and Masser, 'Deconstructing the Simplification of Jury Instructions' (n 59) 285.

92 See generally, Norbert L Kerr and Robert M Bray, 'Simulation, Realism, and the Study of the Jury' in Neil Brewer and Kipling D Williams (eds), *Psychology and Law* (Guilford Press, 2005) 322; James R P Ogloff and V Gordon Rose, 'The Comprehension of Judicial Instructions' in Neil Brewer and Kipling D Williams (eds), *Psychology and Law: An Empirical Perspective* (Guilford Press, 2005) 407.

conclusions made by the investigators'.[93] For example, juror comprehension tests may include paraphrase, multiple-choice, and hypothetical tests that examine aspects of cognition such as remembering, comprehending, and applying directions.[94]

Three significant criticisms of juror comprehension research that often arise within the law are that research:

- comes from another jurisdiction (usually the USA) and therefore is not relevant
- often involves a jury simulation study rather than actual jurors in a real trial, and
- does not involve deliberation processes and is therefore unrealistic.

Is research from another jurisdiction relevant?

Most juror comprehension research emanates from the USA. However, Australia, New Zealand, England and Wales, and Canada have also conducted significant juror comprehension research. When comparing research from different jurisdictions, it is necessary to consider the similarities and differences between the jurisdictions.[95] There are many similarities in the adversarial criminal trial by jury in all five of these common law jurisdictions.[96] This is because of the provenance of the adversarial criminal trial by jury in legal terms and as a historical, social, and cultural phenomenon[97] from England. The similarities are often greatest, and the differences least, when comparing jurisdictions within a federation (eg, within the USA and within Australia where criminal law is primarily a state responsibility).[98]

93 Gary Edmond, 'Judging Surveys: Experts, Empirical Evidence and Law Reform' (2005) 33 *Federal Law Review* 95, 136. See also Richard Lempert, 'Empirical Research for Public Policy: With Examples from Family Law' (2008) 5(4) *Empirical Legal Studies* 907, 925–6.

94 Baguley, McKimmie and Masser, 'Re-Evaluating How to Measure Jurors' Comprehension' (n 70) 55.

95 See, eg, John C Reitz, 'How to Do Comparative Law?' (1998) 46 *American Journal of Comparative Law* 617; Pierre Legrand, 'How to Compare Now' (1996) 16 *Legal Studies* 232; A Esin Orucu, 'Methodology of Comparative Law' in Jan M Smits (ed), *Elgar Encyclopedia of Comparative Law* (Edward Elgar Publishing, 2006) 442.

96 See, eg, John H Langbein, *The Origins of the Adversary Criminal Trial* (Oxford University Press, 2003); New Zealand Law Commission, *Juries in Criminal Trials* (Report No 69, February 2001) 14–24; Neil Vidmar, 'A Historical and Comparative Perspective on the Common Law Jury' in Neil Vidmar (ed), *World Jury Systems* (Oxford University Press, 2000) 1, 13–18; Paul Marcus, 'Judges Talking to Jurors in Criminal Cases: Why US Judges Do It So Differently from Just about Everyone Else' (2013) 30 *Arizona Journal of International & Comparative Law* 1.

97 See, eg, Legrand (n 95) 236–9; Reitz (n 95).

98 See, eg, Stella Tarrant, 'Building Bridges in Australian Criminal Law: Codification and the Common Law' (2013) 39 *Monash University Law Review* 838; Matthew R Goode, 'Constructing Criminal Law Reform and the Model Criminal Code' (2002) 26 *Criminal Law Journal* 152, 152–5.

In the five common law jurisdictions just mentioned (Australia, New Zealand, England and Wales, Canada, and the USA), the primary task of the jury is the same — to determine the issues in dispute between the prosecution and the accused based on the evidence adduced in the case in accordance with the judge's directions. In each jurisdiction, the impartiality of the jury is a central feature, though the method for achieving impartiality may vary between jurisdictions.[99] The investigators, prosecution, defence counsel, and the judge all have essentially the same roles.[100] The similarity in the legal systems means that it is not uncommon for appellate courts in England and Wales, Australia, Canada, and New Zealand to refer to appellate decisions from these other countries, and sometimes from the USA, in deciding how their laws should develop or apply.

However, there are differences between these jurisdictions, such as who is eligible for (or disqualified from) jury service,[101] and with the processes for selecting the jury at court which may include extensive questioning of potential jurors in the USA.[102] There are also differences in the criminal offences, evidence laws, and trial procedures that apply in each jurisdiction. As discussed in Chapter 2, there are also differences between jurisdictions, and within jurisdictions, concerning the judge's summing up, jury directions, and whether judges use SDM aids.[103] There may also be legal and cultural differences between jurisdictions.[104] For example, research into the effects of racial bias in juries may reveal different effects in each jurisdiction and require different strategies for addressing problems.[105] Differences in cultural phenomena and legal procedures may preclude or severely limit meaningful comparison of some aspects of criminal trials. The differences between jurisdictions means that research into juries may not always be relevant, or must be treated with caution, when applying it in another jurisdiction.

99 See, eg, Valerie P Hans and Alyana Jehle, 'Avoid Bald Men and People with Green Socks? Other Ways to Improve the Voir Dire Process in Jury Selection' (2003) 78 *Chicago-Kent Law Review* 1179; Regina Schuller and Neil Vidmar, 'The Canadian Criminal Jury' (2011) 86 *Chicago-Kent Law Review* 497, 500–5; Horan, *Juries in the 21st Century* (n 43) 9–43.

100 Thomas Weigend, 'Criminal Law and Criminal Procedure' in Jan M Smits (ed), *Elgar Encyclopedia of Comparative Law* (Edward Elgar Publishing, 2006) 214, 223–4.

101 See, eg, Horan, *Juries in the 21st Century* (n 43) 15–21; Gregory E Mize and Paula Hannaford-Agor, 'Jury Trial Innovations Across America: How We Are Teaching and Learning from Each Other' (2008) *Journal of Court Innovation* 189, 200–1.

102 See, eg, Mize and Hannaford-Agor (n 101) 208–10; Hans and Jehle (n 99).

103 See, eg, Marcus (n 96); Peter Duff, 'The Scottish Criminal Jury: A Very Peculiar Institution' (1999) 62(2) *Law and Contemporary Problems* 173, 189–90; Lord Justice Moses, 'Summing Down the Summing-Up' (Speech, Annual Law Reform Lecture, Inner Temple, 23 November 2010) 7.

104 See, eg, Simon Bronitt, 'Toward a Universal Theory of Criminal Law: Rethinking the Comparative and International Project' (2008) 27 *Criminal Justice Ethics* 53, 59–62.

105 See, eg, Mark Israel, 'Ethnic Bias in Jury Selection in Australia and New Zealand' (1998) 26 *International Journal of the Sociology of Law* 35; Devine et al (n 2) 673–83, 709–10; Hans and Jehle (n 99).

However, these differences are not as significant as the many challenges that arise in comparing civil and common law jurisdictions, which has been described as like comparing apples and oranges.[106] Further, 'comparative analysis can be undertaken in different ways and for many different purposes'[107] and the fact that there are some differences between jurisdictions may help. Our familiarity with an institution like the jury can make the laws, practices, and procedures in a trial by jury in one's own jurisdiction seem 'inevitable or immutable'[108] or reflective of fundamental principles rather than the 'product of mere historical accident'.[109] Without such insights, it can be more 'difficult to challenge the status quo'.[110]

Research on juries from the five common law jurisdictions mentioned before consistently shows that mock jurors, and jurors when tested, do not understand many of the (often similar) directions as judges traditionally give them.[111] At a higher level of abstraction, this suggests that there is something more fundamental about the conduct of the trial, and the role and task of jurors within it, which produces similarities in research outcomes.[112] It may also reflect that courts in different jurisdictions have used similar approaches to determining what jurors know, how jurors' reason, and therefore how to guide jurors with their task. Some instances of 'judicial knowledge and experience' have developed over centuries and are common to each jurisdiction. For example, the provenance of the courts' mistaken view that a complaint of a sexual offence is 'easy to fabricate, but extremely difficult to refute',[113] can be traced to Chief Justice Hale in the 17th century.[114] Courts have continued to repeat this statement even in recent times.[115]

106 Reitz (n 95) 621. See also Legrand (n 95); H Patrick Glenn, 'Aims of Comparative Law' in Jan M Smits (ed), *Elgar Encyclopedia of Comparative Law* (Edward Elgar Publishing, 2006) 57.

107 Jeremy Horder and David Hughes, 'Comparative Issues in the Law of Homicide' in Jeremy Horder (ed), *Homicide Law in Comparative Perspective* (Hart Publishing, 2007) 1.

108 Erik Luna, 'A Place for Comparative Criminal Procedure' (2003–04) 42 *Brandeis Law Journal* 277, 282.

109 Duff (n 103) 201.

110 Luna (n 108) 282.

111 See, eg, Ogloff and Rose (n 92); Darbyshire, Maughan and Stewart (n 1); Valerie P Hans, 'Jury Systems around the World' (2008) 4 *Annual Review of Law & Social Sciences* 275, 285–7.

112 See, eg, Legrand (n 95) 232, 241.

113 See, eg, *R v Henry* (1969) 53 Cr App R 150, 153 (Lord Salmon). See also *Kelleher v The Queen* (1974) 131 CLR 534, 543 (Barwick CJ); *R v DD* [2000] 2 RCS 275, 302–4 [60]–[63].

114 See generally, Rachael Burgin, 'Persistent Narratives of Force and Resistance: Affirmative Consent as Law Reform' (2019) 59(2) *British Journal of Criminology* 296, 298–9.

115 See, eg, Jennifer Temkin, Jacqueline M Gray and Jastine Barrett, 'Different Functions of Rape Myth Use in Court: Findings from a Trial Observation Study' (2018) 13(2) *Feminist Criminology* 205, 212, 219.

The degree of similarities in trial by jury in the five common law jurisdictions discussed makes it possible, at least at a more general level, to:

- draw upon research about juror comprehension from these different jurisdictions
- consider different practices between jurisdictions to assess their effectiveness, and
- examine changes to trial by jury that are relevant to each jurisdiction.

Research about 'proof beyond reasonable doubt' provides a practical example of the way in which research conducted in one common law jurisdiction may be relevant to other common law jurisdictions. While caution is appropriate when using research from another jurisdiction, the research indicates the similarity in difficulties that jurors in each jurisdiction have with the same concept of 'proof beyond reasonable doubt'. This comparative analysis of the same issue shows that research from one jurisdiction can help in assessing juror comprehension issues in another jurisdiction. This also means that research in one jurisdiction may be relevant in another jurisdiction to assessing juror comprehension and how to address it.

The extent to which research from one jurisdiction illuminates juror comprehension in another jurisdiction requires an assessment of what can reasonably be inferred from the research. What is reasonable to infer depends upon the differences and similarities between the jurisdictions. It also depends upon the methods used in the research. It is also important to consider what inferences can reasonably be drawn from research when determining whether jury simulation studies provide reliable evidence about actual jurors' comprehension.

Do simulation studies realistically reflect a jury trial?

As discussed in Chapter 2, there are significant restrictions on questioning jurors about their deliberations. In England and Wales, and Canada, this severely restricts any research with actual jurors in trials that might involve jury deliberations.[116] While research with actual jurors may be approved in Australia, there are many limitations and practical challenges in obtaining authorisation to conduct this research that make it time consuming and resource intensive.[117] Further, research would not involve asking jurors about their deliberations.

116 *Juries Act 1974* (UK) s 20D; *Criminal Code Act 1986* (Can) s 649. See, also Cheryl Thomas, 'Avoiding the Perfect Storm of Juror Contempt' [2013] (6) *Criminal Law Review* 483; Lewis Ross, 'The Curious Case of the Jury-Shaped Hole: A Plea for Real Jury Research' (2023) 27(2) *The Internartional Journal of Evidence and Proof* 107.

117 See, eg, Jacqueline Horan and Mark Israel, 'Beyond the Legal Barriers: Institutional Gatekeeping and Real Jury Research' (2015) 49 *Australia and New Zealand Journal of Criminology* 422, 426–7.

However, field studies of jurors (from actual trials) have their own limitations including that no two trials are the same, and it can be difficult to identify causal relationships and exclude possible explanations for a result.[118] Further, post-trial interviews with jurors have limitations (eg, 'jurors may forget or distort their recollection of their predeliberation opinions and jury deliberations'[119]). Juror comprehension research could be considerably improved, and may be less contentious, if research were conducted on actual jurors.[120] However, this chapter is more concerned with what use can be made of extant research.

Jury simulation studies provide another way to understand actual jurors and juries. The challenge with jury simulation studies is primarily one of ecological validity, where the simulation attempts to capture the essential features of a jury trial.[121] Jury simulation studies have also been criticised because they only focus on several matters in each study when potentially many components of a jury trial are relevant to juror comprehension of their task. Experimental control in research often isolates each component (eg, the timing of directions, comparing a revised direction with an existing direction, the meaning of proof beyond reasonable doubt) to determine its effect on juror comprehension.[122] This experimental control reflects the tension between controlling a simulation to identify the effect of one or more components compared with the need for a simulation to reflect sufficiently an actual trial to have ecological validity.[123]

Isolating components of a trial may disproportionately highlight the studied component when compared with an actual trial.[124] A meta-analysis of 78 simulation studies found that the variable, or 'treatment effect', often became stronger as the research setting became less realistic.[125] Isolating even a few components for analysis may require a large and complex research study. The research undertaking is much larger and even more complicated when it extends from comprehension of specific directions to the broader question of whether jurors understand the issues they must determine.

Juror comprehension research often focuses on jury directions. However, a broader understanding of the context in which a judge gives directions is

118 See, eg, Kerr and Bray (n 92) 326–9.

119 Kerr and Bray (n 92) 326–9.

120 For a discussion of the importance of conducting research with actual jurors, see Ross (n 116).

121 Ross (n 116) 325–6. See also Jonathan J Koehler and John B Meixner, 'Jury Simulation Goals' in Margaret B Kovera (ed), *The Psychology of Juries* (American Psychological Association, 2017) 161, 163–4.

122 Kerr and Bray (n 92) 326.

123 See, eg, Brian H Bornstein, 'The Ecological Validity of Jury Simulations: Is the Jury Still Out?' (1999) 23(1) *Law and Human Behavior* 75.

124 Geoffrey Kramer and Norbert Kerr, 'Laboratory Simulation and Bias in the Study of Juror Behavior' (1989) 13(1) *Law and Human Behavior* 89, 90.

125 Daniel Linz and Steven Penrod, 'A Meta-Analysis of the Influence of Research Methodology on the Outcomes of Jury Simulation Studies' (Conference Paper, Academy of Criminal Justice Sciences, 1982) cited in Kramer and Kerr (n 124) 90.

essential because the jury functions within a trial system and the courtroom provides jurors with 'cues and . . . ideas of what and what not to do in the trial'.[126] So much is relevant to the overall issue of juror comprehension because the jury is not just another 'micro system' of social dynamics — the judge, lawyers, and the courtroom all play important roles.[127] Many features of the trial process help to transform people into jurors so that they understand their role and how they should undertake it.[128] Simulation studies cannot fully replicate the trial process because a trial is complex, containing multiple components, and requires a jury to return a verdict that has real and significant consequences.[129] This can make it challenging for researchers to determine whether a simulation study reproduces '"real" attitudes and "real" behaviour'.[130]

However, it is also important to be careful in making assumptions about what happens in trials. For example, one assumption is that in a real trial juror comprehension will benefit from repetition, where all the important legal issues will be explained to the jury several times, through opening and closing addresses in addition to the judge's directions.[131] However, this assumes counsel will focus on explaining the law because doing so will be helpful to their client's case. It also depends upon practices that vary between jurisdictions, for example in some jurisdictions the accused may not give an opening address.[132] Indeed, the assumption that counsel's role is to help the jury to understand the law is probably misplaced, and caution is required concerning assumptions about whether counsel, and different presentation styles, improve juror comprehension in the way anticipated.[133]

Simulation studies often involve university students[134] and have been criticised for not being representative of jurors.[135] However, studies comparing undergraduate students and real jurors suggest that undergraduate students provide a realistic measure of juror comprehension.[136] Indeed, because higher education levels correlate with higher levels of comprehension, studies with

126 Geoff Mungham and Zenon Bankowski, 'The Jury in the Legal System' in Pat Carlen (ed), *The Sociology of the Law* (University of Keele, 1976) 202, 206.
127 Mungham and Bankowski (n 126) 211.
128 Marder (n 14) 3.
129 See, eg, Kramer and Kerr (n 124) 89–90.
130 Mungham and Bankowski (n 126) 206.
131 J Alexander Tanford, 'The Law and Psychology of Jury Instructions' (1990) 69(1) *Nebraska Law Review* 71, 105.
132 See chapter 7.
133 See, eg, Lieberman and Sales (n 79) 589.
134 Daniel A Krauss and Joel D Lieberman, 'Managing Different Aspects of Validity in Trial Simulation Research' in Margaret B Kovera (ed), *The Psychology of Juries* (American Psychological Association, 2017) 185, 193, 196.
135 See, eg, Koehler and Meixner (n 121) 168–9.
136 See, eg, V Gordon Rose and James R P Ogloff, 'Evaluating the Comprehensibility of Jury Instructions: A Method and an Example' (2001) 25 *Law and Human Behavior* 409; Brian H Bornstein et al, 'Mock Juror Sampling Issues in Jury Simulation Research: A Meta-Analysis' (2017) 41(1) *Law and Human Behavior* 13 ('Mock Jurors Sampling Issues').

university students only may overestimate the juror comprehension levels of actual jurors (many of whom are not university educated).[137] This does not mean research with students is appropriate for all jury research as for issues beyond general comprehension, the limited demographics of student samples may may be important.[138]

The lack of verisimilitude in jury simulation studies can also cause scepticism about its findings. However, what matters is whether the study has ecological validity so that the findings can be generalised, that is, whether it is reasonable to infer that the findings in the study reflect what real jurors do.[139] There is no right or wrong way to study jurors: there are limitations with both field studies and jury simulation studies and research should employ the best method for their 'purposes and circumstances'.[140] Further, research does not suggest that jury simulation studies are intrinsically flawed or so different from research findings from actual trials that they cannot be relied upon when assessing juror comprehension problems. Indeed, there is a 'paucity of research' showing that these 'deficiencies' make a significant difference to research findings.[141]

Another criticism of the lack of realism of jury simulation studies is that they do not involve jury deliberation processes. This requires closer examination because the deliberative process is central to the jury's task and difficult to replicate.

Is it essential that jurors deliberate together to assess their comprehension levels?

Jury simulation studies that do not include a deliberation process have been criticised for failing to consider the group dynamics of juries where deliberations may rectify individual misunderstandings. This reflects the courts' view of the importance of jury deliberations:

> The robustness of the jury system does not turn on the characteristics, intelligence and understanding of individual jurors but rather on the collective strengths of juries. Individual misunderstandings are likely to be sorted out in the course of collective deliberations.[142]

This view, expressed by New Zealand's Court of Appeal, reflects (collective) judicial knowledge and experience: it flows from the view that the 'genius'

137 See, eg, Rose and Ogloff (n 136) 411; Brian H Bornstein, 'The Ecological Validity of Jury Simulations: Is the Jury Still Out?' (1999) 23(1) *Law and Human Behavior* 75.

138 Lee John Curley and Nicola Peddie, 'A Critique of the Experimental Study of Juror Decision-Making': Challenges and Recommendations' in Nicola Monahan (ed), *Contemporary Challenges in the Jury System: A Comparative Perspective* (Routledge, 2025) 189, 195.

139 See, eg, Kerr and Bray (n 92) 325–31; Koehler and Meixner (n 121) 163.

140 Kerr and Bray (n 92) 351. See also Devine et al (n 2) 698–9; Koehler and Meixner (n 121) 166–7.

141 See, eg, Bornstein et al, 'Mock Juror Sampling Issues' (n 136) 14; Kerr and Bray (n 92) 350.

142 *Wanhalla* (n 78) 597 [47] (William Young P, Chambers and Robertson JJ). See also *Black v The Queen* (1993) 179 CLR 44, 51.

of the jury system is that it draws upon the collective experience of jurors.[143] Although research has primarily focused on individual comprehension without the benefit of group deliberation,[144] research has also considered whether group deliberation improves juror comprehension.

Elwork, Sales, and Alfini found that the deliberation process was helpful in improving comprehension where the starting point was low. In the complex trial discussed earlier in this chapter, the number of correct answers using the original instructions improved from 23% to 40% following deliberation. However, that was well below the 78% comprehension of the twice rewritten instructions. Deliberation did not improve comprehension of the twice rewritten instructions.[145] The authors considered that this reflected the substantial opportunity for improvement with the original instructions, and the lack of opportunity to improve with revised instructions that were 'much closer to the potential maximum level of comprehensibility'[146] achievable with the improvement techniques they used.

Using a simulated study, involving 216 people in juries of 12, Phoebe Ellsworth concluded that while jurors were conscientious, deliberation with other jurors for an hour did not improve their understanding of the law.[147] Deliberating appeared to work well in 'correcting errors of fact but not in correcting errors of law'.[148] Only half of the references to the law during deliberations 'were accurate, even when credit was given for partial accuracy'.[149] Where the jury changed its view about the law, '52 percent of . . . [the changes] involved replacing an erroneous response with a correct one, and 48 percent involved replacing a correct response with an erroneous one'.[150]

This suggests that a jury may not 'recognize the right answer when it hears it'.[151] More general research indicates that a person's subjective confidence in their own judgment is often 'determined by the internal consistency of the information . . . rather than the quality of that information'.[152]

Ellsworth's findings concerning low levels of accuracy about the law, may reflect the influence of jurors' commonsense understanding (or prototypes)

143 *Doney v The Queen* (1990) 171 CLR 207, 214. See also *R v Thompson* [2011] 1 WLR 200, 204–5 [9]–[10].
144 Miko M Wilford and Brian H Bornstein, 'The Disappearing Trial: How Social Scientists Can Help Save the Jury from Extinction' (2023) 29(1) *Psychology, Crime & Law* 1, 10.
145 Elwork, Sales and Alfini, *Making Jury Instructions Understandable* (n 31) 66.
146 Elwork, Sales and Alfini, *Making Jury Instructions Understandable* (n 31) 68.
147 Phoebe C Ellsworth, 'Are Twelve Heads Better Than One?' (1989) 52 *Law and Contemporary Problems* 205, 208–13, 218 ('Are Twelve Heads Better Than One?').
148 Ellsworth, 'Are Twelve Heads Better Than One?' (n 147) 218.
149 Ellsworth, 'Are Twelve Heads Better Than One?' (n 147) 219.
150 Ellsworth, 'Are Twelve Heads Better Than One?' (n 147) 219.
151 Ellsworth, 'Are Twelve Heads Better Than One?' (n 147) 219. See also Rose and Ogloff (n 136) 419.
152 Daniel Kahneman and Gary Klein, 'Conditions for Intuitive Expertise: A Failure to Disagree' (2009) 64(6) *American Psychologist* 515, 522. See also Koehler and Meixner (n 121) 172.

of the law as discussed earlier in this chapter. Jury discussion about the law in Ellsworth's study often concerned matters that jurors' may have had prior knowledge about, like 'first-degree murder' or 'heat of passion'.[153] Ellsworth observed good discussions about the facts during deliberations. However, discussion of the facts did not change verdicts — 'jurors' verdict preferences in the case were rarely a function of a clear mistake on the facts'.[154]

Shari Diamond and Judith Levi rewrote Illinois' death penalty jury instructions for testing in a simulation study involving 170 jury-eligible people, half of whom were allocated to six-person juries. Mock jurors who deliberated improved from 67% to 79% on one of three issues tested but not on the other two issues.[155] The authors concluded that deliberation may 'improve comprehension only when a substantial majority of the members of a jury begin deliberations with a correct understanding of the information at issue'.[156]

As discussed earlier in this chapter, researchers in a New Zealand study found that in 35 of the 48 trials studied (73%), 'fairly fundamental misunderstandings of the law' affected jury deliberations.[157] That study did not detail how many jurors in each jury misunderstood the law and how many understood the law correctly. The researchers concluded that the deliberation process addressed many of these errors and concluded that the legal errors resulted 'in either hung juries or questionable verdicts in only four of the 48 trials', being 8.3%.[158] Compared with other research, this is an exceptionally high error correction rate during the deliberation process,[159] especially given the corrections involved the law rather than the facts.

The Trans-Tasman study, discussed earlier in this chapter, included an examination of the deliberations of 44 mock juries in simulated trials to assess the effect of deliberations on different methods of guiding the jury. In juries that received plain language directions, standard directions, or a checklist, poor pre-deliberation performance was associated with relatively poor post-deliberation performance.[160] However, mock juries given an SDM aid containing fact-based directions (question trails) were 1.4 to 1.7 times more likely to discuss the elements of the offence than juries given other forms of directions and four to six times less likely to discuss elements that were not in dispute.[161] Further, these mock jurors performed equally well at this higher level, following deliberations, regardless of their pre-deliberation performance levels.[162]

153 Ellsworth, 'Are Twelve Heads Better than One?' (n 147) 220.
154 Ellsworth, 'Are Twelve Heads Better Than One?' (n 147) 223.
155 Diamond and Levi (n 4) 226.
156 Diamond and Levi (n 4) 230.
157 NZLC, *Juries in Criminal Trials: Part Two* (n 32) 53 [7.12].
158 NZLC, *Juries in Criminal Trials: Part Two* (n 32) 55 [7.25].
159 Marie Comiskey, 'Initiating Dialogue about Jury Comprehension of Legal Concepts: Can the "Stagnant Pool" Be Revitalized?' (2010) 35 *Queen's Law Journal* 625, 641.
160 Clough et al (n 37) 293.
161 Clough et al (n 37) 291.
162 Clough et al (n 37) 293.

Juror comprehension research indicates that the collective strengths of the jury are important and have a significant role to play with juries,[163] but they are not a cure-all for individual juror comprehension problems. Research on jury deliberations is essential and can play a critical role in improving juror comprehension. However, jury simulation research that does not include a deliberations process can also play a vital role in understanding juror comprehension and assessing strategies for improving juror comprehension.

Conclusion

Whether in the field or in a simulation study, juror comprehension research has limitations. '[R]esearchers are continually faced with a multihorned dilemma. In choosing to avoid one horn, they are invariably gored by another'.[164] The reliability and robustness of each study must be assessed on its merits. Because jurors are different, and each trial is different, there are many issues for research to address. The volume and complexity of interconnected issues to research also presents challenges. Although studies can never be perfect, they can be highly valuable, and they provide the best method available in most jurisdictions for assessing what jurors are likely to understand. The research and its limitations mean that it is not possible to describe the precise extent of juror comprehension problems. Even if research provided such precision, it is still necessary to consider the extent to which it is possible to draw inferences (or generalise) from studies to assess what is likely to happen in actual trials. Drawing inferences from research requires an understanding of both research and its limits and trial procedures. Even if research was conducted on actual juries, it would still be necessary to draw inferences from this research to assess juror comprehension levels in (other) jury trials.[165]

When assessed objectively, research from different jurisdictions provides compelling evidence that many jurors do not understand and correctly apply jury directions (eg, misunderstandings of 'proof beyond reasonable doubt' are common). Comprehension is often about 50% for each direction tested, occasionally rising to 70–80%. As the jurors' task requires comprehension of many directions, overall juror comprehension levels of their task are likely to be lower. Further, the cognitive load on jurors, in learning new information and concepts and then deliberating together to reach a verdict, is significant. Plain language reforms cannot cure all juror comprehension problems — the law itself can be conceptually complex. SDM aids may reduce some conceptual complexity, but they do not address all the sources of juror comprehension

163 Lieberman and Sales (n 79) 635. See also Ogloff and Rose (n 92) 422–3; Ellsworth, 'Are Twelve Heads Better Than One?' (n 147) 219; Devine et al (n 2) 701.

164 Kerr and Bray (n 92) 351.

165 See generally, Valerie P Hans, 'Inside the Black Box: Comment on Diamond and Vidmar' (2001) 87(8) *Virginia Law Review* 1917, 1919–25.

difficulties.[166] What may appear to a judge to be a clear explanation of the law may not be clear to a juror. Jurors are not 'blank slates'. They use their own ideas of the law and their own schemas when trying to understand the judge's guidance.

Research reveals the fiction in both the courts' assumptions about the 'ideal' juror and the pragmatic assumption that jurors do understand and follow the judge's directions. There is a real risk that jurors will not fully understand their task, resulting in trials that are not fair. The strength of this research necessarily indicates that there are significant limitations with the courts' use of judicial knowledge and experience as a basis for determining what jurors know, how they reason, and how best to guide jurors with their task. The consistency of juror comprehension research across jurisdictions reveals that the courts' method for determining what guidance jurors need and how best to guide them — judicial knowledge and experience — is far from adequate.

166 See, eg, Rabeea Assy, 'Can the Law Speak Directly to Its Subjects? The Limitation of Plain Language' (2011) 38(3) *Journal of Law and Society* 376, 384–90.

4 The relationship between the law and social science juror comprehension research

Introduction

There are two sources of knowledge about juror comprehension. Court proceedings provide the traditional source of knowledge about juror comprehension (Chapter 2). With limited opportunities to obtain information directly from jurors, courts rely on indirect measures, such as observing each juror's demeanour and considering jury questions and verdicts. Social science juror comprehension research provides the other source of knowledge (Chapter 3). This research has found that there are significant juror comprehension problems, and that juror comprehension can be improved. However, juror comprehension research has had limited influence in changing criminal trials and laws to improve juror comprehension.

Understanding why juror comprehension research has had limited influence is essential for determining how to develop reforms that give greater weight to this research. Examining this issue raises questions about how the law and the courts assess and use information from social science disciplines about juror comprehension. Given the role of judges in guiding juries, the views that judges' often hold about juror comprehension research are particularly important.

Lord Justice Moses said that '[i]f we understood why we are so resistant to change, we might find less inhibition in changing'.[1] In this chapter I examine views commonly held by judges and lawyers about jurors and juries. I also examine court processes that help to explain why many judges and lawyers only have limited awareness of social science research about juror comprehension, why they may be sceptical about this research, and why they may be concerned about the consequences of accepting this research. I then examine deeper issues concerning the differences between the law and social science research as bodies of knowledge and their different methods for determining the truth.

1 Lord Justice Moses, 'Summing Down the Summing-Up' (Speech, Annual Law Reform Lecture, Inner Temple, 23 November 2010) 11.

DOI: 10.4324/9781003477129-4

Using social science research in the courts to change jury directions and laws

To make or change laws or jury directions, courts need 'adequate information about the suggested change and its legal and practical consequences'.[2] This information may come from other disciplines such as history, economics, and social science. This section is not concerned with expert evidence that helps jurors to understand the facts and consequentially may affect jury directions in individual cases (eg, directions that address misconceptions in a sexual offence case). This section considers how the parties (the prosecution and the defence) may introduce juror comprehension research, and how courts may use juror comprehension research, to change jury directions or the laws that the judge gives directions about.

How parties and non-parties may introduce juror comprehension research into a case

A significant amount of juror comprehension research comes from the USA. The USA also has a well-established process for parties and non-parties to submit social science research in court proceedings that goes beyond the processes used in most other common law jurisdictions.[3] It is 'extremely uncommon' for the High Court of Australia to grant 'leave to a non-party to file or adduce factual material'.[4] Therefore, this section focuses on courts in the USA because their courts should be more likely to admit juror comprehension research.

In the USA, appellate courts may receive social science research through expert witnesses or by using a 'Brandeis brief' — named after the original proponent of these briefs, Louis Brandeis.[5] A Brandeis brief enables social science research (eg, about race, gender, class, bias in testing) to be presented to an appellate court.[6] A Brandeis brief is not usually used at a trial, as a party may instead call expert evidence.[7] Detailed studies of cases in which the Supreme Court of the United States considered social science evidence indicate that this rarely involves juror comprehension (or similar) research.[8] Another study

2 Chief Justice Murray Gleeson, 'Law and Change' (Speech, Flinders University, 19 November 2008).

3 See, eg, George Williams, 'The Amicus Curiae and Intervener in the High Court of Australia: A Comparative Analysis' (2000) 28(3) *Federal Law Review* 365, 369–73.

4 Justice Michelle Gordon, 'Taking *Judging and Judges* Seriously: Facts, Framework and Function in Australian Constitutional Law' (Speech, Monash University Lucinda Lecture, 2 August 2022) 46.

5 *Muller v Oregon* 208 US 412 (1908).

6 See, eg, Jeffrey J Rachlinski, 'Evidence-Based Law' (2011) 96 *Cornell Law Review* 901, 905–6.

7 John Monahan and Laurens Walker, 'A Judges' Guide to Using Social Science' (2007) 43 *Court Review* 156, 157 ('A Judges' Guide').

8 See J Alexander Tanford, 'The Limits of a Scientific Jurisprudence: The Supreme Court and Psychology' (1990) 66 *Indiana Law Journal* 137, 138–9; Mary R Rose, 'How Typical Is *Lockhart v McCree*? Ecological Validity Concerns in Court Opinions' in Margaret B Kovera (ed), *The Psychology of Juries* (American Psychological Association, 2017) 227, 229.

identified seven cases in the US Supreme Court up to mid-2014 which mentioned jury studies but these studies did not involve juror comprehension research.[9] The scarcity of these kinds of cases indicates that it is rare for appellate courts to consider juror comprehension research.

The challenges with using juror comprehension research in courts in the USA is evident in capital punishment cases, where there is considerable evidence of juror comprehension problems.[10] Unusually, the Seventh Circuit of the United States Court of Appeals considered research about the comprehensibility of death penalty jury instructions in *Free v Peters*.[11] Free had been convicted of murder. He challenged the sentence of death on the basis that the instructions provided to the jury were confusing and therefore permitted the 'arbitrary and unguided imposition' of the death penalty.[12]

At the direction of the appellate court in *Free v Peters*, a 'magistrate judge' held an evidentiary hearing to determine the admissibility of research concerning the comprehensibility of the instructions. The research, conducted by Hans Zeisel, involved two sets of mock jurors, involving 238 people already convened for jury service to test their comprehension of instructions that were similar to, or the same as, the instructions used in the *Free v Peters* death penalty hearing. In addition, Free's witnesses in the evidentiary hearing included 'the nation's leading experts in juror comprehension, statistics and linguistics'.[13] Consistent with juror comprehension research generally, the magistrate judge concluded that Zeisel's studies showed very high levels of misunderstanding.[14]

In the Court of Appeals, Chief Judge Posner concluded from his own reading that the instructions were not confusing and found Zeisel's research evidence to be seriously deficient, stating that there were two 'fatal flaws' with the research. First, the ecological setting of the jury simulation test differed from a trial (eg, there were no witnesses, no counsel, and no judge).[15] Second, a control group was not tested with revised instructions to demonstrate whether the instructions could be clarified. Chief Judge Posner said that such a test would then demonstrate that the problem was either the examination setting or that the 'American jury system is entirely hopeless because Americans

9 Rose (n 8) 229.
10 See, eg, Theodore Eisenberg and Martin T Wells, 'Deadly Confusion: Juror Instructions in Capital Cases' (1993) 79 *Cornell Law Review* 1, 5–11; Shari Seidman Diamond and Judith N Levi, 'Improving Decisions on Death by Revising and Testing Jury Instructions' (1996) 79 *Judicature* 224.
11 *Free v Peters*, 12 F 3d 700 (United States Court of Appeals, 1993) ('*Free v Peters*').
12 Free argued that this violated the Eighth amendment: *United States ex rel Free v McGinnis*, 818 F Supp 1098 (1992), 1098 ('*Free v McGinnis*').
13 Kimball R Anderson and Bruce R Braun, 'The Legal Legacy of John Wayne Gacy: The Irrebuttable Presumption That Juries Understand and Follow Jury Instructions' (1995) 78(4) *Marquette Law Review* 791, 795.
14 *Free v McGinnis* (n 12) 1110.
15 *Free v Peters* (n 11) 705–6 (Posner CJ), 707 (Bauer J agreeing).

can't understand even simple jury instructions'.[16] Chief Judge Posner concluded that it was not possible to choose between these options based on the evidence. Therefore, Zeisel's study 'failed to invalidate the instructions given in Free's case'.[17]

Chief Judge Posner's judgment reveals scepticism of the ecological validity of research and a fear that the research may pose fundamental challenges to the role of juries in trials or sentencing hearings. Chief Judge Posner did not subject his own 'knowledge' — that the jury instructions were 'simple' to understand — to the same level of scrutiny as the juror comprehension research.

Around the same time, another appeals court heard an appeal from John Wayne Gacy in which Gacy also sought to rely on Zeisel's research to challenge his death sentence. The court observed that the jury instruction was poorly drafted, containing a quadruple negative:

> If you do <u>not</u> unanimously find from your consideration of all the evidence that there are <u>no</u> mitigating factors sufficient to <u>preclude</u> imposition of a death sentence, then you should sign the verdict requiring the court to impose a sentence <u>other than</u> death.[18]

The court found that Zeisel's research did not matter because courts rely on a presumption that jurors understand and follow jury instructions.[19] However, there have been cases where courts have not applied this presumption — not because of research about juror comprehension, but because judges form their own assessments of the capacity of jurors to follow instructions.[20] Again, the court's own reasoning processes prevailed over social science research.

The difficulties that parties face in introducing juror comprehension evidence in the USA highlight the kind of difficulties that parties are likely to experience in other common law jurisdictions if they try to introduce juror comprehension research. Some scholars have concluded that judges more readily accept research, and do not question its methods (when they could easily be questioned), where research bolsters the decision that the judge was already going to make rather than questions accepted practice.[21] However, research is most valuable, and likely to be questioned, when it identifies problems with existing practices or laws.

16 *Free v Peters* (n 11) 706.
17 *Free v Peters* (n 11) 706.
18 *Gacy v Welborn*, 944 F 2d 305 (7th Cir, 1993), 314 (emphasis added).
19 *Gacy v Welborn* (n 18) 313.
20 See generally Anderson and Braun (n 13) 798–802.
21 Norbert L Kerr and Robert M Bray, 'Simulation, Realism, and the Study of the Jury' in Neil Brewer and Kipling D Williams (eds), *Psychology and Law* (Guilford Press, 2005) 322, 356.

How courts may use juror comprehension research

Instead of a party using a Brandeis brief or calling expert evidence, courts may of their own motion consider research to improve juror comprehension. Research about juror comprehension is not limited to, or usually based on, the circumstances of a current case or the evidence adduced by the parties. Expert evidence about juror comprehension research may not be relevant in a criminal trial because it does not concern 'adjudicative facts' — being 'facts which are in issue or are relevant to a fact in issue' to be determined by the tribunal of fact.[22] However, jury directions will, at least sometimes, fit within the description of 'legislative facts', being facts which go to 'the validity or content of the legal rule or standard by which . . . [a] dispute is to be resolved'[23] and help courts 'to determine what a common law rule should be or how a statute should be construed'.[24]

The terms 'adjudicative facts' and 'legislative facts' have a long tradition in the USA.[25] These terms have also been recognised in Australia, Canada, and New Zealand.[26] However, there is no settled and clear authority governing their use in Australia.[27] The use of these terms in the United Kingdom is even less clear as there is a 'dearth of case law and an unstable and ill-defined approach to legislative facts'.[28]

The laws of evidence, expert evidence, and judicial notice primarily developed for the purposes of determining adjudicative facts. However, courts may take judicial notice of a fact to determine both adjudicative facts and legislative facts. This is the most common method used for determining legislative facts.[29]

The doctrine of judicial notice provides an exception to the requirement to call an expert witness to introduce exogenous knowledge.[30] Judicial notice

22 *Aytugrul v The Queen* (2012) 247 CLR 170, 200 [70] (Heydon J) ('*Aytugrul*'). See also Monahan and Walker, 'A Judges' Guide' (n 7).

23 Stephen Gageler, 'Fact and Law' (2008) 11 *Newcastle Law Review* 1, 23.

24 *Aytugrul* (n 22) 200 [71] (Heydon J).

25 See, eg, John Monahan and Laurens Walker, 'Twenty-Five Years of "Social Science in Law"' (2011) 35 *Law and Human Behavior* 72, 76–7.

26 See, eg, *Woods v Multi-Sport Holdings Pty Ltd* (2002) 208 CLR 460, 478 (McHugh); *Aytugrul* (n 22) 201–2 [71] (Heydon J); *R v Spence* [2005] 3 SCR 458 ('*Spence*'); *Hansen v The Queen* (2007) 23 CRNZ 104, 110 [9] (Elias CJ), 126 [50] (Blanchard J), 149 [132] (Tipping J), and 176–7 [230] (McGrath J) ('*Hansen*').

27 See, eg, Andrew J Serpell, 'Social Policy Information: Recent Decisions of the High Court of Australia' (2011) 21 *Journal of Judicial Administration* 109, 123–5; David Hamer and Gary Edmond, 'Judicial Notice: Beyond Adversarialism and into the Exogenous Zone' (2016) 25 *Griffith Law Review* 291, 300.

28 Christopher Tran, 'Facts and Evidence under the Charter of Human Rights and Responsibilities Act 2009 (Vic) and the Human Rights Act 2004 (ACT)' (2012) 36 *Melbourne University Law Review* 287, 303.

29 Serpell (n 27) 112–13.

30 Hamer and Edmond (n 27) 293–300.

may help the court to better determine the issues in a case consistently with evidentiary principles of 'factual accuracy, efficiency, fairness and institutional integrity'.[31] A court may take judicial notice of a fact if it is 'so generally known that every ordinary person may be reasonably presumed to be aware of it'.[32]

At common law, judicial notice may apply to a wide range of matters. Arguably, anything not proved by formal evidence falls within the description of judicial notice and it may include common sense, general knowledge, and judicial knowledge and experience.[33] The strictness of the tests governing judicial notice for adjudicative facts does not appear to extend to legislative facts.[34] This is important because research about juror comprehension is rarely indisputable beyond the general conclusion that overwhelmingly jurors do not understand jury directions as judges traditionally give them. And, given the nature of juror comprehension research, it is almost inevitable that it is necessary to generalise or draw inferences from research to apply it to (other) trials. Even research specifically tailored to the directions in a case, such as that used in *Free*, was open to some legitimate criticisms. In relation to legislative facts, courts have considered a wide range of social science evidence or information even where it is not common knowledge, or is not incontrovertible:

> [i]t is clear from the cases that judges have felt themselves relatively free to apply their own views and to make their own enquiries of social ethics, psychology, politics and history where relevant without requiring evidence or other proof.[35]

The procedures governing the introduction of matters relied upon to establish legislative facts vary between jurisdictions, are not always clear,[36] and there is considerable uncertainty about whether Australia's uniform evidence laws apply to legislative facts.[37] Uncertainty also arises because courts may not identify when they are using judicial notice to rely on certain evidence or to draw certain conclusions.[38]

David Hamer and Gary Edmond conclude that the 'current state of Australian authority appears to allow and encourage judicial reference to exogenous

31 Hamer and Edmond (n 27) 294.

32 *Holland v Jones* (1917) 23 CLR 149, 153 (Isaacs J).

33 Serpell (n 27) 113.

34 See, eg, Gageler (n 23) 20–2.

35 LexisNexis, *Cross on Evidence* (online at 30 July 2022) 192 [3005]. See also Serpell (n 27) 112–13; Gageler (n 23) 19–20.

36 See, eg, Tran (n 28) 307; Gageler (n 23) 26–9; *Spence* (n 26) 490–1 (Binnie J for Major, LeBel, Deschamps, Fish, Abella and Charron JJ); *Hansen* (n 26) 110 [9] (Elias CJ) and [232] (McGrath J).

37 It is not clear whether section 144 of the *Evidence Act 1995* (Cth) impliedly abolishes the common law doctrine of judicial notice. See, eg, Hamer and Edmond (n 27) 299–304.

38 Tran (n 28) 331.

knowledge on an ad hoc and unprincipled basis'.[39] For example, in one case the Victorian Court of Appeal referred to three articles — about how victims of sexual abuse may react — in deciding what directions a judge should give to assist the jury in understanding why a victim may delay in making a complaint.[40] The court did not receive, nor suggest that it needed to, any expert evidence about the research. The research was referred to in a footnote supporting what appears to be the court's 'knowledge and experience' about delay. The court did not describe its knowledge and experience in those terms, it simply stated matters about delay in sexual offences cases as facts. By contrast, the High Court of Australia has said that expert evidence in the trial court or the intermediate Court of Criminal Appeal was necessary to enable the High Court to consider juror comprehension research about how jurors understand probabilities with DNA evidence.[41]

Other jurisdictions also lack a systematic approach to exogenous knowledge. For example:

- Courts in England and Wales developed directions in sexual offence cases that caution a jury about relying on stereotypes or assumptions about the behaviour of a sexual offence complainant. Courts indicated these directions were based on judges' experience from presiding in such cases, referred to expert material that was available at the Judicial Studies Board, and described the information as being of 'particular notoriety or common knowledge'.[42] The court did not discuss how the directions were based on common knowledge, when their purpose is to address common mistaken stereotypes.
- New Zealand's Court of Appeal changed the content of jury directions about 'proof beyond reasonable doubt', after considering several research studies that indicated that jurors struggled with this concept.[43] However, none of the three judges discussed the basis on which they were entitled to rely on the studies.[44]
- The Court of Appeal in Ontario, Canada, endorsed a judge's decision to provide written instructions 'to enhance juror comprehension of oral instructions'.[45] The appellate court cited three social science studies that

39 Hamer and Edmond (n 27) 313.

40 *R v ERJ* (2010) 200 A Crim R 270, 280. See generally, Greg Byrne, 'Helping Jurors to Understand: Misconceptions about Delay in Making a Complaint' (2022) 47(1) *Alternative Law Journal* 16.

41 *Aytugrul* (n 22) 184 [22] (French CJ, Hayne, Crennan and Bell JJ), 199–200 [66]–[69] (Heydon J).

42 See, eg, *R v D* [2008] EWCA Crim 2557 [9]; *R v Miller* [2010] EWCA Crim 1578 [23]–[24].

43 *R v Wanhalla* [2007] 2 NZLR 573, 585–9 [41]–[45] (William Young P, Chambers and Robertson JJ) ('*Wanhalla*').

44 *Wanhalla* (n 43) 585–9 [41]–[45].

45 *R v Poitras* (2002) 57 OR (3d) 58.

supported the use of written instructions, but without stating the basis on which they did so.

Many of these descriptions of judicial notice also apply to judicial knowledge and experience. Courts use judicial knowledge and experience on an ad hoc basis, they may not state when or how it is relied upon and may not indicate whether it is indisputable or demonstrably reliable. As Hamer and Edmond argue, 'judges' implicit or explicit empirical claims [should] have a more solid basis than their untested subjective "common sense"'.[46] Courts appear comparatively unconstrained in relying on judicial knowledge and experience when determining what is comprehensible to jurors.

Accordingly, courts have rarely used juror comprehension research to assess the effectiveness of jury directions and to change directions or the underlying laws so that courts may give more comprehensible directions. However, even if courts considered more juror comprehension research, significant practical constraints on appellate courts changing jury directions would remain.

Courts have limited capacity to change laws and jury directions. For example, it depends upon there being an appeal in the right kind of case (where the relevant issue can be examined).[47] This may take some years to arise and will depend upon the existence of significant research to identify that there is a problem and that improvements can be made. For example, New Zealand's changes to directions on 'proof beyond reasonable doubt' occurred eight years after the New Zealand Law Commission (NZLC) found that 'many jurors' were uncertain about the meaning of this phrase.[48] In that time, the courts were conducting trials with directions when they knew that jurors were struggling with this fundamental concept. In England and Wales, almost 15 years elapsed between Lord Justice Auld's recommendation that judges provide juries with a 'route to verdict'[49] and practice directions stating that judges should use the route to verdict in nearly all cases.[50] Intermediate appellate courts are further limited in their capacity to change jury directions. For example, because of previous High Court decisions, State and Territory courts in Australia could not change directions on proof beyond reasonable doubt.[51]

46 Hamer and Edmond (n 27) 304 (footnotes omitted).

47 See, eg, Justice Chris Maxwell and Greg Byrne, 'Making Trials Work for Juries: Pathways to Simplification' [2020] (11) *Criminal Law Review* 1034, 1043.

48 New Zealand Law Commission, *Juries in Criminal Trials: Part Two* (Preliminary Paper No 37, November 1999) 54 [7.16] (NZLC).

49 Lord Justice Auld, *A Review of the Criminal Courts of England and Wales* (Report, September 2001) 537–8 [55].

50 *Criminal Practice Direction 2015* (UK) 26K.12. This practice direction has been superseded, but the obligation to provide a route to verdict remains: *R v Atta-Dankwa* [2018] 2 Cr App R 16.

51 See, eg, Maxwell and Byrne (n 47) 1043.

Change would require either the High Court to overturn its previous decisions or legislative intervention in each jurisdiction.[52]

Despite these significant limitations, courts have made some changes to address juror comprehension problems. The most significant changes have occurred outside of the courtroom, where courts have more flexibility to consider social science research.

How courts may use juror comprehension research outside of the courtroom

As discussed in Chapter 2, by drawing on either social science research or their own conclusions about the complexity of the law and juror comprehension problems, courts have sought to improve their guidance to juries, particularly by using SDM aids. The NZLC encouraged the use of question trails based on its observation of two cases but without any evidence that question trails would help jurors.[53] Courts in England and Wales also introduced the 'route to verdict' based on very limited research — a jury simulation study with six mock juries.[54]

Judicial interest in addressing the length and comprehensibility of jury directions in Australia led to the Australian Institute of Judicial Administration (AIJA) commissioning jury research.[55] Judicial interest in improving jury directions generally also contributed to three Australian jurisdictions giving references to law reform commissions on jury directions.[56] Following the VLRC's report, the Department of Justice established the Jury Directions Advisory Group as a partnership between the judiciary and the executive, which advised on significant legislative reforms to jury directions in Victoria over the next ten years.[57] As discussed in Chapter 7, the AIJA processes also led to significant research in Australia and New Zealand to assess whether question trails improved juror comprehension.

However, as discussed in Chapter 2, the extent of change in many jurisdictions has been comparatively limited. In general, these changes have sought to improve juror comprehension outside of specific court cases and without

52 See, eg, Justice Virginia Bell, 'Communication with Juries' (Speech, National Judicial College of Australia Conference, 10 November 2007) quoted in Victorian Law Reform Commission, *Jury Directions* (Report No 17, May 2009) 68 [4.15] (VLRC).

53 New Zealand Law Commission, *Juries in Criminal Trials* (Report No 69, February 2001) 118–19 [313]–[314] (NZLC).

54 Cheryl Thomas, *Are Juries Fair?* (Ministry of Justice, 2010) 38.

55 See, eg, Justice Geoffrey Eames, 'Towards a Better Direction — Better Communication with Jurors' (2003) 24 *Australian Bar Review* 35, 37.

56 VLRC, *Jury Directions* (n 52); Queensland Law Reform Commission, *A Review of Jury Directions* (Report No 66, September 2009) (QLRC); New South Wales Law Reform Commission, *Jury Directions* (Report No 136, November 2012).

57 Greg Byrne and Justice Chris Maxwell, 'Putting Jurors First: Legislative Simplification of Jury Directions' (2019) 43(3) *Criminal Law Journal* 180, 184–5.

questioning the validity of any convictions or the fairness of trial by jury.[58] This kind of change is possible because courts generally control their own procedures in guiding juries. Other changes may involve supporting and expanding directions to give in certain kinds of cases (eg, to address the risk that jurors may rely upon stereotypes or unwarranted assumptions about sexual behaviour in sexual offence cases built upon existing case law in England and Wales) or getting experts in Plain English to review jury directions in bench books.[59]

In summary, it is very difficult to make significant changes to the law or jury directions in court proceedings to improve juror comprehension. There is more scope for courts to make procedural changes or amend bench books where this does not involve any change to existing laws. However, courts have limited capacity to change, and change has been quite limited having regard to the importance and extent of juror comprehension problems.

Judges' and lawyers' views about juror comprehension

The limited nature of changes, and strong judicial comments in some cases, suggest that there may be more fundamental reasons why juror comprehension research has had limited influence. Judges' views about juror comprehension and scepticism about juror comprehension research help to explain why social science juror comprehension research has not driven change more extensively (whether inside or outside of the courtroom). This discussion focuses primarily on judges because of the importance of their role and because information about their views is more readily available. However, references to judges necessarily involve generalisations. References to judges' views are highly likely to be views shared by many (practising) lawyers.

This section examines three sources of information judges may use in forming their views about juror comprehension of their task:

- Judges' own assessment of whether jurors understand their directions
- whether jury verdicts show that juries understand their task, and
- whether appeals against jury verdicts show that juries understand their task.

Assessing whether jurors understand their directions

Like judicial knowledge and experience, surveys of judges' views about juror comprehension challenges are likely to overestimate what is comprehensible to jurors for several reasons. A judge's experience of a jury trial is very different

58 See, eg, Marie Comiskey, 'Initiating Dialogue about Jury Comprehension of Legal Concepts: Can the "Stagnant Pool" Be Revitalized?' (2010) 35 *Queen's Law Journal* 625, 673–3.

59 Judicial College, *The Crown Court Compendium — Part I: Jury and Trial Management and Summing Up* (July 2024) <www.judiciary.uk/wp-content/uploads/2024/07/Crown-Court-Compendium-Part-I-July-2024-1.pdf> 22–13 ('*Crown Court Compendium*').

from a jurors' experience and a judge will almost never have experienced being a juror.[60] Lawyers have the 'curse of knowledge',[61] making it difficult for them to remember what it was like to learn about laws for the first time, and to know what jurors do and do not know. It is therefore difficult for judges and lawyers to know how best to explain the law to those unfamiliar with it.[62] For jurors, the information in jury directions is often difficult to understand because of the nature of the information and because the information is new.[63] Judges and lawyers have often heard the same jury directions for many years, and their assessment of the comprehensibility of a direction is from the perspective of one who already understands the law. As a result, 'it is doubtful that legal professionals can intuitively gauge the degree to which laypeople understand legal language'.[64] Further, when giving jury directions, judges face the 'two audience dilemma'.[65] While judges must guide juries, they may be more focused on a different audience because legal accuracy is essential when facing appellate scrutiny.

Like jurors, judges and lawyers interpret information from a trial through their own knowledge, experience, values, beliefs, and biases.[66] Judges and lawyers are likely to derive their impressions of juror comprehension from information such as jury questions or from 'non-verbal behavioural cues' from jurors when delivering directions.[67] This leads to untested assumptions about jurors and what they understand.

Recognition of juror comprehension problems is likely to be based primarily on judges' and lawyers' own intuitive judgments, observations, and assessments. For example, in a speech to judges about problems in the law affecting juror comprehension, Justice Weinberg said that it is 'unacceptable

60 In most jurisdictions, judges and lawyers are ineligible to serve on a jury. Cf *Juries Act 1974* (UK) s 1.

61 Steven Pinker, *The Sense of Style: The Thinking Person's Guide to Writing in the 21st Century* (Penguin Group, 2014) 57.

62 See, eg, Nancy S Marder, 'Bringing Jury Instructions into the Twenty-First Century' (2006) 81 *Notre Dame Law Review* 449, 460–1; Sara Gordon, 'Through the Eyes of Jurors: The Use of Schemas in the Application of "Plain Language" Jury Instructions' (2013) 64 *Hastings Law Journal* 643, 668–70.

63 John Sweller, Jeroen J G van Merriënboer and Fred Paas, 'Cognitive Architecture and Instructional Design: 20 Years Later' (2019) 31(2) *Educational Psychology Review* 261, 264.

64 Peter Meijes Tiersma, 'Reforming the Language of Jury Instructions' (1993) 22 *Hofstra Law Review* 37, 41.

65 John Gibbons, *Forensic Linguistics: An Introduction to Language in the Justice System* (Blackwell Publishers, 2003) 174.

66 See, eg, Chris Guthrie, Jeffrey J Rachlinski and Andrew Wistrich, 'Inside the Judicial Mind' (2001) 86 *Cornell Law Review* 777; Gary Edmond and Kirsty A Martire, 'Just Cognition: Scientific Research on Bias and Some Implications for Legal Procedure and Decision-Making' (2019) 82(4) *Modern Law Review* 633.

67 Dorean M Loenig, Norbert L Kerr and Dawn Van Joek, 'Michigan Standard Jury Instructions: Judges' Perspectives after Ten Years' Use' (1987) *Cooley Law Review* 347, 365.

for us to continue to direct juries in terms that *we know* make no sense at all'.[68] However, in that 60-page speech there was scarcely any mention of juror comprehension research, and of the 224 footnotes, only five concerned juror comprehension research. Justice Weinberg was clearly aware of juror comprehension research.[69] However, he did not discuss this research in a speech to judges about the problems with jury directions. It is not clear whether this is because he did not think the evidence was important or he did not think his audience would consider it important.

While surveys of judges in Australia indicate that judicial awareness of juror comprehension problems appears to be growing,[70] it is not clear whether juror comprehension research is informing judicial awareness.

Do jury verdicts show that juries understand their task?

Judges may also assess juror comprehension through the lens of whether juries generally reach the 'right' verdict. In a study of 48 trials in New Zealand in the late 1990s, judges agreed with jury verdicts in 50% of cases.[71] This study asked judges what their verdict would be *before* the jury had returned its verdict. However, when judges know the jury's verdict before they express an opinion about the verdict, several studies show that judges agree with a high proportion of jury verdicts — more than 75%.[72] Contextual bias (from knowing the jury's verdict) and hindsight bias (an overestimation of the predictability of past events) may have influenced the judges' perceptions of whether they agreed with the jury's verdict.[73] Studies have shown that when judges are informed of the outcome of an appeal, being one of three possible outcomes, 'they were much more likely to identify that outcome as the most likely to

68 Justice Mark Weinberg, 'Jury Directions on Trial — A Pathway through the Labyrinth?' (Speech, Supreme and Federal Court Judges' Conference, 5–9 July 2014) 59 (emphasis added) ('Jury Directions on Trial'). The reference to 'we know' appears to rely on judicial knowledge and experience.

69 Justice Mark Weinberg, *Simplification of Jury Directions Project* (Supreme Court of Victoria, 2012) <www.supremecourt.vic.gov.au/home/contact+us/publications/simplification+of+jury+directions+project+report> 8–14.

70 Jonathan Clough et al, *The Jury Project 10 Years On — Practices of Australian and New Zealand Judges* (Australian Institute of Judicial Administration, April 2019) 1 ('*The Jury Project 10 Years On*').

71 NZLC, *Juries in Criminal Trials: Part Two* (n 48) 68 [9.3].

72 See, eg, Thomas Eisenberg et al, 'Judge-Jury Agreement in Criminal Cases: A Partial Replication of Kalven and Zeisel's the American Jury' (2005) 2 *Journal of Empirical Legal Studies* 171; Bradley Saxton, 'How Well Do Jurors Understand Jury Instructions? A Field Test Using Real Juries and Real Trials in Wyoming' (1998) 33 *Land and Water Law Review* 59, 102–4.

73 See, eg, James R P Ogloff and V Gordon Rose, 'The Comprehension of Judicial Instructions' in Neil Brewer and Kipling D Williams (eds), *Psychology and Law: An Empirical Perspective* (Guilford Press, 2005) 407, 414; Edmond and Martire (n 66) 637–9, 656; Guthrie, Rachlinski and Wistrich (n 66) 799; Phoebe C Ellsworth, 'Legal Reasoning and Scientific Reasoning' (2012) 63 *Alabama Law Review* 895, 902–3.

have occurred'.[74] Anecdotal evidence is often to similar effect: '[e]xperienced trial judges will tell you that juries mostly get it right'[75] and 'properly-directed juries have over the years shown a remarkable instinct for fairness'.[76] Lawyers have made similar positive statements about jury verdicts.[77] The repetition of these kinds of statements may also inflate perceptions of the truth of the statement.[78]

Judges' and lawyers' views are often based on 'retrospective perceptions and impressions'[79] of jury trials and are 'inevitably coloured in some measure by ideological predispositions'[80] such as supporting trial by jury. These views may also reflect that the jury's verdict accords with what the judge thought, or at least that the jury's verdict was reasonably open on the evidence. Where jurors do not fully understand the judge's directions, they are likely to apply their 'commonsense justice' or prototypes of the law.[81] Especially where jurors' ideas about the law are consistent with the law, jurors are likely to produce a verdict that then appears to be fair to the judge. Trials usually only occur where the evidence is contestable and may involve conflicting accounts, and the standard of proof is high. Further, the jury's possible verdicts are (generally) binary. Accordingly, even the likelihood of chance agreement between judges and jurors is high. Further, the jury's verdict is inscrutable, and the jury does not provide any reasons for its decision. However, in relation to any contested issues, the judge's directions on those issues will provide a reasoned basis, as a simulacrum for the jury's reasons, and make the jury's verdict explicable.[82]

As discussed in Chapter 3, the story model is generally accepted as providing the best explanation of how jurors approach their decision-making task. The story model also helps to understand judges' views about juries. Judges

74 Guthrie, Rachlinski and Wistrich (n 66) 803. This study involved 167 federal magistrate judges in the USA.

75 Justice Peter McClellan, 'Looking Inside the Jury Room' (Speech, Law Society of New South Wales Young Lawyers 2011 Annual Criminal Law Seminar, 5 March 2011) 15. See also Mark Coen et al, 'Respect, Reform and Research: An Empirical Insight into Judge-jury Relations' (2020) 4(2) *Irish Judicial Studies Board* 116, 122.

76 *R v H and C* [2004] 2 AC 134, 146–7 [13] (Lord Bingham).

77 QLRC, *A Review of Jury Directions* (n 56) 163.

78 Edmond and Martire (n 66) 656–7.

79 James R P Ogloff et al, *The Jury Project: Stage 1 — A Survey of Australian and New Zealand Judges* (Australian Institute of Judicial Administration, 2006) 7. See also Coen et al (n 75) 131.

80 John Baldwin and Michael McConville, 'Trial by Jury: Some Empirical Evidence on Contested Criminal Cases in England' (1979) 13 *Law and Society Review* 861, 863.

81 See, eg, Norman J Finkel, 'Commonsense Justice and Jury Instructions: Instructive and Reciprocating Connections' (2000) 6(3) *Psychology, Public Policy, and Law* 591, 608–9; Vicki L Smith, 'Prototypes in the Courtroom: Lay Representations of Legal Concepts' (1991) 61(6) *Journal of Personality and Social Psychology* 857, 869.

82 See, eg, *Taxquet v Belgium* [2010] ECHR 1806 [92]; Jeremy Gans et al, *Criminal Process and Human Rights* (Federation Press, 2011) 444–5.

use their knowledge and experience to decide how well juries perform. Judges usually only have limited information to determine whether juries mostly 'get it right'. When decision-makers have limited information, they intuitively seek coherence in the story they construct.[83] They may also be less inclined to consider other potential sources of information. Further, having decided something, decision-makers tend to be overly confident about the likely correctness of their decision.[84] That juries mostly 'get it right', that courts ensure fair trials, that trial by jury works, can all weave together to make a coherent story. And each verdict that a judge agrees with supports this view, which can make judges more confident that their view is correct.

Do appeals against jury verdicts show that juries do understand their task?

Another way of assessing whether juries 'get it right' is to consider successful appeals against conviction. A number of common law jurisdictions have the so-called 'common form' appeal provisions, based on the *Criminal Appeal Act 1907* (UK).[85] The first limb of the common form appeal provisions provides that the verdict of the jury should be set aside if it is 'unreasonable or cannot be supported having regard to the evidence'.[86] This involves the appellate court making a factual determination about whether the court thinks that 'upon the whole of the evidence it was open to the jury to be satisfied beyond reasonable doubt that the accused was guilty'.[87] The equivalent provision in Canada and New Zealand has been interpreted differently, making it much harder to appeal against a jury's verdict on this ground in those jurisdictions.[88] Therefore, this kind of error should arise more often in Australia than in other jurisdictions.

It is also more likely to be evident in Australia because judges in Australia have less powers to stop a case before a jury considers its verdict. In England and Wales, the judge must stop the case if at the close of the prosecution case the judge considers that a verdict would not be 'safe' — where the evidence is

83 See, eg, Amos Tversky and Daniel Kahneman, 'Belief in the Law of Small Numbers' (1971) 76(2) *Psychological Bulletin* 105, 110.

84 Emma Cunliffe, 'Judging, Fast and Slow: Using Decision-Making Theory to Explore Judicial Fact Determination' (2014) 18 *The International Journal of Evidence and Proof* 139, 144.

85 See, eg Harmonisation of Criminal Procedure Working Group, Standing Committee of Attorneys-General, *Harmonisation of Criminal Appeals Legislation* (Discussion Paper, July 2010) 30–1.

86 See, eg, *Criminal Appeal Act 1912* (NSW) s 6(1); *Criminal Code*, RSC 1985, c C-46 s 686(1)(a)(i); *Criminal Procedure Act 2011* (NZ) s 232(2)(a). This limb falls within the general 'unsafe' test applied in the *Criminal Appeal Act 1968* (UK) s 2.

87 *M v The Queen* (1994) 181 CLR 487, 493 (Mason CJ, Deane, Dawson and Toohey JJ).

88 Greg Byrne, 'The High Court in *Pell v The Queen:* An "Unreasonable" Review of the Jury's Decision' (2020) 45(4) *Alternative Law Journal* 284, 285 ('The High Court in *Pell v The Queen*').

of a 'tenuous character, and taken at its highest, it is such that a jury could not properly convict on it'.[89] That is, the trial judge applies the same test as the appellate court would apply so there is little opportunity to identify a jury's factual error in reaching a verdict in an appeal in England and Wales.[90] In Australia, if at the close of the prosecution case, a judge concludes that the prosecution case taken at its highest 'is capable of supporting a verdict of guilty', the judge must leave the matter for the jury to determine.[91]

Accordingly, in Australia, appeals may arise where the evidence was technically sufficient to prove the charge, but the jury must (or ought to) have had a reasonable doubt about the accused's guilt. In this situation, the fact that the jury convicted the accused suggests that the jury did not fully understand its task. However, even this conclusion is contestable because the appellate court's review process may exclude conclusions of fact that were reasonably open to the jury and in some cases the appellate court may apply a higher standard of proof than the jury was required to apply.[92]

In a review of successful appeals against conviction in Australian trial courts between 1 June 2005 and 31 December 2012, Judge Tilmouth found that this 'unreasonable' ground applied to 83 of the 614 successful appeals. However, this figure included cases where this ground applied to only some of the convictions in the case and where the appellate court substituted lesser alternative verdicts of guilty. Further, the figures may have included appeals allowed because there was fresh evidence or incompetence of counsel.[93] Judge Tilmouth did not identify how many appeals fell within these sub-categories. Appeals on this 'unreasonable' ground do not often succeed because the jury is the 'constitutional tribunal for deciding issues of fact'[94] and it is a 'serious step' to set aside a jury's verdict on this ground.[95]

The qualifications to Judge Tilmouth's figures suggests that errors on this 'unreasonable' ground are not common and rarely provide robust evidence to a judge (or any other observer) that a jury did not understand its task. However, limitations in this evidence do not mean that judges' views about juror comprehension and that juries generally 'get it right' are based on robust evidence.

89 *R v Galbraith* [1981] 1 WLR 1039, 1042.

90 In Scotland, which has the same appeal grounds as in England and Wales, this ground was raised in 11 of 100 cases examined and was only successfully raised in three of those cases: Isla Callander, 'Establishing a Miscarriage of Justice in Scotland: An Analysis of 100 Recent Appeals against Criminal Conviction' [2024] (8) *Criminal Law Review* 520, 535.

91 *Doney v The Queen* (1990) 171 CLR 207, 215; *DPP (Vic) Reference No 1 of 2017* (2019) 267 CLR 350, 370–1 [56].

92 Byrne, 'The High Court in *Pell v The Queen*' (n 88) 287–8.

93 Judge Sydney Tilmouth, 'The Wrong Direction: A Case Study and Anatomy of Successful Australian Criminal Appeals' (2015) 40 *Australian Bar Review* 18, 21.

94 *Hocking v Bell* (1945) 71 CLR 430, 440 (Latham CJ).

95 *R v Baden-Clay* (2016) 258 CLR 308, 329 [65].

The predominant method judges use for assessing whether jurors understand jury directions and the view that juries generally 'get it right', contextualises and minimises concerns about juror comprehension problems. It also provides the starting point within the law that juror comprehension research challenges.

Judges' and lawyers' scepticism about juror comprehension research

Despite notable exceptions of judges who are familiar with jury research,[96] it is not clear that many judges or lawyers are aware of the extent of social science research concerning juror comprehension. Awareness of juror comprehension research appears to be growing.[97] For example, a recent study in Ireland (with 22 judges) found majority support for research about juries 'in which the voices of jurors would be heard'.[98] However, judges and lawyers may be sceptical of juror comprehension research and its implications. This scepticism may limit acceptance of, or the weight given to, this research. There are several reasons for this scepticism.

First, there may be scepticism about whether research assesses the right things. Many of the criticisms of jury simulation studies discussed in Chapter 3 may cause scepticism. For example, that simulation studies lack ecological validity and do not test the many variable factors that arise in a jury trial. Judges and lawyers may not be aware that a significant amount of juror comprehension research is conducted to test 'specific psychological theories or procedural innovations' in a manner that excludes the influence of other potential factors.[99] Further, studies may refer to the comprehension of individual jurors rather than the ability of 12 jurors working together to understand and apply directions.[100]

Second, judges and lawyers may be sceptical about research that conflicts with or seems to criticise established practices, particularly if the judge or lawyers' own view is that jury directions are comprehensible and/or that juries mostly 'get it right'. Anecdotes and personal experience have force because they 'speak to closely held political, social or cultural beliefs',[101] namely, beliefs

96 See, eg, Eames (n 55); James Wood, 'Jury Directions' (2007) 16 *Journal of Judicial Administration* 151 ('Jury Directions'); Moses (n 1); Weinberg, 'Jury Directions on Trial' (n 68).

97 See, eg, Clough et al, *The Jury Project 10 Years On* (n 70) 1; Justice David Watt, *Helping Jurors Understand* (Thomson Carswell, 2007) 17–21.

98 Coen et al (n 75) 132.

99 See, eg, Brian H Bornstein, 'The Ecological Validity of Jury Simulations: Is the Jury Still Out?' (1999) 23(1) *Law and Human Behavior* 75, 88; Justice William Young, 'Summing-Up to Juries in Criminal Cases — What Jury Research Says about Current Rules and Practice' [2003] *Criminal Law Review* 665, 669.

100 See, eg, Marder (n 62) 471.

101 Rachlinski (n 6) 921. See also Tanford (n 8) 145; Gary L Wells, 'Helping Experimental Psychology Affect Legal Policy' in Neil Brewer and Kipling D Williams (eds), *Psychology and Law: An Empirical Perspective* (Guilford Press, 2005) 483, 495.

about the value of trial by jury and the view that juries mostly 'get it right'. As an appellate judge in New Zealand said, describing juries as sausage makers, the 'appellate attitude has generally been: leave the sausage makers alone; the ultimate product is quite acceptable'.[102]

Further, once people form a belief, they become 'highly resistant to change and [this] influences how they perceive and construct future information'.[103] As a result, where robust statistical evidence about juror comprehension is contradicted by one or two vivid personal experiences, the conflict will often be resolved in favour of a person's own logic and experience.[104] The status quo bias may also operate so that judges and lawyers over-value the existing approach and courts knowledge about juror comprehension.[105] Confirmation bias — seeking, believing, and remembering information that is consistent with what we already think[106] — can also be a factor.

These biases are particularly relevant to views about social science research that contradicts, or questions, established legal practices. Judges and lawyers may reject research about juror comprehension that does not accord with their own knowledge and experience.[107] For example, the Queensland Bar Association rejected juror comprehension research, saying that 'whilst not to be disregarded, [it] is no substitute for the views of experienced and effective practitioners in the criminal justice system'.[108] The combined effect of these biases may be powerful. These kinds of decision-making biases make it difficult for judges to fully recognise the limitations of their own knowledge about juror comprehension.[109]

Third, conclusions from the research can be difficult to accept. '[J]udges are loathe to acknowledge any shortcomings in the fairness of the system of

102 *Wanhalla* (n 43) 610 [154] (Hammond J).

103 Joel D Lieberman and Jamie Arndt, 'Understanding the Limits of Limiting Instructions: Social Psychological Explanations for the Failures of Instructions to Disregard Pretrial Publicity and Other Inadmissible Evidence' (2000) 6 *Psychology, Public Policy and Law* 677, 691. This is known as 'belief perseverance'.

104 See, eg, Marder (n 62) 468–70; Phoebe C Ellsworth and Alan Reifman, 'Juror Comprehension and Public Policy: Perceived Problems and Proposed Solutions' (2000) 6 *Psychology, Public Policy and Law* 788, 790.

105 Kylie Burns, 'Judges, "Common Sense" and Judicial Cognition' (2019) 23(3) *Griffith Law Review* 319, 333.

106 See, eg, Ellsworth (n 73) 904; Brian M Barry, *How Judges Judge: Empirical Insights into Judicial Decision-Making* (Routledge, 2021) 15.

107 See, eg, Judge Felicity Hampel, 'Legal Culture, Professional Education and Homicide Law Reform' in Kate Fitz-Gibbon and Arie Freiberg (eds), *Homicide Law Reform in Victoria: Retrospect and Prospects* (Federation Press, 2015) 29, 38.

108 The Bar Association of Queensland's submission to the Queensland Law Reform Commission, quoted in QLRC, *A Review of Jury Directions* (n 56) 144 [7.86]. See also, Jacqueline Horan and Mark Israel, 'Beyond the Legal Barriers: Institutional Gatekeeping and Real Jury Research' (2015) 49 *Australia and New Zealand Journal of Criminology* 422, 430.

109 See, eg, Burns (n 105) 332–3.

criminal justice which they help to administer'.[110] Criticising the competence of the jury therefore challenges trial by jury. Proponents of trial by jury may fear that juror comprehension research will demonstrate 'juror incompetence', based on the assumption that the problem is with jurors rather than the system devised for guiding jurors.[111] Further, there may be a fear that admitting there is a problem with the fairness of trials may be used to argue for the abolition of the jury. Indeed, in the context of evidence laws, Sir John Smith feared the

> revelation that many cases are decided in consequence of material irregularities in the jury room with consequent undermining of public confidence in jury trial. If we are to keep jury trial — and there is an overwhelming sentiment in favour of doing so — it is perhaps better not to know. Is this a case where ignorance is bliss?[112]

Many judges and lawyers have a strong cultural commitment and attachment to trial by jury. Numerous studies show that 'people's cultural commitments affect how they react to social science'.[113] It is much easier to embrace 'evidence' that affirms one's views.[114] It can be difficult to accept juror comprehension research that is inconsistent with one's views, particularly where doing so suggests one has presided over trials that were unfair,[115] or where the evidence might be used to argue for the abolition of the jury.

Another reason for low levels of awareness and scepticism of juror comprehension research arises because the law and social science research involve different systems of knowledge.

Social science research and the law: different disciplines

Judges' and lawyers' views about juror comprehension and juror comprehension research are also influenced by differences between social science juror comprehension research disciplines and the law as a discipline. This section examines three aspects of these differences:

- familiarity with juror comprehension research
- how scientific reasoning and legal reasoning differ, and
- the power of the law as a system of 'truth'.

110 Justice K P Duggan, 'Reform of the Criminal Law with Fair Trial as the Guiding Star' (1995) 19 *Criminal Law Journal* 258, 258.
111 See generally, Ellsworth and Reifman (n 104) 794–5; Moses (n 1) 2; Young (n 99) 678.
112 Sir John Smith, 'Is Ignorance Bliss? Could Jury Trial Survive Investigation?' (1998) 38(2) *Medicine, Science and the Law* 98, 105.
113 Dan M Kahan, 'The Cognitively Illiberal State' (2007) 60(1) *Stanford Law Review* 115, 120–2.
114 Rachlinski (n 6) 922.
115 See, eg, Guthrie, Rachlinski and Wistrich (n 66) 815.

Judges' and lawyers' familiarity with juror comprehension research

Judges and lawyers may be unfamiliar with juror comprehension research because it is generally conducted outside of the discipline of law (eg, psycholinguistics and psychology).[116] The purpose of juror comprehension research may not be to improve understanding of the jury system.[117] The jury itself provides an opportunity to 'extend existing laboratory-based models of decision making to more complex problems and more varied content areas'.[118] This may provide 'insight into adult cognition in a complex, naturally occurring reasoning task'.[119] While this may usefully expand knowledge in these disciplines, it is quite different from the purpose of improving knowledge about the jury to ensure a fair trial. Social science researchers may not be sufficiently familiar with the justice system or policy considerations or know how to write and present their findings for judges and lawyers to understand.[120] Further, where the focus of research is addressing problems with the jury system, criticisms of the methodologies used to research the jury system have been significant.[121]

Judges and lawyers may also not be aware of research published in journals from non-legal disciplines, they may not have (or always have had) access to such journals and may not have the time to read and research these kinds of matters.[122] The breadth and complexity of the law is such that practitioners presenting cases to judges are usually limited to specialising within one or two fields within the law.[123] Judges and lawyers may also find it difficult to understand the research. Required elements of law degrees do not usually include the study of social science research and its methodologies.[124] With research emanating from a different discipline, it may use different research methodologies, statistical analysis, and terms of art which are unfamiliar to

116 See, eg, Fiona Leverick, 'What Do We Know about Rape Myths and Juror Decision Making?' (2020) 24(3) *The International Journal of Evidence & Proof* 255, 256; Sara Gordon, 'All Together Now: Using Principles of Group Dynamics to Train Better Jurors' (2015) 48(2) *Indiana Law Review* 415, 423.

117 Jonathan J Koehler and John B Meixner, 'Jury Simulation Goals' in Margaret B Kovera (ed), *The Psychology of Juries* (American Psychological Association, 2017) 161, 164–6. Cf Kerr and Bray (n 21) 339.

118 Nancy Pennington and Reid Hastie, 'Juror Decision-Making Models: The Generalization Gap' (1981) 89 *Psychological Bulletin* 246, 246.

119 Pennington and Hastie (n 118) 246.

120 See, eg, G Wells (n 101) 486–98; Daniel A Krauss and Joel D Lieberman, 'Managing Different Aspects of Validity in Trial Simulation Research' in Margaret B Kovera (ed), *The Psychology of Juries* (American Psychological Association, 2017) 185, 190.

121 Krauss and Lieberman (n 120) 186.

122 See, eg, Justice Stephen McLeish, 'Challenges to the Survival of the Common Law' (2014) 38 *Melbourne University Law Review* 818; Young (n 99) 669.

123 M Gordon (n 4) 51.

124 See, eg, *Legal Profession Uniform Admission Rules 2015* (NSW) Sch 1. See also Timothy J Berard, 'The Relevance of the Social Sciences for Legal Education' (2009) 19(1/2) *Legal Education Review* 189, 190–3.

most judges and lawyers.[125] There is of course some irony in judges' not fully understanding research about the difficulties that jurors have in understanding the judge's directions.

However, even if juror comprehension research were accessible and easy for judges and lawyers to understand, challenges would remain. This is because of differences between the discipline of the law and social science disciplines that conduct juror comprehension research in terms of goals, methodologies, reasoning processes, and values.

Differences between scientific reasoning and legal reasoning

J Alexander Tanford says that

> [t]he only common ground for psychology and the jurisprudence of trials would seem to be their mutual pursuit of truth. However, the two systems seek and define truth quite differently.[126]

The differences between the law and social science reflect 'different types of thinking — a clash of cultures'.[127] The rival systems theory posits that 'law and social science are rival systems with competing logics'.[128] In this theory, the more closely aligned the values of a social science and the law are, the more likely it is that courts will use information from that social science. Court systems focus on preserving:

- the adversarial system — with trial by jury and a court hierarchy
- the symbolic importance of the courts as 'an essential component of the State's social control apparatus'[129] — this concerns both the courts and the system of trial by jury, and
- social order — a crime control function.[130]

Preserving these aspects of the justice system are generally not important in social science juror comprehension research.

The methodologies used by social science and the law to find the truth also differ. In court, the parties lead the evidence and make arguments in support of their case. The jury does not control the evidence on which it must decide. Trials have a rule-bound process that may exclude potentially relevant

125 See, eg, Tanford (n 8) 144; Young (n 99) 669.
126 Tanford (n 8) 168.
127 G Wells (n 101) 483. See also Andreas Kapardis, *Psychology and Law: A Critical Introduction* (Cambridge University Press, 3rd ed, 2009) 8.
128 Tanford (n 8) 152.
129 Michael McConville, *Criminal Judges: Legitimacy, Courts and State-Induced Guilty Pleas in Britain* (Edward Elgar, 2014) 6–7.
130 Tanford (n 8) 167.

information. The law, or courts, must make final decisions where the results of trials are legally accurate.[131] The development of the law means that it has tended to look backwards to find meaning from cases and to deduce principles from previous decisions.

By contrast, social science juror comprehension researchers control the evidence that they consider. Researchers are not bound by the facts in a case and may consider any data that they consider relevant. Research usually involves conducting numerous trials before a consensus emerges that leads to a verifiable conclusion, without legal consequences (and consequences for parties) flowing from decisions made during research processes.[132] Researchers are not required to reach any conclusions and may conduct further research, if necessary, as their goal is to ensure that research results are empirically verifiable.[133]

Further, methodological limitations may not be well understood from another discipline. For example, practical limitations in social science juror comprehension research may reflect the 'craft-based nature of scientific work', which falls short of the 'idealised images' of how scientific research is properly undertaken.[134] These practical limitations in a research study may provide a basis for a judge to reject valid research.[135] The legal system can frame this in its own terms — it is not exposing and rejecting social science research generally but what it may characterise as a specific failure within the research to meet the (idealised) standards of social science.[136] Research using simulated jury trials and mock jurors inevitably has some limitations. However, the differences between studies, with different methodologies and different strengths and weaknesses, may produce a 'convergent validity' that may then be more powerful than any single study.[137] Thus, a weakness in one study is not necessarily a problem and it may sometimes assist in strengthening overall research.

The need for courts to make final decisions, even when weighing incommensurable matters (eg, in determining the admissibility of evidence) encourages categorical ('either/or') thinking.[138] Social science juror comprehension research does not require categorical thinking, and may express its findings in probabilistic terms.[139] For example, because research consistently shows that comprehension of the law is a problem for many jurors, it is reasonable to infer

131 Tanford (n 8) 168.
132 Tanford (n 8) 157–9.
133 Tanford (n 8) 168. See also Ellsworth (n 73) 897–900.
134 David Mercer, 'The Intersection of Sociology of Scientific Knowledge (SSK) and Law: Some Themes and Policy Reflections' (2002) 6 *Law Text Culture* 137, 145.
135 Ellsworth (n 73) 914–15.
136 Mercer (n 134) 146.
137 Ellsworth (n 73) 914. See, also, Ogloff and Rose (n 73) 425; Bornstein (n 99); Shari Seidman Diamond, 'Empirical Legal Scholarship: Observations on Moving Forward' (2019) 113 *Northwestern University Law Review* 1229, 1238–9.
138 Ellsworth (n 73) 913–15.
139 Ellsworth (n 73) 915–16.

that any jury is likely to include jurors with some comprehension difficulties. However, a judge or appellate court cannot infer from this research that any juror in a particular case did not comprehend the issues that they determined. Considering juror comprehension at the micro level of an individual trial in categorical terms can mask reasonable inferences at the macro level of juror comprehension problems in trials generally.

This discussion raises further questions. Why does the law employ these reasoning processes, how does this occur, and what are the consequences of the way in which the law's knowledge has developed for juror comprehension research?

The power of the law as a system of 'truth'

If courts used scientific reasoning, this would not help to resolve many trials because there is usually no independent means for verifying the truth about events and it is 'almost impossible to prove anything with absolute certainty when reconstructing past events'.[140] Further, it is not possible to replicate disputed events in the way that research studies can replicate events.

Verdicts of guilty and not guilty provide a method through which the law claims 'to establish the truth of [disputed] events'.[141] It is a 'truth certifying' procedure[142] where the jury determines whether certain facts have been proved within a trial system that is framed by the law. The common law has long described this system as providing the 'best method of searching and sifting out the truth'.[143] Knowledge of the 'truth', or factual accuracy, is linked to the process used for determining the truth — the adversarial trial.[144] The legal system presents itself as 'transcend[ing] political and personal biases . . . [through] the objective discovery of facts and impersonal application of rules'.[145] However, this kind of 'truth' is different from reaching a verifiable conclusion in social science research.[146] A 'legal procedure may constitute the

140 This is part of the explanation of 'proof beyond reasonable doubt' in some jurisdictions: see, eg, *Jury Directions Act 2015* (Vic) s 64(1)(c)(i); *Wanhalla* (n 43) 588 [49] (William Young P, Chambers and Robertson JJ); *R v Lifchus* [1997] 3 SCR 320, 321.

141 Carol Smart, *Feminism and the Power of Law* (Routledge, 1989) 10. See also Chief Justice James Spigelman, 'Truth and the Law' (2011) *Journal of New South Wales Bar Association* 99, 102.

142 Zenon Bankowski, 'The Jury and Reality' in Mark Findlay and Peter Duff (eds), *The Jury Under Attack* (Butterworths, 1988) 8, 17.

143 Sir Matthew Hale, *The History of the Common Law of England* (3rd ed, 1739) 255. 'One cannot over-emphasize the commitment of courts of justice to the ascertainment of the truth': *R v Howard* [1989] 1 SCR 1337, 1360 (L'HeureuxDubé J).

144 David Hamer, 'Process and Outcome: The Construction of the *Pell* Acquittals' (2023) 46(2) *Melbourne University Law Review* 372, 374.

145 Mercer (n 134) 144.

146 See, eg, Bankowski (n 142) 8.

truth for the purpose of the law and legal truth is different from a policeman's truth, from lay truth and so on'.[147]

Judicial knowledge and experience emanates from the trial procedures for determining the truth. However, courts do not scrutinise this knowledge and experience in the same way they do juror comprehension research. For example, judicial knowledge and experience would not qualify as expert opinion evidence because:

- judges do not have specialised training or expertise in the subject matter (juror comprehension),[148] and
- judicial knowledge and experience are based on inferences judges draw about juror comprehension (eg, that jurors accurately identify whenever they do not understand something, that jurors will always ask the judge questions if they are uncertain about something, and that judges will fully understand jury questions and the problem they have identified). Other inferences about juror comprehension could reasonably be drawn from this 'evidence'.

The rules of evidence would not permit drawing the inference that jurors do understand their task from this evidence.

The different standard that courts apply to their own sources of knowledge compared with social science research — and especially juror comprehension research — is testament to the power of the courts and their ability to present judicial knowledge and experience as reliable and accurate. In 1908, Hugo Munsterberg framed the challenge of psychology being used in the law as one where the 'lawyer and judge . . . go on thinking that their legal instinct and their common sense supplies them with all that is needed and somewhat more'.[149] This challenge to using social science research to improve the law remains very strong more than a century later.[150]

The phenomenon of judicial knowledge and experience is also consistent with the law's 'ancient sources of authority: case-by-case reasoning and the fundamental role of direct eyewitnessing'.[151] It is also consistent with 'the driving

147 Bankowski (n 142) 8.

148 See, eg, *Evidence Act 2008* (Vic) s 79(1). Applying the common law in England and Wales, the evidence would not have a 'sufficiently reliable scientific basis for the evidence to be admitted': *R v Reed* [2009] EWCA Crim 2698 [111].

149 Hugo Munsterberg, *On the Witness Stand: Essays on Psychology and Crime* (Double Day, 1908) 10–11.

150 Justice Peter McClellan and Amber Doyle, 'Legislative Facts and Section 144 — A Contemporary Problem?' (2016) 12(4) *Judicial Review* 421, 432–5.

151 Sheila Jasanoff, 'Science, Common Sense & Judicial Power in U.S. Courts' (2018) 147(4) *Daedalus* 15, 25.

force of the common law . . . [namely] experience and common sense'.[152] The description of 'corporate'[153] or 'collective'[154] judicial knowledge and experience also aligns with descriptions of the common law, which 'comprised the collective wisdom of multiple generations . . . [making] it superior to other arrangements'.[155] The common law developed by distilling important and universal principles from an examination of case law.

The common law is often 'explained, analysed, and criticized as if . . . [the laws] were transcendental objects unaffected by analyzing subjects'.[156] The law presents itself as being 'largely neutral, as apolitical',[157] and as if the law exists separately from humans. Similarly, courts give their own judicial knowledge and experience the status of some observable truth that is decontextualised from the intuition, knowledge, experiences, and biases of judges who create, develop, and affirm this form of knowledge.[158] The similarities between the common law and judicial knowledge and experience means that the latter may also be susceptible to criticisms that can be made of the common law.

In the second half of the 20th century, jurisprudential movements developed that have criticised attempts to decontextualise the law, arguing that because the law is discriminatory or biased rather than objective, the law ignores insights from other disciplines, and the law fails to take account of the experiences and perspective of 'others'.[159] Further, this modern jurisprudence argues that 'legal institutions and legal analysis itself creates and perpetuates social power'.[160] This jurisprudence comes from law and economics scholars, critical legal studies scholars, feminist scholars, law and literature scholars, and critical race theory scholars, among others.[161] These 'legal scholars examine

152 Lord Neuberger, 'Judges and Professors — Ships Passing in the Night?' (Speech, Max Planck Institute, 9 July 2012) <www.judiciary.uk/wp-content/uploads/JCO/Documents/Speeches/mr-speech-hamburg-lecture-09072012.pdf> 19. See also Oliver Wendell Holmes Jr, *The Common Law* (Little, Brown, 1881) 1.

153 See, eg, *IMM v The Queen* (2016) 257 CLR 300, 346 (Nettle and Gordon JJ).

154 *R v Barker* [2010] EWCA Crim 4 [40]; *R v Miller* [2010] EWCA Crim 1153 [21]; *Crown Court Compendium* (n 59) ch 20.

155 Kunal M Parker, 'The Transformation of the Common Law: Modernism, History, and The Turn to Process' in Markus D Dubber and Christopher Tomlins (eds), *The Oxford Handbook of Legal History* (Oxford University Press, 2018) 695, 699.

156 Gary Minda, 'One Hundred Years of Modern Legal Thought: From Langdell and Holmes to Posner and Schlag' (1995) 28(2) *Indiana Law Review* 353, 381.

157 Jeremiah A Ho, 'Law as Instrumentality' (2017) 101(1) *Marquette Law Review* 131, 175–6.

158 Parker (n 155) 705–8. See also Harry Sanderson, 'Postmodernism and Judicial Notice: How Common is Common Knowledge' (2021) 47(1) *Alternative Law Journal* 41, 42–4.

159 Minda (n 156) 367–70.

160 Minda (n 156) 368. See also Ho (n 157) 170–81; Celia Wells, 'The Impact of Feminist Thinking on Criminal Law and Justice: Contradiction, Complexity, Conviction and Connection' [2004] *Criminal Law Review* 503, 508.

161 Minda (n 156) 367–70. See also Roderick A MacDonald, 'Recommissioning Law Reform' (1997) 35(4) *Alberta Law Review* 831, 841–2.

how legal discourse affirms, excludes, marginalizes and ignores different discourses'.[162] They argue that 'notorious facts reflect the worldview of those in power and ignore valid counter-narratives from those without it'.[163] In a similar vein, feminist legal theory refers to the law presenting as if it arises from (or embodies) a 'point-of-viewlessness'.[164]

These jurisprudential movements provide another explanation for the limited influence that juror comprehension research has had in changing jury trials. Juror comprehension research comes from social science disciplines that the law may exclude, marginalise, or ignore. Further, juror comprehension research seeks to provide an account of the experiences and perspectives of 'others', namely jurors. While jurors play a critical role in jury trials, they are 'others' in terms of the power dynamics that have shaped criminal trials. Over the centuries, the role of the jury, judge, lawyers, and the accused have changed significantly. Power dynamics in the criminal justice system have shaped criminal trials. Juries once played an active and significant role in the trial.[165] However, judges and lawyers progressively took control of the trial process, and the role of the jury decreased. The jury became increasingly passive — where the voices of those with the power to shape the system have drowned out the voices of the powerless.

The system of truth employed by the law has evolved in ways that have rendered the jury largely voiceless and has failed to consider the needs of the jury from the jury's perspective. It is a system of truth where the courts' judicial knowledge and experience of juries remains the authoritative starting point that courts often rely on to understand what jurors know and how they reason. It is difficult for social science to change knowledge about jurors derived from a different 'truth' seeking process, and to change judges' perceptions of juries, their verdicts, and juror comprehension research.

Conclusion

The law has its own methods for determining the truth, often involving judicial knowledge and experience to determine what is comprehensible to jurors. The law's own knowledge and experience can be difficult to identify and to displace. From within the law, the identification of fundamental

162 Minda (n 156) 369.

163 Sanderson (n 158) 43.

164 Regina Graycar, 'The Gender of Judgments: Some Reflections on "Bias"' (1998) 32 *University of British Columbia Law Review* 1, 10.

165 See, eg, John H Langbein, *The Origins of the Adversary Criminal Trial* (Oxford University Press, 2003); Sanjeev Anand, 'The Origins, Early History and Evolution of the English Criminal Trial Jury' (2005) 43 *Alberta Law Review* 407; Angela M Laughlin, 'Learning from the Past? Or Destined to Repeat Past Mistakes? Lessons from the English Legal System and Its Impact on How We View the Role of Judges and Juries Today' (2009) 14 *Widener* 357, 377.

problems from disciplines that reason differently from the law can be challenging to understand and accept. Further, the 'debunking tendency' of empirical research 'may bring it under attack (sometimes in private, less often in public) from members of the legal profession, the judiciary, or government representatives'.[166] The differences between the law and social sciences, their goals, values, methodologies, and reasoning processes help to explain why juror comprehension research has had limited influence in changing criminal trials and laws to address juror comprehension problems.

While the methodologies of courts and social science research may differ, both use their methodologies to seek the truth in their own ways. Legal accuracy is an important goal of trial by jury. Legal accuracy depends upon each juror applying the judge's directions correctly. Juror comprehension research can assist in achieving this objective. However, the courts' method for conducting trials and appeals is not suited to addressing wide-scale pervasive problems where social science research is necessary to identify problems and develop solutions. Courts are not equipped or resourced to undertake this kind of reform process. A different kind of body is required for this kind of reform process.

166 John Baldwin and Gwynn Davis, 'Empirical Research in Law' in Mark Tushnet and Peter Cane (eds), *The Oxford Handbook of Legal Studies* (Oxford University Press, 2005) 880, 897.

5 An interdisciplinary Juries Advisory Council

Introduction

This chapter examines the kind of body needed to address juror comprehension problems in a way that will overcome the challenges presented by the differences between the law and social science disciplines (as discussed in Chapter 4). A Juries Advisory Council (JAC) would be a body that incorporates social science research into reform processes to improve juror comprehension. A JAC would be an interdisciplinary body, blending the expertise of judges and lawyers with experts in jury research. Having an expert JAC would mean that all judges do not need to become juror comprehension experts to address comprehension problems. The JAC would provide new ways of developing research that is more tailored to the needs of the justice system and in ways that are more likely to overcome judges and lawyers' scepticism about juror comprehension research.

No jurisdiction has a JAC. Each jurisdiction should establish a JAC to provide advice on changing laws, practices, and procedures to improve juror comprehension.[1] A JAC could take different forms and perform distinct functions. To some extent this will depend on the jurisdiction and its practices, legal culture, and existing reform processes. The discussion in this chapter examines key issues concerning the composition and functions of a JAC. For example, while research is essential, there will never be enough research to address every combination and permutation of issues that may arise in a trial. Therefore, it is necessary to consider how a JAC will consider research. Legislation provides a vehicle for law reform and improving the justice system. Legislation may change laws, practices, and procedures to improve juror comprehension. However, legislation has been criticised for being too prescriptive and inflexible to change jury directions because directions must be adapted to the needs of each case. This chapter examines this criticism and whether there are ways of employing legislation to address juror comprehension problems. This chapter

1 Greg Byrne, 'A Pathway to Fair(er) Trials: Why We Need a Juries Advisory Council' (2021) 31(2) *Journal of Judicial Administration* 49.

DOI: 10.4324/9781003477129-5

also examines other functions that a JAC could perform that would provide different avenues for addressing juror comprehension problems.

An interdisciplinary Juries Advisory Council

The main reports concerning jury directions over the last 20 years in Australia have given insufficient weight to juror comprehension research and understanding jurors. For example, they generally limit discussion about juror stereotypes or misconceptions to victims in sexual offence cases.[2] The reports generally do not discuss the commonsense justice (or prototypes) that jurors may apply when they seek to understand the law that defines an offence, regardless of the nature of the offence.[3] Further, only the Queensland Law Reform Commission (QLRC) discussed in some detail the assumptions that the law makes about the 'ideal' juror's task and the cognitive load in jury decision-making.[4] Australian reform processes are not unusual in this regard. For example, in the USA, it is 'extremely difficult to show a direct link between specific research efforts and specific reforms'[5] to juries and jury processes.

The limited use of, and weight given to, juror comprehension research may suggest that that policy/decision-makers (including judges, lawyers, the executive and parliament) may not value academic research. The gaps between evidence and policy may reflect a cultural and/or knowledge gap between academics and policy/decision-makers, and these communities may not be used to, or have an incentive to, engage with each other.[6] The extent to which academics and policy/decision-makers interact may be limited but research suggests that this relationship could be developed.[7] What may assist is having a body that values research within the policy/decision-making reform process, understands the needs of policy/decision-makers, and can translate research in ways that are useful for policy/decision-makers.[8]

A JAC could be the body that draws these communities together. It would have the capacity to bridge the gap between social science research and the

2 See, eg, New South Wales Law Reform Commission, *Jury Directions* (Report No 136, November 2012) (NSWLRC) 77 [5.80]; Victorian Law Reform Commission, *Jury Directions* (Report No 17, May 2009) 74 [4.52] (VLRC).

3 Only one Commission discussed this: Queensland Law Reform Commission, *A Review of Jury Directions* (Report No 66, September 2009) (QLRC) 74 [4.100].

4 See, eg, QLRC, *A Review of Jury Directions* (n 3) 22–3 [2.21], 405 [12.15] and 408–9 [12.26].

5 Miko M Wilford and Brian H Bornstein, 'The Disappearing Trial: How Social Scientists Can Help Save the Jury from Extinction' (2023) 29(1) *Psychology, Crime & Law* 1, 9.

6 Paul Cairney and Kirstein Rummery, 'Feminising Politics to Close the Evidence-Policy Gap: The Case of Social Policy in Scotland' (2018) 77(4) *Australian Journal of Public Administration* 542, 544.

7 Joshua Newman, Adrian Cherney and Brian W Head, 'Do Policy Makers Use Academic Research? Reexamining the "Two Communities" Theory of Research Utilization' (2015) 76(1) *Public Administration Review* 24, 30.

8 Newman, Cherney and Head (n 7) 30.

law — and between knowledge derived from the two systems. A JAC would share the values of the courts and the law including preserving the adversarial system, obtaining legally accurate verdicts, and preserving the symbolic importance of the courts and the trial process as part of a system of governing society and preserving social order. However, a JAC's methods would differ from a court.[9] A JAC would not be limited to the issues of one case and would not be required to make a final decision if the evidence is inadequate. It would have a much greater capacity to consider the application of research to many cases rather than to one. A JAC's methods would enable it to provide informed advice based on the best available research. Indeed, the point of using 'exogenous knowledge is to ensure that the development of the law "rest[s] on more than mere intuition, hope, legend, cliché, guesswork, assumption or prejudice"'.[10]

A JAC could also draw these communities together by having a more diverse membership than is typically the case with law reform bodies. It should include members of the judiciary and legal profession as reforms must be consistent with the requirements of a fair trial and to ensure that reforms are practical will require expertise in the justice system. Members should also include academics with expertise in juries and jury research from different disciplines (eg, law, psychology, linguistics) as evidence will be critical in identifying problems and solutions. Former jurors should be involved either as members of the JAC or a consultative body that the JAC uses where juror input would be valuable. In jury reforms conducted in Arizona, Judge Dann said that the 'inclusion of five jurors with recent experience in lengthy trials of complex cases was the most important organizational decision made'.[11] The lived experience of jurors is a form of expertise. Members of the executive, including policymakers, may also be members of the JAC or connected to the JAC, for example, if improving juror comprehension requires changes to laws. Judge Dann said that not including legislators or the executive branch in their committee 'proved to be a flawed decision with long-term detrimental consequences'.[12] The involvement of this broader range of participants in reform processes should help to define problems and generate solutions that better meet the needs of jurors and the justice system.[13]

9 Sir Anthony Mason, 'The Judge as Law-Maker' (1996) 3 *James Cook University Law Review* 1, 6–7.

10 David Hamer and Gary Edmond, 'Judicial Notice: Beyond Adversarialism and into the Exogenous Zone' (2016) 25 *Griffith Law Review* 291, 303 quoting Justice Dyson Heydon, 'Developing the Common Law' in Justin T Gleeson and Ruth C A Higgins (eds), *Constituting Law: Legal Argument and Social Values* (Federation Press, 2011) 93, 99.

11 B Michael Dann and George Logan III, "Jury Reform: The Arizona Experience" (1996) 79 *Judicature* 280, 281.

12 Dann and Logan III (n 11) 281.

13 See generally, Emma Blomkamp, 'The Promise of Co-Design for Public Policy' (2018) 77(4) *Australian Journal of Public Administration* 729, 736.

Aspects of the proposed membership of a JAC can be seen in the approaches to reform adopted in England and Wales and Victoria. In England and Wales, the Editorial Board of the *Crown Court Compendium* included academics such as David Ormerod and Cheryl Thomas. Thomas, a jury researcher, focused on improving the comprehensibility of the language used for jurors and tools that may assist jurors (eg, written directions).[14] In Victoria, the Jury Directions Advisory Group was conducted as a partnership between the courts and the executive.[15] In addition to judges and practitioners, the Advisory Group included academics with extensive jury research expertise, including James Ogloff, a social science academic with extensive experience in juror comprehension research,[16] and jury researchers from within the law, Jonathan Clough and Jacqueline Horan.

The composition of a JAC may shape how it frames the issues[17] and the method(s) it uses.[18] Some law reform commissions adopt a 'lawyer's law reform' approach, concentrating on matters of interest primarily to lawyers, in contrast to 'social law reform', which focuses on matters of broader social policy and community interest.[19] Improving the comprehensibility of the issues for the jury requires legal accuracy (lawyer's law) but will only be effective if it considers social science research (which is more akin to social law reform).

To provide advice on how to change laws, practices, and procedures to improve juror comprehension, a JAC would need relevant and robust juror comprehension research.

A Juries Advisory Council should drive juror comprehension research

A significant challenge in the reform process involves ensuring that research addresses the priorities of the justice system. Jury and juror comprehension researchers have said that

> [p]erhaps the single most important issue that we need to address in the future is an old issue: how do we make our research known to those in

14 See, eg, Cheryl Thomas, *Are Juries Fair?* (Ministry of Justice, 2010).

15 Justice Chris Maxwell and Greg Byrne, 'Making Trials Work for Juries: Pathways to Simplification' [2020] (11) *Criminal Law Review* 1034, 1044–5.

16 See, eg, V Gordon Rose and James R P Ogloff, 'Evaluating the Comprehensibility of Jury Instructions: A Method and an Example' (2001) 25 *Law and Human Behavior* 409.

17 Marcia Neave, 'Institutional Law Reform in Australia' (2005) 23(2) *Windsor Yearbook of Access to Justice* 343, 360–1.

18 Phoebe C Ellsworth and Alan Reifman, 'Juror Comprehension and Public Policy: Perceived Problems and Proposed Solutions' (2000) 6 *Psychology, Public Policy and Law* 788, 815.

19 See, eg, Geoffrey Sawer, 'The Legal Theory of Law Reform' (1970) 20(2) *The University of Toronto Law Journal* 183, 193–4.

the legal system, and even more critically, how do we get them to actually use it?[20]

For research to be known and used requires social scientists to decide what research is relevant and of interest to those in the justice system. This places a heavy burden on social scientists, particularly given the enormous range of potential research topics. Funding for social science research may also not align with the needs of the justice system, for example, research may focus on developing or testing psychological theory.[21] Research may depend upon variables like opportunity, interest, resources, and chance and has tended to be sporadic, often focusing on specific issues.[22]

Existing research processes usually involve researchers from 'within disciplinary divided institutional structures' undertaking interdisciplinary research for use within the law.[23] Social scientists have suggested that researchers need to put themselves in the shoes of policymakers to work out what to research.[24] Researchers then collaborate with lawyers and judges and identify policymakers who are more receptive to scientific evidence.[25] However, why should the onus be on researchers to improve the effectiveness of their research in addressing juror comprehension problems and for social science research funding priorities to align with the purpose of improving the justice system? The justice system is responsible for ensuring that trials are fair. Courts assume that jurors understand their task, reaching verdicts in accordance with the law. Given the evidence of juror comprehension problems, the justice system should not wait for research and then critique the research that emerges. The justice system should be proactive in ensuring that trials are fair, by directing or steering juror comprehension research for its own purposes and needs. However, no jurisdiction has an ongoing process of juror comprehension research that is primarily driven by the justice system to address each jurisdiction's priorities.

20 Edith Greene et al, 'Jurors and Juries: A Review of the Field' in James R P Ogloff (ed), *Taking Psychology and Law into the Twenty-First Century* (Springer, 2002) 225, 270.

21 Margaret B Kovera, 'Conclusion: The Future of Jury Research' in Margaret B Kovera (ed), *The Psychology of Juries* (American Psychological Association, 2017) 287, 288.

22 See, eg, Norbert L Kerr, 'Suggested Do's and Don'ts for Future Jury Research: A Swan Song' in Margaret B Kovera (ed), *The Psychology of Juries* (American Psychological Association, 2017) 257, 270.

23 Alexandra Grey and Laura Smith-Khan, 'Bringing Linguistic Research into Legal Scholarship and Practice' (2021) 46(1) *Alternative Law Journal* 64, 69.

24 Jonathan J Koehler and John B Meixner, 'Jury Simulation Goals' in Margaret B Kovera (ed), *The Psychology of Juries* (American Psychological Association, 2017) 161, 178.

25 See, eg, Daniel A Krauss and Joel D Lieberman, 'Managing Different Aspects of Validity in Trial Simulation Research' in Margaret B Kovera (ed), *The Psychology of Juries* (American Psychological Association, 2017) 185, 201; Kerr (n 22) 278.

Reviews of jury directions by law reform bodies have sometimes commissioned research on juror comprehension.[26] However, this typically involves one-off research rather than forming part of an ongoing process of review. Academic research, which provides the major source of juror comprehension research, requires specific funding for each project.[27] Seeking research grants is not only time consuming, but there is also no central body coordinating research in areas prioritised by the courts or a JAC. By contrast, governments do fund bodies focused on sentencing research (eg, Sentencing Councils) and research and programs for judges' professional development (eg, Judicial Colleges).[28]

A JAC, which conducts and reviews juror comprehension research, should drive the research process, setting the priorities for research, and conduct or commission research.[29] It could help to close the gap between 'questions that social scientists ask and the questions that policy makers want answered'.[30] While not focusing specifically on jurors and juries, a similar point was made by Julia Quilter in relation to the examination of 40 years of sexual offence reforms in New South Wales — if 'we don't undertake systemic empirical research into what is going on in courtrooms, we can't possibly expect to understand why the goals of statutory reforms are not being achieved'.[31] Further, a JAC could transform the findings of researchers by combining it with legal and practice knowledge for judges and policy makers. This would stand in stark contrast to processes requiring researchers to educate decision-makers about juror comprehension research or decision-makers needing to develop social science research expertise.

With a mechanism to proactively drive juror comprehension research, the next issue is how a JAC should use social science research in its decision-making processes.

26 See, eg, New Zealand Law Commission, *Juries in Criminal Trials* (Report No 69, February 2001); Blake McKimmie, Emma Antrobus and Ian Davis, 'Jurors' Trial Experiences: The Influence of Directions and Other Aspects of Trials' in Queensland Law Reform Commission, *A Review of Jury Directions* (Report No 66, 2009) Appendix E.

27 See, eg, Jonathan Clough et al, 'The Judge as Cartographer and Guide: The Role of Fact-based Directions in Improving Juror Comprehension' (2018) 42(5) *Criminal Law Journal* 278 ('The Judge as Cartographer and Guide') where funding was provided by the Australian Research Council, Department of Justice and Regulation (Vic) and the New Zealand Law Foundation.

28 See, eg, Arie Freiberg, 'Bridging Gaps, Not Leaping Chasms: Trust, Confidence and Sentencing Councils' (2021) 12(3) *International Journal for Court Administration* 6, 9–11.

29 Byrne (n 1) 60–9.

30 Koehler and Meixner (n 24) 177.

31 Julia Quilter, 'Getting Consent "Right": Sexual Assault Law Reform in New South Wales' (2021) *The Australian Feminist Law Journal* 1, 23.

A Juries Advisory Council should make decisions informed by social science research

Juror comprehension research will always necessarily have some limitations. Balancing the need for evidence, and understanding the limits of evidence, is crucial to this process. A JAC must determine when it has sufficient information to make an informed decision and how to integrate this information with knowledge of criminal laws and trials to provide robust and effective advice and/or reform.

Lord Justice Moses stated that an impediment to reforming judicial guidance to jurors 'is the perceived need, whenever a sensible proposal is made, to consign the issue to research'.[32] This 'perceived need' may reflect an idealised image of what social science research can prove. Requiring testing with actual jurors in a real case, for complete ecological validity, before changing directions presents a Catch-22 problem — because every case is different, each case only provides ecological validity for a case conducted in identical ways and with identical people. Conducting studies with actual jurors, especially when this involves their deliberations, can be costly and time consuming. It can also be difficult to isolate comprehension of a particular jury direction from other factors that may contribute to its comprehension. Further, in many jurisdictions, legal and institutional barriers may restrict and even prevent research with actual jurors.[33]

Social scientists might also argue that no change should be made until each proposed new direction has been evaluated with jurors and further revised, if necessary, given the desire for certainty in research outcomes.[34] Juror comprehension research is potentially relevant to many issues in a criminal trial. It is not realistic to isolate every issue in every jurisdiction and rigorously analyse it before making any changes. Researchers 'must be cognizant of the complex interactions that might exist between various aspects of the simulation and manipulated variables'.[35] These limitations often lead to researchers stating that additional research is required before policy decisions are made based on the evidence obtained. This is understandable where there is some uncertainty about how changes will work in practice, and that researchers do not wish to

32 Lord Justice Moses, 'Summing Down the Summing-Up' (Speech, Annual Law Reform Lecture, Inner Temple, 23 November 2010) 11.

33 See, eg, *Juries Act 1974* (UK) s 20D; *Criminal Code*, RSC 1985, c C-46 s 649; Jacqueline Horan and Mark Israel, 'Beyond the Legal Barriers: Institutional Gatekeeping and Real Jury Research' (2015) 49 *Australia and New Zealand Journal of Criminology* 422, 424–5; Norbert L Kerr and Robert M Bray, 'Simulation, Realism, and the Study of the Jury' in Neil Brewer and Kipling D Williams (eds), *Psychology and Law* (Guilford Press, 2005) 322, 329–30.

34 John Baldwin and Gwynn Davis, 'Empirical Research in Law' in Mark Tushnet and Peter Cane (eds), *The Oxford Handbook of Legal Studies* (Oxford University Press, 2005) 880, 890–1.

35 Krauss and Lieberman (n 25) 194.

be responsible for changes that may produce unfairness. However, changes will still be made in the justice system.

Undertaking reform only once research conclusively proves a matter (assuming this is even possible) reflects a starting point that the existing system is acceptable until the contrary is proved. And if reform proceeds in the absence of research, decisions will be made based on the law's knowledge and experience. Within the law, this approach would privilege and trust the role of judicial knowledge and experience over research. Indeed, this might reflect an idealised view of knowledge within the law.[36] Because of the overwhelming evidence of juror comprehension problems, James Ogloff and Gordon Rose have postulated that 'it may be time that the burden of establishing that instructions *are* understood should shift to those who wish to maintain the status quo'.[37] While I do not propose such a radical shift, Ogloff and Rose's proposal highlights the need for lawyer-dominated bodies to be aware of the role, power, and limitations of the law's system of truth, of judicial knowledge and experience, and of limits in their thinking about how to change a jury trial by understanding the juror's perspective. The interdisciplinary nature of a JAC is designed to militate against the risk of it being dominated by this kind of thinking. A JAC will often have to make decisions or provide advice where there is insufficient evidence to be certain about how changes will operate in practice.

Studies of decision-making distinguish between 'intuitive' and 'analytical' (or deliberative) decision-making.[38] Using evidence to make decisions does not mean that reform decisions should be, or can be, purely analytical. Policy-making is also driven or influenced by 'values, beliefs and ideology . . . as well as the experience, expertise and judgement of policy makers'.[39] Considering how laws will operate in practice involves some forward-looking predictions about the likely outcomes and this is an essential part of good law reform.[40] This will involve some intuition. Intuitive decision-making is not inherently bad or problematic: it is 'an essential part of how the human brain functions'.[41]

36 See, eg, Gary Edmond and Kent Roach, 'Trial by Theory: A Response to Acharya's "Law's Treatment of Science: From Idealization to Understanding"' (2013) 36(1) *Dalhousie Law Journal* 57, 88.

37 James R P Ogloff and V Gordon Rose, 'The Comprehension of Judicial Instructions' in Neil Brewer and Kipling D Williams (eds), *Psychology and Law: An Empirical Perspective* (Guilford Press, 2005) 407, 426 (emphasis in original).

38 See, eg, Robin M Hogarth, 'A Challenge for Psychological Research on Decision Making' (2010) 21(4) *Psychological Inquiry* 338, 338; Daniel Kahneman and Gary Klein, 'Conditions for Intuitive Expertise: A Failure to Disagree' (2009) 64(6) *American Psychologist* 515, 519.

39 Philip Davies, 'The State of Evidence-Based Policy Evaluation and Its Role in Policy Formation' (2012) 219 *National Institute Economic Review* R41, R42.

40 Michael Tilbury, 'Why Law Reform Commissions: A Deconstruction and Stakeholder Analysis from an Australian Perspective' (2005) 23 *Windsor Yearbook of Access to Justice* 313, 323.

41 Chris Guthrie, Jeffrey J Rachlinski and Andrew Wistrich, 'Blinking on the Bench: How Judges Decide Cases' (2007) 93(1) *Cornell Law Review* 1, 5.

Indeed, 'the key to good judgment is to match task demands and cognitive style'.[42]

While the role of judicial knowledge and experience should not be privileged over research, in the absence of directly applicable research, judicial assessment of what is comprehensible to jurors is relevant. Judges may not be good at 'intuitively gaug[ing] the degree to which laypeople understand legal language',[43] but there is little evidence of judges underestimating what is comprehensible to jurors. While judges may overestimate juror comprehension for many reasons, if judges can identify reasons why jury directions may be difficult for jurors to understand, a JAC should consider their views.

Changes can, and should, be made to improve juror comprehension where this is supported by directly applicable research or is based on reasonable inferences drawn from research. A JAC may use probabilistic reasoning and draw inferences from research on a similar topic or from a similar jurisdiction without necessarily needing research to be conducted on every specific matter. For example, as discussed in Chapter 3, linguistic changes, organisational changes to the hierarchy in which information is presented, and changes to the framework and presentation of directions — by giving integrated directions — are likely to improve juror comprehension.[44] However, reforms may have some unintended consequences.[45] A JAC may conclude that the introduction of an imperfect improvement, or where it is uncertain whether a reform will achieve its goal, is preferable to the status quo. A JAC would need to consider this when introducing, piloting, or providing advice about reforms.

Combining the expertise, and intuition, of judges and lawyers about how proposed changes will work in practice is an essential and established part of law reform processes. Recognising this aspect of existing law reform decision-making provides space in which to incorporate probabilistic reasoning and drawing inferences from social science juror comprehension research. It means that JAC could draw on juror comprehension research to find ways of achieving the law's goals (eg, a fair trial where jurors understand their task) in a way that is consistent with the values of the discipline of law.

In addition to providing advice that integrates social science research and legal expertise, a JAC's functions should be tailored to the many challenges of addressing juror comprehension problems.

42 Hogarth (n 38) 340.

43 Peter Meijes Tiersma, 'Reforming the Language of Jury Instructions' (1993) 22 *Hofstra Law Review* 37, 41.

44 See, eg, Robert P Charrow and Veda R Charrow, 'Making Legal Language Understandable: A Psycholinguistic Study of Jury Instructions' (1979) 79 *Columbia Law Review* 1306; Clough et al, 'The Judge as Cartographer and Guide' (n 27).

45 See, eg, Chantelle M Baguley, Blake M McKimmie and Barbara M Masser, 'Deconstructing the Simplification of Jury Instructions: How Simplifying the Features of Complexity Affects Jurors' Application of Instructions' (2017) 41(3) *Law and Human Behavior* 284.

A Juries Advisory Council's functions

The most common way of improving jury guidance has been to improve bench books, to support trial judges in providing clearer guidance to juries.[46] Under an interdisciplinary JAC, this would continue to be one of the most significant pathways to improving jury guidance. However, bench books cannot change the law. Many problems with jury directions emanate from legislation and appellate decisions and may be difficult to address through court cases.[47]

Providing advice about jurors and juries

A JAC should be independent and not part of the executive arm of government. It would also not be the primary law reform body in a jurisdiction as criminal law reform is often unrelated to juries and juror comprehension. A JAC's work would often focus on changes to court procedures to improve juror understanding. Existing law reform bodies and governments will continue to recommend and/or reform the law and may do so in ways that affect juror comprehension. That reform process should be informed by expert advice provided by a JAC about the likely effect of proposed changes on juror comprehension. For example, in their reviews of sexual offence laws, Law Reform Commissions in New South Wales and Victoria recommended the introduction of jury directions to address misconceptions.[48] However, these recommendations were made without any evidence concerning whether the recommended reforms would be effective. Governments in each jurisdiction introduced laws giving effect to the recommendations. Subsequent research has questioned whether these directions are likely to achieve their objectives.[49]

What the Law Reform Commissions and governments in New South Wales and Victoria needed was expert advice concerning whether jurors would understand and act on the new directions as intended. However, there was no established body that could undertake or direct this research and provide this advice. This does not mean that the JAC would necessarily be providing policy advice — although as discussed in Chapter 9, the purpose of addressing

46 See, eg, Judicial College, *The Crown Court Compendium — Part I: Jury and Trial Management and Summing Up* (July 2024) <www.judiciary.uk/wp-content/uploads/2024/07/Crown-Court-Compendium-Part-I-July-2024-1.pdf>; Courts of New Zealand, *A Guide to the Question Trails* <www.courtsofnz.govt.nz/for-lawyers/question-trails/>.

47 See, eg, Justice Mark Weinberg, 'Jury Directions on Trial — A Pathway through the Labyrinth?' (Speech, Supreme and Federal Court Judges' Conference, 5–9 July 2014) 60 [194].

48 NSWLRC, *Consent in Relation to Sexual Offences* (Report No 148, September 2020) ch 8; VLRC, *Improving the Justice System Response to Sexual Offences* (Report, September 2021) ch 20.

49 Faye T Nitschke, Blake M McKimmie and Eric J Vanman, 'The Effect of Trauma Education Judicial Instructions on Decisions about Complainant Credibility in Rape Trials' (2023) 29(1) *Psychology, Public Policy, and Law* 69.

juror misconceptions is to ensure a fair trial where jurors determine the issues on their legal and factual merits.

There are differences in the extent to which individual judges may consider it is appropriate to be involved in giving policy advice. And the culture and practices of judges being involved in bodies that make policy recommendations varies between jurisdictions. In some jurisdictions, judges may be members of law reform commissions. The JAC's advice could be limited to expert technical advice about how potential reforms may affect juror comprehension that the policy decision-makers should consider — this is a matter that may depend on the membership of the JAC and cultural practices within that jurisdiction.

Bench books may improve a judge's guidance and explanations of the law. However, they cannot change the law. As discussed in Chapter 4, there are significant limitations on the ability of courts to change the law based on juror comprehension research. Another way of changing the law is through legislation.

Recommending legislative reform of jury directions

One of the more challenging issues with juror comprehension reform concerns whether legislation provides an appropriate vehicle for significant jury directions reform. In Australia, legislation has often led reform processes. In other jurisdictions, such as England and Wales and New Zealand, courts have often been at the forefront of change and legislation has played more of a supportive role.[50] This may explain why Australian jurisdictions have been more willing to use legislation to change jury directions. However, there was initially concern that legislation was not appropriate for changing jury directions.

Courts are traditionally responsible for ensuring a fair trial. Using legislation to reform jury directions may involve changes to what courts have decided is necessary for a fair trial. Mandatory jury directions have been criticised for involving 'legislative intrusion into the independence of the judiciary'.[51] Further, reports on jury directions from the QLRC and New South Wales Law Reform Commission (NSWLRC) considered statutory reform to be too inflexible because jury directions need to be tailored to the needs of individual cases and may require statutory amendment. The QLRC and NSWLRC strongly preferred the flexibility of the common law to govern the content of jury directions.[52] While the flexibility of the common law in contrast to

50 Deputy Chief Judge Meryl Sexton, 'Foreword' in Greg Byrne and Jacqueline Horan (eds), *Sexual Assault Trials: Challenges and Innovations* (LexisNexis, 2025) v–vi.

51 Sir John Gillen, *Gillen Review: Report into the Law and Procedures in Serious Sexual Offences in Northern Ireland* (Report, May 2019) 206 [6.94]. See generally, Maxwell and Byrne (n 15) 1044–5.

52 See, eg, QLRC, *A Review of Jury Directions* (n 3) 145–7 [7.91]–[7.98]; NSWLRC, *Jury Directions* (n 2) 41 [2.35].

statute can easily be overstated[53] and it is unusual for the common law to substantially change and simplify jury directions, it is important to examine these criticisms of legislative reform.

Because the evidence in each case may be different, statutory evidentiary directions generally require more flexibility than substantive or general directions. The QLRC and NSWLRC erroneously assumed that legislation would necessarily be too prescriptive about the content of jury directions. Many of the directions reformed in Victoria's *Jury Directions Act 2015* (JDA) involve evidentiary directions.[54] The JDA sets out the 'essential elements' (or minimum content) of jury directions and abolishes many prescriptive requirements of common law directions.[55] The JDA also provides that a judge is not required to use any particular form of words when directing a jury.[56]

In practice, 73% of judges surveyed in Victoria said that the JDA had 'made the process of communicating the law to the jury much simpler, enabling them to provide shorter and more concise directions'.[57] Judges did not express any concern that they were not able to tailor directions to the needs of a case. The prospects of an appellate court deciding that there are matters that must be included in directions that are contrary to its previous decisions presented a low risk in Victoria because the essential elements of most directions originated in appellate court decisions.[58] Further, given that parliament determined that a direction containing the essential elements would be a sufficient direction, it is highly unlikely that an appellate court would then conclude that directions containing those essential elements were insufficient to ensure a fair trial.[59] Since the commencement of the first jury directions reforms in 2013, appellate courts have not identified any deficiencies in the statutory directions.[60] Former justice of the High Court of Australia, Justice Virginia Bell, concluded that the 'Victorian reforms provide a workable template for reform'.[61] And while Sir John Gillen said that he maintained his faith in the

53 Stella Tarrant, 'Building Bridges in Australian Criminal Law: Codification and the Common Law' (2013) 39 *Monash University Law Review* 838, 848–50.

54 For example, there are evidentiary directions concerning post-offence conduct evidence, identification evidence, tendency and coincidence evidence, and unreliable evidence.

55 See, eg, VLRC, *Jury Directions* (n 2) 81 [4.91]; Maxwell and Byrne (n 15) 1045–6.

56 *Jury Directions Act 2015* (Vic) s 6.

57 Jonathan Clough et al, *The Jury Project 10 Years On — Practices of Australian and New Zealand Judges* (Australian Institute of Judicial Administration, April 2019) 1, 56.

58 See, eg, Maxwell and Byrne (n 15) 1045–6.

59 See *PJE v The Queen* (Unreported, High Court of Australia, S154/1995, 9 September 1996) 11, where Brennan CJ said that it was not even arguable 'that a court may decline to exercise its jurisdiction to try a criminal case because it forms the view that a law enacted by the Parliament is unfair'.

60 See, eg, Maxwell and Byrne (n 15) 1054–5.

61 Justice Virginia Bell, 'Jury Directions: The Struggle for Simplicity and Clarity' (Speech, Banco Court Lecture, Supreme Court of Queensland, 20 September 2018) 27.

judiciary and did not consider legislation necessary to address rape myths, he 'believe[d] there is much to be said for the approach adopted in Victoria'.[62]

This does not mean that legislative reform is the only way to improve juror comprehension. As discussed in Chapter 2, England and Wales, and New Zealand, have both changed jury directions and the summing up without legislative intervention. Jurisdictions may vary in the extent to which they use legislation to improve jury directions. What is important is that legislation *can* be an effective method for introducing changes to jury directions to improve juror comprehension. As a JAC would be independent of the executive, its role would be limited to recommending legislative changes to improve jury directions.

However, a JAC would not be limited to providing advice and recommending legislative reforms. It could also potentially perform two other functions tailored to addressing juror comprehension problems.

Developing jury directions and guideline judgments

The first function would involve a JAC developing new jury directions or reforming existing jury directions, provided this did not involve overturning statutory jury directions or appellate decisions. The authority for a body outside of the court and parliament to create jury directions could be like that provided to the Sentencing Council in England and Wales. The Sentencing Council may issue sentencing guidelines that courts must follow unless it is not in the interests of justice to do so.[63] Similarly, in California, a judge must use an instruction that the Californian Judicial Council has approved, 'unless he or she finds that a different instruction would *more accurately state the law and be understood by jurors*'.[64] This function would enable a JAC to directly improve jury directions in a limited but flexible way.

New Zealand has developed a variation on this kind of approach for jury directions that address misconceptions in sexual offence cases. Since December 2022, 'the Judge must give the jury any direction the Judge considers necessary or desirable to address any relevant misconception relating to sexual cases'.[65] To assist judges in giving directions, New Zealand's Te Kura Kaiwhakawā — Institute of Judicial Studies developed examples of directions that judges could give.[66] The resources explain the need for the directions, the content of the directions, and when the judge should give the directions. Judges then need to adapt the examples of directions to each case. The

62 Gillen (n 51) 206 [6.95].

63 *Sentencing Act 2020* (UK) s 59(1).

64 *California Rules of Court*, Title 2, Trial Court Rules, r 2.1050(e) (emphasis added).

65 *Evidence Act 2006* (NZ) s 126A.

66 Te Kura Kaiwhakawā — Institute of Judicial Studies, *Responding to Misconceptions about Sexual Offending: Example Directions for Judges and Lawyers* (2023) <www.courtsofnz.govt.nz/for-lawyers/jury-directions-and-question-trails/>.

Institute developed the resources following consultation with representatives from the judiciary, defence bar, and subject-matter experts from academia. The approach to the content of directions is flexible, acknowledging that as research about misconceptions evolves, the directions may need to be changed.[67] As the resources and jury directions have only recently commenced, there has been no evaluation of this resource and judicial practices.[68] Using this kind of legislative imprimatur, a JAC could perform this kind of function to assist judges in developing directions. However, the legislation and the JAC's function need not be limited to misconceptions in sexual offence cases.

The second function a JAC could perform would be to provide expert assistance to an appellate court that is empowered to provide a guideline judgment on guiding the jury.[69] A guideline judgment could overturn existing appellate decisions or provide further support to drive changes in practice (eg, in how the judge guides the jury with its task). In relation to guideline judgments for sentencing, Victoria's Court of Appeal said that the

> great advantage of a guideline judgment is that it enables this court to deal systematically and comprehensively with a particular topic or topics relevant to sentencing, rather than being confined to the questions raised by particular appeals.[70]

This process might assist in dealing with perennial problems like the length of the judge's summing up. It might also assist with matters such as developing innovative ways for the parties to inform the jury during the trial about how evidence relates to their cases, rather than being limited to opening and closing addresses.

Guideline judgments of this nature would address two limitations in improving jury guidance through the courts that were discussed previously. First, the court's judgment would not be limited to the facts of the case. Second, the court would be assisted by input from a body with expertise in juror comprehension research that could ensure the court is informed about any relevant research.

Conclusion

The introduction of an interdisciplinary JAC would be a meaningful change. It could use social science juror comprehension research in a manner that is consistent with and promotes the law's goals and values (eg, that trials are fair,

67 Te Kura Kaiwhakawā — Institute of Judicial Studies (n 66) 3.

68 Yvette Tinsley, Warren Young and Claire Baylis, 'Jurors' Use of Rape Myths in Aotearoa New Zealand' in Greg Byrne and Jacqueline Horan (eds), *Sexual Assault Trials: Challenges and Innovations* (LexisNexis, 2025) 165, 169.

69 For a more detailed discussion about how this could work, see Byrne (n 1) 68–9.

70 *Boulton v The Queen* (2014) 46 VR 308, 316 [26].

and verdicts are legally accurate). A JAC could identify and drive priority areas for research for the justice system. A JAC could integrate judicial and legal expertise with social science juror comprehension research expertise. It could use probabilistic reasoning to draw inferences from social science research, understanding the limitations of knowledge from both the law and social sciences. This approach is essential to change laws, practices, and procedures to improve juror comprehension.

A JAC would therefore have the capacity, resources, and expertise to address juror comprehension problems. However, having the right kind of body is unlikely to be sufficient to overcome the power of the law's knowledge about juror comprehension and to give appropriate weight to social science juror comprehension research. How should a JAC consider juror comprehension problems and approach this reform process? Chapter 6 develops my method for addressing juror comprehension problems so that jurors understand their task.

6 A jury-centric approach

Introduction

Simply having a Juries Advisory Council (JAC) with social science expertise is unlikely to be sufficient to drive juror comprehension reforms. Jeffrey Rachlinski has asked:

> Why have the evidence-based movements made so much headway in medicine and in business, but not in law? Two principle reasons seem important: first, law has conflicting goals, unlike medicine and business; and second, people do not reason about social phenomena the way they reason about medicine and business.[1]

Rachlinski's observations indicate the significant challenges that evidence-based law reform faces. Meeting these challenges requires a clear goal and a clear process for addressing juror comprehension problems.

In this chapter, I discuss my method for addressing juror comprehension problems in criminal trials. A jury-centric approach is evidence-informed. This is necessary if empirical research is going to 'replace the dominance of myth, anecdote, and judicial hearsay in jury reform'[2] (Chapter 5). The goal is to achieve a fair trial — where jurors understand their task. The process for achieving this goal is the application of a 'jury-centric approach'. Therefore, I define a 'jury-centric approach' and discuss what it means for a jury to be a 'competent' jury. Because ensuring a fair trial is of fundamental importance, I examine how other policy factors should be assessed, including whether anything could preclude or limit a reform that will achieve the fair trial goal that jurors understand their task. The framework also involves an analysis of judicial expertise in juror comprehension and guiding juries and examines what support judges need when introducing changes. In this way, a jury-centric approach provides

1 Jeffrey J Rachlinski, 'Evidence-Based Law' (2011) 96 *Cornell Law Review* 901, 917.
2 Jacqueline Horan and Mark Israel, 'Beyond the Legal Barriers: Institutional Gatekeeping and Real Jury Research' (2015) 49 *Australia and New Zealand Journal of Criminology* 422, 434.

DOI: 10.4324/9781003477129-6

a comprehensive organising framework for assessing all relevant policy factors to reforms intended to assist jurors in understanding their task.

Chapters 7, 8, and 9 provide detailed case studies, based on evidence already available, that apply a jury-centric approach to potential reforms that may improve juror comprehension.

What is a jury-centric approach?

There have been surprisingly few attempts to formulate a method for improving juror comprehension. Where reviews have recognised juror comprehension problems, they usually identify it as important to address and sometimes describe it in terms of being relevant to securing a fair trial for the accused.[3] However, juror comprehension is not usually described as being a ***necessary condition*** of a fair trial. If jurors do not understand their task there cannot be a fair trial. Defining juror comprehension as a necessary condition of a fair trial properly recognises its importance. Further, while the best evidence of juror comprehension problems emanates from outside of the discipline of the law, framing juror comprehension as a fair trial problem grounds this issue within the law in familiar terms.

To improve jury trials, Nancy Marder proposes using a 'jury-centric' perspective:[4]

> a perspective that takes the jury as its starting point and asks: What tools do jurors need in order to perform more effectively the tasks with which they have been charged?[5]

The tools Marder refers to include jurors taking notes and asking questions during the trial, judges giving jurors written copies of jury directions, and utilising technology (eg, through the provision of juror orientation materials and computers).[6] Marder later explained that this perspective also applied to

3 See, eg, Queensland Law Reform Commission, *A Review of Jury Directions* (Report No 66, September 2009) 116 [7.3] (QLRC); Victorian Law Reform Commission, *Jury Directions* (Report No 17, May 2009) 75–9 [4.58]–[4.77].

4 Marder also proposes using a jury-centric perspective for other reasons including challenging popular images or portrayals of juries, to give voice to the views of individual jurors about their role or service: Nancy S Marder, 'Introduction to the Jury at a Crossroad: The American Experience' (2003) 78 *Chicago-Kent Law Review* 909, 917–20 ('Introduction to the Jury at a Crossroad').

5 Marder, 'Introduction to the Jury at a Crossroad' (n 4) 918.

6 Marder, 'Introduction to the Jury at a Crossroad' (n 4) 916. See also Nancy S Marder, 'Juries and Technology: Equipping Jurors for the Twenty-First Century' (2001) 66 *Brooklyn Law Review* 1257, 1283–6.

the drafters of jury instructions who 'must put themselves in the position of lay persons who have not been trained in the law'.[7]

There are several examples where judges and scholars have invoked similar perspectives. For example, reflecting upon jury reforms implemented in Arizona, Judge Dann said that the 'most important organizational decision . . . [occurred because the] jurors convinced the committee of the wisdom of looking at the trial through jurors' eyes in addition to those of a judge or of a lawyer'.[8] In the context of the voir dire selection of jurors in trials in the USA, Mary Rose observed that in 'both legal writings and the social science literature, the documented voice and perspective of the juror is absent'.[9] Judge Bennett from the USA stated that his jury trial practices and innovations have been motivated by asking 'WWJW', that is, 'what would jurors want'?[10] And the terms of reference for the Queensland Law Reform Commission's review of jury directions indicated that the Commission should 'consider how information given to the jury can be presented in the most useful way *from the jurors' point of view*'.[11]

Part way through its jury directions reform process, Victoria published two reports that included a 'jury-centric approach' in the titles.[12] I was responsible for the content and publication of these reports and developed the title.[13] These reports did not define a 'jury-centric approach' and therefore did not analyse each proposal for reform through the five steps of a jury-centric approach discussed in this chapter. It is possible to point to instances where the Victorian jury directions reform process undertook analysis that is consistent with some of the steps in my 'jury-centric approach'. However, at most, the Victorian reform process reveals only a fledgling version of my 'jury-centric approach'. My definition in this book provides a more robust and transparent form of analysis through clearly articulated decision-making criteria.

Marder's 'jury-centric' perspective provides the best method to date for improving juror comprehension by focusing on the tools jurors need and jury

7 Nancy S Marder, 'Bringing Jury Instructions into the Twenty-First Century' (2006) 81 *Notre Dame Law Review* 449, 482.

8 B Michael Dann and George Logan III, 'Jury Reform: The Arizona Experience' (1996) 79 *Judicature* 280, 281.

9 Mary R Rose, 'A Voir Dire of Voir Dire: Listening to Jurors' Views Regarding the Peremptory Challenge' (2003) 78 *Chicago-Kent Law Review* 1061, 1065–6.

10 Judge Mark W Bennett, 'Reinvigorating and Enhancing Jury Trials through an Overdue Juror Bill of Rights: A Federal Trial Judge's View' (2016) 48 *Arizona State Law Journal* 481.

11 QLRC, *A Review of Jury Directions* (n 3) 159 (emphasis in original).

12 Criminal Law Review, Department of Justice & Regulation (Vic), *Jury Directions: A Jury-Centric Approach* (Report, March 2015); Criminal Law Review, Department of Justice & Regulation (Vic), *Jury Directions: A Jury-Centric Approach Part 2* (Report, February 2017).

13 I was the Director of Criminal Law Review, the business unit in the Department of Justice & Regulation (Vic) responsible for writing and publishing these reports and the Chair of the Jury Directions Advisory Group, which was discussed in Chapter 2.

instructions. However, because all information in a trial (including the law, practices, and procedures) is potentially relevant to juror comprehension of their task, I propose building on Marder's definition. I define a 'jury-centric approach' as:

> a perspective that takes the jury as its starting point and asks: *What do jurors need in order to understand their task and the issues that they must determine?*

Expanding Marder's definition in this way changes the nature of the enquiry. In common with Marder's definition, my approach seeks to make qualitative improvements to the ability of jurors to perform their task. However, a jury-centric approach[14] is not limited to 'tools' or jury directions. It may include anything that will assist jurors in performing their task — to decide whether the accused is guilty or not guilty of an offence in accordance with the law. While the need for plain language and clear communication techniques remains, a jury-centric approach rejects the 'judicial myth that juries understand and adhere to every direction of the court, so that all that has to be done is modify the directions to accomplish new judicial objectives'.[15] A jury-centric approach goes beyond the content of jury directions to encompass criminal laws that inform the content of directions and to trial practices and procedures. Indeed, 'every stage at which the judge or court interacts with the jurors creates an opportunity to educate the jurors'.[16] Using this new lens requires an examination of the whole trial to consider ways to simplify the issues that the jury must determine, understand what jurors need to know to perform their task, and determine how best to guide the jury with their task.

Further, a jury-centric approach is not limited to the issues themselves. Jurors do not determine issues in a vacuum. They make their decision within an unfamiliar and tightly controlled environment which they may find stressful (eg, they may be uncertain about their role, evidence may be distressing,[17]

14 Marder has also referred to a 'jury-centric approach' but this did not alter her definition of a 'jury-centric perspective': Nancy S Marder, 'Answering Jurors' Questions: Next Steps in Illinois' (2010) 41 *Loyola University of Chicago Law Journal* 727, 741–2.

15 Jane Goodman-Delahunty, David Tait and Natalie Martschuk, 'Procedural Fairness and Jury Satisfaction: An Analysis of Relational Dimensions' in Denise Meyerson, Catriona Mackenzie and Therese MacDermott (eds), *Procedural Justice and Relational Theory: Empirical, Philosophical, and Legal Perspectives* (Routledge, 1st ed, 2020) 44, 44.

16 Nancy S Marder, 'Jurors and Social Media: Is a Fair Trial Still Possible?' (2014) 67(3) *SMU Law Review* 617, 649.

17 See, eg, Dawn E McQuiston, M Dylan Hooper and Abbey E Brasington, 'Vicarious Trauma in the Courtroom: Judicial Perceptions of Juror Distress' (2019) 58 *Judges' Journal* 32, 33; Kate Warner, Julia Davis and Peter Underwood, 'The Jury Experience: Insights from the Tasmanian Jury Study' (2011) 10(3) *Judicial Review* 333, 338.

and the task of reaching a verdict can be quite stressful[18]). These factors can increase jurors' cognitive load and make determining the issues more difficult. Therefore, helping jurors to understand the issues they must determine also requires consideration of how best to support jurors in their task. To provide the best support for jurors requires an understanding of jurors. This includes how key stages of the jury process, and particularly the trial itself, help to educate jurors about their role, their task, and their responsibility. Marder describes this as the how the 'jury process . . . transforms citizens into jurors'.[19]

Broadening the focus of enquiry in these ways provides a new pathway for improving juror comprehension to ensure a fair trial. However, a jury-centric approach does not only expand our understanding of juror comprehension problems. It provides a method for achieving the goal of improving juror comprehension that is evidence-based and comprehensively assesses policy and practical matters.

An evidence-based approach to improving juror comprehension

Why use an evidence-based approach to improving juror comprehension?

Improving public policy by making policy decisions more rational and evidence-based has been increasingly important since the 1950s.[20] In 2016, the US Congress established the Evidence-based Policymaking Commission. The Commission defined 'evidence-based policymaking as the application of evidence to inform decisions in government'.[21] The Commission said that as the evidence base grows, policy makers should increasingly incorporate evidence into decisions about government funding and programs — 'rigorous evidence' should be a 'routine part of government operations'.[22]

A jury-centric approach involves evidence-based reforms to laws, practices, and procedures relevant to criminal trials. The objective is to 'create better law — law informed by reality'.[23] Evidence-based policy and practice is an approach that

18 See, eg, Noelle Robertson, Graham Davies and Nettleingham, 'Vicarious Trauma as a Consequence of Jury Service' (2009) 48(1) *The Howard Journal* 1; Michelle Lonergan et al, 'Prevalence and Severity of Trauma- and Stressor-Related Symptoms among Jurors: A Review' (2016) 47 *Journal of Criminal Justice* 51, 57.

19 Nancy Marder, *The Power of the Jury: Transforming Citizens into Jurors* (Cambridge University Press, 2022) 2.

20 See, eg, Arie Freiberg and WG Carson, 'The Limits to Evidence-Based Policy: Evidence, Emotion and Criminal Justice' (2010) 69(2) *Australian Journal of Public Administration* 152, 153.

21 The Commission on Evidence-Based Policymaking, *The Promise of Evidence-Based Policymaking* (Report, September 2017) <https://cep.gov/report/cep-final-report.pdf> 11–12.

22 *The Promise of Evidence-Based Policymaking* (n 21) 1.

23 Rachlinski (n 1) 910.

> helps policymakers make better decisions, and achieve better outcomes, by using existing evidence more effectively, and undertaking new research, evaluation and analysis where knowledge about effective policy initiatives and policy implementation is lacking.[24]

Evidence-based policymaking is not governed by, or limited to, a technical or rational data-based analysis. Brian Head argues that in government public policy, knowledge arises from three sources:

(1) 'political know-how;
(2) rigorous scientific and technical analysis; and
(3) practical and professional field experience'.[25]

The second and third sources of knowledge are especially important in a jury-centric approach.[26] As occurs when government policy is evidence-based, it is necessary to integrate 'competing and opposing forms of knowledge . . . to form a coherent policy fabric'.[27] Juror comprehension research cannot determine how all laws should work nor all aspects of how courts should conduct trials. This research is relevant and important because juror comprehension is a necessary condition of a fair trial. However, juror comprehension is not a sufficient condition of a fair trial. There are many principles and objectives at work in the criminal law that cannot be reduced to an evidence-based assessment. Indeed, 'empirical study alone cannot dictate policy'.[28]

Evidence-based law reform focuses on improving the law in practice. Judges have expertise in the law and the conduct of trials that constitutes 'practical and professional field experience'. However, as Rachlinski observed, one reason why evidence-based policy is especially difficult in the law is because people reason differently about the law — the power of anecdote is a 'significant impediment to the development of evidence-based law'.[29] As discussed in Chapter 4, the courts' judicial knowledge and experience is an unreliable source of information that has played a significant role in obscuring or minimising juror comprehension problems identified by social science

24 Philip Davies, 'The State of Evidence-Based Policy Evaluation and Its Role in Policy Formation' (2012) 219 *National Institute Economic Review* R41, R42. See also Adrian Cherney and Brian Head, 'Evidence-Based Policy and Practice: Key Challenges for Improvement' (2010) 45(4) *Australian Journal of Social Issues* 509, 510.

25 Brian W Head, 'Three Lenses of Evidence-Based Policy' (2008) 67(1) *Australian Journal of Public Administration* 1, 5. See also Wayne Parsons, 'Not Just Steering But Weaving: Relevant Knowledge and the Craft of Building Policy Capacity and Coherence' (2004) 63(1) *Australian Journal of Public Administration* 43, 51; Freiberg and Carson (n 20) 155–8.

26 The first source of knowledge is primarily relevant to legislative change.

27 Parsons (n 25) 44.

28 Rachlinski (n 1) 918. See also Davies (n 24) R42.

29 Rachlinski (n 1) 919.

research. Judicial views should not prevail over robust social science research to the contrary when assessing juror comprehension. However, any changes designed to improve juror comprehension must operate within a legal system and a trial process, being areas of legal expertise. It is important to balance the need for the development of law reform based on analysis of legal principles — and 'black letter' law — and the need to consider evidence as to how the law works.

Accordingly, integrating competing and opposing forms of knowledge is critical to an evidence-based approach. Evidence-based policymaking and law reform is not sufficient on its own to produce fair trials and therefore cannot be determinative of policy issues. The term 'evidence-informed' better reflects the role of evidence in the broader policy-making environment employed by a jury-centric approach, which considers reasoned argument, professional judgements, stakeholder interests, and political contexts.[30] Obtaining evidence-informed understanding of jurors' perspectives is therefore critical.

Understanding jurors' perspectives

An evidence-informed identification of juror comprehension problems and solutions to these problems depends on information from and about jurors. This does not mean that jury-centric reform proposals must be limited to what jurors think should be reformed. As discussed in Chapter 3, jurors' subjective assessment of their comprehension of jury directions is not always accurate. A jury-centric approach requires new ways of thinking to develop proposals that will improve juror comprehension.

As discussed in Chapter 4, it can be difficult for judges and those trained in the law to understand a juror's perspective. However, the perspectives of leaders like judges and lawyers are readily accessible and powerful compared to jurors' perspectives.[31] Comparing a juror's views about trial by jury with a legal academic's view helps to illustrate the different perspectives. John Langbein's critique of the adversary trial reflects a lawyer's approach:

> Jurors are untrained in the law and often inexperienced in adjudication, they decide without giving reasons, and they have no continuing responsibility for the consequences of their decisions. Because of the grave risks of error and bias that inhere in using such decision makers, the common law courts have never left juries to their own devices. Rather, the judges have undertaken to guide and oversee the work of the jury.[32]

30 Brian W Head, 'Evidence-Based Policymaking — Speaking Truth to Power?' (2013) 72(4) *Australian Journal of Public Administration* 397, 397.

31 See generally, Milton Derber, 'What the Lawyer Can Learn from Social Science' (1963) 16 *Journal of Legal Education* 145, 150.

32 John H Langbein, *The Origins of the Adversary Criminal Trial* (Oxford University Press, 2003) 321.

By contrast, Malcolm Knox, a juror from a trial in New South Wales described his experience and perspective of the trial process:

> When I was empanelled we were told nothing other than to listen carefully and decide on the evidence. Was I allowed to raise my hand and ask for something to be clarified? How about ask if I'd not heard something clearly? Was I allowed to take notes? . . . I still don't know the answers to any of these questions . . . Our sheriff's officer would not answer any questions except to say that the judge would instruct us fully AT THE END OF THE EVIDENCE (not much use by then! . . .).[33]

The transient nature of jury service and the confidentiality of jury deliberations compounds difficulties in understanding juror perspectives. Juries do not have leaders like a judge. The jury's foreperson (sometimes called a representative or speaker) speaks for the jury in the trial for limited purposes. And like other jurors, the foreperson will not usually have any legal training and will not usually have had experience as a juror.[34]

Jurors do not have an official and ongoing representative, or a 'juror's union', to inform others of their views about how the trial system works for them.[35] The 'jurors' perspective so often gets lost, largely because jurors are not in a position to advocate for themselves'.[36] Jurors may speak out occasionally, but even in the USA where there are significantly fewer restrictions on what a juror may say after a trial about their deliberations, speaking out is quite limited. A juror might write a book or speak to the media, but this is an ad hoc process, often based on an individual juror's experience of one case.[37]

Imagination can add to, rather than replace, evidence about juror comprehension and ways of improving comprehension. Incorporating imagination into the reform process reflects that the 'task of good public policy making is not to reason what is good for others but to envision imaginatively, from diverse standpoints, the present reality and the desirable future'.[38] Under-

33 Malcolm Knox, *Secrets of the Jury Room* (Random House Australia, 2005) 316 (emphasis in original).

34 See, eg, Jane Goodman-Delahunty et al, 'Practices, Policies and Procedures that Influence Juror Satisfaction in Australia' (Research and Public Policy Series No 87, July 2007) 50; BBC News, 'What Is the Chance of Being Called for Jury Service?' (28 April 2016) <www.bbc.com/news/uk-scotland-36140259>.

35 Knox (n 33) 295. See also Greg Byrne, 'Juries and the "Detective Juror": Improving Public Discussion about Juries and Jurors' (2023) 48(3) *Alternative Law Journal* 185, 186–7.

36 Marder, 'Answering Jurors' Questions' (n 14) 742.

37 See, eg, Keith Wagstaff, '5 Books from Jurors Who Cashed in on Their Court Cases' *The Week*, online, 9 January 2015 <https://theweek.com/articles/462172/5-books-from-jurors-who-cashed-court-cases>; Trevor Grove, *The Juryman's Tale* (Bloomsbury, 1998); Knox (n 33).

38 D Don Welch, 'Ruling with the Heart: Emotion-Based Public Policy' (1997) 6 *Southern California Interdisciplinary Law Journal* 55, 85.

standing jurors' 'present reality and the desirable future' involves imagining what jurors need and how the law and jury trials could be different.

There are limits to the extent to which we can fully put ourselves in the position of a juror, let alone all jurors, as we cannot access all of their knowledge and experiences.[39] However, we can improve our 'perspective by stretching . . . [our] imagination to identify and understand the perspectives of others'.[40] Further, '[a]rticulating visions of the future is one way of making explicit our assumptions',[41] and may also assist in identifying when we unintentionally project our experiences or perspective onto others.[42] Projecting in this way is easy to do in relation to jurors because of the confidentiality of jury deliberations. Further, our familiarity with trial by jury can make the procedures used in a trial by jury seem 'inevitable or immutable'[43] or reflect fundamental principles rather than being the 'product of mere historical accident'.[44]

While I do not propose that there should be an advocate for the jury in trial proceedings,[45] it is useful to imagine what a trial would be like if a lawyer, with expertise in juror comprehension research, represented the jury's interests. A jury's representative might propose changing the trial to assist jurors in understanding the issues that the jury must determine. This hypothetical representative could be an advocate in the court, asking questions for and on the jury's behalf, or requesting that counsel present the case, and the judge give directions, in a particular way. This representative might ask counsel to periodically identify, or summarise briefly, how evidence given by witnesses supports their case.[46] This may help jurors to understand the evidence when jurors are evaluating it. In addition to the judge providing written guidance to the jury, a representative might ask that judges provide diagrams and illustrations where possible.[47] This representative might also seek change outside of

39 See generally, Katharine T Bartlett, 'Feminist Legal Methods' (1990) 103(4) *Harvard Law Review* 829, 880–7.

40 Bartlett (n 39) 882. See also, Welch (n 38) 68.

41 Heather Ruth Wishik, 'To Question Everything: The Inquiries of Feminist Jurisprudence' (1985) 1 *Berkeley Women's Law Journal* 64, 76.

42 Bartlett (n 39) 886.

43 Erik Luna, 'A Place for Comparative Criminal Procedure' (2003–04) 42 *Brandeis Law Journal* 277, 282.

44 Peter Duff, 'The Scottish Criminal Jury: A Very Peculiar Institution' (1999) 62(2) *Law and Contemporary Problems* 173, 201.

45 See, eg, Joshua Grew, 'Using Facilitators in Criminal Jury Trials in New South Wales — Undermining "Trial by Jury" or the Way Forward?' (2011) 12(5) *ADR Bulletin*, Article 3.

46 G Thomas Munsterman, Paula L Hannaford-Agor and G Marc Whitehead, National Center for State Courts, *Jury Trial Innovations* (Report, 2006) <www.ncsc-jurystudies.org/__data/assets/pdf_file/0021/7644/jury-trial-innovations-2d-ed-2006.pdf> 134–5 [5.10].

47 See, eg, Firoz Dattu, 'Illustrated Jury Instructions: A Proposal' (1998) 22 *Law and Psychology Review* 67, 76–80, 80–92; Carolyn Semmler and Neil Brewer, 'Using a Flow-Chart to Improve Comprehension of Jury Instructions' (2002) 9 *Psychiatry, Psychology and Law* 262.

individual trials to improve systematically the presentation of information to juries.

Imagining this kind of jury representative also highlights how the law has rendered the jury largely voiceless and has failed to consider the jury's perspective. Power dynamics between judges, lawyers, law reform bodies, and parliaments have shaped criminal trials and our understanding of what is a fair trial. Jurors have been largely voiceless through these changes, with no representative focusing on juror comprehension and juror perspectives.[48] This approach to using imagination, and seeing different perspectives, is like some feminist critiques of the law and 'is more likely to respond to the lives of those whose experiences have been omitted from law's attention'.[49]

An evidence-informed approach should incorporate rather than limit 'imagination, insight and creativity'.[50] Incorporating imagination may help to ask the right research questions and ensure that proposals are not limited by existing processes or conceptions of how trial by jury should work. Using imagination can be challenging. Using imagination, together with research about juror comprehension, should improve understanding of the jurors' perspectives and what they need to understand their task. As discussed in Chapter 5, having former jurors involved in a JAC will help to build understanding of jurors' perspectives. However, while an evidence-informed reform will improve juror comprehension, that does not mean that the reform is necessarily appropriate or desirable.

Using a jury-centric approach to resolve competing policy objectives

As Rachlinski identified, a significant challenge for evidence-based law is that, unlike business or medicine, the law does not have one 'unifying, organizing principle'.[51] Laws usually have multiple purposes, such as efficiency and fairness, which may conflict. A jury-centric approach promotes deeply held values about the jury system: the importance of trial by jury and the importance of a fair trial. Indeed, a jury-centric approach uses research about the problems

48 Having a 'voice' — outside of deliberations — could be based on procedural fairness, because it would give 'citizens' [a] sense of being heard and having their input valued': Goodman-Delahunty, Tait and Martschuk (n 15) 46. It might also be based on models of an employees' voice, where employees may make suggestions for improvement: Paula K Mowbray, Adrian Wilkinson and Herman Tse, 'Evolution, Separation and Convergence of Employee Voice Concept' in Peter Holland, Julian Teicher and Jimmy Donaghey (eds), *Employee Voice at Work* (Springer, 2019) 3, 5.

49 Regina Graycar and Jenny Morgan, 'Law Reform: What's in It for Women?' (2005) 23 *Windsor Yearbook of Access to Justice* 393, 399.

50 Ken Young et al, 'Social Science and the Evidence-Based Policy Movement' (2002) 1(3) *Social Policy and Society* 215, 223.

51 Rachlinski (n 1) 917–18. The goal in medicine 'is a positive outcome for the patient's health' and in business it is the 'bottom line'.

with juror comprehension to strengthen the institution of trial by jury. This should mean that problems that often confront the introduction of evidence-based law reforms should not be as strong with a jury-centric approach.

This section discusses what fair trial principles are, how they evolved and how to resolve conflicts between fair trial principles and human rights more broadly. I then examine how a jury-centric approach provides a framework for assessing other policy factors.

Fair trial principles and a competent jury

The importance of a fair trial is 'so elementary as to need no authority to support it'.[52] The principle of a fair trial informs, and sometimes constrains, criminal trial procedure.[53] It reflects the inherent power of a court to control its own processes and to prevent abuse of those processes.[54] Fair trial principles apply broadly and in many different circumstances. While it is not possible to list all components of a fair trial, some principles are very clear: a judge must ensure that the accused's trial is a fair trial.[55] Fair trial principles govern how the judge guides the jury in its task.

Human rights laws encapsulate some common law fair trial principles, such as the right to a fair trial, or a 'right to a trial as fair as the courts can make it'.[56] For example, Article 14 of the *International Covenant on Civil and Political Rights 1966* (ICCPR) provides that a criminal charge must be determined by a 'competent, independent and impartial' tribunal.[57] In a criminal trial by jury, the jury is the tribunal of fact. Both the ICCPR and domestic human rights legislation[58] encapsulate some essential common law fair trial requirements (eg, the accused's right to a fair hearing). This is because the very notion of a fair trial in the ICCPR derives from the common law and extends back to Magna Carta.[59]

52 *R v Macfarlane; Ex parte O'Flanagan and O'Kelly* (1923) 32 CLR 518, 541 (Isaacs J). (The irony of citing authority is intentional.)

53 See, eg, *Connelly v DPP* [1964] AC 1254, 1347 (Lord Devlin); Chief Justice James Spigelman, 'The Truth Can Cost Too Much: The Principle of a Fair Trial' (2004) 78 *Australian Law Journal* 29, 30.

54 *Jago v District Court of New South Wales* (1989) 168 CLR 23, 28 ('*Jago*').

55 See, eg, *RPS v The Queen* (2000) 199 CLR 620, 637 (Gaudron ACJ, Gummow, Kirby and Hayne JJ); *R v Horseferry Road Magistrates' Court; Ex parte Bennett* [1994] 1 AC 42, 68; *R v H and C* [2004] 2 AC 134, 145 [10] ('*H and C*'); *R v Seaboyer* [1991] 2 SCR 577, 603; *Wilson v The Queen* [2016] 1 NZLR 705.

56 *Jago* (n 54) 49 (Brennan J). See, generally, Jeremy Gans et al, *Criminal Process and Human Rights* (Federation Press, 2011) 378.

57 Article 14 of the *International Covenant on Civil and Political Rights*, opened for signature 16 December 1966, 999 UNTS 171 (entered into force 23 March 1976).

58 See, eg, *Charter of Human Rights and Responsibilities Act 2006* (Vic) s 24; *Human Rights Act 1998* (UK) s 1; *New Zealand Bill of Rights Act 1990* (NZ) s 24(e); *Canada Act 1982* (UK) c 11, sch B pt 1 ('Canadian Charter of Rights and Freedoms') s 11(f).

59 Stefan Trechsel, *Human Rights in Criminal Proceedings* (Oxford University Press, 2005) 81–2.

What does it mean for a jury to be a 'competent' tribunal? The common law developed on the basis that each juror must be competent.[60] For example, if a juror does not understand English, they would not be 'capable of understanding the trial proceedings', and therefore not competent to serve as a juror.[61] If the fact that a juror is not competent is only discovered after the trial has commenced, the jury should be discharged or the verdict set aside.[62] Assessing the competency of an individual juror based on a specific reason (eg, language comprehension) is an important but limited way of assessing the competency of a jury and fails to recognise that juror comprehension problems are more likely to arise from the 'characteristics of the situation' rather than the 'characteristics of the person'.[63]

A 'competent' tribunal usually means a tribunal established by law with jurisdiction to determine a matter.[64] There is no clear definition about what it means for the jury, rather than a juror, to be a competent tribunal. This suggests that courts have given limited attention to such matters and that evidence of such problems does not usually appear in trial proceedings.[65] Further, courts may be reluctant to define such matters because doing so might open new avenues of appeal or subject the jury to unwanted scrutiny. Whether the ICCPR or domestic legislation should define the word 'competent' this broadly is beyond the scope of this book. However, for policy development purposes, 'more attention should be paid to a juror's ability to understand the law of a case as one determining criterion of his/her competence to "judge" that case'.[66] A definition may help to define and highlight the importance of juror comprehension problems in ensuring a fair trial.

As discussed in more detail in Chapter 9, a tribunal is not impartial if a 'fair-minded observer might reasonably apprehend that the judge (or juror) might not bring an impartial mind to the resolution of the question the judge (or juror) is required to decide'.[67] This test focuses on whether there is a 'possibil-

60 *Lal v The King* (1933) 50 TLR 1 ('*Lal*').
61 See, eg, Law Reform Commission of Western Australia, *Selection, Eligibility and Exemption of Jurors* (Final Report, Project No 99, April 2010) 94; New Zealand Law Commission, *Juries in Criminal Trials* (Report No 69, February 2001) 78 [196] (NZLC).
62 *Lal* (n 60) 3–5.
63 Phoebe C Ellsworth and Alan Reifman, 'Juror Comprehension and Public Policy: Perceived Problems and Proposed Solutions' (2000) 6 *Psychology, Public Policy and Law* 788, 794–5.
64 See, eg, Trechsel (n 59) 45–8.
65 See eg, Phoebe C Ellsworth, 'Are Twelve Heads Better Than One?' (1989) 52 *Law and Contemporary Problems* 205, 207.
66 Amiram Elwork, Bruce D Sales and James J Alfini, *Making Jury Instructions Understandable* (Michie Company, 1982) 28.
67 *Ebner v Official Trustee in Bankruptcy* (2000) 205 CLR 337, 344 [6] (Gleeson CJ, McHugh, Gummow and Hayne JJ) ('*Ebner*'). The law is very similar across jurisdictions: see, eg, *Porter v Magill* [2002] 2 AC 357 ('*Porter*'); *Muir v Commissioner of Inland Revenue* [2007] 3 NZLR 495 ('*Muir*'); *R v Lippé* [1991] 2 SCR 114; *RDS v The Queen* [1997] 3 SCR 484 ('*RDS*'); Andrew Higgins and Inbar Levy, 'Judicial Policy, Public Perception, and the Science

ity (real and not remote)' rather than a 'probability' that a juror may not be impartial.[68] Like impartiality, juror competency concerns whether a juror will, or is capable of, deciding a case on its 'legal and factual merits'.[69] Adapting this test to whether a tribunal (the jury) is competent, the test should be whether a fair-minded observer might reasonably apprehend that there is a *real possibility that jurors might not understand their task.*

A fair-minded observer is also an informed observer.[70] An informed observer would consider evidence when assessing whether jurors understand their task. Further, by focusing on a 'real possibility', this obviates the need for juror comprehension evidence about whether each juror in each trial understands their task. Obtaining juror comprehension evidence in each trial would most likely infringe the confidentiality of jury deliberations. Instead, it is possible to draw inferences from jury research about what is likely to happen in each case.

Adapting the test for judge/juror impartiality to assess the competency of the jury as a tribunal highlights the importance of juror competency. An evidence-informed approach to improving juror comprehension to ensure a fair trial therefore must focus on addressing the real possibility (as shown by juror comprehension research) that jurors might not understand their task.

How do fair trial principles evolve?

While the requirement that a tribunal be competent is set out in the ICCPR, common law fair trial principles are broader than those set out in the ICCPR and are relevant to assessing proposals that aim to improve juror comprehension. I generally refer to 'fair trial principles' rather than defined rights or legislative requirements to reflect the full scope, and the flexible and dynamic way in which common law fair trial principles have evolved.[71]

Fair trial principles often appear to be self-evident essential features of the criminal law. However, the development of the criminal law and trial by jury shows that rather than being transcendent qualities, fair trial principles reflect

---

of Decision Making: A New Framework for the Law of Apprehended Bias' (2019) 38(3) *Civil Justice Quarterly* 376, 378.

68 *Ebner* (n 67) 345 [7] (Gleeson CJ, McHugh, Gummow and Hayne JJ) (emphasis in original). See also, *Locabail (UK) v Bayfield Properties Ltd* [2000] QB 451, 475; *RDS* (n 67) 530 [109] (Cory and Iacobucci JJ); *Muir* (n 67) 508–9 [62]. When applying this test retrospectively, in an appeal following conviction, the plurality in the High Court of Australia said that a 'reasonable apprehension' must be formed based on facts found on the balance of probabilities: *HCF v The Queen* (2023) 97 ALJR 978; [2023] HCA 35 [46] (Gageler CJ, Gleeson and Jagot JJ). This gloss on the test does not apply when conducting a forward-looking risk assessment: at [45].

69 *Ebner* (n 67) 345 [8] (Gleeson CJ, McHugh, Gummow and Hayne JJ).

70 *Porter* (n 67) [103].

71 Spigelman (n 53) 30–1.

changing social and political standards.[72] Further, the common law and fair trial principles have some flexibility to evolve with changes in society and societal expectations and can change from decade to decade.[73]

Fair trial principles have helped to shape trial by jury. This includes significant historical shifts in trials: the impartiality of the jury as it changed from being a witness to the facts to a judge of the facts;[74] establishing the jury's independence from the judge;[75] the accusatorial nature of trial proceedings;[76] and the expansion of jury directions to guide the jury in its task. Indeed, the way in which fair trial principles have evolved suggests that they have much in common with judicial guidance of the jury, having both developed based on judicial knowledge and experience and judges' common sense.[77]

Fair trial considerations have often focused on the accused's right to a fair trial. In the latter parts of the 20th century, criticisms of criminal laws and criminal trials from feminist critiques and victims' rights movements[78] have expanded what is necessary for a trial to be fair. Lord Steyn referred to a 'triangulation of interests', reflecting the public interest in a fair trial for the accused, victim, and the community.[79] A jury-centric approach is not limited to ensuring a fair trial for the accused. The purpose is to ensure a fair trial, whether that be from the accused's, the victim's, or the community's perspective. Further, a jury-centric approach can accommodate expansions of fair trial considerations, such as the need for a competent jury (as I have defined it).

Whatever the content and definition of fair trial principles, the most critical issue for a jury-centric approach is what to do if a proposed change that

72 Simon Bronitt and Bernadette McSherry, *Principles of Criminal Law* (Lawbook, 4th ed, 2017) 93.

73 *Dietrich v The Queen* (1992) 177 CLR 292, 328 (Deane J); *H and C* (n 55) 145–6 [11] (Lord Bingham); Spigelman (n 53) 43.

74 See, eg, Edward L Rubin, 'Trial by Battle. Trial by Argument' (2003) 56 *Arkansas Law Review* 261, 276; Langbein (n 32) 320; Valerie P Hans and Neil Vidmar, *Judging the Jury* (Plenum Press, 1986) 27–8.

75 Hans and Vidmar (n 74) 21–2. See also Langbein (n 32) 323–4.

76 See, eg, *CFMEU v Boral Resources (Vic) Pty Ltd* (2015) 256 CLR 375, 394 [61] (Nettle J); *Woolmington v DPP* [1935] AC 462, 481 (Viscount Sankey LC).

77 See generally, Sheila Jasanoff, 'Science, Common Sense & Judicial Power in U.S. Courts' (2018) 147(4) *Daedalus* 15, 25; Kunal M Parker, 'The Transformation of the Common Law: Modernism, History, and The Turn to Process' in Markus D Dubber and Christopher Tomlins (eds), *The Oxford Handbook of Legal History* (Oxford University Press, 2018) 695, 699.

78 Gans et al (n 56) 381. See also Victorian Law Reform Commission, *The Role of Victims of Crime in the Criminal Trial Process* (Report No 34, August 2016) 27.

79 *R v A (No 2)* [2002] 1 AC 45, 65 [38]. See also Phoebe Bowden, Terese Henning and David Plater, 'Balancing Fairness to Victims, Society and Defendants in the Cross-Examination of Vulnerable Witnesses: An Impossible Triangulation?' (2014) 37 *Melbourne University Law Review* 539, 557–60; Greg Byrne, 'Respecting Victims' Rights Through Victim Legal Representation' in Greg Byrne and Jacqueline Horan (eds), *Sexual Assault Trials: Challenges and Innovations* (LexisNexis, 2025) 130, 132–4.

supports the fair trial principle that jurors understand their task conflicts with another fair trial principle or another human right.

Fair trial principles and other human rights and policy factors

Within human rights conventions and legislation, there are different ways of categorising rights. For example, rights may be categorised as absolute or non-derogable rights (eg, freedom from slavery or torture, or the right to due process) or as limited or qualified rights (eg, the right to a private life).[80] Limited or qualified rights may also be distinguished based on whether they involve strong rights (eg, the right to a fair trial).[81] However, in Canada there is no hierarchy of rights, no absolute rights, and 'all must be defined in light of competing claims'.[82]

It is inevitable that each human right will conflict with another human right at some point.[83] I will primarily describe rights as conflicting, though other descriptions are also used (eg, rights being in 'tension' with one another, or infringing or limiting rights).[84] The inevitability of conflicts between human rights is recognised in some human rights legislation which provide that certain rights (eg, strong or qualified rights) may be limited if the limit is reasonable and can be 'demonstrably justified'.[85] This involves considering matters such as the importance and purpose of the right and whether the limit is necessary, proportional, and parsimonious (or no greater than necessary).[86] More compelling reasons are required to limit stronger rights like fair trial rights.[87] Legislation may also set out in more detail the kinds of matters to consider when determining whether a limitation of a right is reasonable. For example, the nature of the right, the purpose of the limitation, the nature and extent of

80 See, eg, Başak Çalı, 'Balancing Human Rights? Methodological Problems with Weights, Scales and Proportions' (2007) 29(1) *Human Rights Quarterly* 251, 257–61.

81 Jeremy Horder, *Ashworth's Principles of Criminal Law* (Oxford University Press, 9th ed, 2019) 77–9.

82 *R v Mills* [1999] 3 SCR 668, 713–14 [61] (McLachlin and Iacobucci JJ).

83 Steven Greer, Laurence W Gormley and Jo Shaw, *The European Convention on Human Rights: Achievements, Problems and Prospects* (Cambridge University Press, 2006) 204–5.

84 See, eg, Patricia Hughes, 'The Reconciliation of Legal Rights' in Shaheen Azmi, Lorne Foster and Lesley Jacobs (eds), *Balancing Competing Human Rights Claims in a Diverse Society: Institutions, Policy, Principles* (Irwin Law, 2012) 271, 276–7.

85 See, eg, *Canada Act 1982* (UK) c 11, sch B pt 1 ('Canadian Charter of Rights and Freedoms') s 1; *New Zealand Bill of Rights Act 1990* (NZ) s 5; *Charter of Human Rights and Responsibilities Act 2006* (Vic) s 7(2).

86 See, eg, *R v Oakes* [1986] 1 SCR 103, 138–9 [69]–[70] (Dickson CJ); Gans et al (n 56) 55–8; Horder (n 81) 78–9, 130–1.

87 Andrew Ashworth, 'Crime, Community and Creeping Consequentialism' [1996] *Criminal Law Review* 220, 229.

the limitation and whether any less restrictive means are available to achieve the purpose of the limitation.[88]

Whether or not legislative criteria apply to conflicts between rights, courts often reconcile conflicting rights through a 'balancing process'.[89] Undertaking a balancing process does not mean that all matters considered are of equal weight. A 'balancing process' involves considering similar matters to those set out in human rights legislation earlier (eg, the objective of the proposed limit on a human right and whether the limitation is necessary to meet that objective, and whether the public interest in that objective outweighs the harm caused to individual rights[90]). In undertaking this process, it is important to clearly articulate the contested nature of the values, legal principles, and empirical evidence considered in this balancing process.

The right to a fair hearing by a competent, independent, and impartial tribunal is a strong right. Indeed, a hearing before a tribunal without these features can never be fair.[91] Fair trial principles operate in two ways. When assessed overall, a trial must be fair.[92] However, a trial is comprised of many components. It may be possible to limit one or more of these components of a fair trial, or a human right, and still have a fair trial overall.[93] For example, the accused's long-established fair trial right to confront their accuser[94] may be limited by providing that an accused cannot personally cross-examine a sexual assault complainant.[95] This limitation is justifiable as it assists 'complainants and witnesses to give their best evidence in a humane procedure which treats them with appropriate concern and respect'.[96] However, overall, the trial may be fair if the accused's lawyer, or a court appointed lawyer, may conduct this cross-examination.

88 See, eg, *Charter of Human Rights and Responsibilities Act 2006* (Vic) s 7; *New Zealand Bill of Rights Act 1990* (NZ) s 5.

89 See, eg, *Jago* (n 54) 33 (Mason CJ), 57 (Deane J); *R v Corbett* [1988] 1 SCR 670, 692 (Dickson CJ); Greer, Gormley and Shaw (n 83) 203.

90 See, eg, Australian Law Reform Commission, *Traditional Rights and Freedoms — Encroachments by Commonwealth Laws* (Report No 129, December 2015) 45 [2.63]. This balancing process is sometimes described as reconciling different rights: Hughes (n 84) 272–3.

91 Trechsel (n 59) 46–7. See also *X7 v Australian Crime Commission* (2013) 248 CLR) 92, 116 [38].

92 See, eg, *H and C* (n 55) 145 [10] (Lord Bingham).

93 See, eg, *Brown v Stott* [2003] 1 AC 681, 704; *Traditional Rights and Freedoms — Encroachments by Commonwealth Laws* (n 90) 230–1 [8.50]–[8.52].

94 See, eg, *R v Davis* [2008] 1 AC 1128, 1137–8 [5]; Mike Redmayne, 'Confronting Confrontation' in Paul Roberts and Jill B Hunter (eds), *Criminal Evidence and Human Rights: Reimagining Common Law Procedural Traditions* (Hart Publishing, 2012) 283.

95 See, eg, *Criminal Procedure Act 2009* (Vic) s 356; *Crimes Act 1914* (Cth) s 15YF.

96 Paul Roberts and Jill B Hunter, 'Introduction — The Human Rights Revolution in Criminal Evidence and Procedure' in Paul Roberts and Jill B Hunter (eds), *Criminal Evidence and Human Rights: Reimagining Common Law Procedural Traditions* (Hart Publishing, 2012) 1, 20.

There are limitations in using a balancing process, debates about whether a 'balancing' process appropriately describes the assessment, and the nature of rights-based discourse has some limitations.[97] While there is no clear alternative process to use, methods for resolving conflicts between rights usefully provide a transparent and familiar framework for analysing conflicts between fair trial principles and other human rights. A jury-centric approach incorporates this human rights framework for dealing with the inevitable conflicts arising from different fair trial considerations and other human rights. This means that a jury-centric approach has a clear goal where jurors understand their task and a method for resolving conflicts between this goal and other goals in the justice system.

Sometimes fair trial policy factors will provide clear choices. For example, suppose that a proposal is made that the accused be compellable to give evidence, enabling the prosecution to cross-examine the accused, in every case. This proposal conflicts with common law immunities that an accused is not a compellable witness in their own trial and cannot be compelled to answer questions.[98] While clear statutory intent may abrogate the privilege against self-incrimination, it is still a strong right,[99] and it is relevant to the fairness of a trial. Therefore, the proposal would not be justifiable to achieve the goal of improving juror comprehension because it would override another strong fair trial principle.

Making the accused a compellable witness in every case may seem an extreme and unlikely proposal. This suggests that strong fair trial considerations are not likely to often conflict with proposals that improve juror comprehension. Because of their genesis in fair trial considerations, many procedural changes that promote a fair trial will not conflict with other strong rights or fair trial principles (eg, the introduction of SDM aids for juries). However, a proposal such as making the accused compellable to improve juror comprehension may also be a Trojan horse for changing the criminal justice system based on other policy or ideological reasons (eg, to make the criminal justice system more favourable to the prosecution). Analysing proposals within a transparent fair trial framework is essential in identifying a policy's real goals.

97 See, eg, Çalı (n 80), 259; Greer, Gormley and Shaw (n 83) 203–13; Bronitt and McSherry (n 72) 156 [2.205].

98 The High Court of Australia has said that it is a 'fundamental principle' that the prosecution cannot compel the accused to assist in the prosecution: *Environmental Protection Authority v Caltex Refining Co Pty Ltd* (1993) 178 CLR 477, 527 (Deane, Dawson and Gaudron JJ).

99 See, eg, Anthony Gray, 'The Right to Silence: Using American and European Law to Protect a Fundamental Right' (2013) 16 *New Criminal Law Review* 527, 532–9; Andrew L-T Choo, '"Give Us What You Have' — Information, Compulsion and the Privilege against Self-Incrimination as a Human Right' in Paul Roberts and Jill Hunter (eds), *Criminal Evidence and Human Rights: Reimagining Common Law Procedural Tradition* (Bloomsbury Publishing, 2013) 239, 249–54.

Other policy factors may play a more prominent role in proposals for changes to substantive laws than with procedural laws. This is because, unlike procedural laws, substantive laws have generally not emerged from, or been shaped by, fair trial principles. For example, when determining what the elements should be for the offence of rape, there are many policy factors that are relevant in defining an offence. Other policy factors may provide another goal of reform, such as improving the justice system's response in sexual offence cases. A jury-centric approach should still be used in this kind of reform process. While it is necessary that jurors can understand or apply the law, comprehensibility to a jury is not a sufficient basis for defining criminal responsibility. The comprehensive nature of a jury-centric approach's organising framework means that all relevant factors need to be considered, even if the initial goal is not focused on improving the jury's understanding of their task.

Because of a judge's primary role in guiding a jury, many reforms will be relevant to the way in which a judge conducts a trial and guides the jury with their task. This raises the question of whether the judge's role should be re-considered in determining whether a change will ensure a fair trial where jurors understand their task.

When should the application of jury-centric reforms depend upon judicial expertise?

Appellate courts have stated that the trial judge is 'in the best position to understand the dynamics of any particular trial and to devise directions that meet the demands of that trial'.[100] This approach gives trial judges some flexibility, based on their expertise, in how they guide the jury in each case to ensure that jurors understand their task.

Whether a judge should give a jury a transcript of the evidence illustrates how a judge may use their discretion in deciding how to guide the jury. In Australia and New Zealand, judges have a discretion to provide the jury with a transcript.[101] The New South Wales Law Reform Commission said this discretion should be exercised in the context of the individual case by reference to the complexity and nature of the matters in issue, the length of the trial, any other measures that might more usefully assist the jury in recalling and

100 New South Wales Law Reform Commission, *Jury Directions* (Report No 136, November 2012) 41 [2.35] (NSWLRC). See also, Judicial Studies Board, *Crown Court Bench Book: Directing the Jury* (2010) <https://issuu.com/forensicmed/docs/crown_court_benchbook_-_judicial_studies_board> 1; *R v Rodgerson* [2015] 2 SCR 760, 785 [52]; *R v Lawrence* [1982] AC 510, 519; *Holland v The Queen* (1993) 117 ALR 193, 200. Cf Lord Justice Moses, 'Summing Down the Summing-Up' (Speech, Annual Law Reform Lecture, Inner Temple, 23 November 2010) 3–4.

101 In England and Wales, a judge may only provide a jury with a transcript during deliberations in exceptional circumstances because of the oral nature of the trial and concerns that it may be given undue weight: *R v Popescu* [2010] EWCA Crim 1230.

considering the issues that they are to decide, whether the jury has requested access to the transcript, and whether it is practicable to supply a transcript.[102]

The discretionary provision of transcripts has resulted in very inconsistent practices. A 2019 survey in Australia found that 35.5% of judges always provide the jury with a transcript.[103] However, this aggregate data masks jurisdictional variations: 89% of Victorian judges surveyed said they always provide the jury with a transcript. Excluding Victorian judges indicates that for the rest of Australia, only 14.5% of judges surveyed always provide the jury with a transcript, 54.5% do sometimes, and 31% never provide the transcript.[104] It may be that part of this disparity reflects practical limitations concerning whether a transcript is available in either hard copy or electronic form. The Victorian result is very similar to New Zealand, where in the same survey, 93.6% of judges surveyed said they always provide the jury with a transcript.[105]

There is unlikely to be anything about a particular trial that would lead a judge to conclude that a transcript of the evidence would assist one jury as opposed to another jury, except perhaps if a trial is short. There is no 'reason in principle why the jury — the principal trier of fact — should be denied the basic record of the evidence that it is required to assess'.[106] And jurors generally want more written materials.[107]

The difference in outcome between (and within) jurisdictions appears to depend primarily upon the views of the judge about what they think will assist the jury. This decision should be informed by research. It should not depend upon a judge's familiarity with, or views about, jury research, or about whether jurors should even have access to a transcript. Further, if judges are not aware of research about the provision of a transcript, judges are more likely to make this decision based on their own knowledge and experience.

Judges make many decisions when determining how best to guide juries. Judges tailor their guidance to juries primarily by drawing on their knowledge and experience, that is, what they have always done or have seen done, or their own preferred learning styles, their intuition and assumptions about jurors, and their observations or impressions of juror demeanour (eg, do they appear to understand). This raises a deeper issue about judicial knowledge and

102 NSWLRC, *Jury Directions* (n 100) 121 [6.41].

103 Jonathan Clough et al, *The Jury Project 10 Years On — Practices of Australian and New Zealand Judges* (Australian Institute of Judicial Administration, April 2019) 40–1.

104 Jonathan Clough et al (n 103) 40–2.

105 Jonathan Clough et al (n 103) 40.

106 QLRC, *A Review of Jury Directions* (n 3) 319 [10.98].

107 See, eg, NZLC, *Juries in Criminal Trials* (n 61) 130–1 [342]; Jacqueline Horan, *Juries in the 21st Century* (Federation Press, 2012) 74–6; Blake McKimmie, Emma Antrobus and Ian Davis, 'Jurors' Trial Experiences: The Influence of Directions and Other Aspects of Trials' in Queensland Law Reform Commission, *A Review of Jury Directions* (2009) Appendix E, 9–10, 24–5.

experience concerning juror comprehension. Does this knowledge and experience reflect judicial expertise? Is it reliable?

As discussed in Chapter 2, there are few clear general statements about what the law assumes jurors know and how they make decisions. What about judges? Judges have expertise in the law. The law assumes that each trial judge possesses the expertise to know what jurors know, how jurors' reason, and how to guide jurors so that they understand their task. The judge's function is particularly challenging because of the volume and complexity of laws that judges must master and explain,[108] the complexities of scientific and technological evidence, changing juror expectations for written and visual aids for presenting information,[109] and juror's familiarity with searching the internet to problem-solve and obtain information.[110]

Examining the role of evidence-based research in medicine assists in understanding the challenge of expecting judges to incorporate juror comprehension research into their decision-making about how to guide juries. The experience of evidence-based medicine is that it is hard 'to translate . . . evidence into improving the quality of practice and outcomes'.[111] Practitioners may be sceptical of, and give little weight to evidence.[112] The 'inherently clinical focus on individual doctors and individual patients can make it difficult for many doctors to think like statisticians and scientists'.[113] Reviewing and synthesising the evidence is a complicated task and methodological issues arise for which there may be no clear answer.[114] Evidence-based medicine requires doctors to integrate their 'individual clinical expertise with the best available external clinical evidence from systematic research'.[115] This involves integrating different fields of knowledge and changes to practice based on that research.

108 See, eg, Justice Stephen McLeish, 'Challenges to the Survival of the Common Law' (2014) 38 *Melbourne University Law Review* 818, 824. See also Judicial College, *The Crown Court Compendium — Part I: Jury and Trial Management and Summing Up* (July 2024) <www.judiciary.uk/wp-content/uploads/2024/07/Crown-Court-Compendium-Part-I-July-2024-1.pdf> viii–ix (Foreword by Baroness Carr of Walton-on-the-Hill, Lady Chief Justice).

109 Horan, *Juries in the 21st Century* (n 107) 74–6.

110 See, eg, Tasmania Law Reform Institute, *Jurors, Social Media and the Right of an Accused to a Fair Trial* (Final Report No 30, January 2020) xv; Jacqueline Horan, 'Jurors as Detectives of Truth and "Don't Search" Instructions in Sexual Assault Trials' in Greg Byrne and Jacueline Horan (eds), *Sexual Assault Trials: Challenges and Innovations* (LexisNexis, 2025) 146, 149–50.

111 Fredric M Wolf, 'Lessons to Be Learned from Evidence-Based Medicine: Practice and Promise of Evidence-Based Medicine and Evidence-Based Education' (2000) 22(3) *Medical Teacher* 251, 253. See also Cherney and Head (n 24) 512.

112 See, eg, David Isaacs and David Fitzgerald, 'Seven Alternatives to Evidence Based Medicine' (1999) 319(7225) *British Medical Journal* 1618, 1618.

113 Rachlinski (n 1) 902.

114 Wolf (n 111) 252.

115 David L Sackett et al, 'Evidence Based Medicine: What It Is and What It Isn't' (1996) 312(7023) *British Medical Journal* 71, 71.

Integrating knowledge and changing practices in the law would also be particularly challenging.

Judges have areas of expertise: they 'have been recognized within their profession as having the necessary skills and abilities to perform at the highest level'.[116] However, a judge may not have expertise in all areas of the law and 'expertise in a domain is not a single skill but rather a large collection of miniskills'.[117] In determining expertise, it is therefore important to focus on the activity undertaken rather than experience across a field more broadly.[118] Does a judge's expertise in criminal law extend to all aspects of guiding the jury? Skilled intuitive judgment only arises in environments that occur regularly, where there are 'valid cues to the nature of the situation', and there is an opportunity to learn those cues.[119]

Judges may receive a limited form of feedback on the quality of their legal analysis in the development of their career and as a judge (eg, from appellate courts and commentary).[120] However, judges receive very little feedback on the effectiveness of their guidance to jurors from jurors, judges, or experts in communicating with juries.[121] While some judges may develop legal and procedural expertise in conducting criminal jury trials, very few judges have expertise in juror comprehension research. Juror confidentiality means judges do not get feedback directly from jurors in any detailed way. Further, even if a judge is subjectively confident in their intuition about what jurors understand, experts are not good at identifying when their intuitions are or are not reliable.[122] This means that 'reliance on subjective confidence may contribute to overconfidence'.[123] Accordingly, judges may not give sufficient weight to the limitations of their own knowledge.[124]

116 James Shanteau, 'Competence in Experts: The Role of Task Characteristics' (1992) 53(2) *Organizational Behavior and Human Decision Processes* 252, 255.

117 Daniel Kahneman, *Thinking, Fast and Slow* (Penguin Books, 2012) 238.

118 Emma Cunliffe, 'Judging, Fast and Slow: Using Decision-Making Theory to Explore Judicial Fact Determination' (2014) 18 *The International Journal of Evidence and Proof* 139, 159.

119 Daniel Kahneman and Gary Klein, 'Conditions for Intuitive Expertise: A Failure to Disagree' (2009) 64(6) *American Psychologist* 515, 520.

120 Cunliffe (n 118) 172. See also Chris Guthrie, Jeffrey J Rachlinski and Andrew Wistrich, 'Blinking on the Bench: How Judges Decide Cases' (2007) 93(1) *Cornell Law Review* 1 ('Blinking on the Bench').

121 See generally, James R P Ogloff et al, *The Jury Project: Stage 1 — A Survey of Australian and New Zealand Judges* (Australian Institute of Judicial Administration, 2006) 36. See also Jeffrey J Rachlinski and Andrew J Wistrich, 'Judging the Judiciary by the Numbers: Empirical Research on Judges' (2017) 13(1) *Annual Review of Law and Social Science* 203, 223.

122 Kahneman and Klein (n 119) 522–3. See also Guthrie, Rachlinski and Wistrich, 'Blinking on the Bench' (n 120).

123 Kahneman and Klein (n 119) 523. For a study of trial judges using intuition rather than analytical or deliberative decision-making, see Guthrie, Rachlinski and Wistrich, 'Blinking on the Bench' (n 120) 16–18.

124 Chris Guthrie, Jeffrey J Rachlinski and Andrew Wistrich, 'Inside the Judicial Mind' (2001) 86 *Cornell Law Review* 777, 815 ('Inside the Judicial Mind').

The environment judges operate in is also challenging. As discussed in Chapters 2 and 3, jury questions do not provide a complete and reliable source of information about juror comprehension and jurors are not good at determining whether they understand a direction. Accordingly, the cues that judges receive from jurors about their comprehension are often unreliable. This kind of environment is called a 'wicked' environment because the feedback judges receive is minimal and what is received is often misleading.[125] Further, there is little that 'can be done about many aspects of the legal system that contribute to judges' "wicked" learning environments'.[126]

The different skills and expertise that judges are or are not likely to have developed, are relevant to determining what matters judges are best placed to determine on a case-by-case basis and what matters should apply automatically, or presumptively. It is not realistic to expect all judges to become experts in juror comprehension research. Therefore, it is important to assess when judges are best placed to determine what guidance will be of most assistance to the jury in understanding its task. To change their guidance to juries, judges may need to change their practices.

What support do judges need when using jury-centric reforms?

A jury-centric approach will inevitably lead to reforms that will require judges to learn new laws, practices, and procedures and to change their practices in conducting a trial. With policy reform generally, 'defensiveness and negativity are as common as cooperation'.[127] Evidence-based medicine has shown that physicians 'do not like change' and 'physician culture and physician behavior change very slowly'.[128] In a similar vein, the legal profession has been described as 'predominantly reactionary rather than proactive'[129] and change can be notoriously difficult.

A jury-centric reform process may occur over many years as research continues to identify juror comprehension challenges and innovative ideas emerge about guiding juries more effectively. Research shows that uptake of evidence-based policy changes improves if the change arises from 'strategies that provide space for policy-makers and practitioners to search, read, contemplate, exchange ideas and discuss research evidence'.[130] This is a model of reform that

125 Kahneman and Klein (n 119) 520. See also Robin M Hogarth, 'A Challenge for Psychological Research on Decision Making' (2010) 21(4) *Psychological Inquiry* 338, 343.

126 Guthrie, Rachlinski and Wistrich, 'Blinking on the Bench' (n 120) 35.

127 Head, 'Three Lenses of Evidence-Based Policy' (n 25) 9.

128 Michael J Goldberg, 'Lessons Learned in 20 Years of Developing Evidence-Based Medicine' (2012) 32(Suppl 2) *Journal of Pediatric Orthopaedics* S193, S193–4.

129 Jacqueline Horan and Shelley Maine, 'Criminal Jury Trials in 2030: A Law Odyssey' (2014) 41 *Journal of Law and Society* 551, 553.

130 Cherney and Head (n 24) 514. See also Judge Felicity Hampel, 'Legal Culture, Professional Education and Homicide Law Reform' in Kate Fitz-Gibbon and Arie Freiberg (eds), *Homicide Law Reform in Victoria: Retrospect and Prospects* (Federation Press, 2015) 29, 40.

a JAC should undertake, drawing on its membership from within the judiciary and legal profession.

Judicial leadership will also be critical in supporting the change process.[131] Judges will need to understand why changes occur, especially where changes depart significantly from accepted practice and judicial knowledge and experience. Research about jurors indicates that it can be difficult to follow and apply new procedures that contradict one's intuitions or preconceptions.[132] Judges are likely to be the same.[133] This suggests that to be effective, strategies to improve juror comprehension must address judges' views, assumptions, and ideas about their role.

Jury-centric changes may involve additional work for judges to acquire new knowledge and develop new resources, skills, and practices. Four years after the commencement of 'integrated directions' in Victoria (a type of SDM aid), only four (20%) Victorian judges surveyed reported having given integrated directions.[134] Two of the judges said that '"inexperience with the format and fear of departure from the charge book discourages use" and that preparation "takes time" and may be "complex"'.[135] These explanations point to the need for judicial support for changes to be made.

To support jurors, Marder asks what tools jurors need to perform their tasks more effectively.[136] Supporting judges through change processes and providing them with the best information to perform their task requires similar consideration. When applying a 'judge-centric' perspective, we should ask what tools and assistance judges need to perform their task of guiding the jury more effectively. Some changes also depend upon practitioners developing new skills and practices. For example, judges need the assistance of practitioners to define the issues in dispute and summarise prosecution and defence cases when using decision-making aids. Therefore, sometimes supporting judges will require supporting practitioners through change processes.

131 See, eg, Justice Chris Maxwell and Greg Byrne, 'Making Trials Work for Juries: Pathways to Simplification' [2020] (11) *Criminal Law Review* 1034, 1056.

132 Bradley Saxton, 'How Well Do Jurors Understand Jury Instructions? A Field Test Using Real Juries and Real Trials in Wyoming' (1998) 33 *Land and Water Law Review* 59, 95.

133 See, eg, Guthrie, Rachlinski and Wistrich, 'Inside the Judicial Mind' (n 124) 816–18. See also, Gary Edmond and Kirsty A Martire, 'Just Cognition: Scientific Research on Bias and Some Implications for Legal Procedure and Decision-Making' (2019) 82(4) *Modern Law Review* 633, 644–9; Australian Law Reform Commission, *Without Fear or Favour: Judicial Impartiality and the Law on Bias* (Report 138, December 2021) ch 4.

134 Judicial College of Victoria, *Jury Directions Act 2015 Evaluation: Judicial Survey Results*, discussed in Greg Byrne and Justice Chris Maxwell, 'Putting Jurors First: Legislative Simplification of Jury Directions' (2019) 43(3) *Criminal Law Journal* 180, 199.

135 Judicial College of Victoria, *Jury Directions Act 2015 Evaluation: Judicial Survey Results*, discussed in Byrne and Maxwell (n 134) 199.

136 Marder, 'Introduction to the Jury at a Crossroad' (n 4) 918.

Evidence-based medicine shows that '[e]vidence alone is insufficient for making good decisions';[137] practitioners must understand the context in which they are operating and tailor their actions to individual situations. It is essential to transform research into useable information for judges.[138] This involves using research from specific juror comprehension studies and combining this with legal knowledge to determine how to improve juror comprehension. This interdisciplinary information must then be transformed into practical information that judges can readily understand and use in a trial setting.

In many jurisdictions, bench books provide some of this final form of information that assists judges in conducting a trial and guiding the jury. Bench books can reduce the burden on judges by avoiding the need for each judge to be an expert on each legal issue. Bench books promote efficiency, consistency, and should improve judicial guidance. However, in their current form, these benefits primarily arise in existing areas of judicial expertise — the law and legal accuracy. Bench books, or something like them, could be used to provide judges with this final form of information about juror comprehension and why new practices are necessary. This would obviate the need for judges to be experts in juror comprehension research, while understanding the rationale for changes, and enable them to guide juries using evidence-informed resources.

Conclusion

A jury-centric approach therefore provides a comprehensive organising framework for assessing evidence-informed proposals to improve juror comprehension. This method involves five steps that ask the following questions:

(1) Is there an evidence-informed basis for concluding that a proposal will improve juror comprehension of the issues that they must determine?
(2) Does the proposal conflict with another fair trial principle or human right, and if so, is it unjustifiable or inappropriate to proceed with the proposal?
(3) Are there any other policy factors to consider, and if so, do they outweigh the benefits of introducing the proposal?
(4) If a proposal involves an area of judicial expertise, is a judge best placed to tailor a solution to an individual case?
(5) Do judges need resources or training (a judge-centric perspective) to implement the new law, practice, or procedure?

As discussed in the introduction to this chapter, Rachlinksi identified conflicting goals and the way in which people reason about law reform as impediments

137 Wolf (n 111) 254. See also Goldberg (n 124) S193; David Isaacs, 'Evidence-Based Medicine' (2014) 50 *Journal of Paediatrics and Child Health* 579, 579.

138 See, eg, Chief Justice Susan Kiefel, 'The Academy and the Courts: What Do They Mean to Each Other Today?' (Speech, Australian Academy of Law Patron's Address, 31 October 2019).

to evidence-informed law reform. A jury-centric approach aims to address these two impediments to evidence-based reforms that address juror comprehension problems.

In relation to the first impediment, it is not possible to remove all conflicting goals in the law. However, a jury-centric approach has a clear goal, to improve juror comprehension because having a competent jury — one that understands its task and therefore decides the issues on their legal and factual merits — is a necessary condition of a fair trial. This goal explains why juror comprehension is important within the terms of fundamental features of the law.

In relation to the second impediment, a jury-centric approach provides a framework for reasoning differently about law reform to address juror comprehension problems. A JAC can conduct a jury-centric reform process by integrating social science research and judicial and legal expertise in a manner that accepts and promotes the essential values of the justice system, such as ensuring a fair trial.

Juror comprehension research is necessary when applying a jury-centric approach. However, it is not sufficient of its own. Understanding when it is reasonable to draw inferences from research and when judicial expertise is critical to reforms provides an approach that values and incorporates evidence but is not limited or dominated by evidence. Just as the solution to juror comprehension is not to make every juror an expert in the law, the solution is not to make every judge an expert in juror comprehension research. Instead, a jury-centric approach recognises judicial expertise, the limits of judicial expertise, and uses a judge-centric approach to ask what tools judges need to perform their task of guiding the jury more effectively.

While the goal is that all jurors understand their task, it is not practical to test whether this goal has been achieved in every case. This means that it is necessary to assess whether there is a real possibility that a jury might not understand their task. This is not a bright line test as proposals generally must be assessed based on the proposal itself and whether the proposal contributes overall to a fair trial. Further, there are often diverse ways of improving juror comprehension and competing policy factors can make it difficult to determine the best reform to introduce. A jury-centric approach provides a framework for considering matters that should be considered in any good reform process. It also expands the matters considered in reform processes to include judicial expertise and incorporates a judge-centric approach to support changes in judicial practice. A jury-centric approach also highlights the critical nature of the goal that jurors understand their task. This approach should make achieving juror comprehension goals much more likely.

A jury-centric approach is potentially relevant to all criminal laws, practices, and procedures that affect whether jurors understand their task. It is not possible to discuss every way in which a jury-centric approach may improve criminal trials in each jurisdiction. Therefore, the next three chapters contain case studies to evaluate whether a jury-centric approach provides a robust, effective, and transparent reform process by examining distinct kinds of potential reforms.

7 Case study one — Structured decision-making aids

Introduction

This chapter provides the first of three case studies examining how a jury-centric approach applies to proposals to improve juror comprehension. Judicial guidance is critical to jurors understanding their task. Therefore, this case study focuses on proposals to improve the structure and content of the judge's guidance.

As discussed in Chapter 2, the traditional approach to summing up the case involves the trial judge providing the jury with blocks of information, where each block has a separate purpose or focus. For example, there may be blocks of general directions, substantive directions, and evidentiary directions, a summary of the evidence, and a summary of the parties' closing addresses.[1] This traditional style of summing up leaves the jury with the challenging task of understanding the law, working out how to apply the law to the facts, and connecting directions with different blocks of information.

Lord Justice Moses described this traditional style of summing up as requiring the jury to follow a path that is 'as obscure, as tortuous and as arduous as could possibly be devised'.[2] Over the last two decades, judges have increasingly provided jurors with SDM aids. SDM aids 'highlight important decision points along a path to an outcome'.[3] In a criminal trial, there are usually several decisions that a jury must make to reach a verdict (eg, did the accused kill the deceased, did the accused intend to kill the deceased, was the accused acting in self-defence). Answering these questions leads the jury to an outcome, namely whether the accused is guilty or not guilty of the offence charged. Judges may structure all their guidance, including references to the evidence and the way in which the parties put their case, around the decision points in

1 Queensland Law Reform Commission, *A Review of Jury Directions* (Report No 66, September 2009) 273 [9.88] (QLRC); Lord Justice Moses, 'Summing Down the Summing-Up' (Speech, Annual Law Reform Lecture, Inner Temple, 23 November 2010) 3.

2 Moses (n 1) 2.

3 Tamsin Ede and Jane Goodman-Delahunty, 'Question Trails in Trials: Structured versus Unstructured Juror Decision-Making' (2013) 37 *Criminal Law Journal* 114, 119.

DOI: 10.4324/9781003477129-7

an SDM aid. This type of guidance departs significantly from the traditional summing up.

The different types of SDM aids and their potential to change the judge's guidance provide an interesting case study to illustrate and assess a jury-centric approach. This case study on guiding the jury examines three SDM aid reform proposals, namely that:

- judges should give integrated directions in all jury trials
- judges should provide a written outline of the issues to the jury when the trial commences, and
- the accused should be required to disclose their defence to the jury when the trial commences.

The proposals draw from existing practices and proposals for change. However, no jurisdiction has introduced all the proposals discussed in this chapter. The second and third proposals each build on the previous proposal. The first proposal will be analysed through all five steps of a jury-centric approach. The second and third proposals will be analysed through only those steps that raise significant additional issues. This analysis is based on existing research — it is not necessary to conduct additional research to examine how a jury-centric approach works in relation to these proposals. However, before discussing these proposals, it is necessary to define important terms used in discussing SDM aids.

Definitions and types of structured decision-making aids

SDM aids provide juries with a pathway to a verdict by identifying each decision point that jurors must determine to reach a verdict. The decision points are based on the elements of the offence charged and any defences. Each decision point is framed as a question with a binary — 'yes' or 'no' — answer. As discussed in Table 7.1, while the questions provide the backbone of all SDM aids, SDM aids vary in two principal ways:

- how the questions are framed — the questions may use legal language, or the judges may embed the law into factual questions, and
- whether information is included with the questions — the questions may or may not be used to provide a framework for general and evidentiary directions, and other information (eg, about how each party puts their case) to the jury.

These two differences have resulted in three different types of SDM aids that I describe as checklists, factual questions, and integrated directions. Jurisdictions generally describe SDM aids by reference to the *process* of using decision points. England and Wales call their decision aid a 'route to verdict'.[4] New Zealand calls their decision aid a 'question trail'.[5] Canada calls their decision aid 'step-directions'.[6] Victoria's 'integrated directions' is the only decision aid described in terms of its content.[7] This section, and Table 7.1, explains differences between these SDM aids.

Table 7.1 Types of SDM aids

Types of SDM aids	*How does the SDM aid work?*
Checklist	The judge turns the elements of the offence and any defence into questions for the jury's consideration. The questions are not adapted, or are only adapted in a minor way, to the facts of the case (eg, name of the accused). The questions are likely to be abstract in nature,[8] referring to the legal issue that must be determined. For example, where two accused are jointly charged with cultivating cannabis, the checklist questions would include: • Did the accused (Green) make an agreement with other people to pursue a joint criminal enterprise (to cultivate cannabis)? • Was the offence (of cultivation) within the scope of the agreement?[9]

(*Continued*)

4 *R v Atta-Dankwa* [2018] 2 Cr App R 16 ('*Atta-Dankwa*'). In Scotland, the 'route to verdict' has a different meaning, indicating that the 'terms of a trial judge's charge to the jury should be such as to enable the informed observer, who has heard the proceedings at the trial, to understand the reasons for the verdict. In other words, there must be a discernible route to the verdict': *CH v Her Majesty's Advocate* [2016] HCJAC 4, [13].

5 See, eg, *R v Dixon* (2007) 23 CRNZ 911; *Rawle v The Queen* [2019] NZCA 249 ('*Rawle*').

6 See, eg, Justice David Watt, *Helping Jurors Understand* (Thomson Carswell, 2007) 93; Marie Comiskey, 'The Jury in Canada: Testing the Comprehensibility of Styles of Jury Instructions and the Effectiveness of Aids' in Sanja Kutnjak Ivković et al (eds), *Juries, Lay Judges, and Mixed Courts: A Global Perspective* (Cambridge University Press, 2021) 174, 179.

7 *Jury Directions Act 2015* (Vic) s 67(3).

8 See, eg, Benjamin Spivak et al, 'The Impact of Fact-Based Instructions on Juror Application of the Law: Results from a Trans-Tasman Field Study' (2020) 101(1) *Social Science Quarterly* 346, 349.

9 These questions are based on the checklist used in Victoria: Judicial College of Victoria, *Criminal Charge Book* <https://resources.judicialcollege.vic.edu.au/article/1053858> [5.3.2]. This does not include every question that would be in the checklist.

Table 7.1 (Continued)

Types of SDM aids	*How does the SDM aid work?*
Factual questions[10]	In a factual question (or 'fact-based' question[11]), the judge embeds the law into the questions to be determined by the jury. Factual questions may start as questions in a checklist that the judge tailors to the particular facts and the issues in the trial. For example, the prosecution will have proved that Green participated in a joint criminal enterprise to cultivate cannabis if the answer to the following questions is 'yes': • Did Green rent the warehouse to Brown? • Did Green know that Brown was using the warehouse to cultivate cannabis?[12] There is no bright line that indicates the extent to which the question must include facts to call it a 'factual question' rather than a question in a checklist. Information (eg, references to evidence or how the parties put their case) may or may not be added to factual questions.
Integrated directions	The term 'integrated directions' describes the combination of factual questions with case information (eg, evidence, evidentiary directions, and how the parties put their case).[13] For example, the factual question, did Green rent the warehouse to Brown, becomes an integrated direction with the addition of the following information: • Red says that Brown paid Green $5000 per month in cash at the warehouse (evidence) • Red's evidence may be unreliable because she says she was a party to the cultivation but received immunity for giving evidence (evidentiary direction), and • the prosecution says surveillance photographs corroborate Red's evidence; the defence says Red cannot be believed because she has a motive to lie (eg, to avoid prison) (how the parties put their case).

10 The term 'factual question' is used in the *Jury Directions Act 2015* (Vic) s 67(2).
11 Jonathan Clough et al, *The Jury Project 10 Years On — Practices of Australian and New Zealand Judges* (Australian Institute of Judicial Administration, April 2019) 50 ('*The Jury Project 10 Years On*').
12 This example draws on question trail guides used in New Zealand, for 'group liability offences': Courts of New Zealand, *A Guide to the Question Trails* <www.courtsofnz.govt.nz/for-lawyers/question-trails/>.
13 *Jury Directions Act 2015* (Vic) s 67(3). The term 'integrated directions' originated from: QLRC, *A Review of Jury Directions* (n 1) 273 [9.88].

Descriptions of SDM aids can be confusing because the practices between jurisdictions and individual judges in those jurisdictions may vary. For example, in England and Wales, the 'route to verdict' may not embed the law into factual questions and therefore may be like a checklist.[14] A route to verdict may be in the form of questions or a flowchart.[15] However, a judge may give jurors 'narrative directions', which summarise the law and key issues, to accompany the route to verdict.[16] Combined, the two documents share some of the features of integrated directions. However, narrative directions may not include evidentiary directions and therefore might not be described as integrated directions. The New Zealand term 'question trail' 'suggests that it is only concerned with directing juries by means of a series of questions'.[17] However, a question trail might, but need not, include references to the evidence, evidentiary directions, and a summary of how the parties put their case.[18]

The differences in the description and content of these SDM aids is important when comparing SDM aids used in each jurisdiction and research about SDM aids. For example, one study said it examined a 'question trail'.[19] However, based on these definitions, the questions in the study would be described as a checklist because the law was not embedded into factual questions.[20] This does not affect the validity of the methodology used in the research but is important in understanding what kind of SDM aid was being assessed when interpreting the results of the study.

The lack of clear definitions and consistent use of labels describing SDM aids presents challenges when comparing SDM aids across jurisdictions. Wherever possible, I will use the terms checklist, factual questions, and integrated directions as used in Table 7.1.

14 Judicial College, *The Crown Court Compendium — Part I: Jury and Trial Management and Summing Up* (July 2024) <www.judiciary.uk/wp-content/uploads/2024/07/Crown-Court-Compendium-Part-I-July-2024-1.pdf> 23–4 ('*Crown Court Compendium*').

15 David Ormerod and Cheryl Thomas, 'Routes to Verdict — What We Know and What We Need to Know' [2021] (8) *Criminal Law Review* 615, 616.

16 See, eg, David Ormerod and Richard Taylor, 'Agreement and Disagreement in Murder and Manslaughter Verdicts' [2022] (3) *Criminal Law Review* 185, 206.

17 Justice R A Hulme, 'Sharpening Up Your Summing Up' (Speech, District Court Annual Conference, 29 March 2016) 12.

18 See, eg, Elisabeth McDonald, *Rape Myths as Barriers to Fair Trial Process: Comparing Adult Rape Trials with Those of the Aotearoa Sexual Violence Court Pilot* (Canterbury University Press, 2020) 402–4.

19 Ede and Goodman-Delahunty (n 3) 124.

20 Ede and Goodman-Delahunty (n 3) 135. For example, the first question was 'Are you sure that the death of Angus McNamara was the result of acts by Lynette McNamara?'.

Proposal one: Giving integrated directions to improve juror comprehension

The first proposal is that judges should give integrated directions in all jury trials. When applying a jury-centric approach, the first step involves assessing whether the evidence indicates that a proposal will improve juror comprehension.

Evidence supporting giving integrated directions in all jury trials

Before discussing specific research on the use of integrated directions, research about what does or does not help to improve juror comprehension of more traditional jury directions creates a basis for hypothesising, or drawing reasonable inferences, that integrated directions should improve juror comprehension.

Hypothesising that integrated directions should improve juror comprehension

The structure used in SDM aids presents information in a logical structure and that may make it easier for jurors to understand. Amiram Elwork, Bruce Sales, and James Alfini identified three key methods for creating a logical structure to present information, all of which are used in integrated directions.[21] These structures are:

- hierarchical — where 'higher level concepts are broken down into their lower-level components and then integrated'[22] (eg, where an offence is broken down into its elements and then each element is turned into one or more factual questions)
- associational — where topics 'connected to one another by a common concept are grouped together'[23] (eg, identifying key evidence in relation to each factual question), and
- algorithmic — where 'instructions are presented in a way that is consistent with the order in which they are to be executed'[24] (eg, the decision points in an SDM aid that need to be answered to reach a verdict).

While the development of factual questions involves a hierarchical approach, the logical sequence of questions presented to a jury in an SDM aid prioritises an algorithmic organisation of materials.[25] Integrated directions then use

21 Amiram Elwork, Bruce D Sales and James J Alfini, *Making Jury Instructions Understandable* (Michie Company, 1982) 149.

22 Elwork, Sales and Alfini, *Making Jury Instructions Understandable* (n 21) 151.

23 Elwork, Sales and Alfini, *Making Jury Instructions Understandable* (n 21) 150.

24 Spivak et al (n 8) 348. See also Elwork, Sales and Alfini, *Making Jury Instructions Understandable* (n 21) 151–2.

25 Spivak et al (n 8) 348. See also Benjamin Spivak, James R P Ogloff and Jonathan Clough, 'Asking the Right Questions: Examining the Efficacy of Question Trails as a Method of Improving

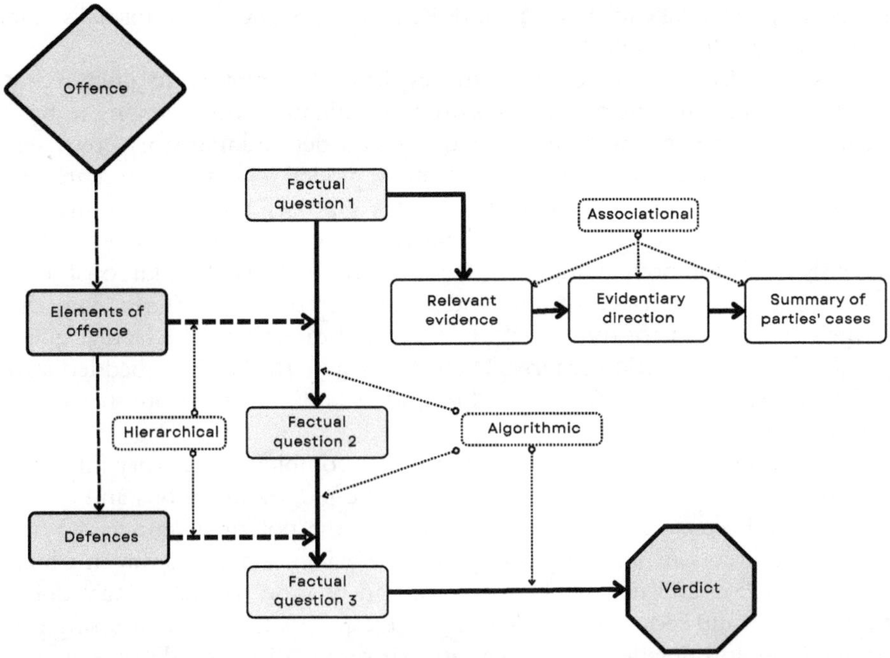

Figure 7.1 The logical structure of integrated directions[26]

an associational structure for information (eg, references to relevant evidence and evidentiary directions about that evidence) that is relevant to each factual question, as shown in Figure 7.1.

The logical structure of integrated directions may also assist jurors to engage in active decision-making, using an evidence-driven rather than a verdict-driven approach to their deliberations. Verdict-driven juries vote early and then 'structure the discussion around available verdict options, seeking to identify the option that is most acceptable to jurors'.[27] As a result, the evaluation of evidence may be disjointed and fragmented.[28] By contrast, integrated directions 'focus and synchronize discussion of the issues so that *all* the jurors are discussing and deciding the *same* issues at the *same* time'.[29] Evidence-driven

Lay Comprehension and Application of Legal Concepts' (2019) 26(3) *Psychiatry, Psychology and Law* 441, 443.

26 Figure 7.2 shows a full set of integrated directions in relation to factual question one. A judge would give associational information for each factual question that is in issue.

27 Brian H Bornstein and Edie Greene, 'Jury Decision Making: Implications for and from Psychology' (2011) 20 *Current Directions in Psychological Science* 63, 65.

28 Reid Hastie, Steven D Penrod and Nancy Pennington, *Inside the Jury* (Lawbook Exchange, 2002) 164.

29 Watt (n 6) 99 (emphasis in original).

juries tend not to take many votes, and the vote at the end acts to formalise the result of their discussion.[30]

Evidence-driven juries evaluate the evidence 'attempting to discern the "truth" from conflicting facts'.[31] This process facilitates jurors bringing to bear their different perspectives on the evidence and determining story construction.[32] As discussed in Chapter 3, the 'story model' is generally accepted as providing the best explanation for how jurors approach their decision-making task.[33] The second stage of the story model of juror decision-making involves learning and comprehending the decision criteria.[34] With traditional jury directions, jurors must learn and understand the decision criteria from the judge's explanations of the law. With integrated directions, the factual questions contain the decision criteria. Therefore, where the law is embedded into factual questions, jurors do not need to understand the law before they apply it to the facts.[35]

The third stage of the story model involves combining the story information to the classifications and definitions in the judge's directions and determining the best match between the story and the potential verdicts.[36] With integrated directions, the judge integrates the evidence and the way in which the prosecution and defence put their case in relation to each factual question. This should reduce the complexity of the juror's task when assessing the prosecution and defence stories (eg, are the prosecution and defence stories 'coherent', that is, consistent, plausible, and complete).

Integrated directions are also consistent with aspects of educational theory. Jurors face a substantial learning task that they must undertake in constrained circumstances. SDM aids provide the scaffolding for jurors' decision-making task. Direct Instruction principles provide that:

- learners should be provided with 'an overview or outline when engaging with unfamiliar material for the first time'

30 See, eg, Bornstein and Greene (n 27); Penny Darbyshire, Andy Maughan and Angus Stewart, 'What Can the English Legal System Learn from Jury Research Published up to 2001?' (Kingston Law School, 2001) <www.sixthformlaw.info/06_misc/pdf_files/penny_darbyshire.pdf> 30.

31 Bornstein and Greene (n 27) 65.

32 See, eg, Darbyshire, Maughan and Stewart (n 30) 30; Bornstein and Greene (n 27) 65.

33 See, eg, Darbyshire, Maughan and Stewart (n 30) 22; Lora M Levett et al, 'The Psychology of Jury and Juror Decision Making' in Neil Brewer and Kipling D Williams (eds), *Psychology and Law: An Empirical Perspective* (Guilford Press, 2005) 365, 373–5.

34 Nancy Pennington and Reid Hastie, 'Evidence Evaluation in Complex Decision Making' (1986) 51 *Journal of Personality and Social Psychology* 242, 253.

35 Jonathan Clough et al, 'The Judge as Cartographer and Guide: The Role of Fact-Based Directions in Improving Juror Comprehension' (2018) 42(5) *Criminal Law Journal* 278, 284 ('The Judge as Cartographer').

36 Pennington and Hastie (n 34) 253.

- decision-making tasks should be broken into smaller steps to help reduce cognitive overload, and
- instructions should be both in writing and given orally.[37]

Jurors will have different learning styles. Some jurors may learn best through listening and watching the judge but for others reading may be a better method of learning. Providing important information in writing (as well as orally) enables jurors to follow written information when the judge directs them, and jurors can read the written document in the jury room.[38] This should help some jurors with their learning task.

Based on this research, there are good reasons for hypothesising that integrated directions should help jurors with their task.

The evidentiary basis for using integrated directions to improve juror comprehension

Until recently, research on SDM aids suggested that they did not, or only marginally, improved juror comprehension and application of the law.[39] Two issues arising from this research concern what is being tested and how it is tested.

First, as just discussed, different descriptions are used for SDM aids. For example, one study found that the 'question trail' tested 'did not reduce cognitive load or improve juror comprehension'.[40] The 'question trail' contained three factual questions, but the fourth (and final) question was not a factual question. The fourth question was a checklist-style question that encompassed all elements of the offence and asked whether the prosecution had proved that the accused committed the offence.[41] This question was redundant as it should have simply reflected the outcome of previous answers rather than being a separate question about their verdict.

Second, SDM aids (except perhaps checklists) need to be evaluated differently from traditional jury directions. Research on traditional directions has

37 Max Rogers, 'Laypeople as Learners: Applying Educational Principles to Improve Juror Comprehension Instructions' (2021) 115 *Northwestern University Law Review* 1185, 1215–18.

38 Nancy Marder, *The Power of the Jury: Transforming Citizens into Jurors* (Cambridge University Press, 2022) 127–9.

39 See, eg, Carolyn Semmler and Neil Brewer, 'Using a Flow-Chart to Improve Comprehension of Jury Instructions' (2002) 9 *Psychiatry, Psychology and Law* 262; Ede and Goodman-Delahunty (n 3) 134 (while noting that scores improved on 'complex comprehension'); Catriona McKay, Mark Nolan and Michael Smithson, 'Effectiveness of Question Trails as Jury Decision Aids: The Jury's Still Out' (2014) 21(4) *Psychiatry, Psychology and Law* 492, 494–5, 505; Clough et al, 'The Judge as Cartographer' (n 35) 282–4.

40 Ryan Essex and Jane Goodman-Delahunty, 'Judicial Directions and the Criminal Standard of Proof: Improving Juror Comprehension' (2014) 24 *Journal of Judicial Administration* 75, 93.

41 Essex and Goodman-Delahunty (n 40) 93.

primarily focused on improving juror comprehension of the law because jurors need to understand the law to apply it correctly. However, where the law is embedded into factual questions, jurors do not need to understand the law to apply it. The important question is whether jurors correctly apply the law.[42] Further, many studies assess individual juror comprehension. One of the main purposes of SDM aids is to assist jurors to structure their deliberations. Therefore, it is important to evaluate whether SDM aids assist deliberations.

The most significant study on SDM aids involved simulated jury trials conducted in Victoria and a field study of trials in Victoria and New Zealand (the 'Trans-Tasman' study). The simulated jury trials involved 1007 people, selected from those called for jury duty. In simulated jury trials, the researchers compared the use of standard directions (not revised), plain language directions, plain language directions combined with a checklist, and 'fact-based directions'.[43] The 'fact-based directions' involved factual questions that were explained by reference to 'concrete examples' from the case wherever possible.[44] This was consistent with the use of question trails in New Zealand. It therefore broadly falls under the description of integrated directions. At that time, standard judicial practice in Victoria was to use checklists.[45]

The Trans-Tasman study found in simulated jury trials that adding a checklist to plain language directions did not improve comprehension and application of jury directions. The study concluded that this is consistent with the '"split-attention" effect; that is, the ability to perform a task decreases where information is presented in different forms that are not integrated'.[46] This suggests that to be helpful, decision points need to be integrated with other judicial guidance. For example, by providing oral directions in the same sequence as the written questions and referring to the list of questions during the oral directions.[47] Research in Canada similarly found that 'there is a significant advantage to integrating legal concepts into factual questions and presenting them in a logical manner to jurors'.[48]

The Trans-Tasman simulated jury trials study involved testing following deliberation. Mock jurors who received fact-based directions had significantly higher scores for correctly applying directions.[49] Further, as shown in Figure 7.2, those who received the fact-based directions 'performed nearly

42 Clough et al, 'The Judge as Cartographer' (n 35) 284.
43 Clough et al, 'The Judge as Cartographer' (n 35) 285.
44 Clough et al, 'The Judge as Cartographer' (n 35) 286.
45 Clough et al, 'The Judge as Cartographer' (n 35) 286.
46 Clough et al, 'The Judge as Cartographer' (n 35) 289. See also, John Sweller, Jeroen J G van Merriënboer and Fred Paas, 'Cognitive Architecture and Instructional Design: 20 Years Later' (2019) 31(2) *Educational Psychology Review* 261, 268.
47 Clough et al, 'The Judge as Cartographer' (n 35) 289.
48 Comiskey (n 6) 187–8.
49 Clough et al, 'The Judge as Cartographer' (n 35) 292.

equally well regardless of their comprehension prior to trial'.[50] This was in marked contrast to the other conditions where poor pre-trial comprehension strongly correlated with poor post-trial deliberation.[51] This suggests that this kind of SDM aid can significantly improve jurors' ability to apply the judge's directions and therefore determine the case in accordance with the law.[52]

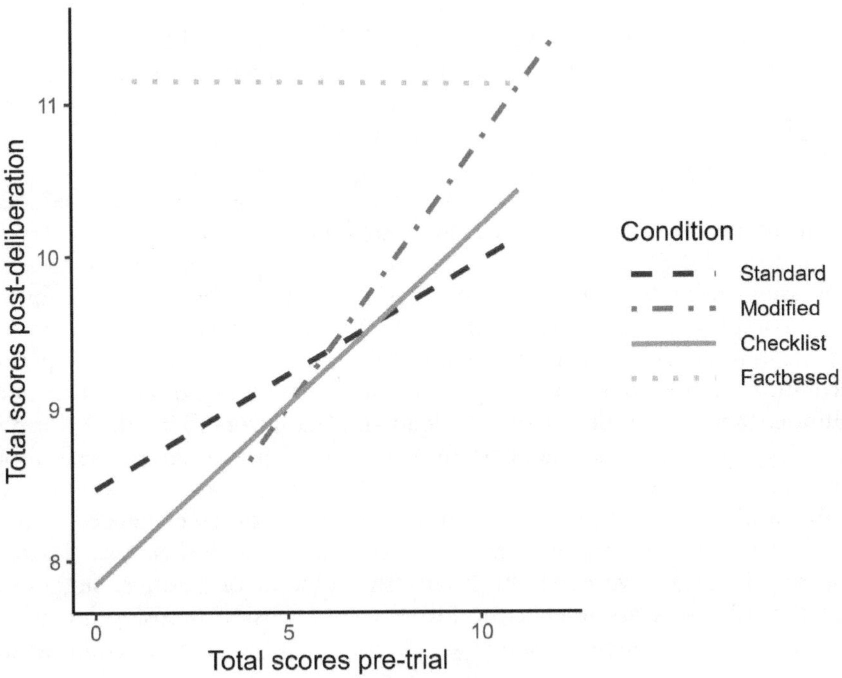

Figure 7.2 Relationship between pre-trial and post-deliberation multiple-choice scores. Lines of best fit based on ordinary least squares regression[53]

50 Clough et al, 'The Judge as Cartographer' (n 35) 293.
51 Clough et al, 'The Judge as Cartographer' (n 35) 293.
52 See also Comiskey (n 6) 185–6. Comiskey's study involving 571 jury-eligible citizens found that step-directions produced better comprehension scores than traditional jury directions.
53 Clough et al, 'The Judge as Cartographer' (n 35) 293. This plot has been reproduced with the authors' permission and I gratefully acknowledge the assistance of one of the authors, Benjamin Spivak, in enabling this plot to be reproduced. This plot is from an article first published by Thomson Reuters in the *Criminal Law Journal* and should be cited as Jonathan Clough et al, 'The Judge as Cartographer and Guide: The Role of Fact-Based Directions in Improving Juror Comprehension' (2018) 42(5) *Criminal Law Journal* 278. For all subscription inquiries please phone, from Australia: 1300 304 195, from Overseas: +61 2 8587 7980 or online at <www.thomsonreuters.com.au/en-au/contact.html>. The official PDF version of this article can also be purchased separately from Thomson Reuters.

The Trans-Tasman study also included a field study involving 463 jurors from 86 trials conducted in Victoria and New Zealand. This part of the study compared New Zealand's question trails with Victoria's checklist approach. New Zealand jurors' application of the law was 18.5% better than Victorian jurors.[54] New Zealand's question trail also assisted jurors to structure their deliberations more efficiently. For example, the question trail:

- provided a clear starting point for deliberations
- provided an 'ongoing framework' for deliberations in 37 of the 43 trials
- helped to order the discussion of evidence and focus on the facts in issue, and
- helped to resolve 'disagreements during deliberations'.[55]

As discussed in Chapter 3, jurors' commonsense justice or preconceived ideas about the law can limit their understanding of directions about the law. Trying to understand the law requires jurors to engage in more 'high level or effortful processing', using 'systematic or central' processing of information.[56] Informational complexity is an important factor that may affect whether a person will engage in high-level effortful reasoning.[57] Reducing informational complexity through fact-based questions which minimise the amount of law jurors need to understand, may reduce cognitive load and lead jurors to invoke a 'form of analytical reasoning that may help override jurors' preconceived ideas about the law'.[58]

Accordingly, in addition to hypothesising from other evidence, there is good evidence that integrated directions assist jurors with their task. To date, research findings have generally been either neutral or positive, suggesting that the risk of adversely effecting juror comprehension by using integrated directions is low. Nonetheless, further research on integrated directions would be helpful: to understand how best to use them in simple and complex cases, for diverse types of substantive jury directions; to assess whether they improve understanding of evidentiary directions through an associational relationship with the relevant evidence; and to determine how they should engage with jurors' commonsense ideas of the law.[59]

As discussed in Chapter 5, a body such as a Juries Advisory Council may draw reasonable inferences from research about how a reform is likely to

54 Clough et al, 'The Judge as Cartographer' (n 35) 295.

55 Clough et al, 'The Judge as Cartographer' (n 35) 295–6.

56 Chantelle M Baguley, Blake M McKimmie and Barbara M Masser, 'Deconstructing the Simplification of Jury Instructions: How Simplifying the Features of Complexity Affects Jurors' Application of Instructions' (2017) 41(3) *Law and Human Behavior* 284, 285.

57 Baguley, McKimmie and Masser (n 56) 285.

58 Ede and Goodman-Delahunty (n 3) 134. However, one study suggests that jurors may continue to use commonsense ideas about the law to construct stories when using question trails and therefore question trails may not reduce cognitive load (at least for some offences): McKay, Nolan and Smithson (n 39) 505–7.

59 See, eg, Spivak et al (n 8) 359; Ormerod and Thomas (n 15) 615; McKay, Nolan and Smithson (n 39) 507–8.

work in practice in its jurisdiction. It is not necessary for research to prove conclusively, in all circumstances, that a proposed reform will improve juror comprehension before reform is recommended. It is also possible to pilot reforms to gather evidence where the evidence is insufficient. For example, the New Zealand Law Commission encouraged the use of question trails after observing their use in two of 41 trials examined.[60] England and Wales relied on two limited studies to support the use of a route to verdict. The first study concerned a written summary of directions that did not involve any logical sequence of questions, but improved juror comprehension of self-defence directions.[61] The second study indicated that jurors perceived written directions were helpful, but did not test whether juror comprehension improved.[62]

Another reasonable inference may be drawn from judicial experience: determining the issues in a trial is a matter that falls within an area of judicial expertise about the law and legal practice. Judges in New Zealand have said that developing question trails helps to focus counsel on the real issues in dispute at an earlier stage in the trial. As a result, 'the trial generally becomes confined to the matters in issue in the question trail'.[63] Focusing clearly and early in a trial on the issues in dispute should help juror comprehension. It should result in jurors having to consider fewer issues and bring the relevant issues into sharper focus at an earlier time.

Research from the Trans-Tasman study now provides a substantial contribution to the evidence-base concerning the use of SDM aids. While the study has some limitations and does not assess all scenarios,[64] it provides a reasonable basis for concluding that integrated directions improve the ability of jurors to perform their task.

Applying fair trial principles to the use of integrated directions in all jury trials

The second step in a jury-centric approach asks whether a proposal conflicts with any other fair trial principle or human rights. Four potential issues to consider are whether:

(1) integrated directions limit the jury's supremacy for determining facts
(2) integrated directions limit the jury's ability to agree on a verdict of acquittal

60 New Zealand Law Commission, *Juries in Criminal Trials* (Report No 69, February 2001) 121 [317] (NZLC).
61 Cheryl Thomas, *Are Juries Fair?* (Ministry of Justice, 2010) 38–9. See also Lily Trimboli, 'Juror Understanding of Judicial Instructions in Criminal Trials' (2008) 119 *Contemporary Issues in Criminal Justice* 1, 8; McKay, Nolan and, Smithson (n 39) 493–4.
62 Cheryl Thomas, 'Avoiding the Perfect Storm of Juror Contempt' [2013] (6) *Criminal Law Review* 483, 497–8.
63 *New Zealand Bench Book*, quoted in Hulme (n 17) 15.
64 See, eg, Ormerod and Thomas (n 15) 616.

(3) integrated directions limit the jury's ability to acquit despite the evidence proving guilt, and
(4) juries should be required to answer specific factual questions in addition to giving a verdict.

Do integrated directions limit the jury's supremacy for determining facts?

To take advantage of the logical structure of an SDM aid, a judge may direct the jury about the order in which they must consider offences (including alternative offences), elements of offences, defences, and matters in issue.[65] This can help jurors because research suggests that jurors want more help with their deliberations[66] and, for example, find alternative verdicts confusing.[67] The High Court of Australia has said that a judge may inform the jury about the order in which their verdicts will be taken, and may suggest — but must not direct — the jury about how to organise their deliberations.[68] This limitation is said to flow from the supremacy of the jury in determining facts[69] and means that a judge must not, for example, direct the jury to consider the most serious offence before considering a lesser alternative offence. If the judge does suggest how the jury should organise its deliberations, the judge must also inform the jury that they are 'free to organise their individual processes of reasoning, or their discussions as a group, in whatever manner appears to them to be convenient'.[70]

Integrated directions usually provide a decision-making pathway from the most serious offence to a lesser alternative offence (eg, if the prosecution has not proved the fault element for murder, the jury then considers manslaughter). The High Court has not considered whether directing a jury to follow the pathway in integrated directions involves directing the jury to use 'a sequence of deliberation' that restricts the jury in the performance of its function.[71] With integrated directions, the decision points used for each offence are even more

65 See, eg, *Jury Directions Act 2015* (Vic) ss 64E and 64F.

66 See, eg, Jane Goodman-Delahunty et al, *Practices, Policies and Procedures that Influence Juror Satisfaction in Australia* (Research and Public Policy Series No 87, July 2007) 139.

67 NZLC, *Juries in Criminal Trials: Part Two* (Preliminary Paper No 37, November 1999) [7.23]–[7.24]. See also D Graham Burnett, *A Trial by Jury* (Alfred A Knopf, 2001) 88–9; Mary Timothy, *Jury Woman: The Story of the Trial of Angela Y Davis — Written by a Member of the Jury* (Emty Press, 1974) 217–18, 239–40.

68 *Stanton v The Queen* (2003) 77 ALJR 1151, 1157 [34]–[35] ('*Stanton*').

69 See, eg, Marder (n 38) 153; Diane E Courselle, 'Struggling with Deliberative Secrecy, Jury Independence, and Jury Reform' (2005) 57 *South Carolina Law Review* 203, 236. The High Court's reasoning is similar to concerns about discussing the evidence with the jury: Paul Marcus, 'Judges Talking to Jurors in Criminal Cases: Why US Judges Do It So Differently from Just about Everyone Else' (2013) 30 *Arizona Journal of International & Comparative Law* 1.

70 *Stanton* (n 68) 1157. See also *Smith v The Queen* [2013] VSCA 112, [40].

71 However, in *Stuart v The Queen* (1974) 134 CLR 426, the High Court commended the trial judge's decision aid which posed questions for the jury and implicitly indicated that follow the questions and that their answers would lead to certain verdict outcomes.

specific than directing a jury to consider the most serious offence first. Consistent with the High Court's decision, the NSWLRC recommended that the judge should direct the jury that 'they are not bound to use it [a question trail] if they prefer to approach their deliberations in some other way'.[72]

If a judge informs a jury that they may follow the integrated directions pathway but are free to organise their discussions as they wish, will a jury follow the pathway anyway? Jury research generally indicates that jurors want more information and assistance, and jurors find their judge's advice to be clear and that 'their' judge was helpful.[73] This suggests jurors will often use the pathway in integrated directions if it is provided even if the judge informs them that they are free to not use it. One simulation study involving 92 participants found that there were differences in the degree to which individuals were willing or motivated to use question trails.[74] However, that study did not involve a deliberation process, and the participants may not have perceived sufficient benefit in using the question trail provided.

The distinction between directions about the order of verdicts and how the jury may organise their deliberations is arbitrary. Directing the jury about the best procedure for considering issues during their deliberations does not suggest what conclusions the jury should reach about factual issues. New Zealand, Canada, and England and Wales have experience using SDM aids.[75] Courts in those jurisdictions have not identified fair trial problems with directing juries to follow SDM aids.

Accordingly, permitting judges to direct the jury on the order that they must consider offences, defences, elements, and issues does not interfere with the independence of the jury. Of course, directing the jury that they must follow the pathway in integrated directions is unenforceable and a jury may still return a verdict even if they choose not to follow the pathway. And because jury deliberations are confidential, it is very unlikely that it would ever be known when a jury did this.

Do integrated directions limit the jury's ability to agree on a verdict of acquittal?

Judge Berman from New South Wales says that there are two defects in question trails.[76] First, there is a possibility that the jury may not agree on one question

72 New South Wales Law Reform Commission, *Jury Directions* (Report No 136, November 2012) 151 [6.168] (NSWLRC). By contrast, Victoria specifically abrogated the High Court's decision: *Jury Directions Act 2015* (Vic) s 64G.

73 See, eg, Jacqueline Horan, *Juries in the 21st Century* (Federation Press, 2012) 74–90; Kate Warner, Julia Davis and Peter Underwood, 'The Jury Experience: Insights from the Tasmanian Jury Study' (2011) 10(3) *Judicial Review* 333, 342–5, 359.

74 McKay, Nolan and, Smithson (n 39) 499, 508.

75 See, eg, Comiskey (n 6) 175–80.

76 Judge Peter Berman, 'Question Trails in Jury Instruction — A Note of Caution' (2012) 24(4) *Judicial Officers Bulletin* 27, 29.

and therefore not consider a subsequent question on which they might all agree. Second, if jurors do continue to deliberate, they may not realise that they must only agree on their verdict and not the reasons for reaching their verdict.[77] New Zealand uses two mechanisms to address these issues.

First, judges may change the order in which the question trail starts, so that the jury considers key issues first.[78] This depends on the judge correctly identifying what is most important to the jury.[79] Where there are several issues in dispute, this may be challenging. Further, because of the logical structure of SDM aids there are limits to the extent to which the order can be changed without losing the benefits of the SDM aid's logical pathway to a verdict.

Second, a judge may direct the jury where necessary (eg, where the jury says it cannot agree) that each juror must answer the questions for themselves.[80] The fact that some jurors reach a verdict of not guilty on question one and others on question two, for example, does not matter. Question trails do not change the law — what matters is whether jurors agree on their verdict rather than why they reached their verdict.[81] The direction given in New Zealand is consistent with a juror's existing obligations in making their own decision about their verdict. Therefore, Judge Berman's concerns can be addressed.

The NSWLRC recommended that a judge should also make clear that 'the question trail is intended for use by each juror individually, as an aide in reaching the verdict that he or she considers justified on the evidence'.[82] This suggests that the question trail is for a juror's individual use and not for a jury to use in structuring its deliberations. This interpretation risks losing one of the key benefits of question trails (and integrated directions) — having all jurors consider the same issues at the same time. Research concerning how jurors understand this direction would be essential to know whether it should be given or refined in some way.

Do integrated directions limit the jury's power to acquit despite the evidence proving guilt?

What if a jury wishes to acquit a person — despite being satisfied that the evidence proves guilt — because they consider that a conviction would be unjust

77 Berman (n 76) 29. See generally, Ormerod and Taylor (n 16) 188.

78 Hulme (n 17) 14.

79 Some jurors have indicated that in the absence of judicial guidance they have found it difficult to know where to start their deliberations: see, eg, Burnett (n 67) 88–9; Timothy (n 67) 217–18, 239–40.

80 Justice Robert Chambers, 'Question Trails: A Reply to His Honour Judge Berman SC's "Note of Caution"' (2012) 24(7) *Judicial Officers Bulletin* 57, 57. The NSWLRC recommended that a direction be given to this effect: NSWLRC, *Jury Directions* (n 72) 151 [6.167].

81 Chambers (n 80) 57. See also Ormerod and Taylor (n 16) 202–9.

82 NSWLRC, *Jury Directions* (n 72) 151 [6.167].

in all the circumstances? This is called jury nullification.[83] Jury nullification links strongly to the idea that juror decision-making involves the application of prototypes or commonsense justice understanding of the law,[84] and usually arises where community sentiment on moral issues differs from the law. For example, juries have refused to convict on abortion laws in Canada[85] and Australia,[86] in political trials in the United Kingdom,[87] and in euthanasia cases in several jurisdictions.[88] Jury nullification played an important role historically in the development of the criminal justice system,[89] but does not arise often in a modern context.[90] The merits of jury nullification are beyond the scope of this book. However, the question is whether using integrated directions changes whatever powers juries currently possess to acquit, despite being satisfied that a charge has been proved.

Consistently with traditional directions, judges giving integrated directions would not inform the jury that they may choose not to follow the law. Further, the decision path may end with a final question such as if your answer is 'yes', your verdict *will* or *must* be one of guilty.[91] The purpose of using factual questions is to increase the likelihood that jurors will understand their task and therefore correctly apply the law to the facts. It is not the purpose of factual questions (or jury directions) to explain the law to the jury so that the jury can decide whether they agree with the law and decide whether it is appropriate to apply the law in all the circumstances.

Factual questions essentially remove the requirement for the jury to understand the law and then apply the law to the facts. However, because factual questions focus on the facts of a case, they do not usually engage with jurors'

83 See, eg, Courselle (n 69) 212; Paula L Hannaford-Agor, 'Judicial Nullification? Judicial Compliance and Non-Compliance with Jury Improvement Efforts' (2002) 28 *Northern Illinois University Law Review* 407, 421; Liana C Peter-Hagene and Chasity L Ratliff, 'When Jurors' Moral Judgments Result in Jury Nullification: Moral Outrage at the Law as a Mediator of Euthanasia Attitudes on Verdicts' (2021) 28(1) *Psychiatry, Psychology, and Law* 27, 27–8.

84 See, eg, Norman J Finkel, 'Commonsense Justice and Jury Instructions: Instructive and Reciprocating Connections' (2000) 6(3) *Psychology, Public Policy, and Law* 591, 595–600; Vicki L Smith, 'Prototypes in the Courtroom: Lay Representations of Legal Concepts' (1991) 61(6) *Journal of Personality and Social Psychology* 857, 869.

85 Regina Schuller and Neil Vidmar, 'The Canadian Criminal Jury' (2011) 86 *Chicago-Kent Law Review* 497, 525.

86 See, eg, Gideon Haigh, *The Racket: How Abortion Became Legal in Australia* (Melbourne University Press, 2008).

87 Nicholas Blake, 'The Case for the Jury' in Mark Findlay and Pete Duff (eds), *The Jury Under Attack* (Butterworths, 1988) 140, 141–2.

88 See, eg, Peter-Hagene and Ratliff (n 83) 43.

89 See, eg, Courselle (n 69) 212; Hannaford-Agor (n 83) 421.

90 See, eg, Peter-Hagene and Ratliff (n 83); Valerie Hans, 'What Difference Does a Jury Make?' (2012) 3 *Yonsei Law Journal* 36, 46–7.

91 See, eg, *Crown Court Compendium* (n 14) 23–4. The wording of the question to the jury varies between jurisdictions. In Canada judges use the word 'must': Watt (n 6) 98. The last question in a standard question trail in New Zealand is, 'if yes, find Mr Smith guilty': *A Guide to the Question Trails* (n 12).

commonsense ideas about the law and how it applies. While factual questions may lead jurors to invoke more analytical reasoning,[92] there is no guarantee that this will remove all commonsense justice from jury decision-making.[93] The jury retains ultimate responsibility for the consequences of their findings of fact as expressed by their verdict. Further, if a jury wished to return a verdict that accorded with their own sense of justice, they may acquit the accused, even though the offence has been proved. If integrated directions make the law or the circumstances in which a person is guilty clearer to the jury, and a jury acquits despite the evidence, it will be clearer that the jury's verdict reflects their views about the law rather than that they did not understand the law.[94]

Therefore, using integrated directions does not change whatever powers juries currently possess to acquit despite being satisfied that a charge has been proved.

Should juries be required to answer factual questions in addition to giving a verdict?

Lord Justice Auld recommended that in addition to returning their verdict, a jury should answer publicly each factual question in an SDM aid.[95] Would publicly answering the factual questions in integrated directions further encourage the jury to use the decision-making pathway and thereby 'induce a more structured debate in the jury room'?[96]

As discussed before, judges may direct jurors that they must follow the pathway in integrated directions. In the Trans-Tasman study, jurors in New Zealand used question trails in 37 out of 43 (86%) trials studied without the court requiring the jury to give answers to each factual question.[97] This suggests that any increase in jury usage of SDM aids arising from requiring answers to factual questions will be marginal. New Zealand's Court of Appeal has said that using question trails does help jurors structure debate in the jury room and 'ensure that they do not get distracted into prejudicial, sympathetic or other impermissible reasoning processes'.[98] However, the court's conclusion appears to reflect judicial knowledge and experience rather than direct knowledge or reasonable inferences drawn from robust research about the structure of jury deliberations. As discussed in Chapter 2, courts do not receive reliable information about the content and quality of jury deliberations.

92 Ede and Goodman-Delahunty (n 3) 134.
93 See, eg, McKay, Nolan and Smithson (n 39) 507–8.
94 Some verdicts that appear to involve jury nullification may be the result of juror comprehension problems: Finkel (n 84) 599–600.
95 Lord Justice Auld, *A Review of the Criminal Courts of England and Wales* (Report, September 2001) 538 [55].
96 Auld (n 95) 536–7 [53]. Lord Justice Auld's reasons for recommending this change were not limited to juror comprehension.
97 Clough et al, 'The Judge as Cartographer' (n 35) 296.
98 *Rawle* (n 5) [18].

Requiring public answers to factual questions might also provide some evidence about whether jurors understood the questions. However, because the answers to factual questions in integrated directions are designed to produce 'yes' or 'no' answers, these answers are unlikely to indicate whether the jury made any errors in reaching those answers unless there is a clear inconsistency in their answers.[99] Further, like a jury's verdict (as discussed in Chapter 4), the jury's answers are likely to be understandable, or retrospectively explicable, and therefore would not obviously indicate jury errors. A qualitative assessment of juror comprehension could only be made if the jury provided reasons for their answers and that is beyond the scope of this proposal, and this book.[100]

A jury's verdict provides accountability in jury decision-making.[101] Requiring jurors to answer specific questions publicly might increase accountability and make jurors think more carefully about the basis of their decision.[102] In the USA, jurors surveyed believed that special verdict forms (which bear some similarities to answering questions in an SDM aid) improved their deliberations.[103] However, the nature of the questions and how jury answers were made public is unclear. Further, the research did not assess whether special verdicts objectively improved juror comprehension, nor did it compare special verdicts with integrated directions.

Further, as already discussed, requiring the jury (and possibly each juror) to answer factual questions publicly may affect deliberations (eg, where jurors are concerned that their answer may be detrimental to a complainant's mental health[104]) or highlight the varied reasons jurors had for reaching their verdict. In turn, this may increase the pressure on jurors to justify their findings. This kind of increased public accountability of jurors raises questions about whether the process would 'maintain the integrity and finality of a formally expressed verdict',[105] protect jurors (and former jurors) from pressure and harassment,[106] and promote public confidence in the integrity of the justice

99 Inconsistent jury verdicts may sometimes reveal a jury error, see, eg, *R v Fanning* [2016] 1 WLR 4175, 4188 [15]–[19]; *MacKenzie v The Queen* (1996) 190 CLR 348, 366–8.

100 See, eg, Richard Lippke, 'The Case for Reasoned Criminal Trial Verdicts' (2009) 22 *Canadian Journal of Law and Jurisprudence* 313.

101 Jury directions function as the jury's reasons: *Taxquet v Belgium* [2010] ECHR 1806.

102 See, eg, Sara Gordon, 'What Jurors Want to Know: Motivating Juror Cognition to Increase Legal Knowledge & Improve Decisionmaking' (2014) 81 *Tennessee Law Review* 751, 773; Chantelle M Baguley, Blake M McKimmie and Barbara M Masser, 'Re-Evaluating How to Measure Jurors' Comprehension and Application of Jury Instructions' (2020) 26(1) *Psychology, Crime & Law* 53, 61–2.

103 Larry Heuer and Steven Penrod, 'Trial Complexity: A Field Investigation of Its Meaning and Its Effects' (1994) 18(1) *Law and Human Behavior* 29, 50.

104 See, eg, Victorian Law Reform Commission, *The Role of Victims of Crime in the Criminal Trial Process* (Report No 34, August 2016) 378 [17.139].

105 *Smith v Western Australia* (2014) 250 CLR 473, 481 ('*Smith*'). Similar rules apply in the United Kingdom and Canada: *R v Mirza* [2004] 1 AC 1118, 1144; *R v Pan* [2001] 2 SCR 344, 373–5 ('*Pan*').

106 *Smith* (n 105) 484.

system.[107] It could also be argued that requiring jurors to identify the basis on which they find the accused not guilty[108] might increase the pressure on jurors to return a verdict of guilty. If this occurs, it may limit the presumption of innocence.[109] However, there is no evidence that requiring jurors to answer factual questions publicly would limit this significant right.

In common with the arguments for requiring the jury to answer factual questions publicly, the arguments against requiring it lack evidence. Evidence to resolve these issues is essential. Requiring the jury (or jurors) to answer publicly each question on its path to a verdict is not justified under a jury-centric approach because there is (currently) a lack of evidence indicating it will improve juror comprehension, and it is possible that it might interfere with presumption of innocence.

Do any general policy factors outweigh the benefits of using integrated directions in all jury trials?

The third step in a jury-centric approach involves examining whether there are any other policy factors to consider, and if so, whether they outweigh the benefits of a proposal. The cost of implementation and whether it adds to delays in courts are policy factors relevant to whether judges should use integrated directions.[110] Judges who have not used question trails or integrated directions have expressed concern that they may require too much work, may be inefficient, and may cause delays in trials.[111]

However, Judge Ingram from New Zealand has said that, with experience, question trials become 'quicker and easier'.[112] Judicial preparation time for the summing up in New Zealand is, on average, half that of judges in Victoria.[113] New Zealand has also developed a large database of draft question trails to support judges in using them.[114] This reduces the burden on individual judges when developing question trails. Therefore, the cost of supporting judges in giving integrated directions is relevant but should not be significant and need not add to delays in court cases once judges (and counsel) are familiar with them. This cost does not clearly outweigh the benefits of using integrated directions to improve juror comprehension.

107 Dorne Boniface, 'Juror Misconduct, Secret Jury Business and the Exclusionary Rule' (2008) 32 *Criminal Law Journal* 18, 24–8; *Pan* (n 105) 373–5.

108 *United States v Spock*, 416 F 2d 165 (1st Cir, 1969), 182. This decision concerned the use of special verdict forms.

109 Courselle (n 69) 235–6.

110 See, eg, Spivak, Ogloff and Clough (n 25) 454.

111 Hulme (n 17) 17. See also Clough et al, *The Jury Project 10 Years On* (n 11) 51–2.

112 Hulme (n 17) 17.

113 Based on research by Professor James Ogloff discussed in Hulme (n 17) 9.

114 *A Guide to the Question Trails* (n 12).

Should each trial judge decide whether to use integrated directions?

The fourth step in a jury-centric approach involves examining whether the decision to use (or not use) integrated directions involves an area of judicial expertise, where a judge is best placed to tailor a solution to an individual case. The traditional view of the judge's role strongly supports each trial judge deciding what how they guide the jury. This view flows from the idea that the 'trial judge is in a unique position to judge the level of comprehension of the jury, as a whole and individually, as the trial progresses'.[115] Therefore, 'the judge should have a wide discretion as to how he or she approaches a particular summing-up . . . to enable the judge to customise his or her approach'[116] to the issues in each case.

As discussed in Chapters 4 and 6, there are many reasons why it is difficult for judges to determine what jurors do or do not understand and what guidance will be most effective. Knowledge of juror comprehension research is not an area of judicial expertise. Instead, judges' views about juror comprehension are more likely to reflect judicial knowledge and experience, which often overestimates juror comprehension levels. While a judge may receive cues from the jury that suggest what jurors do and do not understand (eg, from questions), this is not a reliable source of information.

Research assists in determining whether integrated directions should be used in all cases. In the field component of the Trans-Tasman study, 37 of the 43 (86%) juries studied used the question trail 'as an ongoing framework' during their deliberations.[117] Juries' reasons for not using the question trail included:

> it was too confusing; it was used as a starting point only; the jury had already made up their mind; a single issue case where the question trail was not helpful; and a multiple charge case where the question trail was seen as too long/unwieldy.[118]

Juries did not identify any common reasons for not using a question trail. Further, the reasons provided by jurors are not the kind of reasons that a judge would be able to identify (eg, whether a jury has already made up its mind). However, there may be some single-issue cases where a judge may conclude that jurors are not likely to benefit significantly from using integrated directions.[119] In England and Wales, judges must provide juries with a route to

115 Submission from The Bar Association of Queensland, quoted in QLRC, *A Review of Jury Directions* (n 1) 285 [9.117].

116 QLRC, *A Review of Jury Directions* (n 1) 285 [9.117]. See also *R v Ménard* [1998] 2 SCR 109, 124 [27].

117 Clough et al, 'The Judge as Cartographer' (n 35) 296.

118 Clough et al, 'The Judge as Cartographer' (n 35) 296.

119 However, Justice Robert Chambers discussed an example of a single-issue case in New Zealand in which the jury requested that the trial judge provide them with a question trail:

verdict unless 'the case is so straightforward that it would be superfluous'.[120] Lord Justice Holroyde has said that one should be cautious about concluding that a route to verdict would be superfluous because the discipline of drafting a route to verdict may help to avoid errors and jury confusion about the offences they are determining.[121]

Some judges in Victoria have expressed concern about using integrated directions in complex cases, because the factual permutations may be overwhelming for the jury.[122] Some cases may be quite complicated to describe in integrated directions. However, integrated directions do not make the issues more complicated than they already are. Instead, they lay bare the complexity of the jury's task. Further, the experience of judges in New Zealand in using question trails is that they are best suited to more complex cases where there are multiple accused, charges, and issues, and may lead counsel to refining the issues more clearly for the jury.[123]

This suggests that it will be difficult for a judge to determine when integrated directions might not improve juror comprehension. Does this mean that it should be mandatory for judges to give integrated directions?

A survey of New Zealand judges found that 75% considered that there are no reasons for not using question trails.[124] By contrast, 81% of judges surveyed in Victoria could identify reasons for not using fact-based questions — although only a minority of judges in Victoria had ever directed a jury in this way.[125] Experience in using question trails appears to allay many concerns about their use. However, only five of the 34 judges surveyed from New Zealand considered that question trails are suited to all cases.[126] This is a low level of support for universal usage from judges familiar with the use of question trails. This might be an example of 'reactance theory' (which is usually discussed in relation to jurors), where judges may consider that a mandatory approach would interfere with their 'freedom' to guide the jury in what they consider to be the most appropriate manner.[127] However, judges are also motivated to achieve

Justice Robert Chambers, 'Jury Instruction: New Zealand Methodology and the Forthcoming Australasian Empirical Research' (Speech, 13th International Criminal Law Congress, 13 September 2016).

120 *Atta-Dankwa* (n 4); *R v N* [2019] EWCA Crim 2280, [18].

121 See generally, *Atta-Dankwa* (n 4) [31]–[32].

122 Clough et al, *The Jury Project 10 Years On* (n 11) 52.

123 Clough et al, *The Jury Project 10 Years On* (n 11) 52. See also *New Zealand Bench Book*, quoted in Hulme (n 17) 15.

124 Clough et al, *The Jury Project 10 Years On* (n 11) 51.

125 Clough et al, *The Jury Project 10 Years On* (n 11) 51.

126 Clough et al, *The Jury Project 10 Years On* (n 11) 52.

127 Joel D Lieberman and Jamie Arndt, 'Understanding the Limits of Limiting Instructions: Social Psychological Explanations for the Failures of Instructions to Disregard Pretrial Publicity and Other Inadmissible Evidence' (2000) 6 *Psychology, Public Policy and Law* 677, 694–5.

the 'right' outcome and may (rightly) consider how they tailor their guidance in each case to be critical to this task.[128]

In the absence of more evidence considering the use of integrated directions in different scenarios, it is difficult to be certain that they will improve juror comprehension in every case. Therefore, the use of integrated directions should not be mandatory, but it also should not be left solely to the discretion of the judge. That was the approach adopted in Victoria, and as discussed next, the uptake of integrated directions has been slow. And in Canada, courts do not use step-directions consistently, and usage may vary between Provinces (even though most criminal trials concern federal laws).[129] Instead, there should be a strong presumption that judges give integrated directions, based on the *very* strong presumptions in England and Wales that a judge uses a route to verdict. This could be achieved by legislation, practice directions, or appellate decisions.

If judges identify cases in which they do not consider integrated directions to be necessary, or desirable, further research should be conducted about those cases. This would provide evidence for either recognising those cases as exceptions to the general approach or it may show that judges should use integrated directions in those cases.

Do judges need support when introducing integrated directions?

The fifth step in a jury-centric approach examines whether judges need support such as resources or training to implement new processes.

As the Queensland Law Reform Commission observed, in jurisdictions that do not already do so, using integrated directions requires a shift in thinking for judges and for counsel.[130] Experience in Victoria bears this out. In a survey of judges conducted four years after legislative support for jury directions commenced, only four of the 20 judges surveyed said that they had given integrated directions.[131] Two of the four judges explained that they had not used integrated directions because '"inexperience with the format and fear of departure from the charge book discourages their use", and that preparation "takes time" and may be "complex"'.[132] In another survey, eight out of 20

128 See generally, Christina Mühlberger and Eva Jonas, 'Reactance Theory' in Kai Sassenberg and Michael L W Vliek (eds), *Social Psychology in Action Evidence-Based Interventions from Theory to Practice* (Springer International Publishing, 1st ed, 2019) 79–80.

129 Comiskey (n 6) 175–80.

130 QLRC, *A Review of Jury Directions* (n 1) 279 [9.99].

131 Judicial College of Victoria, *Jury Directions Act 2015 Evaluation: Judicial Survey Results*, ('*Jury Directions Act 2015 Evaluation*' discussed in Greg Byrne and Justice Chris Maxwell, 'Putting Jurors First: Legislative Simplification of Jury Directions' (2019) 43(3) *Criminal Law Journal* 180, 199. Victoria's Court of Appeal has given clear support for judges using integrated directions: *Star v The Queen* [2020] VSCA 331, [43].

132 *Jury Directions Act 2015 Evaluation*, quoted in Byrne and Maxwell (n 131) 199.

Victorian judges said they had tried using fact-based questions when directing juries.[133] More than ten years after legislation supporting the use of integrated directions was introduced, Victoria's *Criminal Charge Book* does not provide any resources that specifically support the development of factual questions. However, the Judicial College of Victoria has taken steps to assist judges with more traditional style jury directions.[134]

By contrast, New Zealand's *A Guide to the Question Trails* includes examples of more than 140 question trails for more commonly prosecuted offences.[135] But resources need to be accompanied by training as even in New Zealand, one judge said that 'some [judges] are more experienced, better than others . . . some make a complete hash of it'.[136] Other jurisdictions need to develop their own similar examples based on offences in their jurisdiction, accompanied by training for judges.[137] Because judges need assistance from counsel in developing integrated directions, training for counsel is also an important part of the process.[138]

While not a panacea for all juror comprehension problems, and further research is required, there is good evidence that the presumption should be that judges give integrated directions to assist the jury with their task. Applying a judge-centric perspective indicates that judges will need resources and training to support this change.

Until now, this analysis has focused on judges giving integrated directions during their summing up. The second proposal builds on the first proposal by examining whether a judge should provide the jury with certain information when the trial commences, to further guide the jury before the judge gives integrated directions during the summing up.

Proposal two: Providing the jury with an 'Outline of Issues' when the trial commences

As discussed in Chapter 2, judges often provide some directions to the jury at the start of the trial and during the trial. For example, approximately 50% of judges surveyed in Australia, and 24% of judges surveyed in New Zealand, said they provide substantive directions during the trial.[139] Judges also regularly

133 Clough et al, *The Jury Project 10 Years On* (n 11) 50. Given the different descriptions used for SDM aids, these figures may have overstated their use.

134 Judicial College of Victoria, 'Judicial Precedent Builders' <www.judicialcollege.vic.edu.au/node/46715>.

135 *A Guide to the Question Trails* (n 12).

136 Clough et al, *The Jury Project 10 Years On* (n 11) 51.

137 See, eg, Greg Byrne, 'A Pathway to Fair(er) Trials: Why We Need a Juries Advisory Council' (2021) 31(2) *Journal of Judicial Administration* 49, 66.

138 See, eg, Victorian Law Reform Commission, *Jury Directions* (Report No 17, May 2009) 125 [6.90] (VLRC); *Dunn v The Queen* [2017] VSCA 371, [63] ('*Dunn*').

139 Clough et al, *The Jury Project 10 Years On* (n 11) 16–20.

give evidentiary directions during the trial.[140] Similarly, in England and Wales judges are encouraged to give general and evidentiary directions at any time during the trial that may be helpful to jurors.[141]

Before closing addresses by the prosecution and defence counsel, judges in New Zealand often provide the jury with the factual questions that will form part of the question trail. Sometimes described as a 'bare question trail',[142] it does not include a summary of the evidence or how parties put their case.[143] The judge settles the question trail and provides the final version to the jury after closing addresses.[144] Judicial knowledge and experience in New Zealand indicates that providing the question trail to the jury before closing addresses, 'allow[s] counsel to structure their addresses around the question trail, and allow[s] the jury to make notes under each question'.[145] Giving the jury a bare question trail just before closing addresses, reflects the development of SDM aids to improve the summing up.

When a trial commences, the Victorian Law Reform Commission (VLRC) recommended that the judge should provide a jury with an 'Outline of Charges'.[146] This Outline would identify the elements of the offence(s) with which the accused is charged and the elements the accused disputes. The Outline of Charges sought to improve the information provided to juries in Victoria. That information included a copy of the indictment[147] and defence's response to the prosecution's opening to the jury, indicating the 'acts, facts, matters and circumstances with which issue is taken and the basis on which issue is taken'.[148] The VLRC's Outline of Charges would be more helpful to the jury than an indictment because the charges in the indictment do not always set out all elements of the offence, and an indictment is drafted in legal terms and for legal purposes rather than for informing a jury of the issues in a case.

140 Clough et al, *The Jury Project 10 Years On* (n 11) 18. Judges surveyed in Australia and New Zealand said they gave evidentiary directions during the trial in 95.7% of trials.
141 *Criminal Procedure Rules 2020* (UK) r 25.14; *Crown Court Compendium* (n 14) 1–4.
142 Hulme (n 17) 12.
143 Hulme (n 17) 12–14. See also *Dunn* (n 138) [67] where the trial judge adopted a similar approach.
144 Hulme (n 17) 12–14.
145 *New Zealand Bench Book*, quoted in Hulme (n 17) 15.
146 VLRC, *Jury Directions* (n 138) 115–18.
147 VLRC, *Jury Directions* (n 138) 116 [6.36]. See also Clough et al, *The Jury Project 10 Years On* (n 11) 42, where Australian and New Zealand judges surveyed said that they always (67% Australia and NZ) or sometimes (26% Australia; 7.4% New Zealand) provide a copy of the indictment to the jury.
148 *Criminal Procedure Act 2009* (Vic) s 183(2). See also *Criminal Procedure Act 1986* (NSW) s 143(1)(c); *Criminal Procedure and Investigations Act 1996* (UK) s 6A; *Criminal Procedure Act 2004* (WA) s 96(3)(c); *Criminal Procedure Act 2011* (NZ) s 88(2)(b).

Adapting the first checklist example discussed in Table 7.1, the Outline of Issues could commence with:

(1) Did the accused (Green) participate in the joint criminal enterprise to cultivate cannabis?
- The accused does/does not dispute this element.

My 'Outline of Issues' differs from the VLRC proposal. The different name reflects that an Outline of Issues is not limited to the charges and seeks to identify the issues that the jury will need to consider to reach a verdict. An Outline of Issues would:

- set out the factual questions
- (briefly) refer to the evidence the prosecution relies upon to prove the allegation in the factual question, and
- identify what is and is not in dispute in the trial.

The Outline of Issues is a type of SDM aid because its purpose is to assist jurors with the decision points that they will need to determine to reach their verdict at the end of the trial.

The discussion in this section assumes that the content of the Outline of Issues does not require the accused to say anything more than what they admit or dispute. This proposal assumes that the judge intends to give integrated directions in the summing up. However, when the trial commences, it is not necessary to signpost the decision path (eg, with 'yes' or 'no' results) for the jury. The Outline of Charges can be transformed into an Outline of Issues by focusing more on the factual issues than the legal issues in a case and by further explaining the elements of the offences and the facts relevant to proving those elements. An example of an Outline of Issues is set out in Table 7.2 (using some of the information provided in the integrated directions example in Table 7.1):

Table 7.2 Outline of Issues

Outline of Issues
(1) Did Green participate in the joint criminal enterprise to cultivate cannabis by renting the warehouse to Brown? • Prosecution: Red witnessed Brown paying Green $5000 per month in cash at the warehouse and there are surveillance photographs of three meetings between Brown and Green • Accused: The accused disputes the prosecution's evidence.

The first, second, and fourth steps in a jury-centric approach are most relevant to assessing an Outline of Issues. No new considerations arise with step three (whether other policy factors outweigh the benefits of introducing the proposal) and step five (whether judges need support to implement the proposal).

The evidentiary basis for providing the jury with an Outline of Issues when the trial commences

Applying the first step in a jury-centric approach, there is no specific evidence indicating whether this proposal will improve juror comprehension. Isolating whether a particular change makes a difference would probably be assessed through simulated jury studies. However, if there is a benefit from providing an Outline of Issues at the start of a trial, this is much more likely to arise in a trial conducted over many days. Such a benefit may be difficult to identify in a jury simulation study as these are normally completed within half a day (at most). Because of these assessment difficulties, it is necessary to consider whether reasonable inferences can be drawn from more general evidence concerning whether this proposal is likely to improve juror comprehension.

Jurors are not blank slates, recording the evidence and then only assessing the evidence (in accordance with the judge's directions) once they retire to consider their verdict. Jurors 'actively process the evidence as it emerges, evaluating it and attempting to fit it into an evolving story which makes sense to them'.[149] This means that if jurors are processing information and developing narratives from an early stage of the trial, '[d]elaying the presentation of critical information until the end of the trial . . . [is] counter-productive'.[150] Opening statements are 'critical and influential because they establish the ground rules and create a framework or schema in light of which jurors evaluate the evidence that follows'.[151] SDM aids can 'assist jurors in organizing and understanding the evidence as they hear it, improve their recall, and reduce the chances of their applying an erroneous rule to the evidence'.[152]

149 Warren Young, Yvette Tinsley and Neil Cameron, 'The Effectiveness and Efficiency of Jury Decision-Making' (2000) 24 *Criminal Law Journal* 89.

150 Valerie P Hans, 'US Jury Reform: The Active Jury and the Adversarial Ideal' (2002) 21 *St Louis University Public Law Review* 85, 90.

151 James R P Ogloff et al, *The Jury Project: Stage 1 — A Survey of Australian and New Zealand Judges* (Australian Institute of Judicial Administration, 2006) 20. See also Krisda Chaemsaithong, 'Speech Reporting in Courtroom Opening Statements' (2017) 119 *Journal of Pragmatics* 1, 2; Shelley C Spiecker and Debra L Worthington, 'The Influence of Opening Statement/Closing Argument Organizational Strategy on Juror Verdict and Damage Awards' (2003) 27(4) *Law and Human Behavior* 437, 438–9, 450–1.

152 B Michael Dann and George Logan III, 'Jury Reform: The Arizona Experience' (1996) 79 *Judicature* 280, 281.

Psychologists distinguish between 'incidental and intentional learning'.[153] Jurors will incidentally learn at least some of what is relevant to their task (including reaching a verdict) from the trial itself. Intentional learning occurs if jurors know at the start of a trial what will be relevant to their verdict. In the absence of guidance about the issues in the case, it is reasonable to assume that 'jurors probably select and evaluate evidence in terms of their own sense of morality and justice'.[154] Providing jurors with a framework would enable them 'to focus on relevant evidence as it is being presented, and later remember it'.[155] When 'judicial communications and instructions concerning the evidence are clear, the influence of individual juror attitudes, personalities and dispositions on verdicts diminishes'.[156] The Outline of Issues may also reduce the cognitive load on jurors by reducing the amount of information they must process.[157] Further, giving jury directions at the start of a simulated trial in addition to the end of a trial has been shown to reduce factual errors.[158]

Juries already get information orally about a case from the prosecution opening, and from the defence in some jurisdictions.[159] Research indicates that when visual information (eg, charts and diagrams) is integrated with complex verbal information, this can help people to engage in more effortful evaluation of evidence.[160] The use of written documents such as an Outline of Issues has the potential to build on the way in which jurors learn by presenting the key information to the jury visually.[161]

Based on the existing research just discussed, it is reasonable to infer that providing the jury with factual questions and identifying what is and is not in dispute at the commencement of a trial should improve juror comprehension (and be more helpful than giving the jury the indictment).

153 Elwork, Sales and Alfini, *Making Jury Instructions Understandable* (n 21) 22.
154 Elwork, Sales and Alfini, *Making Jury Instructions Understandable* (n 21) 23.
155 Elwork, Sales and Alfini, *Making Jury Instructions Understandable* (n 21) 23.
156 Ogloff et al (n 151).
157 Sweller, Merriënboer and Paas (n 46) 262.
158 Amiram Elwork, Bruce D Sales and James J Alfini, 'Juridic Decisions: In Ignorance of the Law or in Light of It?' (1977) 1 *Law and Human Behavior* 163, 177.
159 In Victoria, defence counsel must respond to the prosecution opening: *Criminal Procedure Act 2009* (Vic) s 225. In most jurisdictions, defence counsel is *invited* to respond to the prosecution opening and may accept or decline the invitation, see, eg, *Criminal Procedure Rules 2020* (UK) r 25.9(2)(c); *Criminal Procedure Act 2011* (NZ) s 107(2); *Criminal Procedure Act 1986* (NSW) s 159.
160 See, eg, Emma Rempel et al, 'The Power of Technology: Examining the Effects of Digital Visual Evidence on Jurors' Processing of Trial Information' (2019) 33(6) *Applied Cognitive Psychology* 1288, 1289–90; Sweller, Merriënboer and Paas (n 46).
161 See, eg, Firoz Dattu, 'Illustrated Jury Instructions: A Proposal' (1998) 22 *Law and Psychology Review* 67; Semmler and Brewer (n 39) 263; Seyed Yaghoub Mousavi, Renae Low and John Sweller, 'Reducing Cognitive Load by Mixing Auditory and Visual Presentation Modes' (1995) 87(2) *Journal of Educational Psychology* 319, 331–3.

Fair trial principles and other human rights relevant to providing an Outline of Issues when the trial commences

Applying the second step in a jury-centric approach involves assessing whether providing an Outline of Issues to the jury when the trial commences conflicts with any fair trial principles or other human rights.

The factual questions in an Outline of Issues reflect the elements of the offences that the prosecution must prove, or defences it must negate. However, setting out factual questions in full may be problematic in some cases. For example, in *R v Jones*[162] the trial involved eight accused charged with murder, with 13 possible different routes through which each accused could be convicted of murder or manslaughter.[163] A document setting out all the elements for each offence that each accused is charged with, together with key evidence that the prosecution relies upon, may be overwhelming to the jury when the trial commences and affect whether the trial is fair.[164] A simplified document may be more appropriate to begin with in such cases to avoid overwhelming a jury. For example, the document might not refer to evidence the prosecution relies on, or only at a very high level.

This proposal does not change the accused's existing legal obligations — the accused may indicate that all factual questions are in dispute. Disputing something that the prosecution can obviously prove may reduce the credibility of the accused's disputation of other matters. Defence counsel is therefore more likely to only dispute matters where there is a good reason to do so. Determining whether to dispute a matter involves a forensic decision by counsel rather than something that affects the accused's rights.

However, what if the evidence at the trial differs from the reference to the evidence in the Outline of Issues or the evidence changes what the accused says is or is not in dispute? In any trial, the evidence may vary from what is expected when the trial commences. The Outline of Issues frames the issues and the jury's assessment of the evidence. As discussed, this framework may be more effective than existing processes. Therefore, any differences between the trial and the way in which the evidence is described in the Outline of Issues may be more obvious and better remembered by a jury.

If the change in the evidence is substantial (eg, a key witness totally recants their evidence) then the trial may be unfair because the accused must meet a substantially different prosecution case.[165] As already may occur in such

162 *R v Jones* (2006) 161 A Crim R 511.

163 Justice Geoffrey Eames, 'Tackling the Complexity of Criminal Trial Directions: What Role for Appellate Courts?' (2007) 29 *Australian Bar Review* 161, 170–3.

164 This may be similar to indictments containing so many charges that it may overwhelm the jury. See, eg, *R v Smart* [1983] 1 VR 265; *R v N(P)* [2010] 2 Cr App R 14; *Bauer v The Queen* (2015) 46 VR 382.

165 See, eg, *Patel v The Queen* (2012) 247 CLR 531, 551 [67] (French CJ, Hayne, Kiefel and Bell JJ) where 'the prosecution case changed at a very late point in the trial with the result

circumstances where there is no Outline of Issues, the judge may discharge the jury and order a new trial.

There is no evidence of differences between the trial and the prosecution opening and defence response presenting significant problems in Victoria, probably because it is a manageable risk. The expertise of the judge and counsel will help to minimise the risk of differences between the Outline of Issues and the trial because they should be able to identify most cases where the risk is significant. The risk assessment will involve multiple factors including the kinds of issues in dispute, the evidence which has already been obtained (eg, if witness statements contain multiple inconsistencies), an assessment of the key witnesses, and the case overall. Aided by the prosecution and defence counsel, judges are best placed to manage this risk.

Managing the risk that the Outline of Issues differs significantly from the evidence may affect the content of the Outline of Issues. For example, the prosecution may be more circumspect with how it describes the evidence it relies on, and defence counsel may be less inclined to indicate that a matter is not in dispute until the evidence on that issue has been given. It would also be possible to add to the Outline of Issues once the evidence is clear in the trial.[166] The effectiveness of the Outline of Issues in framing the issues may result in a more cautious approach to reducing information to writing that would usually form part of oral opening addresses but should still provide useful information for the jury in many trials.

Accordingly, providing a jury with an Outline of Issues at the commencement of the trial does not interfere with other fair trial principles and is consistent with existing policy choices several jurisdictions have already made concerning the need for the accused to identify what is and is not in issue at the start of the trial.

Should the trial judge decide in each case whether to provide an Outline of Issues?

The fourth step in a jury-centric approach considers whether judicial expertise should govern use of an Outline of Issues. As discussed with Proposal One, there may be some cases where the judge decides not to give integrated directions, for example, because the case is a simple single-issue case. This may be apparent when the trial commences, and the judge may consider that giving the jury an Outline of Issues would be 'superfluous'.[167] However, other reasons a judge may have for not giving integrated directions may not be apparent when the trial commences.

---

that much of the evidence that had been admitted on the wide-ranging prosecution case no longer remained relevant'.

166 Lord Justice Auld recommended that a similar kind of document be provided to juries in England and Wales and updated as required during the trial: Auld (n 95) 521 [23].

167 *Atta-Dankwa* (n 4).

The main risk with using an Outline of Issues will arise from its reference to evidence. Determining how to manage this risk is a matter that falls within judicial expertise. For example, the judge might decide that the Outline of Issues should not refer to evidence, or that a more general checklist style of questions be used instead of factual questions. Where the risk is with one or two witnesses, the judge could decide that a more detailed Outline of Issues only be provided after that evidence is given. Accordingly, judicial expertise will play a significant role in determining the content of an Outline of Issues provided to the jury at the commencement of the trial.

In most cases a judge should give the jury an Outline of Issues. However, a judge needs a broader discretion than is proposed for a judge to not give integrated directions in the summing up. This is because at the start of the trial, a judge will not know whether potential problems will eventuate. Therefore, a judge should be able to decline to provide an Outline of Issues, or to modify its content if, for example, it is in the interests of justice to do so.

The third proposal in this case study examines whether the accused should be required to disclose their defence in the Outline of Issues. This proposal involves more significant conflict between the goal of improving juror comprehension and the accused's rights.

Proposal three: Requiring the accused to disclose their defence when the trial commences

The Outline of Issues operates on the basis that the accused must indicate whether they admit or dispute parts of the prosecution case.[168] Proposal three examines whether the accused should, in addition, be ***required*** to disclose their defence in the Outline of Issues. This proposal draws on the definition used in England and Wales that if the accused does anything more than put the prosecution to its proof, that constitutes a 'defence'.[169] For example, if an accused is charged with dangerous driving and says anything more than that they did not drive the car (eg, that someone else drove the car), they would be putting a forward a 'defence'.[170] England and Wales uses this definition of a 'defence' for its defence disclosure regime. One of the purposes of that regime is to enable the prosecution to determine whether it possesses any information or evidence that might be relevant to the accused's defence.[171] Improving prosecution disclosure is not relevant to improving juror comprehension. The question for this proposal is whether this aspect of defence disclosure is justified to improve juror comprehension.

168 See, eg, *Criminal Procedure Act 2009* (Vic) s 183.
169 *R v Rochford* [2011] 1 WLR 534 ('*Rochford*').
170 *Rochford* (n 169).
171 David Ormerod, 'Improving the Disclosure Regime' (2003) 7(2) *International Journal of Evidence & Proof* 102, 114.

The traditional view is that the accused is not required to disclose their defence until the close of the prosecution case.[172] There is no common law right preventing the accused from disclosing their defence when the trial commences.[173] However, jurisdictions have different laws concerning whether the accused may give an opening address to the jury when the trial commences and what the accused may say in an opening address.[174]

The first step in a jury-centric approach concerns the evidence supporting a proposal. Would requiring the accused to disclose their defence improve juror comprehension beyond that achieved by proposal two? There is no additional evidence available beyond that discussed in proposal two. At its highest, it would be reasonable to infer that it might improve juror comprehension by bringing the issues in dispute into sharper relief. This may further assist jurors in understanding and focusing on precisely the issues they will need to determine. However, any improvement in juror comprehension is likely to be marginal.

In the absence of additional evidence, I will not discuss this step further. I will also not discuss steps three, four, and five of a jury-centric approach when analysing this third proposal as no significant new issues arise. Accordingly, the second step in a jury-centric approach — whether the proposal conflicts with other fair trial rights — is most relevant to assessing any new issues with proposal three.

Does requiring disclosure of the accused's defence conflict with fair trial principles or other human rights?

The second step in a jury-centric approach asks whether requiring the accused to disclose their defence when the trial commences conflicts with any fair trial principles or other human rights. The defence disclosure regime in England and Wales was based on a report that said that the pre-trial requirement of defence disclosure 'involves no sacrifice to the defendant's legitimate interests'.[175] The principal 'legitimate interest' is whether disclosing the accused's defence when the trial commences limits the privilege against self-incrimination

172 See, eg, Jeremy Gans, Andrew Palmer and Andrew Roberts, *Uniform Evidence* (Oxford University Press Australia and New Zealand, 2019) 392 [14.1.1]. Many jurisdictions recognise exceptions to this (eg, for alibi evidence or evidence from an expert witness).

173 *Hamilton v Oades* (1989) 166 CLR 486, 499 (Mason CJ).

174 For example, in England and Wales, the court may invite the accused to give an opening address: *Criminal Procedure Rules 2020* (UK) r 25.9(2)(c). In Victoria, a legally represented accused must indicate the matters in the prosecution opening with which the accused takes issue and the basis on issue is taken but may not address the jury about their case more generally: *Criminal Procedure Act 2009* (Vic) s 225.

175 Lord Justice Gross, *Review of Disclosure in Criminal Proceedings*, Judiciary of England and Wales (Report, 2011) 76 [140].

(which forms part of the right to silence[176]) or infringes the nature of the accusatorial trial.

The privilege against self-incrimination is 'deep rooted in English law',[177] but 'statutory interference with the right is almost as old as the right itself'.[178] The scope of the privilege and justifications for the privilege are often unclear.[179] Disclosing the accused's defence does not entail disclosing all information in the accused's possession. A defence statement should indicate why the accused is not guilty and the accused is not required to incriminate themselves.

However, might disclosing the accused's defence assist the prosecution to address weaknesses in its case, or to prepare better for the accused's case? In Australia, the High Court has said that the accusatorial nature of a criminal trial means that 'the prosecution cannot compel the accused to assist it to discharge its onus'.[180] The High Court described this as the 'companion principle'.[181] It is a companion to the fundamental principle that the prosecution bears the burden of proving the accused's guilt.[182] The companion principle may apply where the privilege against self-incrimination has been abolished.[183]

The companion principle does not apply to documents that incriminate the accused if the documents speak for themselves (eg, documents created in the normal course of a corporation's affairs).[184] However, the accused's defence statement is a document developed specifically for criminal proceedings — its purpose is to explain the accused's defence. Does the defence statement assist the prosecution in proving its case?

The defence statement requires the accused to put forward their defence, but the accused cannot be compelled to answer questions about their defence. Further, the accused has control over the statement and its purpose, and presumably the content will be exculpatory in nature. At its highest, knowing the accused's defence might enable the prosecution to prepare better for

176 See, eg, *R v Director of Serious Fraud Office; Ex Parte Smith* (1992) 95 Cr App R 191, 199 ('*Director of Serious Fraud Office*'); *Environmental Protection Authority v Caltex Refining Co Pty Ltd* (1993) 178 CLR 477, 503 (Mason CJ and Toohey J), 526 (Deane, Dawson and Gaudron JJ).

177 *Lam v The Queen* (1991) 93 Cr App R 358, 364. See also See also Andrew L-T Choo, '"Give Us What You Have" — Information, Compulsion and the Privilege Against Self-Incrimination as a Human Right' in Paul Roberts and Jill Hunter (eds), *Criminal Evidence and Human Rights: Reimagining Common Law Procedural Tradition* (Bloomsbury Publishing, 2013) 239, 254.

178 *Director of Serious Fraud Office* (n 176) 206. See also *Lee v The Queen* (2014) 253 CLR 455, 466–7 [32]–[33] ('*Lee*'); *CFMEU v Boral Resources (Vic) Pty Ltd* (2015) 256 CLR 375, 387 ('*CFMEU*').

179 See, eg, Mike Redmayne, 'Rethinking the Privilege against Self-Incrimination' (2007) 27(2) *Oxford Journal of Legal Studies* 209, 209–10, 218, 225–6.

180 *CFMEU* (n 178) 387.

181 *CFMEU* (n 178) 387 [35] (French CJ, Kiefel, Bell, Gageler and Keane JJ).

182 *Lee* (n 178) 466–7 [32]–[33].

183 *Lee* (n 178) 466–7 [32]–[33].

184 *CFMEU* (n 178) 388.

the accused's defence. This arguably assists the prosecution, but it does not involve the accused providing evidence that assists the prosecution to prove its case and the prosecution's burden of proof, and the standard of proof, remain the same.

In England and Wales, if the accused puts forward a defence at trial that was not disclosed in their defence statement, the court or another party may comment on this failure and the 'jury may draw such inferences as appear proper in deciding whether the accused is guilty of the offence concerned'.[185] This has been described as an indirect compulsion to speak.[186] The right to silence is not absolute[187] and may be limited by parliament in ways that are consistent with a fair trial. As a result, the jury may draw adverse inferences from what the accused has said or has failed to do provided that the prosecution case does not 'solely or mainly' depend upon these inferences.[188] These inferences may mean that, in some cases, the accused's defence statement assists the prosecution in proving its case.

If a parliament in Australia decided to allow a jury to draw adverse inferences from a failure to disclose a defence in a defence statement, this would interfere with a common law right. For this to be effective (at least in Australia), the principle of legality provides that unambiguous wording is required to give effect to legislation that clearly interferes with common law rights, such as the companion principle.[189]

In summary, applying a jury-centric approach to proposal three demonstrates that:

- the evidence indicating that the proposal will improve juror comprehension is weak but might make a marginal difference, and
- there is a risk that the proposal may involve the accused assisting the prosecution in proving its case.

As a result, requiring the accused to disclose their defence for the purposes of improving juror comprehension is not justified under a jury-centric approach. If proposal three is justifiable on other grounds — not concerning improving juror comprehension — a jury-centric approach would not limit defence disclosure.

185 *Criminal Procedure and Investigations Act 1996* (UK) s 11(5)(b).
186 See, eg, Choo (n 177) 239.
187 *Beckles v United Kingdom* [2003] 36 EHHR 162, 177 [57] ('*Beckles*').
188 *Beckles* (n 187) 178 [58]. See generally Redmayne (n 179) 215.
189 See, eg, *Al-Kateb v Godwin* (2004) 219 CLR 562, 577 [19]–[20] (Gleeson CJ); *R v Secretary of State for the Home Department* [2000] 2 AC 115, 131 (Lord Hoffman); Dennis C Pearce, *Statutory Interpretation in Australia* (LexisNexis Butterworths, 2019) 209–10 [5.3].

Conclusion

The development of question trails in New Zealand and the route to verdict in England and Wales occurred before there was an evidence base supporting their use. Recommendations from the New Zealand Law Commission and Lord Justice Auld supporting these changes were based primarily on policy objectives and intuition rather than on evidence. The recommendations could have been criticised on the grounds that the policy objectives were not shared, or that the reviews had given insufficient weight to other policy factors, or that the reviewers' intuitions were simply wrong.

Requiring proposals to be evidence-informed provides one mechanism for changing the nature of such policy debates. There is now good evidence that in most cases judges should give integrated directions during their summing up to improve juror comprehension. Reasonable inferences can be drawn from existing evidence that giving the jury an Outline of Issues at the commencement of the trial will improve juror comprehension. However, the evidence and inferences that can be drawn from evidence are insufficient to conclude that juror comprehension will improve if the accused is required to disclose their defence when the trial commences. Because this conclusion is based on existing evidence, further evidence might change this conclusion. Assessing the evidence supporting each proposal moves the arguments about their benefits beyond 'the dominance of myth, anecdote, and judicial hearsay in jury reform'.[190]

As discussed in Chapter 6, evidence-based law is difficult because the law has conflicting goals and people do not reason about the law in the same way as they do about medicine and business.[191] The analysis of the three proposals in this chapter demonstrates how framing juror comprehension as a fair trial issue provides a framework for resolving conflicts with other fair trial principles and other human rights. This framework involves conclusions about which people may disagree. However, a jury-centric approach makes analysis of the policy reasons for and against a proposal, and how it should work, more transparent and promotes rigorous analysis. Further, it highlights the interests, and importance, of juror comprehension of the issues, something that can easily be lost in debates about the policy merits of a proposal.

190 Jacqueline Horan and Mark Israel, 'Beyond the Legal Barriers: Institutional Gatekeeping and Real Jury Research' (2015) 49 *Australia and New Zealand Journal of Criminology* 422, 434.

191 Jeffrey J Rachlinski, 'Evidence-Based Law' (2011) 96 *Cornell Law Review* 901, 917.

8 Case study two — Homicide offences

Introduction

Complexity in the law can translate into complexity in jury directions:

> complicated concepts or principles are more difficult to express clearly than simple ones. It is difficult to explain in a single sentence or short paragraph concepts that law students, lawyers, and judges spend months if not years learning.[1]

My second case study examines whether, and if so how, a jury-centric approach is relevant to substantive laws that define criminal offences and defences. Judges have identified complexity in the law as a significant problem: the 'substantive law relating to criminal offences is probably just as much to blame [as the law on jury directions] for the undue complexity that plagues many criminal trials'.[2] As discussed in Chapter 7, a judge can embed substantive laws into factual questions to make the issues in a trial more comprehensible to the jury. To ensure that the jury applies the law correctly, factual questions must be consistent with the law. Therefore, the laws that define offences and defences constrain the content of factual questions.

There are thousands of offences that could be examined to assess the role of a jury-centric approach with offences. Homicide offences provide a useful case study for several reasons. First, while each common law jurisdiction has offences of murder and manslaughter with basic similarities in the offences, there are sufficient differences between jurisdictions to highlight the kinds of issues raised by a jury-centric analysis. Second, despite not being committed often, homicide offences disproportionately appear in appellate cases and academic literature. As one of the most serious criminal offences, murder plays a critical role in defining the law and criminal offences and defences more

1 Justice David Watt, *Helping Jurors Understand* (Thomson Carswell, 2007) 61.
2 Justice Mark Weinberg, 'Jury Directions on Trial — A Pathway Through the Labyrinth?' (Speech, Supreme and Federal Court Judges' Conference, 5–9 July 2014) 60.

DOI: 10.4324/9781003477129-8

generally. Third, there is evidence that juries find homicide trials to be more complicated than trials involving many other offences.[3] Fourth, strong policy arguments shape, and often dominate the discussion of, proposals for defining homicide offences and defences. Therefore, a case study involving homicide offences provides a challenging environment for assessing the role of jury-centric approach in defining criminal offences and defences.

In contrast to the proposals discussed in Chapter 7, criminal offences and defences do not exist to improve juror comprehension. However, offences must be comprehensible to jurors and juror comprehension evidence can play an important role in resolving difficult policy choices when defining offences and defences. The case study in this chapter does not involve a detailed analysis of all issues in relation to homicide offences or each step in a jury-centric approach. Instead, the case study focuses on how the first step in a jury-centric approach (juror comprehension evidence) and the third step (policy choices) are relevant to defining:

- the offence of murder, and
- the partial defence of excessive self-defence.

How a jury-centric approach is relevant to criminal offences and defences

As discussed in Chapter 6, a jury-centric approach takes the jury as its starting point and asks: *What do jurors need to understand the issues that they must determine?* This definition assumes that something else defines 'the issues'. The law, the evidence, and the way in which the parties conduct the case play critical roles in defining the issues. As the law helps to define the issues, this raises the question whether the law itself must be comprehensible to jurors for them to understand the issues they must determine.

Examining the comprehensibility of the law can involve philosophical issues about whether laws must be discoverable, accessible, and foreseeable so that people can avoid breaching the law.[4] However, a jury-centric approach is concerned with the comprehensibility of the law as a question of the practical application of laws. This is similar to Lord Mackay's observation that jury directions should be 'comprehensible to an ordinary member of the public who is called to sit on a jury and who has no particular acquaintance with the

3 Michael Heise, 'Criminal Case Complexity: An Empirical Perspective' (2004) 1(2) *Empirical Legal Studies* 331, 366.

4 See, eg, Joseph Raz, 'The Law's Own Virtue' (2019) 39(1) *Oxford Journal of Legal Studies* 1, 3; Jeremy Horder, *Ashworth's Principles of Criminal Law* (Oxford University Press, 9th ed, 2019) 81–4; Lord Bingham, 'The Rule of Law' (2007) 66 *Cambridge Law Journal* 67, 69 and 71; Sebastian Walker, 'The Foreseeability of Law: How Many Lawyers Should It Take to Understand Your Criminal Liability?' [2021] (2) *Criminal Law Review* 113, 113–16.

law'.[5] This practical focus reflects that jurors must apply the law, and the law assumes that jurors will need assistance with this task.

The practical focus of a jury-centric approach includes consideration of the way the judge guides the jury when explaining how the law applies to the issues in the case.[6] Judges should transform appellate court judgments and legislation into a form that is intelligible to jurors. For example, appellate courts have indicated that complex elements, such as 'malice aforethought'[7] or 'reckless indifference to life'[8] can be explained in more comprehensible terms to a jury.[9] A judge may also be able to turn elements of offences and defences into factual questions to improve juror comprehension.

Accordingly, for a jury-centric approach, it is not necessary that the law defining an offence to be defined in comprehensible terms if it can be transformed into comprehensible jury directions, including factual questions in a SDM aid as discussed in Chapter 7. However, there may be limits to the extent to which factual questions can simplify the elements of offences and defences in a trial.

For example, Victoria's — now repealed — offence of rape was especially complex.[10] Victoria's Court of Appeal said that the offence of rape and associated jury directions were 'so extraordinarily complex as to throw into doubt the expectations on which the system of trial by jury is founded'.[11] Those expectations included that the judge could explain the law to the jury and that the jury could understand the law. Although Victorian judges did not use factual questions when guiding juries at that time, factual questions could not have removed the conceptual complexities inherent in the offence, at least not without glossing over the complexities.

5 *R v Adomako* [1995] 1 AC 171, 189 (Lord Mackay LC). See also *Zoneff v The Queen* (2000) 200 CLR 234, 260–1 [64]–[67] (Kirby J).

6 *Alford v Magee* (1952) 85 CLR 437, 466 ('*Alford*'); *RPS v The Queen* (2000) 199 CLR 620, 637 (Gaudron A-CJ, Gummow, Kirby and Hayne JJ); *R v MacKinnon* (1999) 132 CCC (3d) 545, 555 (Doherty JA).

7 Law Commission, *Murder, Manslaughter and Infanticide* (Report No 304, November 2006) 59 [3.41].

8 *Crimes Act 1900* (NSW) s 18(1)(a).

9 See, eg, *Alford* (n 6) 466; Judicial Commission of New South Wales, *Criminal Trial Courts Bench Book* <www.judcom.nsw.gov.au/criminal/> [5–6310] ('*Criminal Trial Courts Bench Book*').

10 The fault element for rape was that the accused was aware that the complainant was not, or might not be, consenting. An accused's belief that the complainant was consenting was not a defence, but depending on its nature and strength, could prevent the prosecution from proving the fault element beyond reasonable doubt. The accused's belief did not have to be reasonable, but the reasonableness of a belief was relevant to whether the belief was held. See generally, *NT v The Queen* (2012) 225 A Crim R 102, 107 [15]–[16] ('*NT*'); Criminal Law Review, Department of Justice & Regulation (Vic), *Victoria's New Sexual Offence Laws: An Introduction* (Report, June 2015) 3 [2.3.1].

11 *Wilson v The Queen* (2011) 33 VR 340, 343 [2] (Maxwell P). See also *NT* (n 10) 107–8 [19].

The elements of an offence must also be clear when considered alongside alternative offences. As discussed in Chapter 3, one study with mock jurors in the USA assessed whether they understood the difference between attempted murder and the lesser alternative offence of battery with intent to kill. The study used the instructions provided to a jury in an actual trial where the jury convicted the accused of the lesser alternative offence. Only one of 34 mock jurors (3%) in the study could describe the difference between these two offences.[12] By rewriting the instructions twice, 80% of 86 mock jurors correctly described the difference between the two offences.[13]

Alternative homicide offences can also be challenging because the result element — death — is the same in each offence. Therefore, the accused's state of mind will often be the only difference between liability for murder or manslaughter.[14] This may involve relatively fine distinctions about the accused's state of mind.[15] Distinguishing between certain states of mind can also be difficult from an evidentiary perspective. Unless an accused makes admissions, it will often be necessary for a jury to infer an accused's state of mind from their conduct.

Assessing whether jury directions about homicide offences are comprehensible to jurors can also be challenging because jurors are not blank slates. They may already have commonsense ideas of homicide laws which may affect their ability to accurately understand and apply the judge's directions.[16] Jury directions should guide the jury to make decisions in accordance with the law rather than their own subjective morality or viewpoint. Further, criminal laws need to define murder and manslaughter so that 'censure and punishment are deserved and the degree of censure and punishment is proportionate to the degree of wrongdoing we ascribe to the defendant's conduct'.[17] To achieve

12 Amiram Elwork, Bruce D Sales and James J Alfini, *Making Jury Instructions Understandable* (Michie Company, 1982) 51–3.

13 Elwork, Sales and Alfini (n 12) 51–3.

14 Martin Wasik, 'Sentencing in Homicide' in Andrew Ashworth and Barry Mitchell (eds), *Rethinking English Homicide Law* (Oxford, 2000) 167, 180.

15 See generally, Law Reform Commission of Western Australia, *A Review of the Law of Homicide* (Project No 97, September 2007) 80–1 ('LRCWA'); Model Criminal Code Officers Committee of the Standing Committee of Attorneys-General, *Fatal Offences against the Person* (Discussion Paper, June 1998) 51 (MCCOC).

16 See, eg, Vicki L Smith, 'Prototypes in the Courtroom: Lay Representations of Legal Concepts' (1991) 61(6) *Journal of Personality and Social Psychology* 857 ('Prototypes in the Courtroom'); Norman J Finkel, 'Commonsense Justice and Jury Instructions: Instructive and Reciprocating Connections' (2000) 6(3) *Psychology, Public Policy, and Law* 591 ('Commonsense Justice and Jury Instructions'). The majority of the High Court of Australia also seemed to have accepted that jurors may use their commonsense ideas of homicide offences in reaching a verdict: *Gilbert v The Queen* (2001) 201 CLR 414, 421 [16]–[17] (Gleeson CJ and Gummow J) and 441 [101] (Callinan J).

17 William Wilson, 'Murder and the Structure of Homicide' in Andrew Ashworth and Barry Mitchell (eds), *Rethinking English Homicide Law* (Oxford University Press, 2000) 21, 53.

this objective, relying on the 'moral and political response of judge and jury'[18] is inadequate; clear laws are essential.

Therefore, homicide laws must not be too conceptually complex, must distinguish clearly between alternative offences, and enable jury verdicts to identify important differences in culpability in a consistent way. Factual questions may assist but comprehensible laws are not sufficient to make a law appropriate. Further, juror prototypes of the law may affect their comprehension of the law and factual questions. Therefore, it is essential to consider how offences and defences are defined, to assess their comprehensibility to jurors, and to assess how laws are likely to operate in practice.

The case study focuses primarily on Victoria and England and Wales. This is because, out of Australia, New Zealand, England and Wales, and Canada, Victoria introduced the most changes to homicide laws in Australia in recent decades[19] and England and Wales conducted the most significant recent policy review of homicide laws.[20] The different approaches to homicide laws in these two jurisdictions provide a useful case study for considering which offence structure is preferable when analysed through a jury-centric approach.

Applying a jury-centric approach to the offence of murder

The Law Commission's proposals and Victoria's offences

In 2006, the Law Commission of England and Wales ('Law Commission') proposed replacing the common law offences of murder and manslaughter with two offences of murder — called first degree murder and second degree murder — and an offence of manslaughter.[21] The element that the accused caused the harm (death) is common to each offence. The proposed offence of first degree murder contained two alternative fault elements, namely, where the accused (A):

(1) intends to kill B (the deceased), or
(2) intends to cause serious injury to B coupled with an awareness that their conduct involves a serious risk of causing death to B.[22]

Second degree murder contained the same basic structure as first degree murder and differed only in relation to the fault elements. The differences between the fault elements for first and second degree murder (with words deleted from first degree murder marked with strikethrough and additional words in italics) involve where the accused (A):

18 Wilson (n 17) 53.
19 See, eg, Kate Fitz-Gibbon and Arie Freiberg (eds), *Homicide Law Reform in Victoria: Retrospect and Prospects* (Federation Press, 2015).
20 *Murder, Manslaughter and Infanticide* (n 7).
21 *Murder, Manslaughter and Infanticide* (n 7).
22 *Murder, Manslaughter and Infanticide* (n 7) 32 [2.69]–[2.70].

(1) intends to ~~kill~~ cause *serious injury* to B (the deceased), or
(2) intends to cause ~~serious~~ *injury* (or fear or risk of injury) to B coupled with an awareness that their conduct involves a serious risk of causing death to B.

The combination of the offence of manslaughter[23] with the two murder offences provided a three-tiered structure to these homicide offences. The Law Commission's proposals included a third way of committing second degree murder — where the prosecution proves first degree murder, but the accused successfully raises a partial defence such as provocation or diminished responsibility.[24]

The approach used in Victoria's common law offence of murder creates a simpler structure with only one offence of murder and, since 2014, there are no partial defences as provocation and a form of excessive self-defence have been abolished.[25] There are four relevant alternative fault elements for the offence of murder in Victoria. The principal two fault elements involve where the accused (A):

(1) intends to kill or cause really serious injury to B (the deceased), or
(2) acts recklessly 'knowing that it was probable that death or really serious injury [to B] would result'.[26]

There is a high degree of overlap between what amounts to murder in Victoria and first or second degree murder in the Law Commission's proposals.

Policy factors concerning homicide laws

A detailed discussion of the policy issues that arise when determining the scope of homicide offences is beyond the scope of this book. However, outlining important policy factors that have shaped homicide offences illustrates how a jury-centric approach works with policy factors in defining offences. The policy factors shaping homicide offences include:

- when to distinguish between murder and manslaughter
- fair labelling for conduct involving a homicide
- what the maximum penalty for murder should be and the role of mandatory sentencing for murder

23 *Murder, Manslaughter and Infanticide* (n 7) 51 [2.163].

24 *Murder, Manslaughter and Infanticide* (n 7) 32 [2.70]. Since the Law Commission's report, provocation has been repealed and replaced by a defence called 'loss of control': *Coroners and Justice Act 2009* (UK) ss 54–6.

25 Provocation was abolished in 2005: *Crimes (Homicide) Act 2005* (Vic) ss 3 and 6. A form of excessive self-defence introduced in 2005 and then repealed in 2014: *Crimes Amendment (Abolition of Defensive Homicide) Act 2014* (Vic) s 3.

26 See, eg, *Crabbe v The Queen* (1985) 156 CLR 464 ('*Crabbe*'); Judicial College of Victoria, *Criminal Charge Book* <https://resources.judicialcollege.vic.edu.au> [7.2.1] (emphasis omitted).

- whether there should be partial defences to murder, and
- social law reform considerations.

The murder-manslaughter distinction

Even though the 'distinction between murder and manslaughter is almost certainly over 500 years old',[27] debate about what differentiates the offence of murder from manslaughter remains.[28] Victoria's laws and the Law Commission's proposals distinguish between murder and manslaughter in different ways. The differences between these jurisdictions (and other Australian jurisdictions[29]) suggest that there is no bright line or 'easy or perfect solutions' based on legal, policy, or moral grounds that clearly demarcate murder from manslaughter.[30] Because the harm in fatal offences (death) is the same it does not assist in distinguishing culpability. Therefore, the extent of an offender's culpability or moral blameworthiness is central to the distinction between murder and manslaughter. Further, a judge must be able to explain the murder-manslaughter distinction comprehensibly to a jury.

The Law Commission's approach more closely followed the 'correspondence' principle,[31] namely, that the fault element (eg, intention to kill and conduct causing death) relates to the harm done.[32] Common law murder in Victoria departs further from the correspondence principle because it provides that a person commits murder even when they did not intend death or were not aware that there was a serious risk of death. That is, liability extends beyond where death is intended or foreseen to where a person only foresees that really serious injury is the probable result of their conduct.[33]

The fault elements that distinguish murder and manslaughter involve difficult policy issues concerning what is morally equivalent or distinguishable. Moral blameworthiness is also relevant to jurors' commonsense justice and

27 *Murder, Manslaughter and Infanticide* (n 7) 9 [1.32].

28 See, eg, C M V Clarkson, 'Context and Culpability in Involuntary Manslaughter: Principle or Instinct?' in Andrew Ashworth and Barry Mitchell (eds), *Rethinking English Homicide Law* (Oxford University Press, 2000) 133, 143; Wilson (n 17) 25–6.

29 Ian Leader-Elliott, 'Recklessness and Moral Desiccation in the Australian Law of Murder' in Jeremy Horder (ed), *Homicide Law in Comparative Perspective* (Hart Publishing, 2007) 143, 149–50 ('Recklessness and Moral Desiccation').

30 See, eg, Jeremy Horder, 'The Changing Face of the Law of Homicide' in Jeremy Horder (ed), *Homicide Law in Comparative Perspective* (Hart Publishing, 2007) 19, 26–30.

31 *Murder, Manslaughter and Infanticide* (n 7) 34 [2.79].

32 The extent to which there should be correspondence between fault and harm, that is, where they do not fully correspond, is the subject of considerable debate. See, eg, Horder, *Ashworth's Principles of Criminal Law* (n 4) 95–7; Clarkson (n 28) 156–7; Andrew Cornford, 'The Architecture of Homicide' (2014) 34(4) *Oxford Journal of Legal Studies* 819, 820–5.

33 See generally, Horder, *Ashworth's Principles of Criminal Law* (n 4) 95–7, 177.

therefore may be relevant to juror comprehension of judicial guidance explaining the murder-manslaughter distinction.[34]

Fair labelling

'Fair labelling' refers to the 'belief that the label applied to an offence ought fairly to represent the offender's wrongdoing'.[35] Fair labelling can play an important role in defining the offence of murder and differentiating it from other offences. However, defining what is meant by 'fair labelling' is challenging and as Glanville Williams said, '[n]o one could argue that unfair labelling is acceptable'.[36] 'Murder' is a 'highly emotive' label[37] that resonates with the community.[38] For the purposes of 'fair labelling', the key challenge 'is to cut up the murder-manslaughter cake in a way which renders the two wrongs meaningfully distinct'.[39] In this sense, fair labelling may be seen as relevant to offence differentiation rather than an overriding consideration of its own,[40] and is therefore relevant to the murder-manslaughter distinction already discussed. The murder and manslaughter offence labels symbolise condemnation of the offences,[41] and the symbolic power of the offence label — especially for murder — may be diminished if offences are defined in a way that 'strays too far from their paradigm cases'.[42]

Fair labelling primarily arises with statutory offences because enactment provides an opportunity to name an offence. However, the courts have considered fair labelling. In *R v Jogee*,[43] the Supreme Court of the United Kingdom

34 See generally, Norman J Finkel, *Commonsense Justice Jurors' Notions of the Law* (Harvard University Press, 1995) 1–3; Catriona McKay, Mark Nolan and Michael Smithson, 'Effectiveness of Question Trails as Jury Decision Aids: The Jury's Still Out' (2014) 21(4) *Psychiatry, Psychology and Law* 492, 507.

35 Andrew Ashworth, 'Elasticity of Mens Rea' in C F H Tapper (ed), *Crime, Proof and Punishment: Essays in Memory of Sir Rupert Cross* (Butterworths, 1981) 45, 53.

36 Glanville Williams, 'Convictions and Fair Labelling' (1983) 42(1) *Cambridge Law Journal* 85, 86.

37 James Chalmers and Fiona Leverick, 'Fair Labelling in Criminal Law' (2008) 71(2) *Modern Law Review* 217, 241–3.

38 Ian Leader-Elliott, 'Reform and Codification of the Law of Homicide: Reflections on the Victorian Experience' in Kate Fitz-Gibbon and Arie Freiberg (eds), *Homicide Law Reform in Victoria: Retrospect and Prospects* (Federation Press, 2015) 158, 159 ('Reform and Codification of the Law of Homicide').

39 Wilson (n 17) 38.

40 Andrew Cornford, 'Beyond Fair Labelling: Offence Differentiation in Criminal Law' (2022) 42(4) *Oxford Journal of Legal Studies* 985.

41 Chalmers and Leverick (n 37) 226–9.

42 Wilson (n 17) 37. See also Victor Tadros, 'Fair Labelling and Social Solidarity' in Lucia Zedner and Julian V Roberts (eds), *Principles and Values in Criminal Law and Criminal Justice: Essays in Honour of Andrew Ashworth* (Oxford University Press, 2012) 67, 71.

43 *R v Jogee* [2017] AC 387 ('*Jogee*').

overturned 'parasitic accessory liability' for the offence of murder.[44] 'Parasitic accessory liability' is called 'extended common purpose' or 'extended joint criminal enterprise' in Australia.[45] It applies where two or more people embark on a common purpose or joint enterprise to commit an offence (eg, robbery). It makes an accomplice liable for the offence of murder if they foresaw the *possibility* that their accomplice (the principal offender) might kill a person in the course of committing another offence (eg, robbery) which was their common purpose or joint enterprise.

The Supreme Court of the United Kingdom concluded that the development of parasitic accessory liability had progressed without considering 'the fundamental policy question of whether and why it was necessary and appropriate to reclassify such conduct as murder rather than manslaughter'.[46] The Court overturned parasitic accessorial liability on a number of grounds, including general policy considerations such as 'fair labelling and fair discrimination in sentencing'[47] and the 'striking anomaly of requiring a lower mental threshold for guilt in the case of the accessory than in the case of the principal'.[48] The High Court of Australia has declined to reconsider this form of accessorial liability.[49] However, this did not mean that the High Court considered fair labelling irrelevant to policy issues concerning criminal liability.

The policy considerations identified by the Supreme Court of the United Kingdom indicate the importance of fair labelling when defining homicide offences. The offence of murder should be defined in a way that its label broadly reflects moral blameworthiness and therefore ties into comprehensibility issues as discussed concerning the murder-manslaughter distinction.

The maximum penalty for murder

One of the most significant differences between Victoria and England and Wales concerns the penalties. Maximum penalties and the sentences imposed for the offence of murder depend in part on how the offence is defined.[50] Sentencing coherence in homicide depends on offences being arranged hierarchically, and with gradations within those offences being clearly based upon

44 Sir John Smith coined the term 'parasitic accessory liability': Sir John Smith, 'Criminal Liability of Accessories: Law and Law Reform' (1997) 113 *Law Quarterly Review* 453, 455.

45 See, eg, *Clayton v The Queen* (2006) 81 ALJR 439 ('*Clayton*'); Penny Crofts et al, *Waller & Williams Criminal Law: Text and Cases* (LexisNexis, 14th ed, 2020) 925–6 [12.41]–[12.43].

46 *Jogee* (n 43) 414 [74].

47 *Jogee* (n 43) 414 [74].

48 *Jogee* (n 43) 416 [84].

49 See eg, *Clayton* (n 45) 179 [19]; [2006] HCA 58 (Gleeson CJ, Gummow, Hayne, Callinan, Heydon and Crennan JJ); *IL v The Queen* (2017) 262 CLR 268; *Mitchell v The King* (2023) 97 ALJR 172. This form of accessorial liability was abrogated in Victoria in 2014: *Crimes Act 1958* (Vic) s 324C(2).

50 Clarkson (n 28) 144. See also Horder, 'The Changing Face of the Law of Homicide' (n 30) 23.

distinctions in an offender's culpability for causing death.[51] However, as discussed earlier, there is no bright line test that easily distinguishes between degrees of culpability for murder and manslaughter offences. And the way offences are defined may affect the extent to which a jury considers the accused's culpability when deliberating.

In England and Wales, the penalty for murder is a mandatory term of life imprisonment.[52] The Law Commission's reference — and therefore its recommendations — were constrained by the requirement that life imprisonment would remain the penalty for murder.[53] Therefore, the Law Commission sought to provide sentencing coherence by recommending a 'graduated system or hierarchy of offences' to 'reflect the offence's degree of seriousness, without too much overlap between individual offences'.[54] The narrowness of first degree murder reflected that the courts would not have any discretion to fix an appropriate sentence based on the individual circumstances of the case and the offender. The Law Commission proposed that second degree murder be punishable by a maximum of life imprisonment.[55]

In Victoria, the maximum penalty for murder is life imprisonment.[56] However, a court has a discretion to impose less than the maximum penalty and usually does. Between 2017–18 and 2021–22, 18 of the 89 sentences of imprisonment for murder in Victoria were for a period of less than 20 years.[57] Increasing limits on sentencing discretion in Victoria with the introduction of 'standard sentences' in 2017[58] do not appear to have changed the range of sentences imposed. If the Victorian offence had a maximum penalty of mandatory life imprisonment, this would be a significant policy consideration against its simpler murder-manslaughter offence distinction, where the offence of murder is broader than the Law Commission proposed.

When the maximum penalty for the offence of murder is a mandatory term of life imprisonment, the case for a narrower offence of murder[59] is at its strongest. However, this constraint led to the Law Commission proposing two murder offences involving more fine-grained distinctions between offences.

51 Wasik (n 14) 192. See generally, Sentencing Advisory Council (Vic), *Maximum Penalties: Principles and Purposes* (Report, October 2010) 11–13 [3.21]–[3.32].

52 *Murder, Manslaughter and Infanticide* (n 7) 14–15 [1.58]–[1.62].

53 *Murder, Manslaughter and Infanticide* (n 7) 16 [1.66].

54 *Murder, Manslaughter and Infanticide* (n 7) 16 [1.64].

55 *Murder, Manslaughter and Infanticide* (n 7) 32 [2.71].

56 *Crimes Act 1958* (Vic) s 3(1).

57 Sentencing Advisory Council (Vic), *Sentencing Snapshot: Murder* (Report 273, June 2023) 3. The sentence imposed refers to the head sentence, or maximum term of imprisonment, rather than the non-parole period.

58 *Crimes Act 1958* (Vic) s 3(2). The 'standard sentence' is 'the sentence for an offence that, taking into account only the objective factors affecting the relative seriousness of that offence, is in the middle of the range of seriousness': *Sentencing Act 1991* (Vic) s 5A(1)(b). For murder, the 'standard sentence' is 25 years' imprisonment.

59 Horder, 'The Changing Face of the Law of Homicide' (n 30) 23.

Narrower offence distinctions are likely to make juror comprehension of the differences more difficult, but there is no evidence quantifying what this difference might be. Victoria's broader offence of murder expands the role of the judge in making important sentencing decisions about the offender's level of culpability[60] and may result in some comparatively low sentences for murder. Low sentences may raise questions about whether the offence is labelled and/or defined appropriately.[61] These considerations highlight the role sentencing discretion can play in defining offences and sentencing policy choices may affect offence definitions, which in turn may affect juror comprehension.

Partial defences to murder

Constrained by the mandatory penalty of life imprisonment for murder, the Law Commission recommended that partial defences of provocation and diminished responsibility should be available to a charge of first degree murder.[62] These partial defences serve two principal purposes. First, if relevant, they provide a mechanism for a jury to recognise the reduced culpability of the offender.[63] Second, in some jurisdictions, but not under the Law Commission's proposals, partial defences mean that a person will not be labelled a murderer. Under the Law Commission's proposals, the person would be labelled a second degree murderer.

Partial defences only apply to the offence of murder. They developed primarily because of the existence of significant penalties such as capital punishment or mandatory sentences of life imprisonment. The case for partial defences is strongest where there is mandatory sentencing for murder. Where judges have a discretion to impose a lesser sentence than life imprisonment for the offence of murder, as in Victoria, the case for partial defences is not as strong, as discussed later in this chapter.

Partial defences usually mean that juries must make more decisions and more finely balanced decisions about an offender's culpability. The extent to which partial defences align with moral blameworthiness and jurors' commonsense concerning the murder-manslaughter distinction will also be relevant to juror comprehension of each partial defence.

60 See, eg, *Murder, Manslaughter and Infanticide* (n 7) 32 [2.67]; Wasik (n 14) 167–9, 183–4; LRCWA, *A Review of the Law of Homicide* (n 15) 77–9; David Ormerod and Richard Taylor, 'Agreement and Disagreement in Murder and Manslaughter Verdicts' [2022] (3) *Criminal Law Review* 185, 192–6.

61 See generally, Wasik (n 14) 192; Horder, 'The Changing Face of the Law of Homicide' (n 30) 23.

62 *Murder, Manslaughter and Infanticide* (n 7).

63 See, eg, LRCWA, *A Review of the Law of Homicide* (n 15) 217; MCCOC, *Fatal Offences Against the Person* (n 15) 103.

Social law reform

The discussion so far primarily reflects 'lawyer's law reform' (focusing on matters of interest primarily to lawyers) rather than 'social law reform' (focusing on matters of broader social and community interest).[64] Social law reform places particular emphasis on the context in which homicides occur, rather than 'abstract philosophical principles', for determining what homicide laws should be.[65] Empirical evidence is critical both to understanding the circumstances in which homicides occur and the way in which the law applies to those circumstances.[66] This involves beginning with the social problems rather than the legal categories used to address homicides.[67] Social law reform has been particularly important in the context of intimate partner homicides, because they often concern gendered crimes involving an abuse of power. These crimes have not traditionally been well recognised by self-defence laws and by partial defences like provocation which developed primarily in the context of a 'one-off spontaneous encounter' usually involving two men, or in circumstances involving 'breaches of [a man's] honour'.[68]

Social law reform is critical to determining the policy goals of homicide laws and identifying when laws may not accord with moral blameworthiness. For example, the moral blameworthiness of a man who kills his partner because she committed adultery may be inappropriately excused by the partial defence of provocation and self-defence laws may fail to adequately recognise the situation of a woman who kills her partner in response to him repeatedly committing family violence.[69] The law should address, rather than align itself with, mistaken views about moral blameworthiness. Moral blameworthiness is relevant to jurors' commonsense justice and therefore may affect their comprehension of the law and their task. Therefore, a jury-centric approach is relevant to achieving social law reform goals.

64 See, eg, Geoffrey Sawer, 'The Legal Theory of Law Reform' (1970) 20(2) *The University of Toronto Law Journal* 183, 193–4; Kiernan Tranter and Rodney Meyer, 'The Use of Journal Articles by the Queensland Law Reform Commission' (2015) 27 *Bond Law Review* 57, 73.

65 See, eg, the approach adopted in Victorian Law Reform Commission, *Defences to Homicide* (Final Report, October 2004) 4 [1.9] and 15 [1.40] (VLRC).

66 Justice Marcia Neave, 'The More Things Change the More They Stay the Same: Homicide Law Reform in Victoria' in Kate Fitz-Gibbon and Arie Freiberg (eds), *Homicide Law Reform in Victoria: Retrospect and Prospects* (Federation Press, 2015) 9, 16.

67 See, eg, VLRC, *Who Kills Whom and Why: Looking Beyond Legal Categories* (Occasional Paper, 2002) 1–2.

68 VLRC, *Defences to Homicide* (n 65) 21–2 [2.4] and 61 [3.8]. See also Kate Fitz-Gibbon and Sharon Pickering, 'Homicide Law Reform in Victoria, Australia: From Provocation to Defensive Homicide and Beyond' (2012) 52 *British Journal of Criminology* 158; Danielle Tyson et al, 'The Effects of the 2005 Reforms on Legal Responses to Women who Kill Intimate Partners' in Kate Fitz-Gibbon and Arie Freiberg (eds), *Homicide Law Reform in Victoria: Retrospect and Prospects* (Federation Press, 2015) 76.

69 See, eg, VLRC, *Defences to Homicide* (n 65) 55–8 [2.92]–[2.103] and 61–4 [3.8]–[3.14].

Interconnected policy issues

These five policy issues (the murder-manslaughter distinction, fair labelling, the maximum penalty for murder, partial defences to murder, and social law reform) are interconnected. For example, if there is a mandatory life penalty for the offence of murder, this may constrain policy choices when defining murder and whether to recognise partial defences. However, the definition of murder is also tied to moral blameworthiness, the murder-manslaughter distinction, when it is appropriate to label a person a murderer, and to achieving social law reform goals. Definitions, moral blameworthiness and labels are all relevant to what jurors understand about the offence of murder and whether they are likely to apply the law as intended.

To be effective, offences and defences must reflect the resolution of these interconnected policy issues and be capable of being explained comprehensibly to jurors. The first step in a jury-centric approach focuses on the comprehensibility of offences and defences. Juror comprehension evidence therefore provides a critical further interconnected issue to consider when defining homicide offences.

Juror comprehension evidence in relation to murder offences

Reports and proposals for reforms of homicide offences often discuss the need for offences to be comprehensible to jurors. For example, the Law Commission's criteria for distinguishing offences and defences included that they should be clear and certain 'in a way that non-lawyers can understand and accept'.[70] The Law Commission further said that it is important to 'ensure that the law does not become so complex that it cannot be applied by juries, especially when they are faced with a number of defendants running different defences (perhaps in the alternative)'.[71] In assessing its proposal for first and second degree murder and an offence of manslaughter, the Law Commission said that

> [m]ost significantly, prosecutors, defence advocates and judges have not objected to the three-tier structure on the grounds that it would prove to be too complex.[72]

On what basis did prosecutors, defence counsel, and judges conclude that the three-tiered structure was not too complex? They could not draw on direct experience because England and Wales had, and still has, a two-tiered structure of homicide offences. However, they may have drawn inferences based

70 *Murder, Manslaughter and Infanticide* (n 7) 3 [1.10]. See also MCCOC, *Fatal Offences Against the Person* (n 15) 113; VLRC, *Defences to Homicide* (n 65) 103 [3.111].
71 *Murder, Manslaughter and Infanticide* (n 7) 23 [2.25].
72 *Murder, Manslaughter and Infanticide* (n 7) 23 [2.26].

on the extent to which jurors *appear* to understand the two-tiered structure and their general views about what is and is not comprehensible to jurors. For example, the Law Commission endorsed judicial comments that juries do not need 'intention' explained to them[73] and that if the law confused jurors, they 'would expect juries to be consistently sending notes to judges asking for further explanation', which had not been occurring.[74]

As discussed in Chapters 2 and 3, jury deliberations are confidential, and jurors often do not ask questions when they are confused about the law or may mistakenly believe that they do understand the law. Therefore, jury questions to the judge provide an unreliable source of information for assessing juror comprehension. In the absence of direct and reliable information about what jurors understand, courts have inferred what jurors do and do not understand (judicial knowledge and experience) and appear to have used the same approach when assessing the Law Commission's three-tiered structure. The Law Commission also appears to have relied on a similar kind of knowledge and experience. In effect, the Law Commission was drawing inferences from what is already inferred knowledge (judicial knowledge and experience) about what jurors do and do not understand about existing offences. As discussed in Chapter 3, juror comprehension research indicates that there are significant problems with the accuracy and reliability of judicial knowledge and experience in assessing juror comprehension.

Like other reviews of homicide laws,[75] the Law Commission did not refer to social science juror comprehension research. There are no simulated jury studies comparing the comprehensibility of the Law Commission's proposals with either existing laws in England and Wales or in Victoria, or other proposals for reform of homicide laws. Therefore, as discussed in Chapter 5, it is necessary to consider whether reasonable inferences can be drawn from research to compare the comprehensibility of the Law Commission's proposals and the laws in Victoria. Juror comprehension research has identified three areas of inquiry that may assist in comparing the comprehensibility of the Law Commission's proposals with Victoria's laws:

- the difficulties jurors have with linguistic and conceptual complexity
- the cognitive load on jurors, and
- jurors' application of commonsense justice.

73 *Murder, Manslaughter and Infanticide* (n 7) 55 [3.10] and [3.17].

74 *Murder, Manslaughter and Infanticide* (n 7) 58 [3.23].

75 See, eg, MCCOC, *Fatal Offences against the Person* (n 15); LRCWA, *A Review of the Law of Homicide* (n 15); New Zealand Law Commission, *The Partial Defence of Provocation* (Report No 98, September 2007).

Jurors' difficulties with linguistic and conceptual complexity

As discussed in Chapter 3, jurors have difficulty understanding legal jargon, uncommon words, abstract words, and ambiguous words and phrases.[76] This means that words like 'malice aforethought' and 'reckless indifference' which are used in homicide laws in some jurisdictions are problematic unless they are explained in more comprehensible terms.

Conceptual complexity may be more important than linguistic complexity, in determining the comprehensibility of jury directions.[77] Conceptual complexity can arise from the number of, and the nature of the differences between, offences, elements of offences, defences, and partial defences that a jury must understand to return a verdict. Distinguishing between the different fault elements, together with the partial defences in the Law Commission's proposals, increases the conceptual complexity of the jury's task.

Recklessness can be conceptually one of the most complex elements of an offence.[78] Both the Law Commission's proposals and the laws in Victoria rely on forms of recklessness. The Law Commission's proposals require two matters to be proved in relation to the second form of first degree murder (recklessness):

- an intention to cause serious injury, and
- an awareness of a serious risk of causing death.

This is more complicated than recklessness as to death in Victoria which involves proof of only one matter, namely that the accused knew that it was probable that death or really serious injury would result from their conduct.[79]

Studies from the USA have used short vignettes to assess understanding of the Model Penal Code's definitions of intention, knowledge, recklessness, and negligence[80] in either undergraduate students[81] or the general popula-

76 See, eg, Amiram Elwork, Bruce D Sales and James J Alfini, 'Juridic Decisions: In Ignorance of the Law or in Light of It?' (1977) 1 *Law and Human Behavior* 163, 165–9 ('Juridic Decisions').

77 Chantelle M Baguley, Blake M McKimmie and Barbara M Masser, 'Deconstructing the Simplification of Jury Instructions: How Simplifying the Features of Complexity Affects Jurors' Application of Instructions' (2017) 41(3) *Law and Human Behavior* 284, 296; James R P Ogloff and V Gordon Rose, 'The Comprehension of Judicial Instructions' in Neil Brewer and Kipling D Williams (eds), *Psychology and Law: An Empirical Perspective* (Guilford Press, 2005) 407, 428.

78 See, eg, Laurence Severance and Elizabeth Loftus, 'Improving the Ability of Jurors to Comprehend and Apply Jury Instructions' (1982) 17 *Law & Society Review* 153, 180–1.

79 See, eg, *Criminal Charge Book* (n 26) [7.2.1]; Crabbe (n 26).

80 These definitions are generally consistent with those used in Australia and England and Wales. However, recklessness is defined as 'consciously disregard[ing] a substantial and unjustifiable risk': Pam A Mueller, Lawrence M Solan and John M Darley, 'When Does Knowledge Become Intent: Perceiving the Minds of Wrongdoers' (2012) 9(4) *Empirical Legal Studies* 859, 861.

81 See, eg, Robert A Beattey and Mark R Fondacaro, 'The Misjudgment of Criminal Responsibility' (2018) 36(4) *Behavior Sciences & the Law* 457, 463.

tion.[82] The results of these studies have been broadly consistent. In one study, approximately 75% of people considered factual scenarios depicting recklessness or knowledge sufficient to prove that the person acted purposefully.[83] Another study found that people were good at distinguishing between intention, knowledge, recklessness, and negligence,[84] but found knowledge and recklessness the most difficult to distinguish.[85] However, in some studies, subjects chose from a list of the four different states of mind rather than considering whether one or two states of mind (eg, intention and recklessness) had been proved, as would usually occur in a trial.[86]

Research also found that the greater the harm described in the vignette (eg, homicide), the more likely it was for participants to find that a lesser state of mind was sufficient to prove purpose (intention).[87] Research suggests that when making a moral judgement about conduct, and assessing liability (including punitive damages), people treat knowing and reckless acts as if they amount to intentional acts.[88] Further, moral culpability was more important than findings of intentionality in predicting awards of punitive damages.[89]

The second part of the Law Commission's definition of recklessness for first degree murder is that a person is *aware* that their conduct involves a serious risk of causing death.[90] Another study from the USA involving 186 people, using vignettes, suggests that this description of recklessness is better understood than several other ways of explaining recklessness:[91] 65% of those surveyed correctly identified this level of risk involved recklessness.[92] However, improvements in identifying recklessness did not result in any changes to the punishment that the subjects would have imposed for the conduct.[93] Further, none of the descriptions of recklessness tested in the USA involved a two-part definition concerning mental states of intention and awareness of

82 See, eg, Francis X Shen et al, 'Sorting Guilty Minds' (2011) 86(5) *New York University Law Review* 1306, 1334; Mueller, Solan and Darley (n 80) 867; Matthew R Ginther et al, 'The Language of Mens Rea' (2014) 67(5) *Vanderbilt Law Review* 1327, 1350 ('The Language of Mens Rea'); Matthew R Ginther et al, 'Decoding Guilty Minds: How Jurors Attribute Knowledge and Guilt' (2018) 71(1) *Vanderbilt Law Review* 241, 279 ('Decoding Guilty Minds').
83 Beattey and Fondacaro (n 81) 466.
84 Mueller, Solan and Darley (n 80) 875–7. See also Ginther et al, 'The Language of Mens Rea' (n 82); Ginther et al, 'Decoding Guilty Minds' (n 82).
85 Mueller, Solan and Darley (n 80) 876. See also Shen et al (n 82) 1354; Michelle I Bertrand and Richard Jochelson, 'Mock-Jurors' Self-Reported Understanding of Canadian Judicial Instructions (Is Not Very Good)' (2018) 66 *Criminal Law Quarterly* 137, 151–3.
86 Shen et al (n 82) 1332–3. See generally, Beattey and Fondacaro (n 81) 461–2.
87 Beattey and Fondacaro (n 81) 466.
88 Mueller, Solan and Darley (n 80) 875.
89 Mueller, Solan and Darley (n 80) 877.
90 *Murder, Manslaughter and Infanticide* (n 7) 32 [2.69].
91 For example, it was better understood than 'conscious of the likelihood that harm will occur but simply doesn't care': Ginther et al, 'The Language of Mens Rea' (n 82) 1356.
92 Ginther et al, 'The Language of Mens Rea' (n 82) 1356.
93 Ginther et al, 'The Language of Mens Rea' (n 82) 1360.

the kind proposed by the Law Commission for recklessness in first and second degree murder. The more complex the test is, the harder it will be for jurors to understand. Therefore, it is very unlikely that the Law Commission's test would also achieve a comprehension rate of 65%.

Victoria simplifies the directions on fault elements by not requiring the judge to direct the jury about recklessness unless it is necessary to do so on the facts.[94] It is rarely necessary for the judge to do so because the fault element of *intending to cause a really serious injury* substantially overlaps with the fault element concerning recklessness as to death.[95] When reconstructing a past event, there is presumably little difference between finding that a person intended to cause a really serious injury (eg, stabbing another person in the chest) and finding that the person knew that their conduct would probably cause death. Research indicates that where conduct causes harm, people are more likely to attribute intentionality than if no harm resulted from the conduct.[96] By contrast, under the Law Commission's proposals, similar fault elements help to distinguish between first and second degree murder. As a result, a judge (applying the Law Commission's proposals) would often need to explain recklessness to the jury.

While the data is limited, the findings are of concern where murder-manslaughter distinctions rely on fine differences between fault elements and where it is not known whether jurors' moral judgements (or commonsense justice) align closely with legal categories of culpability. While understanding the complexity of individual components of the jury's task is important, the overall cognitive load of the jury's task also affects their ability to deal with complexity in the law.

The cognitive load on jurors

As discussed in Chapter 3, the cognitive load of the juror's task can be high. Cognitive load refers to 'the mental activity imposed upon an individual's finite working memory'.[97] There are limits to each juror's working memory which may affect their capacity to understand their task, including understanding jury directions.[98] Some cognitive load is inevitable in any trial as

94 *Criminal Charge Book* (n 26) 7.2.1 [36]; *Pemble v The Queen* (1971) 124 CLR 107.

95 See, eg, *Crabbe* (n 26); *Criminal Charge Book* (n 26) [7.2.1].

96 Ginther et al, 'Decoding Guilty Minds' (n 82) 275.

97 Ryan Essex and Jane Goodman-Delahunty, 'Judicial Directions and the Criminal Standard of Proof: Improving Juror Comprehension' (2014) 24 *Journal of Judicial Administration* 75, 77. See generally, John Sweller, Jeroen J G van Merriënboer and Fred Paas, 'Cognitive Architecture and Instructional Design: 20 Years Later' (2019) 31(2) *Educational Psychology Review* 261.

98 See, eg, Carolyn Semmler and Neil Brewer, 'Using a Flow-Chart to Improve Comprehension of Jury Instructions' (2002) 9 *Psychiatry, Psychology and Law* 262.

jurors are often unfamiliar with their task, including the law and the evidence that they must assess. '[S]tress, emotions and uncertainty' may reduce working memory.[99] Research suggests that the greatest stress for jurors comes from the decision-making task itself,[100] given comprehension difficulties with the task and the consequences of a verdict for the people involved in the case.[101] Further, research suggests that juries generally find homicide trials to be more complicated than trials involving other offences.[102] Juror stress in a murder trial is therefore already significant irrespective of how the offence is defined.

The complexity of the jury's task is relevant to determining jurors' cognitive load. The 'intrinsic cognitive load is determined by both the complexity of the information and the knowledge of the person processing that information'.[103] As discussed, with the Law Commission's proposals, a jury would often need to distinguish between first and second degree murder. There are two fault elements for each degree of murder and the second fault element for each degree also requires assessment of the dangerousness of the conduct. The comparative complexity of the jury's task in applying the Law Commission's proposals is shown in Table 8.1.

Table 8.1 Fault elements for murder

Victoria	*Law Commission*
Murder • Intention to kill • Intention to cause really serious injury	Murder (first degree) • Intention to kill • Intention to cause serious injury coupled with an awareness that their conduct involves a serious risk of causing death Murder (second degree) • Intention to cause serious injury • Intention to cause some injury coupled with an awareness that their conduct involves a serious risk of causing serious injury

99 Sweller, Merriënboer and Paas (n 97) 285.

100 See, eg, Noelle Robertson, Graham Davies and Nettleingham, 'Vicarious Trauma as a Consequence of Jury Service' (2009) 48(1) *The Howard Journal* 1, 6; Michelle Lonergan et al, 'Prevalence and Severity of Trauma- and Stressor-Related Symptoms among Jurors: A Review' (2016) 47 *Journal of Criminal Justice* 51, 57.

101 Brian H Bornstein et al, 'Juror Reactions to Jury Duty: Perceptions of the System and Potential Stressors' (2005) 23(3) *Behavioral Sciences & Law* 321, 335–6. See also, Heise (n 3) 366.

102 Heise (n 3) 366.

103 Sweller, Merriënboer and Paas (n 97) 264.

Further, a jury may also need to determine whether the prosecution has disproved partial defences beyond reasonable doubt. Determining partial defences that place the burden of proof on the accused, as occurs in England and Wales with diminished responsibility, can be even more challenging for jurors.[104] The more issues that arise in a trial (eg, where there are parties to an offence who allegedly perform different roles and/or there are difficult evidentiary issues), the greater the increase in information provided to jurors and matters that the judge must explain. This informational complexity contributes to the overall cognitive load for jurors.

It is reasonable to infer that the cognitive load associated with the Law Commission's proposed offences would be greater than that involved with Victoria's offences. This cognitive load is likely to reduce the extent to which jurors can understand and accurately apply the judge's directions to return a verdict in accordance with the law.[105] When jurors do not fully understand the law, there is a greater chance that their preconceived ideas about the law will play a more significant role.

Commonsense justice

Jurors' preconceived ideas of the law, or commonsense justice, may differ from the law that jurors must apply.[106] If jurors do not understand the judge's directions, they may instead rely on their commonsense understanding of the law.[107] If jurors understand the judge's directions but the directions conflict with their commonsense understanding of the law, 'jurors' may be resistant to change their views or accommodate new information.[108]

Knowing when the law departs from jurors' commonsense justice is relevant to understanding how to effectively direct the jury. The judge may need to address jurors' misconceptions about the law and explain why their ideas are wrong, to enable jurors to set aside their misconceptions.[109] A judge cannot address a misconception about the law if the judge does not — at least in a general sense — know what jurors' commonsense ideas of the law are or are likely to be. If the judge uses SDM aids to guide the jury, this may reduce

104 To see this set out in a route to verdict involving existing murder and manslaughter offences in England and Wales, see Ormerod and Taylor (n 60) 207–8.

105 Baguley, McKimmie and Masser (n 77) 296.

106 See, eg, Severance and Loftus (n 78) 194; Smith, 'Prototypes in the Courtroom' (n 16) 869.

107 Walter W Steele Jr and Elizabeth G Thornburg, 'Jury Instructions: A Persistent Failure to Communicate' (1988) 67 *North Carolina Law Review* 77, 96. See also Finkel, 'Commonsense Justice and Jury Instructions' (n 16) 608–9; Vicki L Smith, 'When Prior Knowledge and Law Collide: Helping Jurors Use the Law' (1993) 17(5) *Law and Human Behavior* 507, 509 ('When Prior Knowledge and Law Collide').

108 See, eg, Severance and Loftus (n 78) 194; Smith, 'Prototypes in the Courtroom' (n 16) 870; Bradley Saxton, 'How Well Do Jurors Understand Jury Instructions? A Field Test Using Real Juries and Real Trials in Wyoming' (1998) 33 *Land and Water Law Review* 59, 95.

109 Phoebe C Ellsworth and Alan Reifman, 'Juror Comprehension and Public Policy: Perceived Problems and Proposed Solutions' (2000) 6 *Psychology, Public Policy and Law* 788, 800.

informational complexity and lead jurors to invoke a 'form of analytical reasoning that may help override jurors' preconceived ideas about the law'.[110] However, the effectiveness of SDM aids may be limited if they do not engage with jurors' commonsense ideas of justice for more 'morally ambiguous' offences like murder.[111] This is because the morally ambiguous nature of offences may lead jurors to 'make reference to morally based commonsense notions of justice' even when the judge has not discussed such matters.[112]

The Law Commission identified public opinion about what constitutes murder as a relevant factor in defining the offence of murder.[113] In particular, research in England and Wales revealed that 'the public assumes that murder involves an intention to kill or its moral equivalent'.[114] What constitutes the moral equivalent of an intention to kill is debatable,[115] but the Law Commission considered it to be a 'total disregard for human life'[116] and considered recklessness for first degree murder reflected that moral equivalence.

Working out Victorian jurors' commonsense ideas of what constitutes murder is difficult. The Victorian Law Reform Commission (VLRC) did not refer to any research about what Victorians or other Australians consider constitutes murder when reviewing defences to homicide.[117] The Law Reform Commission of Western Australia only referred to research from England and Wales together with anecdotal views presented in parliament in its review of homicide laws.[118] Further, what constitutes murder and manslaughter differs in each jurisdiction in Australia.[119] As a result:

> [o]ne might guess that members of the jury are more likely to be guided by a global view of the circumstances of the death and their intuitive sense of what it takes, morally speaking, for a killing to amount to murder rather than a lesser form of unlawful homicide.[120]

110 Tamsin Ede and Jane Goodman-Delahunty, 'Question Trails in Trials: Structured versus Unstructured Juror Decision-Making' (2013) 37 *Criminal Law Journal* 114, 134.

111 McKay, Nolan and Smithson (n 34) 505–8. Other 'morally ambiguous' offences include kidnapping and indecent assault.

112 McKay, Nolan and Smithson (n 34) 507.

113 *Murder, Manslaughter and Infanticide* (n 7) 5 [1.21].

114 *Murder, Manslaughter and Infanticide* (n 7) 5 [1.21].

115 See, eg, LRCWA, *A Review of the Law of Homicide* (n 15) 83. See generally Victor Tadros, *Criminal Responsibility* (Oxford University Press, 2007) 113.

116 *Murder, Manslaughter and Infanticide* (n 7) 5 [1.21].

117 VLRC, *Defences to Homicide* (n 65).

118 LRCWA, *A Review of the Law of Homicide* (n 15) 76–7.

119 Leader-Elliott, 'Recklessness and Moral Desiccation' (n 29) 149–50, 174.

120 Leader-Elliott, 'Recklessness and Moral Desiccation' (n 29) 161. In a welcome change, the Queensland Law Reform Commission (QLRC) 'commissioned a state-wide survey and focus group research to understand community views' on the laws it is reviewing: QLRC, *Review of Particular Criminal Defences: Community Attitudes to Defences and Sentences in Cases of Homicide and Assault in Queensland* (Research Report 1, November 2024), Preface. How this research will influence the QLRC's report is not yet known.

Using a jury-centric approach to determine homicide laws

Evidence directly comparing juror comprehension of the Law Commission's proposals and Victoria's homicide laws, and jury-eligible citizens' views about what should constitute murder, would assist in choosing between these options. However, by drawing on existing evidence and reasonable inferences from the evidence, this part of the case study shows how a jury-centric approach, in particular juror comprehension evidence, is relevant to determining the policy content of homicide laws.

The available evidence suggests that the simpler Victorian approach of having only one offence of murder, where the jury does not usually need to be directed about recklessness, and does not need to consider any partial defences, is likely to be easier for jurors to understand and apply. It is more likely that Victoria's murder-manslaughter distinction can be explained comprehensibly to a jury. It involves fewer decision points and less information for jurors to understand thereby reducing their cognitive load. However, it is unclear whether the Law Commission's proposals or Victoria's offences more fairly label murder (for each jurisdiction) to reflect moral blameworthiness and therefore how jurors' commonsense justice may affect the comprehensibility of each set of laws.

The case study shows that a jury-centric approach provides transparency in challenging policy decision-making environments. If the policy choice is made that life imprisonment should be mandatory, then a more complex offence structure, potentially with partial defences, is much more likely to be warranted. However, the complexity of the resulting murder-manslaughter offence structure will make the jury's task more difficult and increases the risk that there will not be a fair trial because jurors do not fully understand their task. Victoria's broader offences increase judicial responsibility for assessing levels of culpability. Differentiating culpability depends upon courts having sufficient sentencing discretion. Therefore, improving juror comprehension can provide a relevant policy reason for rejecting mandatory sentencing such as life imprisonment for murder.

Provided that a court has sentencing discretion, applying a jury-centric approach based on the available evidence indicates that Victoria's simpler homicide laws are preferable to the Law Commission's proposals. This does not mean that Victoria's laws produce the best possible policy outcome for all jurisdictions and for all types of homicide. The discussion of policy factors that are interconnected with each other and with juror comprehension shows that defining homicide offences is a difficult task. Further, the case study focused on only two sets of laws and did not consider whether Victoria's laws could be improved from either a policy perspective or a juror comprehension perspective.[121]

121 See Greg Byrne, 'Simplifying Homicide Laws for Complex Situations' in Kate Fitz-Gibbon and Arie Freiberg (eds), *Homicide Law Reform in Victoria: Retrospect and Prospects* (Federation Press, 2015) 144, 156–7.

This discussion has referred to the role of partial defences in defining homicide offences. The next section involves the second part of the case study, an examination of one partial defence, excessive self-defence.

Applying a jury-centric approach to excessive self-defence

The idea underpinning self-defence — recognising that a person may do what is reasonably necessary to defend themselves — makes 'good sense' and 'good law'[122] and should be easy to explain. Self-defence is a complete 'defence' to the offence of murder.[123] In addition to self-defence, three Australian jurisdictions recognise a partial defence of 'excessive self-defence'.[124] In recent decades, some law reform bodies have recommended the introduction of excessive self-defence,[125] and others either have recommended against it or have recommended its repeal.[126] This part of the case study examines whether a jury-centric approach is relevant to the policy decision of whether to recognise excessive self-defence.

What is excessive self-defence?

Self-defence laws in many common law jurisdictions essentially involve two elements:

(1) the accused believed their conduct was necessary,[127] and
(2) the accused's conduct was a reasonable response in the circumstances.[128]

122 *Palmer v The Queen* [1971] AC 814, 831 ('*Palmer*').

123 While often described as a 'defence', self-defence usually forms an element of the offence that the prosecution must disprove beyond reasonable doubt (eg, that the killing occurred without lawful justification or excuse): *Criminal Charge Book* (n 26) [7.2.1].

124 *Crimes Act 1900* (NSW) s 422; *Criminal Law Consolidation Act 1935* (SA) s 15(2); *Criminal Code Act 1913* (WA) s 248(3).

125 See, eg, VLRC, *Defences to Homicide* (n 65); LRCWA, *A Review of the Law of Homicide* (n 15); The Law Commission recommended a different model — modifying provocation to recognise excessive self-defence in certain circumstances: Law Commission, *Partial Defences to Murder* (Final Report No 290, August 2004).

126 *Partial Defences to Murder* (n 125) 80 [4.31]; Criminal Law Review, Department of Justice (Vic), *Defensive Homicide: Proposals for Legislative Reform* (Report, September 2013) (CLR, '*Defensive Homicide*') 33–5 [2.9]; New Zealand Law Commission, *Understanding Family Violence: Reforming the Criminal Law Relating to Homicide* (Report No 139, May 2016) 72 [6.4] ('NZLC, *Understanding Family Violence*') 159–60 [10.108]–[10.110].

127 See, eg, Judicial College, *The Crown Court Compendium — Part I: Jury and Trial Management and Summing Up* (July 2024) <www.judiciary.uk/wp-content/uploads/2024/07/Crown-Court-Compendium-Part-I-July-2024-1.pdf> 18–1 ('*Crown Court Compendium*'); *Crimes Act 1958* (Vic) s322K(2); *Crimes Act 1900* (NSW) s 418; *Criminal Code Act 1913* (WA) s 248(4)(a); Simon Bronitt and Bernadette McSherry, *Principles of Criminal Law* (Lawbook, 4th ed, 2017) 353–4.

128 See *Crimes Act 1958* (Vic) s322K(2). Common law self-defence in Australia and in England and Wales is quite similar: Crown Court Compendium (n 127) 18–1. See also *Crimes Act 1900* (NSW) s 418.

Under the common law in Australia, the second limb is expressed in terms of whether the accused had reasonable grounds for believing that their response was necessary.[129] Whether a response must be a proportionate response depends upon the jurisdiction.[130]

In general terms, excessive self-defence applies where the accused believed that their conduct was necessary, but their response was not reasonable (or was not proportionate).[131] Excessive self-defence operates as a partial defence to the offence of murder and reduces a person's liability to a lesser offence, such as manslaughter.[132] Before examining how excessive self-defence works in practice, the next section discusses why some jurisdictions recognise excessive self-defence and others do not.

Policy factors concerning recognition of excessive self-defence

Excessive self-defence 'has been in and out of favour in Australian law for over half a century'.[133] Both supporters and opponents of excessive self-defence often agree that a person who acts in excessive self-defence is less morally blameworthy if they believed that their use of lethal force was necessary, and they had a right to act in self-defence.[134] However, supporters and opponents disagree about how the law should respond. Both supporters[135] and opponents[136] of excessive self-defence can refer to an impressive number of law reform bodies and appellate decisions that support their respective viewpoints.

In 2004, the VLRC recommended the introduction of excessive self-defence, as part of a package of reforms designed to address gender bias in legal responses to intimate partner homicide.[137] Excessive self-defence is not limited to addressing gender bias in legal responses, but the strongest (social law reform) policy arguments for it arise in this situation. When considering

129 *Zecevic v DPP (Vic)* (1987) 162 CLR 645, 661 (Wilson, Dawson and Toohey JJ) ('*Zecevic*').

130 Some laws expressly recognise that force may be disproportionate: *Criminal Justice and Immigration Act 2008* (UK) s 76(5A) (for a householder against a trespasser) and *Crimes Act 1958* (Vic) s 322M (in the context of family violence).

131 See *Crimes Act 1900* (NSW) s 421(1); *Criminal Code Act 1913* (WA) s 248(3). See also Penny Crofts, *Waller & Williams Criminal Law: Text and Cases* (LexisNexis, 15th ed, 2025) 915–16 [14.17]–[14.19].

132 See, eg, Stanley Yeo, 'Revisiting Excessive Self-Defence' (2000) 12(1) *Current Issues in Criminal Justice* 39, 41.

133 Kellie Toole, 'Defensive Homicide on Trial in Victoria' (2013) 39(2) *Monash University Law Review* 473, 478.

134 See, eg, Yeo (n 132) 40–2; Fiona Leverick, *Killing in Self-Defence* (Oxford University Press, 2006) 174.

135 See, eg, VLRC, *Defences to Homicide* (n 65) 93 [3.90]; Law Commission, *Criminal Law: A Code for England and Wales* (LC 177, 1989) cl 59; Yeo (n 132) 40–2.

136 See, eg, NZLC, *Understanding Family Violence* (n 126). Courts have also rejected excessive self-defence: *Zecevic* (n 129); *Palmer* (n 122); *R v Faid* [1983] 1 SCR 265, 270–4 (Dickson J for the Court) ('*Faid*'); *McNaughton v The Queen* [2014] 2 NZLR 467.

137 VLRC, *Defences to Homicide* (n 65) xxiv.

excessive self-defence in the context of women who kill in response to family violence, three key policy issues arise:

- the limitations of self-defence
- community views about killing in response to family violence, and
- how to recognise excessive self-defence.

The limitations of self-defence

The VLRC said that the 'all or nothing' nature of self-defence can result in inappropriate convictions for murder, particularly for women who kill in response to family violence.[138] As a result, it may discourage women from arguing self-defence at trial, resulting in pleas of guilty to manslaughter when a woman should be fully acquitted.[139] The existence of excessive self-defence may encourage women to argue self-defence.[140] The VLRC described excessive self-defence as providing a 'halfway house' where self-defence is not successfully raised in full.[141] The VLRC was concerned that self-defence may not succeed where jurors do not fully understand the dynamics of family violence.[142] For example, women who kill an intimate partner in response to long-term family violence 'typically do not respond during a violent attack, and as they are often smaller and less experienced in physical combat that their victims, frequently use a weapon when retaliating'.[143]

However, the New Zealand Law Commission said that the very existence of partial defences, and especially excessive self-defence, may produce perverse outcomes and undermine the operation of self-defence.[144] This is because it provides juries with compromise options, suggests that a woman's response to family violence may not be reasonable, and provides a way for the parties to negotiate a plea rather than have a jury consider self-defence.[145]

138 VLRC, *Defences to Homicide* (n 65) 102 [3.106].

139 VLRC, *Defences to Homicide* (n 65) 102–3 [3.106]–[3.111]. See also Tyson et al (n 68) 87–91; Sophie Kate Howes, Katy Swaine Williams and Harriet Wistrich, 'Women Who Kill: Why Self-Defence Rarely Works for Women Who Kill Their Abuser' [2021] (11) *Criminal Law Review* 945, 949–50.

140 VLRC, *Defences to Homicide* (n 65) 102 [3.108]. LRCWA, *A Review of the Law of Homicide* (n 15) 164–7.

141 VLRC, *Defences to Homicide* (n 65) 94 [3.91]. See also NZLC, *Understanding Family Violence* (n 126) 137 [10.4].

142 See, eg, VLRC, *Defences to Homicide* (n 65) 135–6 [4.20], 171 [4.89], 190 [4.146].

143 Kellie Toole, 'Self-Defence and the Reasonable Woman: Equality before the New Victorian Law' (2012) 36 *Melbourne University Law Review* 250, 256–7 ('Self-Defence and the Reasonable Woman').

144 NZLC, *Understanding Family Violence* (n 126) 141 [10.23].

145 NZLC, *Understanding Family Violence* (n 126) 141 [10.23].

Community views about killing in response to family violence

The VLRC said that if jurors do not acquit on the grounds of self-defence, because they find it difficult to understand why a woman may kill in response to family violence, a jury could return a verdict of manslaughter on the grounds of excessive self-defence.[146] However, if a jury returned a verdict of manslaughter despite not fully understanding family violence, it would suggest that the verdict is based on jurors' commonsense[147] or intuitive ideas about what the verdict should be. If the jury's verdict is based on commonsense ideas of how the law should apply, the jury may return a verdict of manslaughter irrespective of whether excessive self-defence exists.[148] A jury can do this by finding that the accused lacked the necessary intent for the offence of murder.[149]

How the law recognises excessive self-defence

Excessive self-defence is anomalous because, unlike self-defence, it only applies to the offence of murder.[150] For non-fatal offences, courts — rather than juries — recognise the reduced culpability of an offender who uses excessive self-defence when imposing a sentence. Through sentencing discretion, a judge can more fully recognise the range of defensive conduct that is excessive in the sentence imposed without needing a jury's verdict.[151] Recognising a partially exculpatory matter through a jury verdict has been described as the 'second-best' way of assessing mitigating circumstances[152] because it requires a jury to make a binary choice about matters that are often one of degree.[153] There 'is no way of articulating the distinction between what is properly regarded as a partial defence, and what is "merely" a mitigating circumstance' for the sentence imposed.[154]

However, the VLRC said that excessive self-defence is qualitatively different from other factors concerning culpability at the sentencing stage, such as provocation. This is because the person intended to act lawfully and their liability is based on an error of judgement.[155] Therefore, the offender should

146 See, eg, VLRC, *Defences to Homicide* (n 65) 102 [3.109]; Howes, Williams and Wistrich (n 139) 952–3.

147 Steele and Thornburg (n 107) 96. See also Finkel, 'Commonsense Justice and Jury Instructions' (n 16) 608–9; Smith, 'When Prior Knowledge and Law Collide' (n 107) 509.

148 See, eg, Byrne (n 121) 151–2.

149 Bradfield has said that 'lack of intent appears to be used as a "de facto" defence of domestic violence': Rebecca Bradfield, 'Women Who Kill: Lack of Intent and Diminished Responsibility as the Other "Defences" to Spousal Homicide' (2001) 13(2) *Current Issues in Criminal Justice* 143, 144.

150 NZLC, *Understanding Family Violence* (n 126) 144 [10.37].

151 MCCOC, *Fatal Offences against the Person* (n 15) 113.

152 See generally, NZLC, *Understanding Family Violence* (n 126) 143–4 [10.38]–[10.40].

153 NZLC, *Understanding Family Violence* (n 126) 143–4 [10.38]–[10.40].

154 *The Partial Defence of Provocation* (n 75) 162.

155 VLRC, *Defences to Homicide* (n 65) 101 [3.104].

not be labelled as a 'murderer'. Further, labelling the offender as a 'murderer' may dilute the power of the label for those who should be described as a 'murderer'.[156] In addition to the label, a jury's verdict (recognising excessive self-defence) may legitimise in a public way the offender's reduced culpability and the imposition of a more lenient sentence.[157]

Accordingly, there are strong policy arguments both for and against recognising excessive self-defence as a partial defence to murder. This may explain why it has found favour in some jurisdictions but not others and why the policy debate surrounding it has continued for many decades. One of the criticisms of excessive self-defence is that it is too complicated for juries. Before considering research on this issue, it is necessary to discuss how a judge explains excessive self-defence to a jury.

How excessive self-defence works

Australia's Model Criminal Code Officers' Committee (MCCOC) said that 'if excessive self-defence is to be re-introduced, the Committee favours a test'[158] based on the test set out in *R v Howe*:[159]

> it is manslaughter and not murder if the accused . . . in honestly defending himself . . . used greater force than was reasonably necessary for his self-protection and in doing so killed his assailant.[160]

While the test in *R v Howe* appears to be straightforward, MCCOC recognised that juries would require more guidance to understand this test. However, MCCOC concluded that when that is done, 'the result tends to be an unworkably complicated test more apt to confuse than assist'.[161] South Australia and Victoria introduced statutory forms of excessive self-defence in 1997 and 2005 respectively.

In South Australia, excessive self-defence applies to conduct that the accused believed to be necessary and reasonable, but where the conduct was not reasonably proportionate to the threat faced.[162] Justice Duggan, formerly of the Supreme Court of South Australia, said he had used a nine-page handout to explain excessive self-defence and said that in some cases the law was 'frighteningly complex'.[163]

156 See generally, Yeo (n 132) 41–2; NZLC, *Understanding Family Violence* (n 126) 138–40 [10.12]–[10.19]; Tyson et al (n 68) 91.
157 *The Partial Defence of Provocation* (n 75) 52.
158 MCCOC, *Fatal Offences Against the Person* (n 15) 111–13.
159 *R v Howe* (1958) 100 CLR 448 ('*Howe*').
160 *Howe* (n 159) 477 (Menzies J).
161 MCCOC, *Fatal Offences Against the Person* (n 15) 113.
162 *Criminal Law Consolidation Act 1935* (SA) s 15(2).
163 'Justice Kevin Duggan' *The Law Report* (ABC Radio National, 2 August 2011) <www.abc.net.au/radionational/programs/lawreport/justice-kevin-duggan/2928124>. In Canada,

Victoria introduced excessive self-defence in 2005[164] and then repealed it in 2015.[165] Victoria's laws were more heavily scrutinised than in other jurisdictions.[166] Victoria's experience therefore provides valuable insights into the operation of excessive self-defence. Victoria enacted excessive self-defence as an offence called 'defensive homicide', rather than as a partial defence. This created some additional problems,[167] but the main problems were inherent in the tests involved when considering excessive self-defence.

A significant problem with excessive self-defence stems from the burden of proof. In Victoria, the jury first considered whether the prosecution had proved beyond reasonable doubt that the accused *did not believe* that their conduct was necessary to defend themselves or another from the infliction of death or really serious injury.[168] What if the jury found that it was *possible* that the accused held this belief but did not positively conclude that the accused *did not believe* their conduct was necessary?

The judge cannot ask the jury what conclusions they have drawn from the evidence and only then direct them about this possibility. Therefore, the Victorian Court of Appeal said that in this situation, the jury 'should *assume* . . . that the accused did hold the asserted belief'.[169] The jury then considered the second limb of the test, whether the prosecution had proved beyond reasonable doubt that the accused did not have reasonable grounds for their (assumed) belief that their conduct was necessary.[170] The Victorian Court of Appeal said that directions explaining how the law worked 'would not need to be excessively complex'.[171] However, requiring the jury to make assumptions about the existence of a belief made the Victorian provisions and the jury's task more complicated.

Simplifying guidance about excessive self-defence

Some of the complexity in the Victorian provisions was a consequence of the second limb (whether there were reasonable grounds for a belief) being tied

---

Dickson J said that excessive self-defence would require 'prolix and complicated jury charges': *Faid* (n 136) 271. See also Semmler and Brewer (n 98) 263.

164 *Crimes (Homicide) Act 2005* (Vic) s 9AC.

165 *Crimes Amendment (Abolition of Defensive Homicide) Act 2014* (Vic) s 3.

166 See, eg, CLR, *Defensive Homicide* (n 126); Kate Fitz-Gibbon, 'The Offence of Defensive Homicide: Lessons Learned from Failed Law Reform' in Kate Fitz-Gibbon and Arie Freiberg (eds), *Homicide Law Reform in Victoria: Retrospect and Prospects* (Federation Press, 2015) 128; Byrne (n 121); Leader-Elliott, 'Reform and Codification of the Law of Homicide' (n 38).

167 See generally: Criminal Law Review, Department of Justice (Vic), *Defensive Homicide: Review of the Offence of Defensive Homicide* (Discussion Paper, August 2010) 53–5 [235]–[248].

168 This test was based on the common law definition of self-defence: *Zecevic* (n 129).

169 *Babic v The Queen* (2010) 28 VR 297, 318 [95] (Neave and King JJA) (emphasis added) ('*Babic*').

170 *Crimes (Homicide) Act 2005* (Vic) s 9AD.

171 *Babic* (n 168).

to the first limb (what the accused believed). If the second limb had instead focused on whether the accused's response was reasonable in the circumstances, as the VLRC had recommended,[172] a jury could make this assessment without needing to make assumptions about what the accused believed. This latter form of excessive self-defence (and self-defence) is preferable because it involves fewer complex issues for a jury to consider.[173]

As discussed in Chapter 6, one way to simplify substantive jury directions is to use factual questions. Factual questions can improve juror comprehension by removing directions about the law, making the issues that the jury must determine more concrete. With excessive self-defence, the jury's task is to apply evaluative standards — for example, did the accused believe their conduct was *necessary* and their response *reasonable*? A factual question for self-defence might refer to the facts that the accused relies on — for example, are you satisfied[174] that Green (the deceased) was carrying a baseball bat when Green approached Red (the accused)? However, even if the jury accepts that Green was carrying a baseball bat (which may be disputed), that fact is not sufficient to satisfy the test for self-defence. Instead, the jury must determine whether they are satisfied that Red did not believe it was *necessary* to kill Green, and that killing Green was not a *reasonable* response in the circumstances. These two questions involve a more complex and qualitative assessment of all the facts than simply whether Green was carrying a baseball bat.

Evaluative standards cannot be replaced by case-specific facts, or if they are, there is a real risk that they will not be accurate. This is reflected in the examples of self-defence in question trails used in New Zealand which continue to use the evaluative standards of *necessary* and *reasonable*.[175] These evaluative standards provide 'the portal through which all the social . . . [and] cultural understandings of what is justifiable' are assessed and they are integral to self-defence laws.[176] They enable the jury to be 'the thermometer of community sentiment'.[177] However, the thermometer is necessarily evaluative and cannot be replaced by the concrete terms necessary for factual questions.

Factual questions do not change the burden or standard of proof. Because the prosecution must disprove self-defence, great care would need to be taken

172 VLRC, *Defences to Homicide* (n 65) 87–90.

173 See, eg, Yeo (n 132) 49–50; VLRC *Defences to Homicide* (n 65) 87–90.

174 'Satisfied' is used here as a shorthand description for proof beyond reasonable doubt.

175 Courts of New Zealand, *A Guide to the Question Trails* <www.courtsofnz.govt.nz/for-lawyers/question-trails/>.

176 Stella Tarrant, 'Self Defence in the Western Australian Criminal Code: Two Proposals for Reform' (2015) 38(2) *University of Western Australia Law Review* 1, 10. See also Jeremy Horder, 'Killing the Passive Abuser: A Theoretical Defence' in Stephen Shute and Andrew Simester (eds), *Criminal Law Theory: Doctrines of the General Part* (Oxford University Press, 2002) 283, 292–3 who describes these kinds of evaluative elements as seeking to 'distribute evenly the burden of risks' faced by defenders and attackers.

177 MCCOC, *Fatal Offences against the Person* (n 15) 103. The Committee made this comment in relation to provocation, but it is also relevant to evaluations of self-defence.

to ensure that a factual question did not make it any more difficult for the accused to argue that they acted in self-defence. For example, in the scenario just outlined, the accused does not have to prove that Green had a baseball bat. The question for the jury is whether the prosecution can prove that Red did not believe that it was necessary to act in self-defence having regard to all the circumstances.

The capacity of the factual questions used in the SDM aid to simplify the application of excessive self-defence is therefore limited but should still assist jurors by contextualising the evaluative standards by reference to the evidence in the case. While policy debates about excessive self-defence and its form have continued, the first step in a jury-centric approach focuses on juror comprehension evidence about excessive self-defence.

Juror comprehension evidence about excessive self-defence

As discussed in relation to juror comprehension evidence about murder offences, law reform bodies have generally discussed the complexity of excessive self-defence through the prism of their own assessment of what is comprehensible.[178] This perspective is like the courts' judicial knowledge and experience. It often draws from comments made by courts about the complexities of excessive self-defence. Further, inferences drawn from jury verdicts involving self-defence and excessive self-defence often assume that the jury's verdict is the result of jurors correctly understanding and applying the law.[179]

The VLRC said that jurors may not understand, or find it difficult to understand why a woman would:

- use fatal force (which may appear disproportionate) in response to family violence, and
- be acting in self-defence where the threat is not immediate.[180]

The VLRC referred to research concerning how mock jurors assess evidence of family violence and the importance of expert evidence in understanding family violence.[181] However, the VLRC made no reference to juror comprehension research generally or to specific research on self-defence. It should be easier to explain self-defence to jurors than to also explain how excessive self-defence modifies self-defence.

178 See, eg, VLRC, *Defences to Homicide* (n 65) 95 [3.94]; LRCWA, *A Review of the Law of Homicide* (n 15) 178.

179 See, eg, Charlotte King et al, 'Did Defensive Homicide in Victoria Provide a Safety Net for Battered Women Who Kill? A Case Study Analysis' (2016) 42(1) *Monash University Law Review* 138, 167–8; Toole, 'Self-Defence and the Reasonable Woman' (n 143) 271–85.

180 See, eg, VLRC, *Defences to Homicide* (n 65) 102 [3.109], 135–6 [4.20], 140 [4.30].

181 VLRC, *Defences to Homicide* (n 65) 171 [4.89].

A 2002 study in South Australia involving 234 mock jurors assessed their comprehension of South Australia's self-defence laws[182] using different techniques for instructing 'jurors' (eg, instructions only, instructions and referring to a judge's summary during testing, and instructions and referring to a flowchart during testing).[183] The best mean correct score from the different techniques was 2.31 out of 4 (with one point each for identifying that the defendant believed there was a threat, the defendant believed their response was both necessary and reasonable, and that their response was reasonably proportionate).[184] Further, mock jurors' comprehension of self-defence affected their conclusions about the facts. Mock jurors who understood all four components of self-defence, said that self-defence did not apply 66.7% of the time.[185] Mock jurors, who only understood one component of self-defence, said that self-defence did not apply 41.9% of the time. There were some limitations with the methods used in the study (eg, the instructions were tape recorded and played to the mock jurors, and it involved some testing of comprehension through paraphrasing rather than application).[186] However, the findings were generally consistent with other juror comprehension research about self-defence and excessive self-defence.[187]

Jury simulation research on self-defence in England and Wales in 2010 involved 797 people called for jury service but who did not serve on a trial.[188] This research demonstrated the challenges of explaining self-defence involving two limbs, namely, whether the accused believed it was necessary to defend themselves and whether the accused used reasonable force).[189] The study used a traditional self-defence scenario where the victim pushed the defendant before the defendant punched the victim.[190] Only 31% of the participants correctly identified both limbs of self-defence, and an additional 48% correctly identified one limb. About one quarter of the participants were provided with written directions. Comprehension improved but remained poor with only 48% of participants correctly identifying both limbs and a further 36% correctly identifying one of the limbs.[191]

Although Victoria recognised excessive self-defence between 2005 and 2014, no research was conducted on jurors in Victoria to assess their

182 *Criminal Law Consolidation Act 1935* (SA) s 15A.
183 Semmler and Brewer (n 98) 264–5.
184 Semmler and Brewer (n 98) 265.
185 Semmler and Brewer (n 98) 265.
186 Semmler and Brewer (n 98) 264, 266–7.
187 Neil Brewer, Sophie Harvey and Carolyn Semmler, 'Improving Comprehension of Jury Instructions with Audio-visual Presentation' (2004) 18(6) *Applied Cognitive Psychology* 765, 765–6.
188 Cheryl Thomas, *Are Juries Fair?* (Ministry of Justice, 2010) 7–8.
189 Thomas (n 188) 36.
190 Thomas (n 188) 36–7.
191 Thomas (n 188) 36–8.

comprehension of excessive self-defence (defensive homicide) jury directions, despite the offence being reviewed and abolished, in part because of its complexity for jurors.[192] However, one study involved detailed interviews with judges and practitioners after Victoria's laws had been in operation for more than five years. The necessary jury directions were described by prosecutorial respondents as 'mind-boggling' and 'unbelievably convoluted', and by judicial respondents as 'incomprehensible', 'too complex', and 'very complicated'.[193]

As discussed in Chapter 4, judges are likely to overestimate juror comprehension. Research about juror comprehension of self-defence and excessive self-defence laws is consistent with general juror comprehension research that suggests self-defence will be challenging for jurors. As discussed in Chapter 3, jurors have difficulty understanding words with excessively flexible meanings (eg, necessary, reasonable belief, and reasonable response). This does not mean that flexible words and concepts (evaluative standards) must never be used. However, the 'need for flexibility in the law is the antithesis of the specificity required for comprehension'.[194]

The version of excessive self-defence jury directions used in research in South Australia contained the words 'reasonable', 'reasonably', or 'reasonableness' 23 times.[195] Further, the prosecution must prove a negative proposition (that the accused did not act in self-defence): jurors find negative propositions more difficult to understand.[196] While double negatives in self-defence are unavoidable, the second limb of excessive self-defence — where the prosecution has 'failed to prove that the accused did not have [the necessary] belief'[197] — further increases the complexity of understanding this partial defence.

The cognitive load in determining self-defence in the context of family violence is also significant. Jurors must:

- understand a broad range of factors that may have occurred over many years that constitute family violence
- determine whether that history of family violence meant that the accused believed it was necessary to use lethal force when they acted, and
- determine whether that was a reasonable response in the circumstances.

Understanding the dynamics of family violence may require learning and applying new information, resulting in significant cognitive load. Adding complex excessive self-defence laws to these facts further increases the cognitive

192 See CLR, *Defensive Homicide* (n 126) 13–22 [2.5].
193 Fitz-Gibbon and Pickering (n 68) 168.
194 Watt (n 1) 61.
195 Semmler and Brewer (n 98) 268–9.
196 See, eg, Elwork, Sales and Alfini, 'Juridic Decisions' (n 76) 167; Peter M Tiersma, 'Communicating with Juries: How to Draft More Understandable Instructions' (2005–2006) 10 *The Scribes of Journal Legal Writing* 1, 20–1.
197 *Criminal Trial Courts Bench Book* (n 9) [6–465].

load for jurors. This scenario is likely to be much more difficult to understand than a claim of self-defence that traditionally involved an assault involving two roughly equal males with no history between them.

Therefore, the available evidence indicates that jurors are likely to have significant difficulty understanding excessive self-defence jury directions. This is consistent with general research about juror comprehension, research about juror comprehension of self-defence, and criticisms expressed by judges and practitioners about the comprehensibility of excessive self-defence jury directions.

Using a jury-centric approach to determine whether to recognise excessive self-defence

There are strong policy arguments both for and against excessive self-defence. These arguments must be considered within the context of other laws in that jurisdiction.[198] For example, the case for excessive self-defence is stronger if a jurisdiction has a mandatory penalty for murder, such as life imprisonment.

It is not necessary to analyse excessive self-defence through all five steps of a jury-centric approach. Most analysis of excessive self-defence focuses on when a person may be excused for taking the life of another person. These policy issues concerning criminal responsibility fall under the second and third steps in a jury-centric approach. Applying the first step in a jury-centric approach changes this analysis by examining the importance of evidence concerning whether jurors are likely to understand excessive self-defence. Juror comprehension studies about self-defence suggest that a significant proportion of jurors are unlikely to understand and/or apply excessive self-defence laws correctly. Factual questions are unlikely to improve the comprehensibility of laws that jurors must apply given they include evaluative standards that are integral to excessive self-defence. The inherent complexities of this partial defence cannot be avoided. Therefore, applying a jury-centric approach means that there is a real possibility that a trial will not be fair to (at least one of) the accused, victim, and the community because jurors will not fully understand their task.

However, the problem identified by the VLRC remains, namely, whether jurors fully understand the dynamics of family violence and the application of self-defence laws for killings in response to family violence. Other reforms must therefore be considered to achieve this policy objective. For example, by introducing laws that support the admission of family violence social context evidence, using jury directions to address misconceptions about family violence, calling expert evidence about family violence, and providing more support

198 See generally, NZLC, *Understanding Family Violence* (n 126) 64 [4.59].

for women (accused) to give evidence in trials about family violence.[199] These kinds of reforms require evaluation to assess their effectiveness in addressing misconceptions about family violence.[200]

Conclusion

Major reviews of homicide laws discussed in this chapter focused primarily on complicated interconnected policy issues. Grappling with these policy issues is critical to ensuring that offences and defences work appropriately in a wide range of situations, where the offence is labelled fairly, and the punishment fits the crime. However, it is rare for these reviews to examine juror comprehension research even though juror comprehension is necessary for a fair trial and critical to understanding how these laws should be defined. More specific research about homicide offences and excessive self-defence (and other defences and excuses) would be helpful. However, the research that is available, combined with juror comprehension research about linguistic and conceptual complexity, cognitive load, and commonsense justice indicates that jurors are unlikely to understand finely nuanced distinctions of criminal responsibility.

The case study of murder and excessive self-defence shows that a jury-centric approach is relevant to determining the content of criminal offences and defences. Further, it highlights the importance of juror comprehension research in resolving difficult policy issues. This research even provides an argument against a mandatory penalty for murder because the case for more fine-grained murder offences and partial excuses is strongest where the penalty is mandatory.

The examination of excessive self-defence also reveals limitations in the capacity of factual questions to simplify substantive jury directions that involve an assessment of an evaluative standard (eg, did the accused believe it was *necessary* to act or was the accused's response *reasonable*). Evaluative standards are common in defences (eg, sudden or extraordinary emergency, duress, and diminished responsibility) and in some offences (eg, sexual offences involving indecency). These evaluative standards are essential for laws to be fair through the incorporation of community views about what is justifiable or inappropriate. Therefore, it is important to consider the comprehensibility to jurors of the words and concepts used in defining offences and defences.

199 See, eg, Byrne (n 121) 149–53; Heather Douglas, 'Social Framework Evidence: Its Interpretation and Application in Victoria and Beyond' in Kate Fitz-Gibbon and Arie Freiberg (eds), *Homicide Law Reform in Victoria: Retrospect and Prospects* (Federation Press, 2015) 94; Tyson et al (n 68).

200 Tyson et al (n 68) 90–1.

9 Case study three — Misconceptions in sexual offence trials

Introduction

While the issues that the jury must determine in a trial are shaped by evidence and laws, jurors are not blank slates. Indeed

> the purpose and the genius of the jury system is that it allows for the ordinary experiences of ordinary people to be brought to bear in the determination of factual matters. It is fundamental to that purpose that the jury be allowed to determine, by inference from its collective experience of ordinary affairs, whether and, in the case of conflict, what evidence is truthful.[1]

Chapter 3 discussed how jurors assess the plausibility of evidence and stories in a trial against their own knowledge and experience of the world and what, in their experience, usually happens.[2] The credibility of the complainant is often critical in sexual offence trials.[3] Jurors assess the plausibility and credibility of the complainant's evidence against their own knowledge and experience of the world and what usually happens. Jurors' knowledge and experience of the world may in part be based on misconceptions (eg, in relation to race, gender, young people, or understanding family violence and how memory works). Some misconceptions may be relevant to sexual offence trials. What if a jurors' ordinary experience and knowledge of the world is mistaken, and this mistake affects whether a juror is impartial?

1 *Doney v The Queen* (1990) 171 CLR 207, 214 ('*Doney*'). See also Justice David Watt, *Helping Jurors Understand* (Thomson Carswell, 2007) 4–8; Sara Gordon, 'All Together Now: Using Principles of Group Dynamics to Train Better Jurors' (2015) 48(2) *Indiana Law Journal* 415 ('All Together Now').

2 Nancy Pennington and Reid Hastie, 'Evidence Evaluation in Complex Decision Making' (1986) 51 *Journal of Personality and Social Psychology* 242, 247 ('Evidence Evaluation').

3 See, eg, Victorian Law Reform Commission, *Sexual Offences: Law and Procedure* (Final Report, July 2004) 82–7 [1.12]–[1.17] (VLRC).

DOI: 10.4324/9781003477129-9

In recent years, many significant reviews have considered the risk that jurors' misconceptions may affect their decision-making in sexual offence cases, resulting in juries not considering the issues fairly.[4] The policy goal of addressing misconceptions should be to ensure:

- an impartial jury, and
- a competent jury (one that understands its task).

However, addressing misconceptions may make comprehension of the issues more difficult for jurors.[5] Addressing misconceptions may challenge a juror's existing schema — comprised of their 'accumulated knowledge, beliefs, and experiences'[6] — requiring jurors to learn and use new schema, thereby making the juror's task more difficult.

The two main strategies to neutralise, or ameliorate, the influence of misconceptions in juror decision-making in sexual offence trials involve expert evidence[7] and jury directions.[8] Jury directions:

- may have similar efficacy to expert evidence in addressing misconceptions in sexual offence cases,[9] and
- may be preferable to expert evidence where the directions involve simple and irrefutable propositions.[10]

4 See, eg, New Zealand Law Commission, *The Justice Response to Victims of Sexual Violence: Criminal Trials and Alternative Processes* (Report No 136, December 2015) ('NZLC, *The Justice Response to Victims of Sexual Violence*'); New South Wales Law Reform Commission, *Consent in Relation to Sexual Offences* (Report No 148, September 2020) (NSWLRC); Sir John Gillen, *Gillen Review: Report into the Law and Procedures in Serious Sexual Offences in Northern Ireland* (Report, May 2019); Lord Justice Clerk's Review Group, *Improving the Management of Sexual Offence Cases* (Final Report, March 2021); Victorian Law Reform Commission, *Improving the Justice System Response to Sexual Offences* (Report, September 2021).

5 See, eg, Duane T Wegener et al, 'Flexible Corrections of Juror Judgments: Implications for Jury Instructions' (2000) 6(3) *Psychology, Public Policy, and Law* 629, 632; Bradley Saxton, 'How Well Do Jurors Understand Jury Instructions? A Field Test Using Real Juries and Real Trials in Wyoming' (1998) 33 *Land and Water Law Review* 59, 95.

6 Sara Gordon, 'Through the Eyes of Jurors: The Use of Schemas in the Application of "Plain Language" Jury Instructions' (2013) 64 *Hastings Law Journal* 643, 650 ('Through the Eyes of Jurors').

7 See, eg, *R v DD* [2000] 2 RCS 275 ('*DD*'); *DH v The Queen* [2015] 1 NZLR 625 ('*DH*'); *Evidence Act 2006* (NZ) s 25; *Evidence Act 2008* (Vic) s 79.

8 NZLC, *The Justice Response to Victims of Sexual Violence* (n 4) 117 [6.54]; Faye T Nitschke, Blake M McKimmie and Eric J Vanman, 'The Effect of Trauma Education Judicial Instructions on Decisions about Complainant Credibility in Rape Trials' (2023) 29(1) *Psychology, Public Policy, and Law* 69, 70–1.

9 See, eg, Jane Goodman-Delahunty, Anne Cossins and Kate O'Brien, 'A Comparison of Expert Evidence and Judicial Directions to Counter Misconceptions in Child Sexual Abuse Trials' (2011) 44(2) *Australian & New Zealand Journal of Criminology* 196, 211–13; Annie Cossins, 'Expert Witness Evidence in Sexual Assault Trials: Questions, Answers and Law Reform in Australia and England' (2013) 17 *International Journal of Evidence & Proof* 74, 91; Jane Goodman-Delahunty et al, 'Greater Knowledge Enhances Complainant Credibility and Increases Jury Convictions for Child Sexual Assault' (2021) 12 *Frontiers in Psychology* 624331, 17.

10 See, eg, *DD* (n 7) 306 [66]–[68]; *DH* (n 7) 652 [111].

Addressing misconceptions through jury directions also involves changes to the judge's role and responsibilities in a trial. Accordingly, this chapter focuses on using jury directions to address misconceptions to assess the application of a jury-centric approach to a difficult and critical issue in criminal justice systems.

Because there are many misconceptions relevant to sexual offence trials, the case study in this chapter will primarily focus on the approach used to address misconceptions about 'delay' — which may be anything from hours to years — in reporting a sexual offence in Victoria.[11] This involves one of the oldest misconceptions, namely, that a 'real' sexual offence complainant will complain at the first reasonable opportunity to do so.[12] Victoria's approach combines aspects of the approaches used in many other common law jurisdictions.

In discussing sexual offences, terminology is important and depends upon the context in which it is used. As this chapter focuses on criminal trials, I will primarily use terminology commonly used in the law for:

- offences — rape and sexual assault, and
- victim-survivors — the complainant.[13]

However, this chapter refers to research, discussion, and commentaries from disciplines other than the law where different terminology is appropriately used (eg, 'rape myths' instead of misconceptions and 'victim-survivor' rather than complainant).

A competent, independent, and impartial jury

An impartial tribunal

It is fundamental to the common law system of adversarial trial that a criminal charge must be determined by a 'competent, independent and impartial' tribunal.[14] A tribunal is not impartial if a 'fair-minded observer might reasonably apprehend that the judge (or juror) might not bring an impartial mind to the resolution of the question the judge (or juror) is required to decide'.[15]

11 Julia Quilter, Luke McNamara and Melissa Porter, 'The Most Persistent Rape Myth? A Qualitative Study of "Delay" in Complaint in Victorian Rape Trials' (2023) 35(1) *Current Issues in Criminal Justice* 1, 3–4.

12 Quilter, McNamara and Porter (n 11) 1.

13 For a discussion of different views concerning the appropriateness of different terms used, see, eg, Rachael Burgin, 'Persistent Narratives of Force and Resistance: Affirmative Consent as Law Reform' (2019) 59(2) *British Journal of Criminology* 296, 297–8.

14 Article 14 of the *International Covenant on Civil and Political Rights*, opened for signature 16 December 1966, 999 UNTS 171 (entered into force 23 March 1976). See also *Ebner v Official Trustee in Bankruptcy* (2000) 205 CLR 337, 343 [3] (Gleeson CJ, McHugh, Gummow and Hayne JJ) ('*Ebner*'); *Gassy v The Queen* (2008) 236 CLR 293, 323 [97] (Kirby J); *Brown v Stott* [2003] 1 AC 681, 708 (Lord Steyn).

15 *Ebner* (n 14) 344 [6] (Gleeson CJ, McHugh, Gummow and Hayne JJ).

The law is very similar across many common law jurisdictions.[16] The principle that a tribunal is impartial is, in Australia, referred to as the 'apprehension of bias principle'.[17] In this context, bias 'connotes the absence of impartiality',[18] a 'state of mind that is in some way predisposed to a particular result or that is closed with regard to particular issues'.[19] Bias exists when a decision-maker 'holds a view on issues relevant to a case . . . [and that view] tends against one party to a dispute without good reason'.[20] Understood in this way, the apprehension of bias principle applies to misconceptions in sexual offence cases. What is critical in legal terms is whether the bias 'might lead a judge (or juror) to decide a case *other than on its legal and factual merits*'.[21]

Misconceptions in sexual offence trials

Literature from different social science disciplines often describes misconceptions in sexual offence trials as 'rape myths'. 'Rape myths' are 'descriptive or prescriptive beliefs about rape (ie, about its causes, consequences, perpetrators, victims, and their interaction) that serve to deny, downplay or justify sexual violence that men commit against women'.[22] These myths are 'deeply embedded tropes, narratives and structures for understanding and making sense of the world, often operating in unconscious ways'.[23] These myths may include 'prejudicial, stereotyped, or false beliefs about rape, rape victims and rapists'.[24] While stereotypes about rape, for instance, are often empirically wrong, sometimes they may align with the truth (eg, a rape victim might yell 'no' and fight back).[25]

16 See, eg, *Porter v Magill* [2002] 2 AC 357; *Muir v Commissioner of Inland Revenue* [2007] 3 NZLR 495 ('*Muir*'); *R v Lippé* [1991] 2 SCR 114; *RDS v The Queen* [1997] 3 SCR 484 ('*RDS*'); Andrew Higgins and Inbar Levy, 'Judicial Policy, Public Perception, and the Science of Decision Making: A New Framework for the Law of Apprehended Bias' (2019) 38(3) *Civil Justice Quarterly* 376, 378.

17 *Ebner* (n 14) 334–5 [6] (Gleeson CJ, McHugh, Gummow and Hayne JJ).

18 *Ebner* (n 14) 348 [23] (Gleeson CJ, McHugh, Gummow and Hayne JJ). See also *R v Abdroikov* [2007] 1 WLR 2679, 2687 [14] (Lord Bingham of Cornhill) ('*Abdroikov*').

19 *RDS* (n 16) 528 [105] (Cory and Iacobucci JJ).

20 Mark Aronson, Matthew Groves and Greg Weeks, *Judicial Review of Administrative Action and Government Liability* (Thomson Reuters, 6th ed, 2017) 644.

21 *Ebner* (n 14) 345 [8] (Gleeson CJ, McHugh, Gummow and Hayne JJ) (emphasis added).

22 Heike Gerger et al, 'The Acceptance of Modern Myths about Sexual Aggression Scale: Development and Validation in German and English' (2007) 33(5) *Aggressive Behavior* 422, 425. See also Fiona Leverick, 'What Do We Know about Rape Myths and Juror Decision Making?' (2020) 24(3) *The International Journal of Evidence & Proof* 255, 256–8; Ellen Daly, *Rape, Gender and Class: Intersections in Courtroom Narratives* (Palgrave Macmillan, 2022) 15–19.

23 Julia Quilter, 'Getting Consent "Right": Sexual Assault Law Reform in New South Wales' (2021) *The Australian Feminist Law Journal* 1, 16.

24 Martha R Burt, 'Cultural Myths and Supports for Rape' (1980) 38(2) *Journal of Personality and Social Psychology* 217, 217.

25 Daly (n 22) 17–18; Daivd J Hayes, 'Are Rape Myths "Myths"?' (2024) 44(1) *Oxford Journal of Legal Studies* 156, 158–9.

Schemas are essential to a juror's task. Jurors need 'sufficient knowledge of the life experiences of those before them to make sense of testimony and motivations'.[26] Jurors 'rely on commonsense knowledge, on ordinary experience, and on a practiced sense of what is credible and what is not'.[27] Judges encourage jurors to assess the evidence by applying their 'common sense' and 'experience of the world'.[28] This is generally an essential and desirable feature of jury trials. But a juror's common sense and experience may be inconsistent with empirical knowledge, and this may be a cause of injustice.[29] For example, common sense and experience may include rape myths: these myths involve 'oversimplified schemas [that] supply a structure around which information provided in a trial can be organized'.[30]

As discussed in Chapter 3, jurors seem to understand, organise, and complete a story by assessing the plausibility of a story against their own knowledge of the world and what usually happens.[31] This may include a significant component of a juror's personal experience, attitudes, and beliefs, including stereotypes about what constitutes 'appropriate' or 'normal' conduct or behaviour.[32] In the story model, the coherence of a story is critical.[33] Coherence 'refers to a story's logical resilience and is presumably a joint function of three elements: consistency, completeness and plausibility'.[34] Each juror uses their own schema to assess the coherence of a story.

Assessing the coherence or plausibility of a story involves comparing the victim, the accused, or the act, in an individual case with a 'real rape'. Where

26 Martha Minow, 'Stripped Down Like a Runner or Enriched by Experience: Bias and Impartiality of Judges and Jurors' (1992) 33 *William and Mary Law Review* 1201, 1205.

27 Kim Lane Scheppele, 'Manners of Imagining the Real' (1994) 19(4) *Law and Society Inquiry* 995, 1010.

28 See, eg, Elisabeth McDonald, *Rape Myths as Barriers to Fair Trial Process: Comparing Adult Rape Trials with Those of the Aotearoa Sexual Violence Court Pilot* (Canterbury University Press, 2020) 392–5; Peter M Tiersma, 'Asking Jurors to Do the Impossible' (2009) 5(2) *Tennessee Journal of Law and Policy* 105, 117–21; Doney (n 1) 1, 214.

29 See generally Kylie Burns, 'Judges, "Common Sense" and Judicial Cognition' (2016) 25(3) *Griffith Law Review* 319, 320–1, 331–2.

30 Blake M McKimmie, Barbara M Masser and Renata Bongiorno, 'What Counts as Rape? The Effect of Offense Prototypes, Victim Stereotypes, and Participant Gender on How the Complainant and Defendant Are Perceived' (2014) 29(12) *Journal of Interpersonal Violence* 2273, 2275 (references omitted).

31 See, eg, Pennington and Hastie, 'Evidence Evaluation' (n 2) 247; Louise Ellison and Vanessa E Munro, '"Telling Tales": Exploring Narratives of Life and Law within the (Mock) Jury Room' (2015) 35(2) *Legal Studies* 201, 216 ('Telling Tales').

32 See, eg, Pennington and Hastie, 'Evidence Evaluation' (n 2) 247; Lisa Dufraimont, 'Myth, Inference and Evidence in Sexual Assault Trials' (2019) 44(2) *Queen's Law Journal* 316, 330; Olivia Smith and Tina Skinner, 'How Rape Myths Are Used and Challenged in Rape and Sexual Assault Trials' (2017) 26(4) *Social & Legal Studies* 441, 458.

33 Dennis J Devine, *Jury Decision Making: The State of Science* (New York University Press, 2012) 27–8. See also Nancy Pennington and Reid Hastie, 'A Cognitive Theory of Juror Decision Making: The Story Model' (1991) 13 *Cardozo Law Review* 519, 528.

34 Devine (n 33) 28.

the 'real rape' comparison involves a rape myth, this creates the risk that a juror, or a jury, will not reach a verdict based on the legal and factual merits of the case.

Does addressing misconceptions in jury directions create an unfair trial?

As part of a juror's schema, jurors may have misconceptions before a trial starts. However, the presumption in most common law jurisdictions is that jurors are not biased.[35] This presumption depends primarily on the process of randomly selecting jurors to represent the wider community.[36] Jurors bring a diversity of life experiences to their task. Combining this with group decision-making processes may reduce, balance, or counter-act some prejudices[37] and thereby produce accurate fact-finding.[38] However, research has questioned the assumption that the representativeness of juries effectively combats misconceptions in sexual offence trials. If misconceptions are prevalent, other jurors may share the misconceptions and/or not have sufficient accurate knowledge to avoid being influenced by the misconceptions or be able to persuade other jurors to not accept the misconceptions.[39]

John Willis and Marilyn McMahon argue that if a representative jury is inadequate to address misconceptions, this means that random selection and impartiality are separate issues and using directions to address impartiality 'constitute[s] an implicit but profound challenge to the role and existence of the jury'.[40] However, the representativeness of the jury is a means to achieving, rather than a guarantee of, the impartiality of a jury.[41] The risk of bias in randomly selected jurors has been recognised in evidentiary jury directions that warn jurors about impermissible reasoning processes. For example, courts developed directions to address factual misconceptions (eg, that eye-witness

35 See, eg, Jeremy Gans et al, *Criminal Process and Human Rights* (Federation Press, 2011) 428; *Rojas v Berllaque (A-G for Gibraltar intervening)* [2004] 1 WLR 201, 206 [14] (Lord Nicholls).

36 See, eg, *Cheatle v The Queen* (1993) 177 CLR 541; *Abdroikov* (n 18) 2697 [47] (Baroness Hale of Richmond), 2702 [66] (Lord Carswell).

37 See, eg, *AK v Western Australia* (2008) 232 CLR 438, 477–8 [103]; Minow (n 26) 1209–13; Gordon, 'All Together Now' (n 1); Gary Edmond and Kirsty A Martire, 'Just Cognition: Scientific Research on Bias and Some Implications for Legal Procedure and Decision-Making' (2019) 82(4) *Modern Law Review* 633, 658–9.

38 Sara Gordon, 'What Jurors Want to Know: Motivating Juror Cognition to Increase Legal Knowledge & Improve Decisionmaking' (2014) 81 *Tennessee Law Review* 751, 761 ('What Jurors Want to Know').

39 See, eg, Gordon, 'All Together Now' (n 1) 440–4.

40 John Willis and Marilyn McMahon, 'Educating Juries or Telling Them What to Think? Credibility, Delay in Complaint, Judicial Directions and the Role of Juries' (2017) 41 *Criminal Law Journal* 27, 48.

41 See, eg, VLRC, *Jury Empanelment* (Report No 27, May 2014) 36–7 [3.117]–[3.121].

identification is highly reliable[42]) and errors in reasoning processes (eg, that an accused who has lied, is a liar, and therefore any explanation they provide will be a lie;[43] or that their decision must not be based on sympathy or prejudice[44]). These kinds of directions assume that jurors are capable of being fair but may hold certain misconceptions and/or may reason inappropriately. In these kinds of situations, courts use jury directions to address misconceptions, and this does not profoundly challenge the role of the jury.

These kinds of evidentiary directions have traditionally focused on ensuring a fair trial for the accused. However, fair trial considerations in criminal trials have been evolving.[45] A fair trial now involves a triangulation of interests, which include the rights and interests of the accused, victims, and the community.[46] This means that to ensure a fair trial, a trial judge's duty has evolved to include ensuring that a trial is fair for victims and the community.[47]

This evolving and broader focus of fair trial interests has been criticised. Anthony Duff et al have argued that the criminal trial is 'under attack'[48] by victim-oriented changes that 'threaten to erode traditional conceptions of the criminal trial'[49] and 'may compromise the very function and purpose of the trial in the first place'.[50] This narrow purpose ascribed to criminal trials tends to reinforce existing processes by focusing on the rights of the accused and does not sufficiently take account of the need to consider a triangulation of interests.[51] However, even if the arguments presented by Duff et al

42 See, eg, Judicial College, *The Crown Court Compendium — Part I: Jury and Trial Management and Summing Up* (July 2024) <www.judiciary.uk/wp-content/uploads/2024/07/Crown-Court-Compendium-Part-I-July-2024-1.pdf> ch 15 ('*Crown Court Compendium*'); Judicial College of Victoria, *Criminal Charge Book* <https://resources.judicialcollege.vic.edu.au/article/1053858 > [4.12].

43 See, eg, *Criminal Charge Book* (n 42) [4.6]; *Edwards v The Queen* (1993) 178 CLR 193 ('*Edwards*').

44 See, eg, *Criminal Charge Book* (n 42) [1.5.1]; *Crown Court Compendium* (n 42) 4–2; *R v The Queen* [2019] 29 CRNZ 267.

45 *Dietrich v The Queen* (1992) 177 CLR 292, 328 (Deane J); *The State (Healy) v Donoghue* (1976) IR 325, 350; *R v H and C* [2004] 2 AC 134, 145–6 [11] (Lord Bingham); Chief Justice James Spigelman, 'The Truth Can Cost Too Much: The Principle of a Fair Trial' (2004) 78 *Australian Law Journal* 29, 43.

46 See, eg, *Jago v District Court of New South Wales* (1989) 168 CLR 23, 33 (Mason CJ), 49–50, 54 (Brennan J); *R v A (No 2)* [2002] 1 AC 45, 65 [38] (Lord Steyn) ('*A (No 2)*'); Laura Hoyano, 'What Is Balanced on the Scales of Justice? In Search of the Essence of the Right to a Fair Trial' [2014] (1) *Criminal Law Review* 4, 12.

47 See, eg, *KRI v The Queen* [2012] VSCA 186, [100] (Neave JA and King AJA); *A (No 2)* (n 46) 65 [38] (Lord Steyn).

48 Anthony Duff et al, *The Trial on Trial: Volume 3 Towards a Normative Theory of the Criminal Law* (Hart Publishing, 2007) 1.

49 Duff et al (n 48) 1–2.

50 Tyrone Kirchengast, 'Recent Reforms to Victim's Rights and the Emerging "Normative Theory of the Criminal Trial"' (2010) 56(1–2) *Criminal Law Quarterly* 82, 88.

51 See, eg, Kirchengast (n 50); Jacqueline Horan, '#Letherspeak: Victims as Catalysts for Law Reform in Sexual Assault Trials' (2021) 47(2) *Monash University Law Review* 48.

are accepted, their criticisms of victim-oriented changes should not preclude changes to ensure an impartial tribunal which produces accurate verdicts.[52] The fairness of the tribunal is fundamental to whether there can be a fair trial.

Although a judge's guidance to a jury primarily focuses on the law and the evidence, it can also include general (framework) information (sometimes called 'social framework' information).[53] Misconceptions form part of a person's schema. General information focuses on improving jurors' schemas 'rather than seeking to eliminate them from the decision-making process'.[54] General information has an educative purpose, challenging the framework jurors may use when assessing evidence.[55] This information should be general in nature, helping to 'correct erroneous beliefs or assumptions'[56] and helping jurors to 'evaluate behaviour that might otherwise be found incomprehensible or counterintuitive'.[57]

In most trials, judges give jurors directions to set aside any feelings of sympathy or prejudice that they may have.[58] For this general direction to combat misconceptions in sexual offence trials, jurors must accurately identify their own misconceptions, recognise that they may involve sympathy or prejudice, and then be willing and able to set aside any misconceptions they have.[59] Expecting jurors to identify and address biases or misconceptions in this way has been described as 'psychologically implausible'.[60] Further, these directions have been shown to be poor at helping jurors to detect and correct bias when given to jurors as part of the jury selection process in the USA.[61]

Judges may also give juries more specific directions about misconceptions in sexual offence trials. For example, Victoria has jury directions that aim to address potential bias in jurors in sexual offence trials by explaining why a complainant might delay in reporting a sexual offence. Willis and McMahon argue that these directions tend to assist the prosecution and that this 'raises an issue

52 Accurate verdicts are of fundamental importance to Duff et al: Duff et al (n 48) 5.

53 See, eg, Laurens Walker and John Monahan, 'Social Frameworks: A New Use of Social Science in Law' (1987) 73(3) *Virginia Law Review* 559, 560; David Hamer and Gary Edmond, 'Judicial Notice: Beyond Adversarialism and into the Exogenous Zone' (2016) 25 *Griffith Law Review* 291, 306.

54 Catriona McKay, Mark Nolan and Michael Smithson, 'Effectiveness of Question Trails as Jury Decision Aids: The Jury's Still Out' (2014) 21(4) *Psychiatry, Psychology and Law* 492, 508.

55 Louise Ellison and Vanessa E Munro, 'Turning Mirrors into Windows? Assessing the Impact of (Mock) Juror Education in Jury Trials' (2009) 49(3) *British Journal of Criminology* 363, 365 ('Turning Mirrors into Windows').

56 *DH* (n 10) 631 [2].

57 Ellison and Munro, 'Turning Mirrors into Windows?' (n 55) 365.

58 See, eg, *Criminal Charge Book* (n 42) [1.5.1]; *Crown Court Compendium* (n 42) 4–2; *R v The Queen* [2019] 29 CRNZ 267.

59 See, eg, Wegener et al (n 5) 637; Minow (n 26) 1204; Anna Roberts, '(Re)forming the Jury: Detection and Disinfection of Implicit Juror Bias' (2012) 44(3) *Connecticut Law Review* 827, 844.

60 Wegener et al (n 5) 631. See also Roberts (n 59) 844–5.

61 Roberts (n 59) 840.

in relation to the impartiality of the judge'.[62] The Victorian Court of Appeal described these directions as 'ensur[ing] that a jury does not engage in impermissible reasoning that might be to the disadvantage of the prosecution'.[63] Some directions may benefit the accused and some directions may benefit the prosecution or the complainant. However, analysing directions that address misconceptions in terms of benefits to a party diminishes their importance and misconstrues their purpose. Their purpose is to address the risk of bias in the jury when assessing the evidence and to ensure that the trial is fair to all, including the accused and the complainant.

As discussed in Chapter 4, there are differences between adjudicative facts and legislative facts. General information that addresses misconceptions does not involve adjudicative or legislative facts. Legislative facts help to understand how the common law or legislation should or may apply. Information addressing misconceptions is similar in that it helps jurors to understand and evaluate adjudicative facts.[64] Importantly, general information should not invite reasoning that because the victim behaved in the same way as many victims behave, that makes it more likely that the victim is telling the truth.[65] The conclusions drawn about the adjudicative facts in each case remain a matter for the jury.[66] Accordingly, jury directions can address misconceptions without affecting the impartiality of the judge (regardless of whether they assist the prosecution).

Before considering the use of jury directions to address misconceptions in the case study, the next section discusses whether there is evidence that jurors will hold misconceptions in a sexual offence case resulting in a jury that may not be impartial.

Assessing the risk that misconceptions about sexual offences may affect jury decision-making

If random selection does not guarantee jury impartiality, how should the risk of impartiality be assessed? In most common law jurisdictions, there is virtually no regulation of jurors' background knowledge, and no information about whether they accept rape myths.[67] As discussed in Chapter 2, laws governing

62 Willis and McMahon (n 40) 29.

63 *Jacobs v The Queen* [2019] VSCA 285, [73].

64 Neil J Vidmar and Regina A Schuller, 'Juries and Expert Evidence: Social Framework Testimony' (1989) 52(4) *Law and Contemporary Problems* 133, 135.

65 Ellison and Munro, 'Turning Mirrors into Windows?' (n 55) 365; Ian Freckelton, 'Child Sexual Abuse Accommodation Syndrome: The Travails of Counterintuitive Evidence in Australia and New Zealand' (1997) 15 *Behavioral Sciences and the Law* 247, 263–4.

66 Dufraimont (n 32) 345–8.

67 Hamer and Edmond (n 53) 311. The exception to this is the USA where questioning of jurors about their pre-trial knowledge is permitted and might reveal such information: Rose, 'A Voir Dire of Voir Dire' (n 40).

the confidentiality of jury deliberations either prevent or substantially restrict research on jurors in actual sexual offence trials, including whether misconceptions influenced their decision-making. Even if such research were possible

> it would be entirely reliant on [jurors] self-reporting verdict preferences and there would be no opportunity to hold the trial stimulus constant, in order to isolate the effect of pre-existing juror attitudes on verdict choices.[68]

It may also be difficult to identify when a misconception influences decision-making (eg, in deciding that evidence is not relevant, or the weight given to evidence). A juror's conclusions about specific facts may not reveal whether a misconception influenced their conclusion. As Justice Mason observed in the context of judicial fact-finding and the determination of legal principles, prejudice does not 'walk out self-announced'.[69]

Another approach would be to assess whether jurors hold misconceptions, rather than whether misconceptions affect their decision-making. However, the trial process itself may affect how a juror thinks about misconceptions. In a mock juror study, Louise Ellison and Vanessa Munro observed that despite participants recognising the seriousness of rape by an acquaintance, 'jurors' found it more difficult to 'convict' where the complainant and defendant had been in a previous relationship.[70]

The courts' approach to assessing the risk of bias can be applied to assessing the role of misconceptions. The courts' approach to bias provides that:

> whether a judicial officer (or juror) *might* not bring an impartial mind to the resolution of a question that has not been determined requires no prediction about how the judge or juror will in fact approach the matter. The question is one of possibility (real and not remote), not probability.[71]

This test accommodates evidentiary limitations that arise in relation to juror misconceptions. The test can then be adapted so that the issue is whether there is a real, and not remote, possibility that a juror will hold a misconception that might lead them to decide a case on a basis other than its legal and factual

68 Leverick (n 22) 258.

69 Justice K Mason, 'Unconscious Judicial Prejudice' (2001) 75 *Australian Law Journal* 676, 679–80.

70 Louise Ellison and Vanessa E Munro, 'Better the Devil You Know? "Real Rape" Stereotypes and the Relevance of a Previous Relationship in (Mock) Juror Deliberations' (2013) 17(4) *The International Journal of Evidence & Proof* 299, 309–10 ('Better the Devil You Know?').

71 *Ebner* (n 14) 345 [7] (Gleeson CJ, McHugh, Gummow and Hayne JJ) (emphasis in original). See also *Locabail (UK) v Bayfield Properties Ltd* [2000] QB 451, 475; *RDS* (n 16) 530 [109] (Cory and Iacobucci JJ); *Muir* (n 16) 508–09 [62].

merits. Relying on jury simulation studies and other research enables reasonable inferences to be drawn to determine what jurors might know or believe. The next section therefore examines:

- evidence of misconceptions in sexual offence trials
- evidence of misconceptions outside of the courtroom
- assessing the risk that jurors will hold misconceptions, and
- the influence of misconceptions on jury deliberations.

Evidence of misconceptions in sexual offence trials

Counsel often rely on misconceptions when presenting their case. This suggests that counsel believe (in the absence of direct evidence from jurors) that jurors may rely on misconceptions in their decision-making and they hope 'to activate or trigger the biasing effects of these stereotypes'.[72] Research conducted in both Australia and England revealed that counsel (and others in the criminal justice system in the Australia research) believed that jurors are influenced by rape myths.[73]

Based on a review of 75 sexual offence trials in New South Wales, and comparison with previous reports in that jurisdiction, there is evidence of 'entrenched trial practices and narratives' in sexual offence trials across decades.[74] Research concerning 25 sexual offence trials in Victoria reached similar conclusions.[75] A study comparing cross-examination used in 21 rape trials in New South Wales in the 1950s and 21 rape trials in New Zealand in the 2000s revealed that cross-examination topics and strategies used were quite similar.[76] The similarities included comparing the complainant to a 'real rape'

72 Elaine Craig, 'The Ethical Obligations of Defence Counsel in Sexual Assault Cases' (2014) 51 *Osgoode Hall Law Journal* 427, 442. See also Jennifer Temkin and Barbara Krahé, *Sexual Assault and the Justice Gap: A Question of Attitude* (Hart Publishing, 2008) 111; Yvette Tinsley, Claire Baylis and Warren Young, '"I Think She's Learnt Her Lesson": Juror Use of Cultural Misconceptions in Sexual Violence Trials' (2021) 52(2) *Victoria University Wellington Law Review* 463, 472.

73 Wendy Larcombe et al, 'I Think It's Rape and I Think He Would Be Found Not Guilty: Focus Group Perceptions of (un)Reasonable Belief in Consent in Rape Law' (2016) 25(6) *Social and Legal Studies* 611; Dominic Willmott and Lara Hudspith, 'Jury Trials and Rape Myth Bias: Exploring the Research Evidence, Stakeholder Perspectives and Effective Solutions' in Nicola Monahan (ed), *Contemporary Challenges in the Jury System: A Comparative Perspective* (Routledge, 2024) 167, 174–5.

74 See, eg, Julia Quilter and Luke McNamara, 'Experience of Complainants of Adult Sexual Offences in the District Court of NSW: A Trial Transcript Analysis' (2023) 259 *Crime and Justice Bulletin* 1, 2 ('District Court of NSW').

75 Julia Quilter and Luke McNamara, *Qualitative Analysis of County Court of Victoria Rape Trial Transcripts: Report to the Victorian Law Reform Commission* (Final Report, August 2021) ('*County Court of Victoria*').

76 Sarah Zydervelt et al, 'Lawyers' Strategies for Cross-Examining Rape Complainants: Have We Moved Beyond the 1950s?' (2016) *British Journal of Criminology* 551.

victim based on misconceptions about the complainant's lack of physical resistance, sexual history, and delay in reporting the alleged rape.[77] Another study in New Zealand found that in at least 14 of the 18 trials examined, defence counsel referred to misconceptions about false allegations of sexual offending or 'reinforced aspects of the "real rape" paradigm during cross-examination or in closing submissions'.[78]

Further, in a study of eight trials in England and Wales that tested for the presence of 13 different myths or stereotypes, the defence mentioned myths or stereotypes 38 times, with an average of 4.75 myths referred to in each trial.[79] In another study of 18 adult rape and sexual assault trials in England and Wales, 'rape myths were used extensively in every trial'.[80] In a study of 30 trials in England and Wales, rape myths were used in at least 26 trials.[81] Another study of trials in the 2000s in England and Wales revealed that in many sexual assault trials, defence counsel explicitly relied on discredited misconceptions.[82] These kinds of findings have been replicated in other case studies of actual trials in different jurisdictions.[83]

Consistent with the belief of counsel that misconceptions affect *real* juror decision-making, courts in Australia, Canada, New Zealand, the UK, and the USA have all accepted that there is a risk of misconceptions influencing juries.[84] Research conducted with mock jurors provides another way of determining whether it is possible that actual jurors rely on misconceptions in their decision-making.

77 Zydervelt et al (n 76) 562–5. See also Rachel Zajac, Nina Westera and Andy Kaladelfos, 'The "Good Old Days" of Courtroom Questioning: Changes in the Format of Child Cross-Examination Questions Over 60 Years' (2018) 23(2) *Child Maltreatment* 186, 191.

78 Yvette Tinsley, Warren Young and Claire Baylis, 'Jurors' Use of Rape Myths in Aotearoa New Zealand' in Greg Byrne and Jacqueline Horan (eds), *Sexual Assault Trials: Challenges and Innovations* (LexisNexis, 2025) 165, 174.

79 Jennifer Temkin, Jacqueline M Gray and Jastine Barrett, 'Different Functions of Rape Myth Use in Court: Findings from a Trial Observation Study' (2018) 13(2) *Feminist Criminology* 205, 210.

80 Smith and Skinner (n 32) 448–9.

81 Ruth Durham et al, *Seeing is Believing: The Northumbria Court Observers Panel Report on 30 Rape Trials 2015–2016* (Report, 2016) 15.

82 Craig (n 72) 437.

83 See, eg, Tinsley, Baylis and Young (n 72); Burgin (n 13); Terese Henning, 'Beyond "Beyond Reasonable Doubt": Wrong Decisions in Sexual Offences Trials' (2000) 15 *Australian Journal of Law and Society* 1; McDonald (n 28); Anastasia Powell et al, 'Meanings of "Sex" and "Consent": The Persistence of Rape Myths in Victorian Rape Law' (2013) 22(2) *Griffith Law Review* 456; Smith and Skinner (n 32).

84 Jacqueline Horan and Jane Goodman-Delahunty, 'Expert Evidence to Counteract Jury Misconceptions about Consent in Sexual Assault Cases: Failures and Lessons Learned' (2020) 43(2) *University of New South Wales Law Journal* 707, 710. See also Dufraimont (n 32) 331–2.

Evidence of misconceptions obtained from outside of the courtroom

Research in Australia indicates that 'myths and misconceptions about sexual assault and discriminatory attitudes towards women and children' who make a complaint about sexual assault are common,[85] and are prevalent among jury-eligible members of the community.[86] Extensive international studies of rape myths over several decades have found evidence of rape myths influencing juror decision-making.[87]

However, some conclusions about the prevalence of misconceptions have been criticised for relying primarily on data from the 1980s and 1990s,[88] arguing that the prevalence of rape myths in jury-eligible citizens has significantly declined since then.[89] Some caution is also required when considering evidence from other jurisdictions because rape myths vary between societies and cultures and over time.[90] However, there have been many studies this century across different jurisdictions that indicate that rape myth acceptance continues to be a significant challenge.[91]

Research conducted by Cheryl Thomas in England and Wales criticised claims of widespread 'rape myths' in that jurisdiction for their lack of empirical support. This is the most recent significant challenge to findings about the prevalence of sexual offence misconceptions among jurors.[92] Drawing primarily on Thomas's research and a study that found attitudes towards women are

85 Australian Law Reform Commission, *Family Violence — A National Legal Response* (Report No 114, October 2010) [26.38].

86 Jane Goodman-Delahunty, Natalie Martschuk and Annie Cossins, 'What Australian Jurors Know and Do Not Know about Evidence of Child Sexual Abuse' (2017) 41 *Criminal Law Journal* 86.

87 See, eg, Leverick (n 22) 273. See also Sokratis Dinos et al, 'A Systematic Review of Juries' Assessment of Rape Victims: Do Rape Myths Impact on Juror Decision-making?' (2015) 43(1) *International Journal of Law, Crime and Justice* 36.

88 See, eg, Amy Grubb and Emily Turner, 'Attribution of Blame in Rape Cases: A Review of the Impact of Rape Myth Acceptance, Gender Role Conformity and Substance Use on Victim Blaming' (2012) 17(5) *Aggression and Violent Behavior* 443, 450.

89 See, eg, Helen Reece, 'Rape Myths: Is Elite Opinion Right and Popular Opinion Wrong?' (2013) 33(3) *Oxford Journal of Legal Studies* 445.

90 See, eg, Megan Hermolle, Samantha J Andrews and Ching-Yu S Huang, 'Rape Stereotype Acceptance in the General Population of England and Wales' (2022) 37 *Journal of Interpersonal Violence* NP23155; Grubb and Turner (n 88) 445.

91 See, eg, Burgin (n 13); Ellison and Munro, 'Telling Tales' (n 31); Goodman-Delahunty, Martschuk and Cossins (n 86); Horan and Goodman-Delahunty (n 84); McDonald (n 28); Olivia Smith, *Rape Trials in England and Wales: Observing Justice and Rethinking Rape Myths* (Palgrave Macmillan, 2018); Temkin, Gray and Barrett (n 79); Leverick (n 22).

92 Cheryl Thomas, 'The 21st Century Jury: Contempt, Bias and the Impact of Jury Service' [2020] (11) *Criminal Law Review* 987, 998 ('The 21st Century Jury'). Thomas has said that this research is ongoing: Cheryl Thomas, 'A Response to "The Jury Is Still Out"' [2021] (9) *Criminal Law Review* 772, 772.

'gradually improving' in Australia,[93] the Queensland Law Reform Commission concluded that it 'is very difficult to determine whether false preconceptions have an effect upon jury verdicts . . . [and] that the influence of some of the "rape myths" may be overstated'.[94] It is therefore important to consider Thomas's research and to consider broader issues raised by her research.

Thomas's research involved people from 65 juries (post-verdict) involving 771 jurors.[95] The former jurors indicated low levels of agreement with rape myths such as:

- A rape probably didn't happen if the victim has no bruises or marks (3%)
- A woman who wears provocative clothing puts herself in a position to be raped (4%)
- It is difficult to believe rape allegations that were not reported immediately (7%)[96]
- Many women who claim they were raped agreed to have sex and then regretted it afterward (12%)
- Children often make up stories about being sexually abused (3%).

Some answers did suggest the prevalence of rape myths. For example, 43% agreed (and 35% were not sure) that they would expect a complainant to be very emotional when giving evidence about a rape.[97] As can be seen, the questions involve overt examples of rape myths.

However, based on her analysis of sexual offence trials in England in 2019, Ellen Daly said that:

> Rape myths often were not referred to in overt terms, rather they subtly infused the overarching trial narratives at various points, helping to build an overall picture of a rape or assault that did not conform to the 'real rape' prototype and a victim-survivor who did not fit with the notion of an 'ideal victim'.[98]

For example, questioning the complainant about whether they resisted (physically or verbally) are based on rape myths concerning how a 'real' rape victim is supposed to behave.[99] In most jurisdictions, resistance is irrelevant to whether

93 Kim Webster et al, *Australians' Attitudes to Violence against Women and Gender Equality: Findings from the 2017 National Community Attitudes Towards Violence against Women Survey (NCAS)*, ANROWS (Report, March 2018) 8.

94 Queensland Law Reform Commission, *Review of Consent Laws and the Excuse of Mistake of Fact* (Report No 78, June 2020) 209 [8.28].

95 Thomas, 'The 21st Century Jury' (n 92) 1001.

96 Thomas, 'The 21st Century Jury' (n 92) 1002.

97 Thomas, 'The 21st Century Jury' (n 92) 1003.

98 Daly (n 22) 59. See also Willmott and Hudspith (n 73) 171.

99 For examples of the subtle ways in which this and other narratives based on rape myths were used in trials, see Daly (n 22) ch 2.

the complainant consented and takes no account of research that estimates that approximately half of all victims of sexual assault experience freezing (also known as 'tonic immobility').[100] Questions were also based on the idea that 'flirting signals consent, which positions women as gatekeepers of consent'.[101] Research in Victoria revealed cases in which minimal and seemingly irrelevant acts were said to constitute flirting and thereby consent (eg, changing into pyjama shorts at bedtime, flirting in photos taken at a 7-Eleven, walking and sitting close to the accused).[102]

Thomas stated that a key reason why her study was much more reliable than other studies was because it used 'real jurors who actually serve[d] on trials' in contrast to mock jury studies and opinion polls that rely on volunteers.[103] Most (87%) of the participants in her study said they would not have performed jury service if attendance were voluntary.[104] By contrast, 65% of 4,765 jury-eligible citizens surveyed in Australia said that they would be keen or very keen to serve on a jury.[105] Thomas says that her survey resulted in a more accurate demographic of serving jurors and avoided any self-selection bias.[106] Although the participants were required to attend court, and there was a 99% participation rate, they all 'agreed to take part in an anonymous and voluntary post-verdict survey before leaving court'.[107]

However, many other studies have specifically focused on identifying juror eligible participants.[108] For example, a 2017 survey of 1931 people summoned but dismissed or excused from jury service in New South Wales assessed the extent to which they accepted misconceptions about child sexual abuse.[109] The survey found that with eight of the 18 misconceptions assessed, more than half of those surveyed did not disagree with the misconception. For most of these eight misconceptions, approximately 40% of people said they were uncertain about whether they agreed or disagreed with the misconception.[110] Accord-

100 Jane Goodman-Delahunty and Mark A Nolan, 'The Quality of Autobiographical Memories of Sexual Assault' in Greg Byrne and Jacqueline Horan (eds), *Sexual Assault Trials: Challenges and Innovations* (LexisNexis, 2025) 45, 57.

101 Daly (n 22) 34.

102 Steven Tudor and Greg Byrne, 'Affirmative Consent Reforms: Problems with How the New Obligation to Ascertain Consent Works in Victoria' in Greg Byrne and Jacqueline Horan (eds), *Sexual Assault Trials: Challenges and Innovations* (LexisNexis, 2025) 29, 36–7.

103 Thomas, 'The 21st Century Jury' (n 92) 1005.

104 Thomas, 'The 21st Century Jury' (n 92) 1006.

105 Jane Goodman-Delahunty et al, *Practices, Policies and Procedures That Influence Juror Satisfaction in Australia* (Research and Public Policy Series No 87, July 2007) 130–1.

106 Thomas, 'The 21st Century Jury' (n 92) 1007.

107 Thomas, 'The 21st Century Jury' (n 92) 1001 and 1005.

108 See, eg, James R P Ogloff and V Gordon Rose, 'The Comprehension of Judicial Instructions' in Neil Brewer and Kipling D Williams (eds), *Psychology and Law: An Empirical Perspective* (Guilford Press, 2005) 407; Ellison and Munro, 'Better the Devil You Know?' (n 70) 306–7; *Improving the Management of Sexual Offence Cases* (n 4) 100 [5.31].

109 Goodman-Delahunty, Martschuk and Cossins (n 86) 92.

110 Goodman-Delahunty, Martschuk and Cossins (n 86) 94–5.

ingly, the fact that most participants did not volunteer to attend court before participating in the study does not appear to explain why the conclusions from Thomas's study differed from many other studies.

However, as discussed in Chapter 3,[111] examining the assumptions and methods in Thomas's study may explain the different findings from her study.

Thomas's study only asked one question concerning each misconception, rather than several differently worded questions that test for the same attitude.[112] The assessment scale used by Thomas was quite simple (agree/disagree/not sure) rather than five or seven point scales used in other studies of rape myths that measure the degrees or strength of agreement/disagreement with propositions.[113] Where the question points towards a more socially acceptable answer, participants may be less willing to express (self-report) agreement with a rape myth.[114] Further, Thomas equated an answer of 'not sure' with meaning that a rape myth is not held. For example, while only 7% agreed that 'it is difficult to believe rape allegations that were not reported immediately', a further 20% were not sure about this statement.[115] Similarly, while only 3% agreed that children often make up stories about being sexually abused, 33% of those surveyed were not sure.[116] Where a juror is unsure about a rape myth, there may be greater scope for rape myths to be invoked during a trial.[117]

Additionally, the test used by Thomas involved jurors being able to recognise a rape myth in an abstract form. When responding to such questions, the person may answer the questions with a particular rape scenario in mind (eg, stranger rape). However, research suggests that the way in which misconceptions arise will vary depending upon the scenario examined.[118] Thomas's study does not reveal what scenario each person was envisioning when answering the survey questions.

Finally, examining mock juror deliberations following jury trial simulations provides a more detailed and nuanced picture of how misconceptions may be

111 See also Gary Edmond, 'Judging Surveys: Experts, Empirical Evidence and Law Reform' (2005) 33 *Federal Law Review* 95, 136.

112 Ellen Daly et al, 'Myths about Myths? A Commentary on Thomas (2020) and the Question of Jury Rape Myth Acceptance' (2021) 7(1) *Journal of Gender-Based Violence* 189.

113 See generally, Leverick (n 22) 258; Daly et al (n 112); Gerger et al (n 22) 424–6, 434–6; Jon A Krosnick, 'Improving Questionnaire Design to Maximize Reliability and Validity' in David L Vannette and Jon A Krosnick (eds), *The Palgrave Handbook of Survey Research* (Springer International Publishing, 1st ed, 2018) 95, 99–100.

114 See, eg, Gerger et al (n 22) 424; Reece (n 89) 455; Kim Webster et al (n 93) 87; Krosnick (n 113) 98; Daly et al (n 112).

115 Thomas, 'The 21st Century Jury' (n 92) 1002.

116 Thomas, 'The 21st Century Jury' (n 92) 1004.

117 See, eg, Goodman-Delahunty, Martschuk and Cossins (n 86) 97; Ellison and Munro, 'Better the Devil You Know?' (n 70) 310.

118 Louise Ellison and Vanessa E Munro, 'A Stranger in the Bushes, or an Elephant in the Room? Critical Reflections upon Received Rape Myth Wisdom in the Context of a Mock Jury Study' (2010) 13 *New Criminal Law Review* 781, 793–4 ('A Stranger in the Bushes').

relied upon during deliberations.[119] People who express low agreement with (or uncertainty about) rape myths in an abstract form may still 'express highly problematic views when discussing a concrete case'.[120] Similarly, research with actual jurors in New Zealand suggests that even when jurors do not appear to believe misconceptions, they may still draw on misconceptions when assessing the evidence.[121] This highlights the limitations of 'uncritical extrapolation from attitudinal responses to predictions of deliberative process or outcome in concrete rape cases'.[122] Accordingly, Thomas's assumptions and methodological limitations with her study, rather than the reason why subjects participated in the study, is more likely to explain the differences in the results from her study concerning the prevalence of misconceptions when compared with other research. This discussion is not to suggest that there are no limitations with studies that do identify misconceptions.[123] Instead, the discussion explains why the results of Thomas's research are so different from other research.

If there is a risk that jurors may have misconceptions, a challenging issue is to determine when the risk is such that it should be addressed.

Assessing the risk that jurors hold misconceptions in sexual offence trials

If, as Thomas concluded, the risk of a juror holding misconceptions in a sexual offences trial is small, and amounts to less than one person on any jury,[124] is there any need to address this risk? The conclusion that this is an acceptable risk, or a risk that does not need to be addressed, involves several assumptions. More than one rape myth may arise in each trial. There is no information about the distribution of misconceptions among jurors. For example, if four myths are raised in a trial, will that mean there is one juror who holds all the misconceptions, or might there be four jurors who each hold one misconception?

Normally courts assess the risk of bias in a tribunal in relation to a particular jury or juror (or judge). However, the risk of a juror holding a misconception(s) is based on a statistical probability rather than evidence about a particular juror. Even if it is most likely that only one juror will hold all relevant misconceptions, there is a real possibility that more than one juror in a small percentage of juries will hold relevant misconceptions. With no way of determining which jury that will be, even a low rate of jurors holding misconceptions means that

119 Ellison and Munro, 'A Stranger in the Bushes' (n 118) 799. See also Leverick (n 22) 259; Vanessa E Munro, 'A Circle That Cannot Be Squared? Survivor Confidence in an Adversarial Justice System' in Miranda A Horvath and Jennifer M Brown (eds), *Rape: Challenging Contemporary Thinking — 10 Years On* (Milton, 2022) 212–13.

120 Leverick (n 22) 256. See also Ellison and Munro, 'A Stranger in the Bushes' (n 118) 794–5.

121 Tinsley, Baylis and Young (n 72) 471.

122 Ellison and Munro, 'A Stranger in the Bushes' (n 118) 799. See also Tinsley, Baylis and Young (n 72) 469; Daly et al (n 112).

123 See, eg, Leverick (n 22) 266–7; Thomas, 'A Response to "The Jury's Still Out"' (n 92).

124 Thomas, 'The 21st Century Jury' (n 92) 1004.

there is a real possibility that any jury empanelled might not be an impartial jury because of the real risk that it may contain a juror who is not impartial.

Another assumption is that where only one juror is likely to hold misconceptions, other jurors will 'neutralise' this juror's bias during deliberations and reach an impartial verdict.[125] For example, Lord Carswell said that

> [u]nconscious prejudices and bias can be insidious in their operation on people's minds, but the number and diversity of people on a criminal jury constitute a safeguard against such prejudice or bias on the part of any one juror exercising sufficient influence to determine the outcome of the trial.[126]

Research on the dynamics of group decision-making suggests that it is difficult for a juror in the minority to voice their dissent and they may change their views to conform with the majority.[127] However, this research does not mean there is no risk of minority views influencing verdict choices and it involves relying on other jurors or jury deliberations to ensure an impartial jury. Further, 'neutralising' a juror's bias seems to assume that the juror will discuss the case in ways that reveal their misconceptions. Jurors are likely to discuss the case in terms of which facts or stories they do or do not accept. Misconceptions may affect what evidence a person recalls and considers plausible. Therefore, just as Daly found that misconceptions may be 'subtly infused' in trial narratives,[128] jurors may not discuss the evidence in a way that reveals misconceptions for other jurors to correct. Jurors may only discuss the specific facts of the case, even though the facts discussed may be affected by misconceptions.

What if jurors do discuss a misconception during their deliberations? An Australian mock jury trial study involving 885 people called for jury service in New South Wales examined the influence of deliberation on people not provided with any information about child sexual assault (CSA) and people provided with information about CSA from an expert witness or jury directions. The study found that '[d]eliberation provided an opportunity for many jurors to repeat and reinforce CSA misconceptions introduced by [the] defense lawyer during cross-examination of the complainant, or by other deliberating jurors'.[129] The study did not find evidence that jurors with mistaken views about CSA were being corrected by those with less knowledge about CSA.

125 This assumption is implicit in Thomas's research: Thomas, 'The 21st Century Jury' (n 92) 1004.

126 *Abdroikov* (n 18) 2702–3 [67].

127 See generally, Gordon, 'All Together Now' (n 1) 440–4.

128 Daly (n 22) 59.

129 Goodman-Delahunty et al (n 9) 15.

Research suggests that jurors are better at making factual corrections than legal corrections.[130] However, a factual correction is quite different from an assessment of what facts seem plausible and whether a story seems coherent. Further, the capacity of deliberations to correct errors must be treated with some caution.[131] For a juror to correct another juror's misconceptions during deliberations, the first juror would need to be able to identify and correct any misconceptions and have the confidence and persuasive ability to do so. Further, it is not open to a juror to conduct research to refresh or strengthen their existing knowledge as they might normally do outside of a jury trial. Relying on deliberations to correct misconceptions also assumes that there is no unacceptable risk that a juror who holds misconceptions will influence other jurors (and thereby exacerbate the influence of misconceptions on a jury's impartiality). This risk of one juror influencing the other jurors also limits the ability of majority verdict provisions to overcome an individual juror's views. Accordingly, while the jury as a collective entity may sometimes be able to address the risk of juror misconceptions, relying on this method provides an unsatisfactory and unreliable means of ensuring an impartial jury.

Therefore, even where the levels of misconceptions are quite low, there is a real possibility that a juror(s) may have misconceptions in a sexual offence case. If some jurors are likely to accept some misconceptions, how might this influence their verdict?

Do misconceptions influence jury verdicts in sexual offence trials?

Misconceptions are more likely to be influential in sexual offence trials because of the 'unique characteristics of sexual offences'.[132] These characteristics often involve the exercise of power by a person known to the complainant and offences are often committed in private where there are no other eyewitnesses or corroborating evidence. As a result, jurors often need to draw inferences from the available facts and the credibility of the complainant will usually be central to jury deliberations.

As discussed in Chapter 3, the first step in the story model indicates that jurors use their knowledge and experience to understand the evidence in a trial and develop a narrative story to organise that information. This is a step that courts encourage when they tell jurors to use their common sense and

130 Phoebe C Ellsworth, 'Are Twelve Heads Better Than One?' (1989) 52 *Law and Contemporary Problems* 205, 218–19.

131 See also Phoebe C Ellsworth and Alan Reifman, 'Juror Comprehension and Public Policy: Perceived Problems and Proposed Solutions' (2000) 6 *Psychology, Public Policy and Law* 788, 806; Shari Seidman Diamond and Judith N Levi, 'Improving Decisions on Death by Revising and Testing Jury Instructions' (1996) 79 *Judicature* 224, 232.

132 VLRC, *Sexual Offences: Law and Procedure* (n 3) 82–7 [1.12]–[1.17]. See also McDonald (n 28) 42.

experience and knowledge of human behaviour.[133] Cognitive science suggests that misconceptions may inform a juror's knowledge and experience. A person's knowledge and experience are likely to be influenced by their beliefs, for example about whether a complainant is telling the truth.[134] This belief may be informed by, for example, mistaken views about a juror's ability to detect whether a complainant is lying, or the prevalence of false complaints about sexual offences. Further, if the evidence in a case is consistent with a person's beliefs and feelings, the evidence is easier to accept because it requires less cognitive effort to understand.[135] Therefore, where jurors do have misconceptions about sexual offences, evidence that fits with such a narrative is likely to be more easily processed and accepted.

Misconceptions about the victim, the act, and the perpetrator, may result in jurors regarding the complainant's allegation with unwarranted scepticism.[136] Further, 'those who believe in rape myths are more likely to find the defendant not guilty, to believe that the complainant consented, and to place at least some of the blame for events upon the complainant'.[137] Research studies 'are near unanimous in finding a significant relationship between scores on RMA [rape myth acceptance] scales and judgments about victim/perpetrator blame in a specific scenario'.[138] The more misconceptions a person holds, the less credible they perceive the victim to be.[139] Conversely, those who hold few misconceptions are more likely to view the complainant as a credible witness.[140]

Because of the number of different misconceptions and the ways in which they may affect juror assessments of the evidence in a case, it can be difficult to assess the degree to which misconceptions improperly affect juror

133 See, eg, *Doney* (n 1) 1, 214; *R v S (RD)* [1997] 3 SCR 484; *R v Olugboja* [1982] QB 320, 327; McDonald (n 28); Tiersma, 'Asking Jurors to do the Impossible' (n 28) 117–21.

134 Rebecca K Helm, 'Constructing the Truth in the Jury Box in Serious Sexual Offence Cases' [2023] (6) *Criminal Law Review* 399, 404–6.

135 Helm (n 134) 406.

136 Temkin, Gray and Barrett (n 79) 205–6. See also, McDonald (n 28) 42; Craig (n 72) 457–60; Annie Cossins and Jane Goodman-Delahunty, 'The Application of the Uniform Evidence Law to Delay in Child Sexual Assault Trials' in Andrew Roberts and Jeremy Gans (eds), *Critical Perspectives on the Uniform Evidence Law* (Federation Press, 2017) 104, 104–5.

137 Temkin, Gray and Barrett (n 79) 207. See also Lily Trimboli and Judy Cashmore, 'Child Sexual Assault Trials: A Survey of Juror Perceptions' (2006) (102) *Crime and Justice Bulletin* 1, 9; Goodman-Delahunty, Cossins and O'Brien (n 9) 775–7.

138 See, eg, Leverick (n 22) 262; Dinos et al (n 87) 39–40; Jade L Stirling, Peter J Hills and Liam Wignall, 'Narrative Approach to Understand People's Comprehension of Acquaintance Rape: The Role of Sex Role Stereotyping' (2022) 13(2) *Psychology and Sexuality* 129.

139 See, eg, Goodman-Delahunty, Cossins and O'Brien (n 9) 779–80; Dinos et al (n 87) 46; Horan and Goodman-Delahunty (n 84) 709.

140 See, eg, Ellison and Munro, 'Better the Devil You Know?' (n 70) 310.

decision-making.[141] Fiona Leverick concludes from her literature review of research involving female complainants and male defendants that

> there is overwhelming evidence that jurors take into the deliberation room false and prejudicial beliefs about what rape looks like and what genuine rape victims would do and that these beliefs affect attitudes and verdict choices in concrete cases. This evidence is both quantitative and qualitative.[142]

What is more difficult to determine is the 'extent of influence that misconceptions had in deliberations and their contribution to eventual verdicts'.[143] This is partly because of the nature of criminal trials, sexual offences and because jurors may construct different stories from the same evidence because of their different 'experiences, expectations, values, and beliefs'.[144] However, where these stories and conclusions are based on the extent to which jurors hold misconceptions about rape and sexual assault, there is a problem.[145] The trial will not be fair because the jury's decision-making will be influenced by inaccurate information, rather than being decided on its legal and factual merits.

The next question is whether a jury-centric approach can help in determining how to address this fair trial problem. Further, courts typically apply the apprehension of bias rule in individual cases where there is a case-specific reason for doing so. However, it is not realistic to examine each potential juror before empanelling a jury, or after completing a trial, to assess what misconceptions they may hold. The risk that a juror may hold misconceptions is real, but that risk must be assessed based on probabilities rather than inquiries about individual jurors. As a result, broader strategies are required to guard against an unacceptable risk of bias.[146] Jury directions provide one of those broader strategies that could be used.

Applying a jury-centric approach to jury directions addressing misconceptions about 'delay' in making a complaint

To demonstrate how a jury-centric approach is relevant to rape myths or misconceptions, the following case study analyses the use of jury directions to ensure an impartial jury by addressing misconceptions about 'delay' in making

141 See, eg, Tinsley, Baylis and Young (n 72) 479–82.

142 Leverick (n 22) 273.

143 Tinsley, Young and Baylis (n 78) 166.

144 Brian H Bornstein and Edie Greene, 'Jury Decision Making: Implications for and from Psychology' (2011) 20 *Current Directions in Psychological Science* 63, 64–5.

145 Leverick (n 22) 262–3. See generally, Bornstein and Greene (n 143) 64–5; Gordon, 'Through the Eyes of Jurors' (n 6); Dinos et al (n 87) 39.

146 See generally, Australian Law Reform Commission, *Without Fear or Favour: Judicial Impartiality and the Law on Bias* (Report No 138, December 2021) 134 [4.83].

a complaint. The word 'delay' implies that there is an appropriate time to make a complaint and therefore in some ways reflects the misconception itself. Because much of the literature and cases refer to delay in making a complaint, I have also (reluctantly) used that terminology.

Using jury directions to address misconceptions about delay in making complaint

Misconceptions about delay in making a complaint are based on the belief that a 'real' rape victim will make a complaint of rape at the first reasonable opportunity to do so.[147] This belief persisted as part of the law for much of the last century.[148] If a woman 'failed' to complain, this carried 'a strong, but not conclusive, presumption that her testimony was false or feigned'.[149] Extensive empirical research shows that this belief is a misconception.[150] It is common for victims of sexual assaults, and in particular child victims,[151] to delay in reporting or to not report at all. For example, complaints by 45% of male children and 25% of female children occurred more than 20 years after the sexual abuse was alleged to have occurred in an Australian institutional setting.[152] By itself, delay in making a complaint says nothing about the truth of a complaint or the complainant's credibility 'because both true and false complaints may be either immediate or delayed'.[153] However, it is common for defence counsel to rely on evidence of delay in making a complaint as a basis for not accepting a complainant's account. For example, in 70% of the 120 cases examined in an Australian study, defence counsel challenged the complainant's account because of delay in making a complaint.[154] In a study of 75 trials in New South

147 Sir Matthew Hale, *Historia Placitorum Coronae: The History of the Pleas of the Crown* (1736) 633. See generally, Willis and McMahon (n 40) 38–9; Dufraimont (n 32) 343–5.

148 *DD* (n 10) 303 [61]. See also Craig (n 72) 433–4; Ellison and Munro, 'A Stranger in the Bushes' (n 118) 783–4.

149 *R v Lillyman* [1896] 2 QB 167, 171. See also *Kilby v The Queen* (1973) 129 CLR 460; Cossins and Goodman-Delahunty (n 136) 106–7.

150 See, eg, Australian Institute of Health and Welfare, *Sexual Assault in Australia* (Report, August 2020); Cristine Roternberg and Adam Cotter, *The Canadian Centre for Justice Statistics, Police-Reported Sexual Assaults in Canada before and after #MeToo, 2016 and 2017* (Report, November 2018) 7.

151 Judith Cashmore et al, *The Impact of Delayed Reporting on the Prosecution and Outcomes of Child Sexual Abuse Cases* (Royal Commission into Institutional Responses to Child Sexual Abuse, 2016) 32.

152 Cashmore et al (n 151) 32. See also Isabel Grant and Janine Benedet, 'The "Statutory Rape" Myth: A Case Law Study of Sexual Assaults against Adolescent Girls' (2019) 31 *Canadian Journal of Women and the Law* 266, who found that almost 20% of girls aged 12–17 reported sexual abuse more than 10 years after the last alleged incident: at 284.

153 *DH* (n 7) 639 [45]. See also *DD* (n 7) 305 [65]; Dufraimont (n 32) 345–8.

154 Martine Powell et al, *An Evaluation of How Evidence Is Elicited from Complainants of Child Sexual Abuse, Royal Commission into Institutional Responses to Child Sexual Abuse* (Report, 2016) 213. See also, Quilter and McNamara, *County Court of Victoria* (n 75) 111–20; Daly (n 22) 46–9.

Wales (2014–20) defence counsel cross-examined the complainant about not complaining immediately in 84% of trials.[155]

This case study primarily focuses on Victoria's approach to addressing this misconception. The three potential components of Victorian jury directions on delay in making a complaint involve:

- providing general (or framework) information about misconceptions concerning delay in making a complaint[156]
- stating that there may be 'good reasons' for delay in making a complaint,[157] and
- providing examples of 'good reasons' for delay in making a complaint.[158]

Most other common law jurisdictions use the first two components of the Victorian approach.[159] The third component is similar to guidance judges provide in England and Wales and Canada but goes further than any other Australian jurisdiction. As in some other jurisdictions, parties in Victoria may call expert evidence about delay in making a complaint.[160] Further, a complainant may give evidence of their reasons for not complaining at an earlier time. However, the focus of this case study is on the information that a judge may give to a jury about delay in making a complaint.

General information about misconceptions concerning delay in making a complaint

The 'general information' direction in Victoria provides that the trial judge must inform the jury that experience shows that:

(a) people may react differently to sexual offences and there is no typical, proper, or normal response to a sexual offence; and
(b) some people may complain immediately to the first person they see, while others may not complain for some time and others may never make a complaint; and
(c) delay in making a complaint in respect of a sexual offence is a common occurrence.[161]

155 Quilter and McNamara, 'District Court of NSW' (n 74) 21.
156 *Jury Directions Act 2015* (Vic) s 52(4).
157 *Jury Directions Act 2015* (Vic) s 53.
158 See, eg, *R v ERJ* (2010) 200 A Crim R 270 ('*ERJ*').
159 See, eg, *Evidence Act 2006* (NZ) s 127(2); *Criminal Procedure (Scotland) Act 1995* (c.46) s 288DA(2); *Criminal Procedure Act 1986* (NSW) s 294(2)(b).
160 *Evidence Act 2008* (Vic) s 79(2). See also *Evidence Act 2006* (NZ) s 25; Danny Sullivan and Diana Piekusis, 'Expert Mental Health Evidence and Its Limits' in Greg Byrne and Jacqueline Horan (eds), *Sexual Assault Trials: Challenges and Innovations* (LexisNexis, 2025) 67, 79.
161 *Jury Directions Act 2015* (Vic) s 52(4).

Judges need not use the precise words used in Victoria's *Jury Directions Act 2015* when directing the jury.[162] However, Victoria's *Criminal Charge Book* does not elaborate on the content or suggest that trial judges should elaborate on the content of this information.[163] The first two paragraphs of the direction are based on similar information given in England and Wales that was developed by courts and then refined in the *Crown Court Compendium*.[164] The general information in England and Wales then provides that:

- '[w]hen you consider why this allegation was not made earlier, you must not assume that because it was delayed it is untrue',[165] and
- the 'defence say that because the complaint was not made at the time this means W is not telling the truth and that W has made up the story'.[166]

The additional information provided in England and Wales highlights two challenges in addressing misconceptions.

First, repeating the rape myth makes clear why the judge is discussing the issue. However, repeating the rape myth risks entrenching the myth in jurors' minds. If a juror already holds a misconception, that misconception is easier to understand and remember than the information discrediting it.[167]

Second, it is essential to distinguish between general information that addresses a misconception and the specific facts of a case. The second piece of information provided in England and Wales suggests that defence counsel may legitimately rely on the misconception based only on the fact of the delay. This suggests that delay, by itself, may be relevant to whether a complaint is true. The *Crown Court Compendium* gives examples of reasons for rejecting this conclusion based on the specifics of the case (eg, because the complainant thought they would not be believed).[168] It is essential to differentiate between challenging the misconception at the general level and explaining why delay might be relevant when considered in combination with other evidence that is specific to a case.

'Good reasons' for delay in making a complaint

In the second component of Victoria's directions, the judge may inform the jury that there may be 'good reasons' why a victim may delay in reporting, or

162 *Jury Directions Act 2015* (Vic) s 6.
163 *Criminal Charge Book* (n 42) [4.8].
164 *Crown Court Compendium* (n 42) 20–1, 20–6.
165 *Crown Court Compendium* (n 42) 20–6.
166 *Crown Court Compendium* (n 42) 20–6. 'W' refers to the witness (who may also be called the complainant).
167 Jennifer Temkin, '"And Always Keep a-Hold of Nurse, for Fear of Finding Something Worse": Challenging Rape Myths in the Courtroom' (2010) 13(4) *New Criminal Law Review* 710, 725. See also NSWLRC, *Consent in Relation to Sexual Offences* (n 4) [8.39].
168 *Crown Court Compendium* (n 42) 20–6.

not report, a sexual offence.[169] The purpose of the direction is to alert the jury to the

> difficulty that many complainants, particularly children, have first in bringing such matters to light, and then in articulating in the witness box the painful self reflections that they may have felt after the offence occurred . . .[170]

This direction operates primarily at the level of general information. It is abstract in nature but operates to alert jurors to think about why there may be good reasons for delay in making a complaint.

Similar directions in New South Wales and Scotland contextualise their 'good reasons' direction by indicating that delay in complaint does not *necessarily* indicate that an allegation is false.[171] The use of the word *necessarily* implies that sometimes delay in complaint, of itself, may mean that an allegation is false. This is incorrect and reinforces misconceptions about delay. The word *necessarily* was, appropriately, removed from the Victorian provisions for that reason.[172]

In each jurisdiction, the 'good reasons' direction may be given irrespective of whether the complainant is able to articulate any reasons for their delay in making a complaint.[173] Where there is evidence in the trial explaining why the complainant delayed in reporting a sexual offence, the judge may refer to that reason(s) when guiding the jury.[174] However, in the absence of specific evidence, judges in many jurisdictions are not permitted to elaborate on what those 'good reasons' may be.[175]

169 Legislation to this effect exists in other jurisdictions, see, eg, *Evidence Act 2006* (NZ) s 127(2); *Criminal Procedure (Scotland) Act 1995* s 288DA(2); *Criminal Procedure Act 1986* (NSW) s 294(2)(b).

170 *Williams v The Queen* (1999) 104 A Crim R 260, 265 [25] ('*Williams*').

171 *Criminal Procedure Act 1986* (NSW) s 294(2)(a); *Abusive Behaviour and Sexual Harm (Scotland) Act 2016* (asp 22) s 288DA(2)(b) (emphasis added).

172 Department of Justice (Vic), *Rape Law Reform Evaluation Project* (Report, 1994) [Recommendations 34 and 35] cited in Victorian Law Reform Commission, *Sexual Offences: Law and Procedure* (Discussion Paper, 2001) 152 [8.121]. See also Rachel Bain, 'Jury Directions Under the Abusive Behaviour and Sexual Harm (Scotland) Act 2016: A Long-Needed Success for Tackling Rape Myths or Another Measure Falling Short?' (2018) 8 *Aberdeen Student Law Review* 39, 52.

173 See, eg, *Williams* (n 170) 265 [24].

174 See, eg, Judicial Institute for Scotland, *e-Jury Manual* (2024) <www.judiciary.scot/docs/librariesprovider3/judiciarydocuments/judicial-institute-publications/jury-manual-pdf-version-29-july-2024.pdf?sfvrsn=21823400_0> [4.30–4.31/133] ('*Jury Manual*'); *DH* (n 10) 640 [48]; *Williams* (n 170) 265 [24]–[26] (Wood CJ at CL); *ERJ* (n 158) 280; *Hermanus v The Queen* (2015) 49 VR 486, 492 [18] (Osborn JA) and 525 [160] (McLeish JA) ('*Hermanus*').

175 See, eg, *Williams* (n 170) 265 [22]–[23] (Wood CJ at CL); *R v LTP* [2004] NSWCCA 109, [132] (Howie J); McDonald (n 28) 405; *Jury Manual* (n 174) [44.2/133].

Providing examples of 'good reasons' for delay in making a complaint

Victoria's legislative power to give a 'good reasons' direction empowers judges to elaborate on what those 'good reasons' may be, and the judge is not limited to reasons given by the complainant in evidence.[176] This elaboration has been justified on the basis that the complainant may not articulate these reasons when giving evidence (eg, because of the age or experience of the complainant, their level of personal insight, or the stress of giving evidence).[177] Judges in England and Wales and in Canada may provide similar kinds of information to juries.[178]

Victoria's *Criminal Charge Book* lists exemplifications of good reasons for delay in making a complaint that a judge may give to a jury. The exemplifications include:

- being ignorant about the nature, quality and character of the act performed upon them
- feeling powerless (particularly where, as is usually the case, the offender is a family member or close acquaintance)
- trusting the offender, or being emotionally dependent on them
- fearing family dissolution or punishment for the offender
- continuing to be in a sexual relationship with the offender
- feeling that the relationship with the offender is special
- being sworn to secrecy or compelled to secrecy by threats
- feeling responsible, guilty or to blame for the acts
- feeling shame and embarrassment, and
- fearing discouragement or disbelief on the part of family and of officials.[179]

Like expert evidence on such matters, this general information is intended to 'neutralise the erroneous perception that a victim of a sexual offence would complain immediately'.[180] However, one exemplification goes beyond providing general and incontrovertible information, raising questions about whether it is appropriate.

One exemplification provides that a complainant may delay in making a complaint because of 'being sworn to secrecy or compelled to secrecy by threats'. This exemplification does not expressly state that the accused swore or compelled the complainant to secrecy but that is an inference jurors may

176 *ERJ* (n 158) 280; *Hermanus* (n 174) 492 [18] (Osborn JA) and 525 [160] (McLeish JA). Section 52(4A) of the *Jury Directions Act 2015* (Vic) s 52(4A) now expressly provides the power to give examples.

177 *ERJ* (n 158) 280 [51].

178 See, eg, *R v MM* [2007] EWCA Crim 1558, [14]; *Crown Court Compendium* (n 42) 10–29; *DD* (n 7) [65]–[68].

179 *Criminal Charge Book* (n 42) [7.3.1.4].

180 *Bian v The Queen* (2015) 27 CRNZ 627, 637 [51]. See also *R v Bhatt* [2022] EWCA Crim 926.

readily draw.[181] This reason may suggest the judge knows something (negative) about the accused's conduct that the jury does not. It would be unfairly prejudicial to the accused for the judge to give this reason if there is no evidentiary foundation for it in a trial. In the absence of such evidence and the opportunity for the accused to challenge it, a judge would be inviting the jury to speculate about the accused's conduct, and this is not appropriate.

Victoria's *Criminal Charge Book* previously included another exemplification — that a complainant may 'employ psychological strategies to cope with the abuse, such as repression or suppression of the acts'.[182] In psychology, a 'repressed memory' refers to 'the idea that a traumatic memory can be stored yet inaccessibly blocked away from conscious knowledge'.[183] Whether repressed memories exist, and if so, what their role is in memory, is controversial.[184] This fact alone makes it an inappropriate explanation of 'good reasons'. Further, memory 'suppression' is a term of art in psychology. In one case, a trial judge in Victoria added to this exemplification stating that a complainant may also employ 'disassociation' to cope with abuse.[185] This is a medical term and expert evidence should be required to support such directions.[186] A similar idea is expressed in more common terms in England and Wales, namely that a child may 'simply blank what happened out and get on with their lives until the point comes when they feel ready or the need to speak out'.[187] This kind of layperson's description avoids the problems of (undefined) medical terms of art being used and does not involve the controversy of 'repressed' memory.[188]

Accordingly, the proposal in this case study does not include either of these two exemplifications of Victoria's good reasons directions. This proposal will be analysed through the relevant aspects of the five steps of a jury-centric approach.[189]

181 *Criminal Charge Book* (n 42) [4.8.3].

182 This exemplification was removed from Victoria's *Criminal Charge Book* some time after the publication of my article criticising this exemplification was published in 2022: Greg Byrne, 'Helping Jurors to Understand: Misconceptions about Delay in Making a Complaint' (2022) 47(1) *Alternative Law Journal* 16.

183 Lawrence Patihis et al, 'Memory Experts' Beliefs about Repressed Memory' (2018) *Memory* 1.

184 Patihis et al (n 183) 5. See also Richard J McNally, *Remembering Trauma* (Belknap Press, 2005) 1.

185 *Ford v The Queen* (2020) 63 VR 405, [22].

186 These exemplifications could also have been expressed more clearly. For example, the exemplification referred to the 'suppression of the acts'. It is the memory of the act, not the act itself, that the victim may seek to suppress. This could have been described in terms of 'not thinking about the acts or trying to forget about the acts'.

187 *Crown Court Compendium* (n 42) 10–27.

188 See generally Sullivan and Piekusis (n 160) 79–80.

189 The final step in a jury-centric approach (whether judges need resources and training to implement the proposed changes) is not critical for the purposes of this case study.

The evidence-base for addressing misconceptions about delay in making a complaint

The first step in a jury-centric approach is to examine whether there is an evidence-informed basis for concluding that a proposal will improve juror comprehension of the issues that the jury must determine. It is implicit within this step that jurors must determine the issues in accordance with the law. In this case study, the primary purpose of the proposal is to ensure that juries are impartial: deciding cases on their legal and factual merits. Addressing misconceptions may make comprehension more difficult for jurors because they must learn and employ new schema to understand the evidence and decide the issues.[190] While juror comprehension is a necessary condition of a fair trial, it is not a sufficient condition of a fair trial. Therefore, evidence that jury directions are effective in addressing juror misconceptions is essential to assess whether they assist jurors to be competent and impartial.

Simply telling people to disregard their biases (schema) or any previous ideas they had about the law does not seem to diminish their effect.[191] Schemas are resilient, and people continue to use them even when they are told that the evidence supporting the schema is false — this is known as the 'perseverance effect'.[192] Directly addressing a misconception and then explaining how the law applies in that situation has been shown to be more effective.[193]

Research in Australia has compared the effectiveness of expert evidence and jury directions in addressing child sexual assault misconceptions. In a study with mock jurors (118 undergraduate psychology students), researchers found that using either general scientific expert evidence or clinical expert evidence (where the expert met with the victim) and jury directions (whether given at the start of the trial or during the summing up), all helped to reduce misconceptions and led to significant increases in knowledge about child sexual abuse cases.[194]

In England and Wales, Ellison and Munro assessed the effectiveness of judicial information about delay involving nine trials with 24–26 jury-eligible mock jurors for each trial variation.[195] Those who received the judicial information — which was similar to the first two components of Victoria's directions — 'were significantly more likely to say that they were untroubled by the three-day

190 See, eg, Wegener et al (n 5) 632.

191 Gordon, 'Through the Eyes of Jurors' (n 6) 658. See also Vicki L Smith, 'When Prior Knowledge and Law Collide: Helping Jurors Use the Law' (1993) 17(5) *Law and Human Behavior* 507, 532 ('When Prior Knowledge and Law Collide').

192 Gordon, 'Through the Eyes of Jurors' (n 6) 656.

193 See, eg, Vicki L Smith, 'When Prior Knowledge and Law Collide' (n 191) 530–1; Wegener et al (n 5) 634–5, 646.

194 Goodman-Delahunty, Cossins and O'Brien (n 9) 208.

195 Ellison and Munro, 'Turning Mirrors into Windows?' (n 55) 366.

delay in . . . [the] trial scenario'.[196] However, Ellison and Munro found 'striking evidence of [mock] jurors' willingness to construct hypothetical explanations for events when information presented at trial was deemed incomplete or otherwise deficient'.[197]

There is no research assessing the effectiveness of the third component of Victoria's directions — exemplification of the 'good reasons' direction. Drawing on general research, it is reasonable to infer that exemplifications could assist jurors because concrete examples — in contrast to abstract information — help jurors to understand new information.[198] Providing jurors with relevant general information about what good reasons there might be in a case might reduce the extent to which jurors use their own 'commonsense knowledge', intuition, and imagination — which may be informed by misconceptions — to understand the delay.[199] The information contained in a judge's exemplifications may also assist jurors because it can be difficult for jurors to 'know where assumptions, knowledge, and inferences from their common sense and experience end and speculation begins'.[200] Further, explaining why the information is provided may assist jurors to reach a just and accurate verdict, which is a 'core social motive that influence[s] the cognition of all jurors'.[201] It may also lead jurors to 'engage in more careful and elaborate thinking, and reduce bias'.[202] However, in the absence of evidence it is also not known whether, for example, jurors might mistakenly use the exemplifications as evidence (eg, because it comes from the judge who is a trusted source).

There is research about the effectiveness of educational jury directions concerning misconceptions generally, rather than about delay, specifically, in sexual offence scenarios. A review of six studies in which mock jurors were provided educational jury directions to neutralise misconceptions found that there was no clear evidence that the directions effectively intervened to neutralise the misconception.[203] Research in the United Kingdom suggests that there is some evidence, but not convincing evidence, that jury directions may have an impact on jury decision-making.[204] This research suggests that some

196 Ellison and Munro, 'Turning Mirrors into Windows?' (n 55) 370. The number of participants troubled by the delay dropped from 58% to 23%.

197 Ellison and Munro, 'Telling Tales' (n 31) 221.

198 See, eg, Peter M Tiersma, 'Communicating with Juries: How to Draft More Understandable Instructions' (2005–06) 10 *The Scribes of Journal Legal Writing* 1, 7, 25–6.

199 Ellison and Munro, '"Telling Tales"' (n 31) 222. See also McDonald (n 28) 392–5.

200 Byrne (n 182) 21. See also Steven Lubet and Kevin Chang, 'Stupid Juror Questions?' (2013) 37(2) *American Journal of Trial Advocacy* 315, 329–33.

201 Gordon, 'What Jurors Want to Know' (n 38) 753.

202 Gordon, 'What Jurors Want to Know' (n 38) 770.

203 Faye T Nitschke and Blake M McKimmie, 'The Effectiveness of Educational Jury Directions in Adult Sexual Assault Trials' in Greg Byrne and Jacqueline Horan (eds), *Sexual Assault Trials: Challenges and Innovations* (LexisNexis, 2025) 179, 188.

204 Willmott and Hudspith (n 73) 185.

caution should be exercised in drawing general inferences about the effectiveness of jury directions in addressing misconceptions about delay.

It is also important to consider when a judge should give a jury information addressing misconceptions. In Victoria and England and Wales, judges can give this information early in the trial. For example, in Victoria, a judge may give general information to jurors about delay in making a complaint before any evidence is adduced in the trial.[205] Research suggests that measures taken early in a trial to address misconceptions will be more effective than measures taken late in the trial.[206] This is because jurors 'select from and interpret the evidence as it begins to emerge'[207] and this 'may serve as a powerful organizing theme for interpreting new information presented subsequently in the trial'.[208] If the direction is given later in the trial, jurors may have already reached conclusions about the evidence using their own (unchallenged) framework without being informed of the correct legal framework for considering the evidence.[209] Jurors may treat subsequent information about delay in making a complaint as something to be integrated within their existing framework and any factual conclusions they may have already drawn (which may have been influenced by their misconceptions).[210]

Further, learning is an active process. Jurors are not passive blank slates. Giving all relevant information to the jury at the end of the trial conflates knowledge goals (understanding the task) with performance goals (returning a verdict). The performance goal can limit the effectiveness and focus on knowledge goals.[211] This means that framing the instructions as a knowledge task, at the start of the trial, rather than a performance task at the end of the trial, may help comprehension.[212] This enables jurors to 'actively engage with information at the encoding stage, which is when they are able (and willing) to implement strategies to comply with judicial directions'.[213] Giving directions

205 *Jury Directions Act 2015* (Vic) s 52(1). See also *Crown Court Compendium* (n 42) 1–3, 20–5.

206 See, eg, Saul M Kassin and Samuel R Sommers, 'Inadmissible Testimony, Instructions to Disregard, and the Jury: Substantive versus Procedural Considerations' (1997) 23(10) *Personality and Social Psychology Bulletin* 1046, 1050; Vicki L Smith, 'Impact of Pretrial Instruction on Jurors' Information Processing and Decision Making' (1991) 76(2) *Journal of Applied Psychology* 220.

207 NZLC, *Juries in Criminal Trials: Part Two* (n 1) 16.

208 Goodman-Delahunty, Cossins and O'Brien (n 9) 780.

209 See, eg, *R v PZG* (2007) 171 A Crim R 62, [20]; [2007] VSCA 54.

210 Goodman-Delahunty, Cossins and O'Brien (n 9) 780.

211 Gordon, 'What Jurors Want to Know' (n 38) 781.

212 Gordon, 'What Jurors Want to Know' (n 38) 778–82.

213 Rachel K Cush and Jane Goodman Delahunty, 'The Influence of Limiting Instructions on Processing and Judgments of Emotionally Evocative Evidence' (2006) 13(1) *Psychiatry, Psychology, and Law* 110, 121.

early in the trial and repeating them during the summing up may provide the best approach.[214]

Giving directions at the start of a trial may also limit the extent to which defence counsel exploit misconceptions in sexual offence cases. Victorian trial judges have said that giving the jury a direction about delay before the prosecution adduces any evidence changes the way in which defence counsel present their case. They rely less on misconceptions about delay (eg, that a real victim would report an offence immediately).[215]

However, the effectiveness of exemplifications in addressing misconceptions and changing the conduct of the trial to reduce parties raising misconceptions has not been assessed. The prospect that trial practises may be changed by such directions seems limited in light of research that trial practices and narratives (including reliance on delay) remain entrenched,[216] and that judges often do not give such directions early, despite being permitted to do so.[217] Further, there is no research testing some of the refinements proposed earlier to the way in which the information is presented (eg, avoiding or limiting references that repeat the misconception).

In addition to research on addressing misconceptions about delay in making a complaint in sexual offence cases, it is highly likely that other misconceptions will arise in a trial. Strategies addressing multiple misconceptions may increase jurors' cognitive load and thereby reduce the effectiveness of individual strategies to address misconceptions.[218] Further research is essential to determine whether exemplifications are effective. Research might also indicate whether other strategies to address misconceptions may complement, or be more effective than, jury directions.[219]

As discussed in Chapter 5, a Juries Advisory Council may be able to draw inferences from the available research and use its knowledge and intuition to assess the likelihood that misconceptions are currently causing problems and the likely effectiveness of some proposals (eg, that general information and 'good reasons' directions may assist in addressing misconceptions about delay in making a complaint). However, while general research suggests

214 Harrison D H Lee et al, 'The Effects of Victim Testimony Order and Judicial Education on Juror Decision-Making in Trials for Rape' (2022) 30(6) *Psychology, Crime & Law* 509.

215 Justice Chris Maxwell and Greg Byrne, 'Making Trials Work for Juries: Pathways to Simplification' [2020] (11) *Criminal Law Review* 1034, 1052. For examples of how a judge may give directions early in a trial, see Julia Quilter, Luke McNamara and Melissa Porter, 'New Directions for Sexual Offence Trials in New South Wales: The Importance of Timing' (2022) 46 *Criminal Law Journal* 138, 148–50.

216 Quilter and McNamara, 'District Court of NSW' (n 74) 2.

217 See, eg, Quilter, McNamara and Porter (n 215) 150, Temkin, Gray and Barrett (n 79) 220; Smith and Skinner (n 32) 459–60.

218 See, eg, Dorne Boniface, 'The Common Sense of Jurors vs the Wisdom of the Law: Judicial Directions in Sexual Assault Trials' (2005) 28(1) *University of New South Wales Law Journal* 261, 270.

219 See, eg, Tinsley, Baylis and Young (n 72) 483–5; Quilter (n 23) 21–4.

exemplifying on the 'good reasons' direction might assist in addressing juror misconceptions, there is no specific evidence supporting their use. Applying a jury-centric approach provides transparency concerning this aspect of the policymaking process.

Does addressing misconceptions about delay in making a complaint conflict with fair trial principles or other human rights?

The second step in a jury-centric approach involves determining whether the proposal concerning misconceptions about delay in making a complaint conflicts with, or limits, other fair trial or human rights. This raises two key issues. First, does exemplifying a 'good reasons' direction about delay in making a complaint affect the fairness of a trial? This question focuses on exemplifications rather than the first two components of Victoria's directions (giving general information and 'good reasons' directions) because it draws out more potentially conflicting fair trial considerations. Second, how should courts deal with misconceptions about delay that may (mistakenly) *enhance* the complainant's credibility, because the complainant made a complaint immediately?

Does exemplifying a 'good reasons' direction affect the fairness of a trial?

Willis and McMahon argue that Victoria's exemplifications of 'good reasons' involve the judge determining the facts and inviting the jury to speculate.[220] They argue that this results in the judge intruding into the jury's fact-finding role.

As discussed earlier in this chapter, there is one remaining instance where Victoria's exemplification of 'good reasons' risks introducing (or appearing to introduce) evidence that is not part of the case — being sworn to secrecy or compelled to secrecy by threats — and therefore a judge should not give this exemplification. This section discusses the remaining exemplifications which include: being ignorant about the nature and quality of the act; feeling powerless, responsible, guilty, or embarrassed; and fearing disbelief, family dissolution, or punishment.

The first question is how an exemplification of 'good reasons' should be characterised — is it evidence, a direction, a comment,[221] an example,[222] or are they 'statements of fact dressed up as law'?[223]

In *Hermanus v The Queen*,[224] Osborn JA indicated that the exemplification of 'good reasons' for delay was analogous to directions concerning post-offence conduct where the judge must explain that there might be reasons

220 Willis and McMahon (n 40) 46–7.
221 *Crimes Act 1958* (Vic) s 61(2) (now repealed).
222 *Jury Directions Act 2015* (Vic) s 52(4A).
223 Lord Carloway, quoted in Bain (n 172) 57.
224 *Hermanus* (n 174).

why the accused, for example, told lies.[225] The High Court of Australia has described these kinds of exemplifications about lies as *directions*.[226] While the judge should refer to any reasons given in evidence, the judge should also offer explanations that were not mentioned in the evidence (eg a lie may be told out of panic).[227] This is to prevent the jury from reasoning that because the accused lied this must have been because the accused is guilty. Other jurisdictions have adopted a similar approach to lies and to providing explanations not based on the evidence.[228]

Victoria's model jury directions previously recommended telling jurors that the exemplifications were 'directions', but this was removed from Victoria's *Criminal Charge Book*.[229] Describing exemplifications as directions would intrude into the jury's fact-finding function because that would mean that, as a matter of law, there are (or must be) good reasons why the complainant (in this case) delayed in making a complaint. This interpretation also implies that the allegation is true. The purpose of challenging misconceptions is 'to restore the complainant's credibility from a debit balance because of jury misapprehension, back to a zero or neutral balance'.[230] The directions should not enhance the complainant's credibility.

Unlike a direction, exemplifications do not contain any procedural or substantive law, but they do invite the jury to consider certain factors before deciding what evidence to accept. Where the exemplification provides general information that is not based on evidence in the case, it may help jurors to understand or analyse the evidence in the case — but it is not evidence. A jury may properly consider whether a complainant would have, for example, felt embarrassed, powerless, fearful about the impact of a complaint on their family, without requiring evidence specifically to that effect. And the jury may do so regardless of whether the judge says that they may. These kinds of considerations are commonly and properly considered by jurors in bringing their life experience to the jury room when assessing the evidence. This does not involve speculating about the evidence.

The Victorian Cout of Appeal has also described exemplifications as 'comments',[231] perhaps to distinguish them from directions. However, exemplifications are different from comments about the evidence because comments

225 *Hermanus* (n 174) 492 [19]–[22].

226 See, eg, *Edwards* (n 43) 211 (Deane, Dawson and Gaudron JJ).

227 See, eg, *Criminal Charge Book* (n 42) 4.6 [110]–[111].

228 See, eg, *R v Goodway* (1994) 98 Cr App R 11, 15. See also *R v Kalajdic* (2005) 157 A Crim R 300, 306 [26]–[27]; *R v Calnen* [2019] 1 SCR 301, 352 [117] (Martin J).

229 This description of exemplifications was removed from Victoria's *Criminal Charge Book* some time after the publication of my article criticising the description in 2022. However, I do not know whether my article was influential in that regard: Byrne (n 182) 19–20.

230 New Zealand Law Commission, *Evidence: Evidence Code and Commentary* (Report No 55, August 1999) 67 [C111].

231 *Briggs v The King* [2024] VSCA 80, [106].

involve opinions or observations about what significance to attach, or not attach, to evidence adduced in a trial.[232] Comments should be used to help ensure that the 'facts of the case are put "accurately and fairly" to the jury'.[233] However, given the scope that trial judges have to guide juries, and that a judge may link what are clearly comments about the evidence to an exemplification, it can sometimes be difficult to draw a bright line between exemplifications and comments.

Accordingly, exemplifications are not directions or comments. Provided that a judge does not describe exemplifications as directions or comments, a judge may give exemplifications without affecting, or being seen to affect, the judge's impartiality.

Addressing misconceptions about delay in making a complaint reflects a broader notion of a fair trial which includes the interests of the victim, the prosecution, and the community. While most discussion focuses on how misconceptions may unfairly affect juror assessments of a complainant's credibility, what if the prosecution relies on misconceptions to bolster its case?

Misconceptions that may enhance the complainant's credibility

Misconceptions involve an assumption about what happens in a 'real' sexual offence case. One of the challenges with misconceptions is that sometimes sexual offences do occur in what jurors may believe are stereotypical circumstances. For example, some complainants do make a complaint of rape at the first reasonable opportunity to do so. However, just like a truthful complaint, a person may make a false complaint immediately or at a later time.[234]

Where evidence is consistent with a juror's schema, a misconception does not risk jurors inappropriately rejecting or not understanding the evidence. Therefore, jurors should not treat the evidence with unwarranted scepticism. Jurors do not need directions or expert evidence to ***understand*** evidence that is consistent with a stereotype because the evidence is not counterintuitive.

However, misconceptions may be relevant to juror reasoning processes. Evidence of stereotypical behaviour should not invite jurors to reason that, because the victim behaved in the same way as victims often behave, or are thought to behave, it is more likely that the victim is telling the truth. Courts prohibit this kind of reasoning when a victim behaves counterintuitively. This kind of reasoning should also be prohibited in relation to evidence of stereotypical behaviour to ensure a fair trial for the accused. Examples of directions in England and Wales state that 'a complaint is not necessarily true just

232 See, eg, *Azzopardi v The Queen* (2001) 205 CLR 50, 70 [50] (Gaudron, Gummow, Kirby and Hayne JJ).

233 *McKell v The Queen* (2019) 264 CLR 307, 313 (Bell, Keane, Gordon and Edelman JJ). See also *Broadhurst v The Queen* [1964] AC 441, 464.

234 *DH* (n 7) 639 [45]. See also *DD* (n 7) 305 [65].

because it was made immediately'.[235] There is no research concerning how a judge should give a direction in this situation to ensure that it is both effective and comprehensible.

It is important for 'well-informed public debate to document and explore the legitimacy of all uses of rape mythology during the trial process'.[236] The prevalence of misconceptions contributes to a justice system that fails to respond to sexual offences adequately and appropriately.[237] Prosecution reliance on misconceptions is, understandably, considered much less often than defence reliance on misconceptions. However, prosecution reliance on misconceptions may perpetuate reliance on misconceptions by the defence.[238] In England and Wales, in almost half of the 28 trials examined in 2010 and 2012, 'defence barristers . . . argued that their discussion of rape myths was legitimate because the prosecution used them as supporting evidence where possible'.[239] Dealing comprehensively with misconceptions in sexual offence cases therefore also involves ensuring that the jury acts impartially and does not inappropriately rely on misconceptions in its reasoning process towards convicting an accused.

Judicial expertise concerning directions addressing misconceptions about delay in making a complaint

The fourth step in a jury-centric approach examines judicial expertise — whether a judge is best placed to determine whether jurors are likely to have a misconception and if so, how to address that misconception.

Like all human beings, judges have their own biases[240] and may have misconceptions about sexual offences, for example, about how a 'real' victim would behave. Judicial biases may emerge more clearly in judge-alone trials. For example, a trial judge in Canada had a reasonable doubt about a complainant's evidence because she did not 'demonstrate behaviours consistent with that abuse or at least some changes in behaviour such as avoiding the perpetrator'.[241] The Court of Appeal of Alberta concluded that the judge relied 'on an impermissible stereotype, or myth, about the behaviour of sexual assault victims in assessing the complainant's credibility and ultimately acquitting the

235 *Crown Court Compendium* (n 42) 20–6.
236 McDonald (n 28) 52.
237 Temkin and Krahé (n 72) 9–10.
238 McDonald (n 28) 52.
239 Smith and Skinner (n 32) 455.
240 See, eg, Andrew J Wistrich, Jeffrey J Rachlinski and Chris Guthrie, 'Heart versus Head: Do Judges Follow the Law or Follow Their Feelings?' (2015) 93(4) *Texas Law Review* 855; Edmond and Martire (n 37) 644–9; Chief Justice Gerard Brennan, 'Why Be a Judge?' (1996) 14 *Australian Bar Review* 89, 92.
241 *R v ARJD* [2017] ABCA 237 ('*AJRD*').

accused.[242] In New South Wales, a trial judge concluded that there were reasonable grounds for the accused to believe the complainant was consenting because the complainant did not say 'stop' or 'no' or physically try to move away from the accused.[243] Further, while many judges may be aware of many misconceptions about sexual offences, they may have differing levels of knowledge about the risk of jurors having misconceptions about sexual offences and how best to address such misconceptions.

A study of eight sexual offence trials in England in 2010 found that between three and seven rape myths (including delay in making a complaint) were employed in seven of the eight trials.[244] Of the 34 myths identified in the trials studied, the Bench Book provided directions concerning 19 of those myths.[245] Judges gave warnings concerning 11 of those 19 myths, four of which the researchers described as 'perfunctory'.[246] While the *Crown Court Compendium* does not limit the type of directions that may be given, no judges attempted to address misconceptions that were not listed in it.[247] This might be because the judges did not identify the misconceptions[248] or because they were uncertain whether addressing the misconceptions would survive appellate scrutiny. An expert reference committee in New Zealand also concluded that there was 'unevenness' in the content of directions concerning sexual offence misconceptions and whether judges gave any such directions.[249]

In Victoria, the trial judge:

- must give directions (general information and 'good reasons') if the judge considers that there is likely to be evidence, or there is evidence 'that suggests that the complainant delayed in making a complaint'[250]
- may give given an exemplification of the good reasons direction.[251] No separate criteria governs whether a judge exemplifies the 'good reasons' direction.

The Victorian approach minimises the judge's discretion. The issue the judge must determine is whether there is likely to be evidence suggesting that the complainant delayed in making a complaint. Whether the issue of delay in making a complaint arises from the evidence is a matter of judicial expertise and

242 *ARJD* (n 241) [5]. The Supreme Court of Canada affirmed this decision: *R v ARJD* [2018] 1 SCR 218, 219 [2].
243 *R v Lazarus* (2017) 270 A Crim R 378, 399–400 [110]. See Horan (n 51) 70–1.
244 Temkin, Gray and Barrett (n 79) 210.
245 *Crown Court Compendium* (n 42) ch 20.
246 Temkin, Gray and Barrett (n 79) 220.
247 Temkin, Gray and Barrett (n 79) 220.
248 Smith and Skinner (n 32) 459–60.
249 NZLC, *The Justice Response to Victims of Sexual Violence* (n 4) 119 [6.62].
250 *Jury Directions Act 2015* (Vic) s 52(1).
251 *Jury Directions Act 2015* (Vic) s 52(4A).

does not require expertise about how common misconceptions are likely to be in a jury, or what might activate a misconception in jurors during the trial. This approach recognises that judicial expertise concerning sexual offence misconceptions and their influence in jury trials may be variable. However, even with this approach, researchers found that in most of the 21 cases examined involving delay in Victoria, judges did not give this direction during the trial.[252]

Neither Victoria's *Jury Directions Act 2015* nor Victoria's *Criminal Charge Book* indicates when a judge should exemplify upon a 'good reasons' direction. The absence of guidance risks the judge's personal views and knowledge about misconceptions and juror misconceptions playing a more significant role in assessing what is necessary to ensure an impartial jury. However, exemplifications depend very much on the facts of each case and whether there is evidence in the trial explaining why the complainant may have good reasons for not complaining at an earlier time. It would be difficult to limit judicial discretion over such matters without risking requiring judges to provide information that is not helpful to jurors in some cases. In the context of sexual offence cases, where judges give many other directions, it is important to recognise the cognitive load imposed on jurors and not overburden them with information that is not important or may be unnecessary to their task. Further evidence is essential in determining whether judges should have less discretion, or be provided with more guidance, in deciding whether, and if so when, to give the second and third components of Victoria's directions.

Conclusion

This chapter began by asking what happens if jurors' ordinary experience and knowledge of the world is mistaken, and this mistake affects whether a jury is impartial. There is overwhelming evidence that the life experiences and the schema some jurors use when assessing evidence and making decisions may include misconceptions in sexual offence trials (at least where the complainant is female, and the defendant is male). These misconceptions mean that there is a real possibility that a jury will include a juror(s) who will not be impartial. If the tribunal of fact is not impartial, there cannot be a fair trial. However, jury directions may address misconceptions in a way that addresses the risk that a jury will not be impartial. This is consistent with the rationale for jury directions: jurors need guidance to make decisions in accordance with the law and to prevent them from making errors in their reasoning processes.

It is essential to assess whether proposed jury directions achieve their objectives of a competent and impartial jury. This has occurred in relation to the general information and 'good reasons' direction in England and Wales. However, exemplifications of the good reasons direction have not been evaluated. The combined effect of directions and exemplifications on juror comprehension

252 Quilter and McNamara, *County Court of Victoria* (n 75) 140.

has also not been tested. Directions to address misconceptions about the probative value of immediate complaints that the prosecution may rely upon, have also not been tested. Therefore, evidence about the comprehensibility of directions intended to ensure an impartial jury is inadequate even for one of the oldest and better recognised misconceptions in sexual offence cases.

Jeffrey Rachlinksi said that conflicting goals have hindered evidence-based law reform.[253] The discussion in this chapter shows the primacy of the goal of ensuring a fair trial. Two key components of a fair trial are that a jury is competent and impartial. These goals do not conflict because both goals are necessary conditions of a fair trial. However, individual strategies designed to achieve each goal may conflict. The conflict between strategies may be significant because trying to change a person's schema (misconceptions) may make juror comprehension of their task more difficult. However, because the goals do not conflict, this provides a clearer framework for making policy choices between different strategies. A jury-centric framework highlights the importance of evidence about both the problem (the risk that jurors may have misconceptions that affect their impartiality) and the solution (whether jury directions effectively address misconceptions).

The case study in this chapter demonstrates that a jury-centric approach provides a robust and effective method for analysing proposals to ensure a competent and impartial jury. The case study highlights the need for an evidence-informed approach at multiple stages in the development and implementation of proposals to ensure an impartial jury where jurors understand the judge's directions. The case study also highlights the breadth of the challenge in guiding the jury in a way that recognises the rights of the accused and the interests of victims and the community in a fair trial. Addressing misconceptions is challenging, but it is a task that each jurisdiction must undertake to ensure fair trial.

253 Jeffrey J Rachlinski, 'Evidence-Based Law' (2011) 96 *Cornell Law Review* 901, 917.

10 Conclusion — Employing a jury-centric approach

Addressing juror comprehension problems

Trial by jury is facing significant challenges, especially in relation to sexual offences, where serious questions have been raised concerning whether trial by jury is appropriate.[1] In all kinds of jury trials, it is increasingly challenging for judges to guide jurors in their task. Longer trials, new criminal offences, scientific and technological advances in evidence, and legislative and appellate requirements can lead to longer and more complex jury directions. And jurors' expectations about the presentation of information are changing. Reviews in several common law jurisdictions have sought to improve judicial guidance of jurors. However, in most jurisdictions changes from these reviews have been relatively modest. Few judges and other senior people in the justice system are aware of the breadth and depth of juror comprehension problems revealed by social science research. This is despite decades of research identifying juror comprehension problems and that it is fundamental to a fair trial that jurors understand their task.

Law reform bodies sometimes consider whether proposals will be comprehensible to jurors, for example, in relation to homicide laws (Chapter 8). This consideration often occurs through the prism of judicial (or legal) knowledge and experience where the law reform body makes its own assessment of what should be comprehensible to jurors. However, law reform bodies rarely consider general juror comprehension research or research specific to the issues being examined.

Within a criminal trial, juror comprehension problems can be difficult to observe and assess. Based primarily on judges' own observations and intuitions, judicial knowledge and experience developed to determine what jurors need to know and how best to guide them. Courts assume that jurors understand the judge's guidance, that jurors are conscientious and faithful to their oath, and that juries generally 'get it right'. These empirical assumptions

1 See, eg, Lord Justice Clerk's Review Group, *Improving the Management of Sexual Offence Cases* (Final Report, March 2021) 89–92.

DOI: 10.4324/9781003477129-10

should be assessed empirically. When they are tested, research discussed in Chapters 3 and 4 indicates that jurors struggle to understand and follow the judge's guidance, despite being conscientious, and the extent to which they 'get it right' is contestable.

The confidentiality of jury deliberations limits methods of obtaining information directly from jurors. Judicial knowledge and experience provides the default form of 'evidence' about juror comprehension without any apparent awareness of its limitations and the assumptions that constrain its conclusions. Social science juror comprehension research enables us to understand jurors' perspectives without piercing the confidentiality of jury deliberations.

Using social science juror comprehension research

Juror comprehension problems are evident in both general juror comprehension research (Chapter 3) and research concerning more specific matters such as the use of SDM aids, understanding fault elements and self-defence in the offence of homicide, and in misconceptions that jurors have in sexual offence cases (Chapters 7, 8, and 9 respectively). Juror comprehension research can also significantly improve our knowledge about jurors: what they find difficult to understand, and how best to guide them. Change is essential to address the difference between what the evidence shows about juror comprehension and the standard expected of a competent jury to ensure a fair trial.

Juror comprehension research is usually not accepted when it contradicts judicial (and legal) knowledge and experience and indicates that there are fundamental problems with the fairness of jury trials. Social science juror comprehension research can be difficult for judges and lawyers to access and to understand because it comes from different disciplines, with different systems of knowledge, goals, values, and methodologies. However, the law should utilise this valuable information. Working out how to employ this research and change laws and trials is challenging.

We have a systemic problem that needs a systemic solution. Evidence is crucial to understanding the problem and identifying solutions. Juror comprehension research is sufficiently mature and robust to play a vital role in improving criminal laws and jury trials. However, research could be improved. The most obvious way in which it could be improved is by permitting more research with actual jurors.[2] As a judge in Ireland said about jury research: 'Are we ever really going to know what might work better if we don't talk to them themselves?'[3] Not only do we need to hear what jurors say, but we must understand what they need to perform their task. While many jurisdictions

2 Lewis Ross, 'The Curious Case of the Jury-Shaped Hole: A Plea for Real Jury Research' (2023) 27(2) *The Internartional Journal of Evidence and Proof* 107.

3 Mark Coen et al, 'Respect, Reform and Research: An Empirical Insight into Judge-Jury Relations' (2020) 4(2) *Irish Judicial Studies Journal* 116, 132.

have laws that severely curtail or prohibit research with actual jurors, these laws can and should be changed. New Zealand's experience is informative. New Zealand conducts research that involves actual jurors and there is no evidence that this has negatively affected the quality of jury deliberations. It is also not surprising that the jurisdiction that often leads in jury-informed research is also more open to change based on research. Research involving actual jurors in other jurisdictions might also lead to greater acceptance that there are juror comprehension problems and whether proposed solutions are appropriate.

Whatever kind of research is used, incorporating this research requires an innovative approach to reform processes, but it does not require all judges to become juror comprehension research experts.

A Juries Advisory Council

The limitations of existing approaches to addressing juror comprehension problems indicates the need for a Juries Advisory Council (JAC). A JAC would be an interdisciplinary law reform body that sits outside of the courts to undertake a process of continuous improvement to address juror comprehension problems in criminal trials.

A JAC would be best placed to understand and incorporate social science juror comprehension research within a reform process (Chapter 5). Research is the lifeblood of a jury-centric reform process. Courts and governments have been insufficiently proactive in addressing known juror comprehension problems that affect whether trials are fair. Expecting, or waiting for, social science researchers to determine what research courts and governments need highlights problems with existing approaches to addressing juror comprehension problems. A JAC should set the research agenda, could lead the research process, and transform research findings into a form that is easier for judges and lawyers to understand and use. However, research and data alone are insufficient to address juror comprehension problems. Changing the framing and response to juror comprehension problems is essential.

A jury-centric approach

My definition of a jury-centric approach builds on Marder's definition of a jury-centric perspective by broadening the focus of enquiry into the causes of, and potential solutions to, juror comprehension problems. My definition frames juror comprehension problems within terms familiar to the law: juror comprehension is a necessary condition of a fair trial. Further, defining what it means for a jury to be a 'competent' tribunal provides a familiar test that is based on the test for determining whether a tribunal is 'impartial'. Applying my test for a 'competent' tribunal (Chapter 6), a fair-minded observer might reasonably apprehend that juror comprehension research indicates that there is a real possibility that jurors might not understand their task. Therefore, there is an unacceptable risk that a jury might not be a 'competent' tribunal.

Plain language techniques provided the first major attempt to improve guidance to jurors. However, conceptual complexity in the law limits the effectiveness of plain language techniques. SDM aids like integrated directions can overcome some conceptual complexities by embedding the law into the facts and improving the organisation of information. However, integrated directions can contextualise but cannot embed the law in general or evidentiary directions into the facts. Further, with substantive directions that involve an evaluative standard (eg, whether conduct in self-defence was a 'necessary' and a 'reasonable' response) the law cannot be fully embedded into the facts. Integrated directions are not a panacea for all juror comprehension problems. Where a judge cannot reduce the conceptual complexity of the law by embedding the law into the facts, it is essential to consider the content and wording of laws to assess their comprehensibility to jurors. Therefore, a jury-centric approach is not something that is only applied after policy choices about laws have been made.

Existing law reform processes have not made sufficient use of existing juror comprehension research when determining the content of laws. The second case study (on murder and excessive self-defence) demonstrates how a jury-centric approach can incorporate juror comprehension research into policy decision-making about offences and defences. Further, focusing on what is comprehensible to jurors may affect policy choices in defining the law (eg, the scope of the offence of murder, its maximum penalty, and whether the law should recognise excessive self-defence). However, being able to explain the law comprehensibly is not sufficient to make good laws.

Research also reveals the fiction in the law's assumptions about the 'ideal juror'. Jurors are not blank slates. Their knowledge and experience are integral to their value in representing the community. However, being cognisant of jurors' prototypes about the law and views about human behaviour means we cannot ignore misconceptions that jurors may have. To ensure a fair trial, it is essential to address the risk that jurors may not be impartial. Evidence about the biases jurors may possess (eg, concerning misconceptions in sexual offence cases) and whether a direction is likely to be effective in explaining the law or addressing a misconception, is essential.

The complexity of addressing juror comprehension problems in an interdisciplinary way provides the context and need for developing a comprehensive approach to addressing juror comprehension problems. This approach begins by having a clear policy goal: juror comprehension of their task is a necessary condition of a fair trial. Having a clear policy goal is one of the key challenges in evidence-informed law reform.[4] The first step in a jury-centric approach focuses on the evidence. Using an evidence-informed approach to criminal

4 Jeffrey J Rachlinski, 'Evidence-Based Law' (2011) 96 *Cornell Law Review* 901, 917.

laws and criminal trials is not standard practice. It should be. This is essential for laws, practices, and procedures to work as intended and for trials to be fair.

The second step in a jury-centric approach asks whether a proposal conflicts with any other fair trial principles, or other human rights. Improving juror comprehension drives a jury-centric approach. However, the case study on counteracting misconceptions (Chapter 9) demonstrates that a jury-centric approach can be applied to proposals that — to meet the fair trial requirement that a jury be impartial — may make juror comprehension more difficult. A jury-centric approach can help to achieve this strong fair trial requirement, providing a helpful method for adopting comprehensible reforms so that jurors determine the issues on their legal and factual merits.

The third step in a jury-centric approach highlights the importance of policy considerations in the law and law reform. For example, the primary purpose of homicide offences and excessive self-defence is not juror comprehension. Policy considerations can be essential in determining what decisions to make and may preclude some options that successfully improve juror comprehension. This highlights that juror comprehension is a necessary but not a sufficient condition for laws and trials to be fair.

In addition to providing a new way of understanding issues from the jury's perspective, the fourth step in a jury-centric approach challenges conceptions of the judge's role. Courts have long said that the trial judge is in the best position to tailor jury directions to the specific circumstances of each case. A trial judge is best placed to determine the issues in a trial. Indeed, in 2001, Dennis Devine et al said that juror comprehension research was so extensive that it was 'nearly impossible to review comprehensively'.[5] It is not fair or reasonable to expect judges to be experts about jurors and juror comprehension. Therefore, to improve the judge's guidance to jurors, it is important to recognise the limits of judicial expertise when determining whether a judge is best placed to decide how to guide jurors with their task.

The fifth step in a jury-centric approach focuses on supporting judges when introducing jury-centric changes. Just as informing jurors what the law is does not mean that they will understand and apply it, simply passing a new law does not mean that judges will implement it as intended. Without the right support, judges may be slow to adopt new processes and skills (eg, integrated directions in Victoria) or may use them inconsistently (eg, SDM aids in England and Wales and New Zealand[6]). Adapting Marder's definition of a 'jury-centric' perspective, the fifth step involves a 'judge-centric' perspective, by asking what tools and assistance judges need to perform their tasks more effectively.

5 See, eg, Dennis J Devine et al, 'Jury Decision Making: 45 Years of Empirical Research on Deliberating Groups' (2001) 7 *Psychology, Public Policy and Law* 622, 625.

6 See, eg, David Ormerod and Cheryl Thomas, 'Routes to Verdict — What We Know and What We Need to Know' [2021] (8) *Criminal Law Review* 615, 616. Jonathan Clough et al, *The Jury Project 10 Years On — Practices of Australian and New Zealand Judges* (Australian Institute of Judicial Administration, April 2019) 51.

The structure of the five steps in a jury-centric approach prioritises juror comprehension as a reform goal. However, other policy factors may drive the reform process (eg, with offences or addressing misconceptions in sexual offence cases). These other policy factors may also provide the starting point for analysis of the available options. This means that the third step in a jury-centric approach — considering policy factors — may be examined before turning to the first step. The order in which the steps are undertaken is not critical. What is critical is that each step forms part of the review process.

Overall, the five steps in a jury-centric approach provide a rigorous and transparent framework for making decisions about how best to improve criminal laws and trials to ensure that jurors understand their task. It is relevant to all criminal laws, practices, and procedures that affect whether jurors understand their task. This means that a jury-centric approach applies to both new reform proposals and to existing laws, practices, and procedures.

***Should* a jury-centric approach be used to address juror comprehension problems?**

The application of a jury-centric approach may not produce the same laws, practices, and procedures in each jurisdiction. Each jurisdiction is different — the nature of problems, research about problems, what is comprehensible to jurors, and policy goals may all differ between jurisdictions. Each jurisdiction will need to determine when it needs to conduct its own research. The amount of research required to assess the comprehensibility of all existing and all new criminal laws, practices, and procedures in each jurisdiction would be enormous. And this undertaking would take many years to complete — assuming it could ever be completed given the justice system continues to change. The question *should* a jury-centric approach be used to address juror comprehension problems raises two further questions:

- should jurisdictions stop all trials until research proves that jurors do understand all aspects of their task?
- should a jurisdiction make changes even if the evidence does not indicate whether a proposed change is comprehensible to jurors?

Should all trials be stopped until the necessary evidence is obtained?

Applying a jury-centric approach does not require changing every criminal law, practice, and procedure so that it is guaranteed that *every* juror will understand everything. The goal of a jury-centric approach is a competent jury: this involves an assessment of whether there is a real possibility that a jury might not understand its task — to decide whether the accused is guilty or not guilty of an offence in accordance with the law. This assessment, whether based on research from a simulated study or a field study, always involves an element of generalisation from research to conclude what is likely to happen in a future trial, knowing that every trial will be different in some way. The evidence does not suggest that jury trials are irredeemably flawed. However, jury trials could work much better. And given the consequences of a jury's verdict for the accused, victims, and the community, and the difficulty of the task jurors face, it is essential that trials are improved. It is not realistic, nor necessary, to stop all trials until juror comprehension research is conducted on every issue, and necessary reforms introduced, to address all juror comprehension problems.

However, just because the goal of removing a real possibility that a jury might not understand its task is either unattainable with certainty in every trial, or involves a lengthy process of continuous improvement, this does not mean that a jury-centric approach should be abandoned. This conclusion is consistent with accepting that a perfectly fair trial may be unattainable and instead focusing on a trial which is 'fundamentally fair', or 'as fair as the courts can make it'.[7] Accordingly, the courts' pragmatic assumption that jurors follow jury directions therefore must remain — but this should not stymie research or prevent the reform process.

Fair trial requirements may change and evolve over time. A jury-centric approach can and should accelerate the improvement of juror comprehension and therefore the fairness of trials. Further, if the fairness of a trial can be evidence-informed, it should be. Social science research about juror comprehension, rather than judicial (or lawyers') knowledge and experience, should drive efforts to improve juror comprehension. A jury-centric approach provides the process for improving juror comprehension within a legal framework. What is critical is that courts and governments undertake a process of continuous improvement to address juror comprehension problems.

As discussed in Chapter 5, a body like a JAC is essential to undertaking this process of improvement.[8] There is sufficient evidence to identify many issues that jurors are likely to find difficult to understand. Just as difficult issues in the law provide a focus for researchers, they should also be priorities in seeking to improve juror comprehension. This approach to addressing juror comprehension problems will mean that evidence will progressively support the courts' pragmatic assumption that jurors understand and follow jury directions. Using a jury-centric approach is essential to bridge the gap between the courts' assumption and reality. Demonstrably bridging this gap should also improve public confidence in trial by jury.

While trials should continue despite juror comprehension problems, a related problem is whether changes should be introduced where there is no evidence, or insufficient evidence, about whether a proposed change will improve comprehension.

7 *R v O'Connor* [1995] 4 SCR 411, 517 [193] (McLachlin J); *Jago v District Court of New South Wales* (1989) 168 CLR 23, 49 (Brennan J).

8 See also Greg Byrne, 'A Pathway to Fair(er) Trials: Why We Need a Juries Advisory Council' (2021) 31(2) *Journal of Judicial Administration* 49.

Introducing changes that are not evidence-informed

The case study on misconceptions in sexual offence cases (Chapter 9) concluded that there is insufficient evidence about juror comprehension of exemplifications of the direction that there may be good reasons for delay in making a complaint (eg, that the complainant may have felt ashamed or to blame for the acts). Whether jurors understand the exemplifications, and whether they work as intended, is not known. Further, there is a risk that discussing misconceptions about delay may unintentionally entrench the misconception. This scenario — deciding what to do to improve juror comprehension in the absence of robust evidence — is likely to be a widespread problem given the myriad issues that arise in criminal jury trials.

As discussed in Chapter 9, research is available concerning other matters connected to misconceptions about delay (eg, some jurors are likely to hold misconceptions about delay in making a complaint and delay is commonly referred to in sexual offence trials as a reason for disbelieving a complainant). It is therefore possible that this misconception might affect whether a juror brings an impartial mind to their task. General juror comprehension research and information about addressing juror misconceptions will assist in formulating options that are more likely to operate as intended. However, there are limits to the extent to which inferences can be reasonably drawn — research remains critical. Where there is good evidence of a problem, or a strong belief that there is a problem, governments may decide that reform is necessary even without evidence that proves that an intervention will work as intended. As discussed in Chapter 5, this occurred in New South Wales and Victoria where governments introduced jury directions to address certain misconceptions in sexual offence cases. Where the evidence is insufficient, but governments are determined to introduce reform, the remaining four steps in a jury-centric approach should then still be used to analyse proposals for change.

The application of a jury-centric approach provides transparency to the policy decision-making process. It may reveal whether a reform proposal conflicts with any other fair trial requirements or other human rights. It might also be relevant to how a proposal is structured. For example, the basis for giving a direction about misconceptions could be whether (1) there is evidence that may invoke the misconception, or (2) whether jurors are likely to be influenced by evidence invoking the misconception. The second basis depends on all judges having the necessary expertise to make such an assessment. Further, if the basis for giving the direction depends upon matters that fall outside of judicial expertise (eg, the likelihood of misconceptions being triggered in jurors), judges will need more support (step five) so that they understand misconceptions and when they are likely to arise in jurors' assessment of the evidence.

A JAC could assess the risks of using exemplifications to address misconceptions in the absence of sufficient evidence about their effectiveness. Good decision-making will require integrating social science juror comprehension research expertise (eg, using probabilistic reasoning, drawing inferences from the available research) with legal expertise (eg, about how an issue arises and how counsel may use an issue in presenting their case in a trial). However, if the evidence is insufficient, unlike a court, a JAC need not make a final decision. It could seek more evidence and/or could pilot changes to obtain better evidence.

This scenario highlights the ability of a jury-centric approach to apply, and to improve, decision-making to ensure a fair trial in a flexible and practical manner. It also highlights the importance of an ongoing interdisciplinary JAC to undertake tasks involving the law, practice, and social science research. The case for using a jury-centric approach is compelling.

Changing conceptions of responsibility for ensuring a fair trial

A JAC should play a key role in driving research about juror comprehension and developing changes to criminal laws, practices, and procedures. While the extent to which jurisdictions use legislation to introduce change will vary, legislation is likely to perform a significant role.

The establishment of a JAC and the use of legislation to engender a fair trial challenges the traditional paradigm where courts have primarily been responsible for ensuring a fair trial. Traditionally, trial judges are responsible for tailoring their guidance to the issues and to their assessment of the jury's needs in each case. This case-by-case responsibility has resulted in trial judges bearing much of the responsibility for engendering change to improve juror comprehension. This traditional responsibility of trial judges and the courts was evident when Scotland's Cabinet Secretary for Justice admonished the courts, saying that legislation was necessary to address misconceptions in sexual offence cases because 'the courts have not been sufficiently innovative in this area'.[9]

Governments and courts have always shared some of the responsibilities for ensuring a fair trial. Using a jury-centric approach may change the balance of these traditional responsibilities. Courts need to be willing to allow governments to be involved in some areas that have traditionally fallen within the exclusive province of the court, to ensure a fair trial.[10] Governments must respect the role and independence of the courts and undertake improvements

9 Scottish Parliament, *Official Report* (Michael Matheson, 22 March 2016) 94.

10 This requires trust between the judiciary and the executive: Greg Byrne and Justice Chris Maxwell, 'Putting Jurors First: Legislative Simplification of Jury Directions' (2019) 43(3) *Criminal Law Journal* 180, 200.

to criminal laws and jury trials because courts are not equipped for this task. A jury-centric approach shows that:

- to better understand jurors' perspectives and to improve jury guidance a JAC (or similar) is needed to drive the research agenda
- a JAC will require government funding, and
- a JAC should use a jury-centric approach to provide advice to courts and the government about how to address juror comprehension problems to ensure a fair trial.

Supporting a jury-centric approach in this way will give courts more confidence when effectively ceding some of their traditional responsibilities for ensuring a fair trial. Like courts, governments must accept responsibility and change their role in supporting courts to address juror comprehension problems. To borrow from the words of Scotland's Cabinet Secretary for Justice, governments have not been sufficiently innovative in this area.

Courts, laws, and trials must change. As Hans and Vidmar said, '[a]daptability has been the key to . . . [the jury's] survival. It should remain open to experimentation and modification'.[11] Ideas about what is necessary for a fair trial continue to evolve and a jury-centric approach can drive fair trial changes. We owe it to those accused, to victims, to witnesses, and to the community to do better in ensuring fair criminal trials. Listening to the voices of jurors and understanding their perspective is critical to the application of a jury-centric approach. By applying a jury-centric approach, a JAC can develop proposals necessary to improve the fairness of trials so that jurors understand their task and determine the issues on their legal and factual merits.

11 Valerie P Hans and Neil Vidmar, *Judging the Jury* (Plenum Press, 1986) 251.

Index

FSC
www.fsc.org
MIX
Papier | Fördert gute Waldnutzung
FSC® C083411

Kolibri 360 GmbH
Ferdinand-Jühlke-Straße 7
99095 Erfurt, Deutschland
produktsicherheit@kolibri360.de